Master Introductory Psychology

Complete Edition

by Michael Corayer

Text, illustrations, and cover design by Michael Corayer

Copyright © 2016 Michael Corayer

Psych Exam Review Press

ISBN 978-0-9970053-7-0

www.psychexamreview.com

Preface

This book is designed to bridge the gap I see between textbooks and study guides. Generally textbooks are overwhelming, as authors attempt to pack in more information than any one student could manage to remember. On the other hand, many study guides are nothing more than glorified term lists, with simple definitions and multiple choice questions that never really get to the heart of psychology. So while there is a great deal of factual information in these pages, the emphasis is on why concepts matter and why certain studies and theories are important. Your approach to using this book should be similar: focus on the purpose and meaning of the information, rather than obsessively studying the terms and definitions. Once you understand the underlying concepts and the practical applications of these ideas, you'll find it easier to remember the terminology.

A Note about Images

As you'll notice, this book is a bit different from other textbooks and study guides in that it is heavy on text and light on images, charts, and boxes. You'll find a few simple images. Are they amazingly detailed and visually stunning? Certainly not. Are some of them so bad that they just might stick in your head and help you remember the material? I hope so. I've focused on simple drawings I could actually draw on the board in a classroom, rather than trying to find (and license) the "perfect" image. Consider that your average textbook licenses hundreds of images, cartoons, and diagrams (thus inflating the price) that a Google search can instantly reveal to you for free. If you want to see Hermann von Helmholtz or what scanning-electron-microscope images of your stereocilia look like, I'm sure you're resourceful enough to find out. Don't just stick to one confusing textbook diagram when you can find thousands of stunning images in a matter of moments.

If you want a little guidance in tracking down the images that help bring psychology to life, you can start by checking out my Pinterest boards at **www.pinterest.com/psychexamreview** for hundreds of images (as well as articles and videos) on psychology, all organized by topic. For even more resources, check out **www.psychexamreview.com**

Table of Contents

Chapter 1
History & Approaches

What is Psychology?

Psychology is the scientific study of thought and behavior. This means asking why we do the things that we do and think the thoughts that we think. If you've ever wondered why you need to spend so much time sleeping, why visual illusions occur, or how to figure out whether or not that cute classmate has a crush on you, you've considered psychological questions. While current research may not be able to definitively answer the many questions we pose, it can certainly help us to investigate the plausibility of the explanations we generate.

You see, whether you study psychology formally or not, there are questions that you will undoubtedly confront throughout your life. We all wonder about the world we live in and in doing so, we ask the type of questions that psychology attempts to answer. We wonder about the causes of events and behaviors, why some people seem to dance on silver-lined clouds while others are left lamenting the rain, or how some otherwise-rational person can so fervently disagree with our own point of view. I mean, what is wrong with that guy?!

You shouldn't think of psychology as a separate subject, neatly compartmentalized from all others. What I hope this book will show you is that psychology is **life**. The study of psychology will lead you from statistics to sociology, philosophy to pharmacology, epistemology to economics, mathematics to meditation, and biology to basket-weaving. Attempting to understand our own thoughts and behaviors inherently ties us to **all** of human endeavor. Never can one say that the field of psychology isn't relevant to one's personal life. No matter what you're interested in, psychology can help you to understand it. And if you aren't interested in anything at all, psychology will have something to say about that too.

While psychology as a field of academic study may be relatively new, our natural human desire to understand the world means that we have been asking psychological questions since the dawn of our existence.

Nature versus Nurture?

One of the key philosophical influences underlying research in psychology is the attempt to understand how we know what it is we know. Is our knowledge and understanding of the world inborn, or is it acquired through our experiences?

This question goes back thousands of years, long before scientific concepts of genetics or elite preschools. **Plato** (427-347 BCE) believed that we are born with all of our knowledge already inside us, simply waiting to be rediscovered. This concept that knowledge is innate or inborn is known as **nativism**. While there aren't many psychologists today who adhere to strict nativism, we still see this line of thinking in attempts to understand certain types of behavior. Are some people simply born to be sociopathic criminals or loving parents? Predestined for a life of worry-free bliss or chronic depression?

Or perhaps there's something about our experiences and living environment that shapes who we are? **Aristotle** (384-322 BCE) challenged Plato with the concept of **philosophical empiricism;** the belief that all knowledge is acquired through experience. We are born with nothing; a "blank slate" (or if you prefer the Latin phrase, as John Locke did, a *tabula rasa*) waiting to be written upon by our environment.

Once again, there are few staunch philosophical empiricists arguing for the sole influence of environment today. But we may all still wonder what our lives would be like if we were raised in a different neighborhood, a different family, or a different culture. How would we be the same and how would we differ? Just how much does environment shape us?

So while the question of nativism versus empiricism goes back thousands of years, we still don't have a definitive answer, except perhaps to say that most traits and behaviors arise from a complex interaction of both **nature and nurture** or **genes and environment**.

It's not so much a question of "versus" as a question of how the two combine and collaborate to create each unique person. This attempt to determine exactly how our innate characteristics are shaped and expressed by interactions with our environment is still very much an area of inquiry in psychology today, whether we are attempting to determine why it is that some people suffer from mental illnesses and others don't, or simply trying to figure out why some people come to prefer chocolate ice cream to vanilla.

Mind and Body – Cartesian Dualism

Without a doubt, you're familiar with some of the work of **René Descartes** (1596-1650). Perhaps you recognize his famous quote "*Cogito ergo sum*" - "I think therefore I am." Or if you've ever plotted (x, y) points on a graph in geometry class then you've used the *Cartesian* coordinate system. Descartes has had a profound influence on mathematics and Western philosophy, but one of his major contributions to psychology actually came from being wrong.

Descartes believed in **dualism**, the belief that the world could be divided into two main categories: the mental (mind) and the material (body). He believed the mind (or soul) was not a physical substance, but controlled the body, which operated mechanistically. With this belief in mind, Descartes searched for the "seat of the soul" where the non-material mind interacted with the material body. He believed he had found this in the pineal gland near the center of the brain, and that the pineal gland controlled the body via the cerebrospinal fluid. As we'll see, Descartes was wrong about the function of the pineal gland, and most psychologists today believe he was wrong about the mind being separate from the body as well.

With all the names in this chapter, how can we remember Descartes was associated with the concept of dualism? Fortunately, history has left us with an unforgettable memory aid. To remember that Descartes believed mind and body were separate, we need only recall the unfortunate events which followed his death.

Descartes died in Sweden in 1650, where his body was buried. 16 years later, however, it was decided that the great French philosopher's body would be better buried in his native land and his corpse was exhumed. In the process of transferring the remains, the French ambassador to Sweden decided to collect a macabre souvenir for himself in the form of Descartes' right index finger. But this was only a minor disgrace compared to what followed. The larger (and more memorable) disgrace was that Descartes' head was chopped off and his skull never actually made the journey back to France. It remained in private ownership in Sweden until 1821 when it was finally returned to France and placed at the Musée de l'Homme in Paris. You can find his skull there today, separate from the rest of his body, and covered with carved inscriptions from its former owners. How's that for separation of mind and body?

So if Descartes was wrong about dualism, why do we still care hundreds of years later? I don't bring up Cartesian dualism just so I can smugly mock an intellectual icon a paragraph later. Descartes should serve as a reminder that even the greatest of minds can be misled. This is something that we all know, and yet we are still surprised each time we see it occur.

The fact that dualism feels right but is actually wrong shows us that our intuitions about psychology cannot always be trusted. So while I may feel that my mind is separate from my body, that doesn't mean that it is so. Similarly, just because I feel like a treatment is doing something that doesn't mean it's actually an effective medical intervention. While a great deal of psychological research may seem intuitive or even obvious after the fact, we cannot always trust the subjective experience of our own minds. Descartes' misguided search for the seat of the soul should serve to show that even the greatest of geniuses can be fooled.

Throughout these units we will find many examples of great minds gone wrong, of brilliant intellectual leaders so convinced of their views that they fail to consider alternate explanations. These examples should serve as a warning to us all. We have to remember that all minds can be led astray. Without a doubt, future scholars will see some of our current understanding of psychology as feeble, biased, or even backward. This is the great march of intellectual progress, and it doesn't care if you're René Descartes, Sigmund Freud, or B.F. Skinner; it will find and eventually expose your biases and mistakes. In some cases it seems only the long, slow passage of time can shed light on all our shortcomings. So throughout this book I don't bring up the past failings of eminent minds so we may laugh at their wrong-headedness, but rather so that we may see how they were misled and remember that we too are always prone to error. We too may come to believe an idea so firmly that we forget or ignore other alternatives. In attempts to minimize this risk, psychology has gradually adopted a more scientific approach to conducting its inquiries, though we shall still see quite a number of missteps along the way.

In contrast to Cartesian dualism, **monism** (from the Greek *mono* - "one") makes the assumption that everything can be explained as having one source: physiology (for all you philosophy types, this particular type of monism is known as "materialism"). Monism holds that all of our thoughts, behaviors, emotions, and traits can be explained by our physiology. There is no mind or soul separate from the body. We may experience having a mind, but that experience arises from complex processes of the physical body. Or as Descartes' contemporary, Thomas Hobbes, believed, everything is simply "bodies in motion".

The widespread adoption of monism in psychology marked a shift to thinking of your mind and all your inner thoughts as simply experiences derived from the physiological activity of your body. This is generally the guiding approach for modern psychology, and all manner of mental experiences are believed to have physiological counterparts.

Another Error, Another Insight

Jumping ahead a few centuries to the 1820s, we find another example where an error of the past has helped to inform our present understanding.

Franz Josef Gall (1758-1828) became curious about the shape of the brain and how our brain structure might influence our personality traits and abilities. Since brain scanning technologies were still more than a century away, Gall used the most logical method of measuring the brain he had available; measuring the skull. He looked for patterns among the many bumps and dents in skulls, hoping to map out the skull shapes associated with mechanical ability, poetic talent, and other "fundamental faculties". Gall referred to this type of research initially as cranioscopy (Greek *cranium* - "skull" and *scopos* - "vision") but it later became known as ***phrenology*** (Greek *phrenos* - "mind" and *logos* - "study"). Gall believed that bumps and dents in the skull corresponded to underlying brain areas, and that these brain areas corresponded to different mental abilities.

This approach was eventually discarded, because it turns out that your skull shape is not a very good indicator of your underlying brain structure. But while phrenology came to be seen as the pseudo-science it was, its importance should not be ignored. It was one of the first approaches with the guiding assumption that specific brain areas perform specific tasks, known as ***localization of brain function.*** What Gall was really trying to show, despite his flawed approach, was that different areas of the brain do different things. This was a new idea at the time, but one that would eventually become a key concept underlying neurological research.

Psychological Science

Throughout the 19th century and into the 20th century, attempts at answering psychological questions began to take on a more scientific approach. Advances in technology played a role in this development. For example, ***Hermann von Helmholtz*** (1821-1894) began investigating speed of reaction time and was able to get more precise measurements than had previously been possible. He was able to find that the speed in reacting to a stimulus touching a person's toe is ever-so-slightly slower than the speed reacting to a stimulus touching the thigh. This tiny difference has profound implications. It demonstrates that our mental life is not instantaneous. While we may feel that we are aware of things happening to our body as they occur, the truth is that those messages must physically travel to the brain, and different distances to the brain will necessarily mean different arrival times.

So when a mosquito bites your shoulder, your brain finds out faster than when one bites your toe, even though you may not be consciously aware of the time lag. Helmholtz's research can also be seen as validation of the view of **monism** because it demonstrates the physiological limits imposed upon our conscious awareness, rather than suggesting that there is a **dualist** mind separate from the body (a non-material mind could presumably detect any body sensations equally quickly because it would not be bound by the rules of the material world).

Wilhelm Wundt (1832-1920) was impressed by Helmholtz's data-driven approach to researching mental processes, and investigated similar phenomena. Wundt started a research laboratory in Leipzig with the goal of breaking consciousness down into manageable chunks that could be measured. By understanding the structural components of consciousness, Wundt hoped to uncover how the mind operated as a whole. This approach, known as **structuralism**, soon had a number of devoted researchers hoping to find these building blocks of mental experience.

One key tenet of Wundt's structuralism was **introspection**. Introspection is a process of trying to isolate the individual components of perception in order to understand consciousness. For example, participants in the lab might be asked to describe the experience of viewing a single colored tile or a single black spot on a piece of paper. **Edward Titchener** (1867-1927), who studied under Wundt, took this approach to its extreme. Titchener worked for years to create a 44,000 term list of the essential elements of consciousness after laboriously collecting data via introspection.

Unfortunately for Titchener, his comprehensive list didn't actually reveal much about how the mind works. Introspection's inevitably subjective responses meant that it was difficult or impossible to discern different experiences from different descriptions of the same experience. This is a problem that still plagues psychology to this day, as psychiatrists may wonder if two patients are suffering from different symptoms or merely describing the same underlying symptom in different terms. But that's another discussion for later in the book, for now, let's see how structuralism and introspection faded in favor of **functionalism**.

Functionalism's main proponent was **William James** (1842-1910), a Harvard professor who believed that consciousness couldn't be understood by breaking it apart. Instead, James believed that we needed to understand the function of our mental abilities and experiences in order to understand how the mind works. William James was influenced by the ideas of **Charles Darwin** (1809-1882), whose *On the Origin of Species* (1859) emphasized understanding an organism's physical traits and abilities by understanding the adaptive purposes they served. James believed that the same notion that underscored this **natural selection** for physical traits could be used to understand our mental abilities and experiences. For example, when considering an emotional experience like fear, James would look to understand how fear serves an adaptive purpose (such as motivating us to avoid certain situations) rather than focusing on the experience of fear itself (as structuralists might have done).

Looking for the Unseen

Around the same time that functionalism was overtaking structuralism in the United States, another man in Vienna, Austria was contemplating a different approach to understanding mental life. This approach gradually came to the forefront of psychology in the 20th century and the man is now recognized as perhaps psychology's most famous name: **Sigmund Freud** (1856-1939). Freud was a physician, who became interested in understanding patients suffering from mental illness and anxiety (often referred to as **neurosis** at the time).

Freud believed that these afflictions were the result of early childhood experiences which continued to impart influence unconsciously. The Freudian **unconscious** contained the person's deepest wishes, desires, and fears, and unchecked conflicts in the unconscious could reverberate into the patient's conscious thoughts and behaviors, manifested as anxiety and disturbance. By engaging in therapy, the patient would gradually resolve these unconscious conflicts and therefore reduce the anxiety.

Freud's approach, known as the **Psychoanalytic Approach** became the dominant way of thinking about mental illness for decades and also influenced the realms of art, history, and literature. This not only secured Freud's place as a leading figure, it also got people thinking about mental processes that may be happening in the recesses of the unconscious mind. Though most of Freud's theories have been rejected by modern researchers, this notion that there are unconscious influences on our thoughts, behaviors, and emotions was a fundamental new insight for understanding the mind.

Behaviorism

From around 1920-1960, psychological research shifted to an emphasis on observable behavior as a more objective approach, since mental states and unconscious processes were deemed too difficult to assess scientifically. Led by behaviorists like *John B. Watson* (1878-1958), and later, *B.F. Skinner* (1904-1990), (if you can remember that both have a **B.** in their name it can remind you of **B**ehaviorism) psychologists looked to quantify how the environment shapes us. Researchers focused on how systems of rewards and punishments worked to modify behaviors. This emphasis on external rewards and punishments placed behaviorists almost completely in the "nurture" camp when it came to explaining the causes of behavior. The positive and negative consequences of our past experience with the world would determine our future behavior.

During this time, a great number of studies were conducted on animals like rats and pigeons, which were assumed to be simplified proxies for human subjects. By focusing on observable behavior, these researchers believed that psychology needn't worry itself with hidden motives or fleeting emotions. Behavior was believed to be the surest and most objective way to quantify psychological processes. After several decades as the leading view in psychology, behaviorism gradually fell out of favor beginning in the 1960s, in part due to great advances in computer technology.

Modern Approaches to Psychology

The diversity of questions that psychology aims to answer necessarily requires a diversity of approaches. In attempts to answer questions on all nature of human experience, psychology gleefully borrows or steals from other disciplines, creating a quilt of sub-fields with the overall aim of understanding all thought and behavior. As psychology has grown to incorporate these many sub-fields, greater specialization is required of psychological researchers. No longer can one researcher be familiar with the happenings and developments in all areas of psychological inquiry. As a result, most psychologists today probably fall into one of the following categories.

Following behaviorism's decline, the role of mental processes which were not directly observable became an area of greater research. *Cognitive psychology* looks to understand how our thoughts influence our behavior. The way we think, use language, frame questions, and consider context can affect our decision-making, our ability to solve problems, and our emotional state.

Darwin would be proud to see that his legacy lives on in psychology, even if the functionalism of William James has faded. The drive to understand the adaptive purposes of our mental abilities continues today in the form of *evolutionary psychology*. While Darwin didn't have knowledge of specific mechanisms of heredity (like genes), modern day evolutionary psychologists continue to use his approach to uncover how our psychological traits have been selected for throughout human history. One key idea used in evolutionary psychology today is that the mind consists of specialized modules, each with different functions, which have been selected for over millions of years of evolution. For example, an evolutionary psychologist may consider how the human brain seems innately equipped for language acquisition, and therefore examine the role language may have played in our species' survival. Evolutionary psychologists may also look to understand the role of genes and evolution in shaping our relationships, interactions, and social behavior in a closely related sub-field known as *sociobiology*.

If you've ever wondered how children come to learn language or how the myriad changes of puberty affect the teenage brain, these lines of inquiry will quickly lead you to *developmental psychology*. Acknowledging that our mental and physical lives change throughout our lifespan, developmental psychologists seek to understand the progression of these changes in our biology and cognition from the nursery all the way to the nursing home.

Neuroscience looks to understand the links between our brain activity, our thoughts, (*cognitive neuroscience*) and our behaviors (*behavioral neuroscience*). This is an area where some of the greatest strides in psychology have occurred in recent years, thanks in large part to major advances in brain imaging and scanning technology. Armed with the ability to monitor brain function nearly as it happens, we finally have a window into the mind that can reveal patterns of activation and specific regions of specialization in far greater detail than ever before.

As John Donne wrote, "no man is an island" and some psychologists have taken this notion to heart. *Social psychology* looks to understand the complexity of our interpersonal interactions, ranging from the perils of stereotypes, aggression, and conflict, to the heart-warming moments of empathy, altruism, and bonding. Our daily interactions and personal relationships with others can have important influences on our thoughts, behaviors, and emotions and we should never forget that we are inherently social animals.

Enterprising psychologists have set their sights on the workplace, looking to understand how to improve worker morale, productivity, and well-being in a sub-field known as *industrial-organizational psychology*.

Psychology has also grown in its understanding of culture and how society as a whole shapes who we are. In our globalized world, understanding the role of culture on one's behaviors, interpretations, and expectations is no longer just the concern of diplomats, ambassadors, and royal families. Now we are all interacting on a global scale, and the results can be both rewarding and perplexing. Borrowing from anthropology and sociology, *cultural psychology* has looked to tease apart the influences of culture on our thoughts, emotions, and behaviors, showing the ways that culture defines us, as well as the ways we all share one human experience.

And of course, a chapter on approaches in psychology would be remiss not to mention the sub-field that most people bring to mind when they hear the term psychology, and that is *abnormal psychology*, the study of mental illness. This field incorporates many of the approaches above in considering how our minds can go wrong and what we can do to fix them. This field brings together researchers from all approaches in a number of different capacities from medical doctors trained to diagnose mental illness and prescribe medication (*psychiatrists*) to therapists and counselors who may specialize in cognitive or behavioral therapies for particular types of illness or conflict. These may be *clinical psychologists* who focus on mental illness or they may be *counseling psychologists* who focus on other types of conflict such as anxiety or stress related to work and school, interpersonal relationships and family issues, or certain types of addictions.

What's the "best" approach?

If this dizzying array of approaches is stressing you out, remember to step back and consider the purpose for each. Each individual approach is just another way of attempting to answer a psychological question. Should we focus our research on possible genes responsible or childhood experiences? On hormones or cultural influences? Remember that each focus temporarily ignores the others in order to simplify what are very complex questions. It's easier to ask how genes might relate to depression than to try to understand everything about depression all at once.

These different approaches are really just ways to structure our thinking, and we need to be careful not to become trapped in a particular structure. Staying isolated in one of these "boxes" can be useful for making progress and staying focused when dealing with complex interactions, but we need to remember that each box is just part of the picture. We should remember that a strictly biological explanation may be ignoring crucial cognitive factors, or that a psychoanalytic approach may be biased in its cultural understanding of illness. As I described in the introduction, psychology is inherently multidisciplinary. It cannot be reduced to a single approach. While each individual approach is helpful, we want to avoid seeing any single approach as THE approach. So while you may be inclined to prefer one approach, be careful not to be dismissive of the others, as they just may hold the puzzle pieces you're missing.

Chapter Summary – History and Approaches

- *Psychology* is the scientific study of thought and behavior, meaning that psychological inquiry encompasses a wide range of topics.

- Forces shaping behavior can be broadly categorized as *nature* (inheritance, genes) and *nurture* (environment). Rather than thinking in terms of "either/or" distinctions or "versus" we should consider how these two forces of heredity and experience interact with one another to influence behavior.

- Most psychologists today adopt a *monist* approach when thinking about the mind and body, and all thoughts, emotions, and behaviors are assumed to have underlying physiological components.

- Early approaches to psychology included *structuralism*, which attempted to identify the structural components of consciousness, *functionalism*, which emphasized the purpose or function of traits and behaviors, and the *psychoanalytic approach*, which focused on unconscious influences for understanding the mind.

- Modern approaches are varied and psychology can be divided into many different sub-fields, none of which should be considered the "best" approach, as each offers unique insights for improved understanding of thought and behavior.

Notes

Chapter 2
Research Methods

A Challenging Task

As we saw in Chapter 1, we cannot always trust our own experience to determine what is true. With this in mind, psychology has adopted methods for collecting data, analyzing results, and reporting findings that aim to eliminate bias and get more objective information.

There are a few reasons for the greater difficulty that psychology faces compared to other sciences. Human behavior is especially complex. It can be difficult or impossible to narrow something like happiness or aggression down to a single measurement. In addition, psychologists often aim to measure states that are variable and fleeting. Your subjective emotional response to a particular question or task may be markedly different from the participants before and after you. A happiness rating may not represent how you will feel 10 minutes later. Strong feelings of aggression may last only a few moments. Imagine trying to measure the length of a desk that was constantly changing. Psychological research must try to accommodate for the variation between individuals as well as the variation that occurs within a single individual, whose level of happiness, aggression, or depression may be in constant flux.

Psychology must also deal with the fact that measuring people can actually change those people. A desk doesn't shrink in fear or expand with pride when you attempt to measure it, but you may find that human subjects do react to your curious prodding. They may exaggerate their happiness to put you at ease, or downplay their joy to reduce your potential jealousy. They may constrain their aggression to fit social expectations, or they may lash out to display their dominance. Circumstances which create the possibility that participants may be adjusting their responses are known as **demand characteristics** and this reactivity poses a number of challenges to psychological research. One particular example of a demand characteristic is **social desirability**, which is when a participant will give a response that they believe to be more socially acceptable or "correct" even if that response does not accurately reflect the truth.

Imagine that I were to conduct a study on illegal drug use among all of my students. I arrange to have each student come to a personal interview in my office, along with their parents, and supervised by a school administrator. After collecting my data I proudly declare that not a single one of my students has ever used or even considered using illegal drugs. Do you see the problem with my approach? Of course! No one is going to admit to that behavior in that situation. The demand characteristics are overwhelming, and as a result I will end up with bad data. This example may seem obvious, but we must remember that demand characteristics can sneak into any scenario. Depending on the context, people may want to seem more depressed or less depressed, more anxious or less anxious, more responsible or less responsible, and it is the researcher's responsibility to design situations which reduce these influences.

Sometimes even the very act of measuring can cause changes in participants and it can be difficult to assess whether those effects are the result of the measurement process itself or the experimental change in the environment. From 1924 to 1933 a number of experiments on worker productivity were conducted at The Hawthorne Works, a Western Electric factory outside Chicago. When investigating workplace conditions, researchers found that increases in illumination improved productivity. Strangely, they also found that dimming the workplace lighting increased productivity. Both increases stalled after the study ended, however, which suggests that the productivity increases were due to being observed, or perhaps feeling attended to, rather than directly related to lighting levels. Similar experiments involving modifications to work areas, cleanliness, and workspace re-locations also found temporary changes in productivity which lasted only a few weeks then returned to baseline. This effect of changes in the environment (regardless of what the changes are) is referred to as *the Hawthorne Effect* and demonstrates the difficulties of measuring complex variables like work performance.

With all of these potential biases and effects, collecting psychological data is tricky. Yet we still want to know things, so we try to do the research anyway, eyes open to the difficulties we will inevitably face.

What Can We Believe?

The most important aspect of conducting or considering psychological research is adopting an attitude of *skepticism*. We cannot simply believe whatever we read or hear. In science, all claims are immediately met with questioning.

I find it helpful to understand the skeptical mindset by looking at claims that we may naturally be more skeptical of. Claims of psychics, paranormal activity, and ESP represent cases where many people may naturally be more skeptical (though perhaps not as many people as we might hope). For example, when we hear someone claim the ability to bend metal with his mind, we probably find ourselves adopting a skeptical posture. We shouldn't settle for just hearing the claim, we should want to see a thorough investigation, followed by evidence either supporting or refuting the claim. James Randi, a magician and promoter of greater skepticism in education (through the James Randi Educational Foundation) has spent decades exposing psychic frauds (like the metal-bending Uri Geller) by designing carefully controlled studies which prevent the use of deception and trickery. Since 1964 Randi has offered a cash prize (which has grown to $1,000,000) to any person whose paranormal claims can meet the terms of scientific testing. No psychics, mentalists, or mediums have ever claimed the prize, and most won't even agree to testing, knowing full well that they would quickly be exposed as charlatans.

While it may be easier for us to be skeptical of paranormal claims, we should take the same approach when considering the more "normal" types of claims we see on a daily basis. We are constantly faced with claims that psychologists might want to scientifically investigate, from brain enhancement and sleep improvement to happiness boosters and mate-attraction strategies. What claims are being made and who is making them? How can we assess the validity of these claims? Who is collecting the data, how are they collecting it, and how are they analyzing and presenting the results? Developing a skeptical mindset and insisting on evidence will not only help us to avoid scams, it will help us to understand the world.

Even when we have carefully reviewed the evidence and come to a belief about a claim, we must remain humble. We must avoid overconfidence and be willing and in fact eager to accept new knowledge that overturns what we've come to believe. The goal in science is not to always be right but to always seek better explanations. Should a result support our hypothesis, that's great, we have some evidence that the hypothesis applies to this particular situation. Should the result fail to support our hypothesis, that's great too, we now have evidence that a new explanation may be needed. By remaining open to contradiction and critique we remain open to new ideas and new discoveries.

In our humility, we also recognize that we are human, and just like our participants, we are prone to bias and error. In 1963, **Robert Rosenthal** and **Kermit Fode** published the results of a study demonstrating that researchers themselves are prone to error. In this study, introductory psychology students were given rats to care for and run in some experiments. Half of the students were told they had "maze bright" rats who were bred and selected for excellent maze abilities. The other half were told they had "maze dull" rats, selected for poor maze skills. The students then ran a number of maze tests with their rats over the course of 5 days. Not surprisingly, they found that the "maze bright" rats outperformed their "maze dull" counterparts by a significant margin in both correct completions and speed. While the student experimenters weren't surprised by this difference, they should have been. What they didn't know was that all of the rats were randomly selected from the same group and therefore should have all performed comparably. There were no bright or dull rats and it was the pre-existing beliefs of the students that were responsible for the different measurements.

How could this be? Perhaps the result was due to a number of small unconscious differences in the treatment of the rats that ended up having a cumulative effect. Anything from gentler handling, a subtle push at the start of the maze, encouragement along the way, or a faster trigger-finger on the stopwatch may have influenced the results. These tiny unconscious influences created a significant difference between the groups, making it appear that there really were bright and dull rats. We must realize that *our expectations can influence our observations*. This is an example of **observer bias**.

One way of reducing both demand characteristics and observer bias is a ***double-blind study***, in which neither the participants nor the observers who are collecting the data (perhaps a computer, research assistants, etc.) know about the true purpose of the study or which group a participant is in. In Rosenthal and Fode's case, if the students hadn't known whether their rat was "bright" or "dull", they probably would not have found a difference between the groups of rats.

Defining Properties

With any psychological question, what we are really trying to establish is better understanding of a property. We want to know about properties like happiness, depression, aggression, intelligence, etc. The problem with wanting to know about psychological properties is that they can be especially difficult to measure.

In other sciences, it can often seem easy to determine how to define a particular measurement. For example, the general property of length can be defined in terms of centimeters. It's important to remember, however, that centimeters themselves are really just one way of talking about length, they are not the property itself. In other words, ***measures do not detect properties***, they simply provide more convenient representations for us to talk about.

It's simply been agreed upon that centimeters are a good way to talk about length and ideally your centimeter is the same as my centimeter (if not, the measure would become useless). When I decide to measure in centimeters, this is my ***operational definition*** for the property of length. We may say that the property of length has been ***operationalized*** as number of centimeters. Someone else may choose miles, nanometers, or furloughs, which would just be different operational definitions for the same property (length). Depending on the situation, some operational definitions may be more appropriate than others. So if we're at IKEA it's easier for me to tell you that a desk is 80 centimeters in length rather than tell you that the desk is 0.000497097 miles. Even though both of these may be accurate, one is better for helping you decide if the desk will fit in your bedroom.

The same concept is true in psychological research. We may refer to particular measures like depression scales, personality inventories, or satisfaction-with-life assessments, and these are ways of attempting to agree on measurements of psychological properties. As you might guess, however, agreeing on how to define a property like happiness is far more difficult than agreeing to define length in centimeters. I may choose to measure happiness by counting smiles, recording laugh time, completing a survey from -5 to +5, or by looking at patterns of brain activity.

No matter which approach I use to measure happiness, I'm hoping to have **construct validity**. Construct validity means that the operational definition that I've chosen has a clear relationship with the property in question. For example, we might say that using smiles as a measure of happiness has construct validity because we know that there is a relationship between being happy and smiling. In fact, this is an operational definition we probably use quite often when assessing happiness in daily life. We see someone smiling and immediately assume he is happy. Or we try to make someone happy and gauge how successful we are based on whether or not they smile. This doesn't mean that smiling always represents happiness (as there are fake smiles and happy non-smilers) but in general the relationship seems clear.

If instead of counting smiles I chose to count cars as my measure of happiness, the relationship may not seem as clear. While I may argue that owning cars makes some people happy and therefore more cars equal more happiness, chances are that many people would disagree with me, citing happy bikers or depressed millionaires with garages full of vehicles. Or they may even cite the car dealer who is happiest each time a car leaves his possession. In this case, my operational definition (measuring happiness as # of cars owned) would be criticized as having **low construct validity,** meaning that it does not represent the property I'm hoping to study.

Types of Studies

Just as there are many ways of defining properties, there are many ways to go about collecting our data. One approach is to focus on unique situations or special individuals and then study these cases in-depth. This is known as a **case study.** The advantage here is that we can study a participant in detail and use many different operational definitions. For example, if I study one person who is extremely happy, I can consider their happiness in terms of many behaviors, thoughts, and feelings and get a fuller picture of what happiness means for that person.

The problem, however, is that a single individual will only tell me about happiness for that one person. I cannot assume that this is representative of happiness for all people, who may experience it differently. Unfortunately, case studies only tell us about individuals, and we can't necessarily use that information to know about the "average" person. Knowing that an approach works for one person may be nice, but we also want to know about whether the approach will work for others. Still, case studies are important when we want to understand remarkable traits (like high IQ or rare ability) or when we want to study events or situations that we couldn't ethically impose on someone (like brain damage, extreme stress, or rare diseases).

The Survey Method

Instead of a case study, I might decide to collect survey data from a much larger number of people. This will give me a better idea of the average, though I probably won't be able to get nearly as much detail from each individual in my study. I need to bear in mind that demand characteristics may influence my survey and how people respond. How I choose to word my questions may have a subtle but important effect on the responses I receive. For example, asking whether an organization should "limit access to inappropriate websites" may sound more agreeable than asking if they should "censor web content". Even though both questions refer to the same idea, the different framing of the question may shift the results in a particular direction. This shift may mean results do not accurately represent how people actually think.

I should also consider that there may be something different about the people who actually took the time to respond to my survey. This is known as *reporting bias*. For example, if most depressed people fail to return my survey on happiness, but happy people all report back, I may end up with an overly optimistic view of average happiness. This might bring me to consider more carefully who is participating in my research. Researchers want to know about a particular *population* of people and the term population refers to anyone in that group who *might* be studied. This *target population* might be teenagers, the elderly, college students, patients suffering from depression, or soldiers returning from combat. Ideally we could study every individual in a population, but in most cases, the populations we want to know about are far too large. So while the population includes everyone we might study, the group of people that we actually manage to study is known as the *sample*, and this sample is used to represent the entire population.

The best way to create our sample would be to choose individuals from the population at random. This *random sampling* technique would ensure that every member of the population had an equal chance of being selected. Theoretically this is ideal, but in practice this approach is often unrealistic or impossible to implement. Instead we may use an *opportunity sample* or *convenience sample*, based on those members of the target population that are readily available to us. For example, if I want to know about college students I may choose a nonrandom sample from one local college, rather than attempting to randomly select from all college students everywhere.

Researchers may also want to use *stratified sampling* to ensure that sub-populations within the population are well-represented in the sample. For example, I may want an equal number of males and females in my study or proportional representation of different ethnic groups, and a truly random sample would not guarantee this.

So while random samples are the ideal, most studies don't use random sampling. In fact, many studies are criticized for not even having a ***representative sample*** because the participants tend to be college students, which means they are often younger, better-educated, wealthier, and whiter than the population they are meant to represent.

But rather than throwing up our hands in frustration because we can't get a sample that will represent all people from New York to New Guinea, we just do the research, non-representative sample and all. In many cases, non-representative data is better than no data. We can't expect every study to find a representative sample, and we might still learn something from the study. Finding that a particular effect happens in just one limited sample may be interesting on its own. Or we might be able to gauge the representativeness by comparing a large number of non-representative samples from many different studies. So if I only study white, middle-class suburban teenagers and someone else only studies recent immigrants living in a large metropolis, we can compare our findings to see if the results generalize from one sample to another. Finally, sometimes we may not care if a sample is representative because we can assume that the results apply anyway. For example, if a new drug killed all the people who took it you would be wise not to try it, even if everyone in that sample was a different gender, age, or ethnic group than you.

Correlational Studies

Our minds are constantly looking to connect ideas. We want to know how things are related, so we naturally look for patterns in the world around us. Most of the time, this pattern-seeking works well and allows us to make intuitive predictions about how the world works. Of course, our minds don't work perfectly all the time, and as a result, we may occasionally make errors in connecting two ideas, seeing a pattern where no pattern actually exists. This is known as an ***illusory correlation***. For example, I may notice that when I aced my psychology exam I was wearing a blue shirt. I realize I was also wearing a blue shirt when I did well on a math exam. I may come to believe that there is a relationship between wearing blue and performing well. While this is a silly example, it does happen in real-life (think lucky charms and gambling superstitions) and illusory correlations can become far more troublesome when they involve incorrect assumptions about gender or race. I may notice a particular behavior being performed by a person of a particular ethnic group on more than one occasion and then come to believe there is a relationship between the behavior and the entire ethnic group.

This can be dangerous, because once we come to believe an illusory correlation we may pay more attention to examples that fit our belief and disregard or ignore any contradictory examples. This is known as ***confirmation bias***, and it can strengthen our belief in patterns that aren't actually there. In order to safeguard ourselves from these false patterns, we may need to actually collect and analyze data to better understand the relationship between two variables. When doing so, we are performing a ***correlational study***.

In a correlational study, researchers simply measure two variables and then look for a ***pattern of variation***. One way of looking at the measurements from correlational research is to create a ***scatterplot***, which simply plots the scores from each variable, one on the x-axis and one on the y-axis. Just by looking at a scatterplot, we can see if there is a general pattern between the variables. Perhaps as one variable increases we see that the other variable increases or decreases in a predictable manner. Of course, seeing isn't quite enough and we want to have a way to quantify the strength of the relationship between the variables. To do this we calculate the ***correlational coefficient*** (represented by the letter *r*). The r value can range from -1 to +1. Positive r values indicate ***positive correlations***. In a positive correlation, as one variable increases the other also increases. In a ***negative correlation***, as one variable increases the other decreases.

We can think of the r value as telling us how accurately we could predict one of the variables if we knew the other. The closer to 1 or -1, the greater the accuracy of our predictions. As we move closer to 0, the ability to make predictions becomes less accurate. An r value of +1 indicates a **_perfect positive correlation_**, and -1 indicates a **_perfect negative correlation_**, both of which mean that one variable predicts the other variable perfectly accurately (the difference between positive and negative is just whether the other variable increases or decreases).

In perfect correlations, each data point falls neatly on a line, with no exceptions. Naturally, this type of relationship is rare and exceptions are common. As exceptions build up, the line becomes more and more spread out, until it no longer resembles a line at all. An r value of **_0_** indicates no relationship between the two variables, meaning that the data are completely random. As we can see from the scatterplots below, the closer our data are to a line (closer to +1 or -1) the stronger the relationship, and the more spread out the line, the weaker the correlation. (Note that the example in the second diagram shows a negative correlation, and thus the line slants downward, as X increases Y decreases).

Perfect Positive Correlation

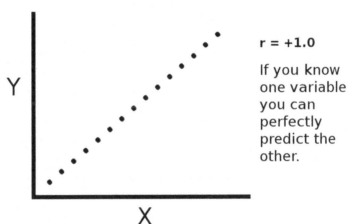

r = +1.0

If you know one variable you can perfectly predict the other.

Moderate Correlation

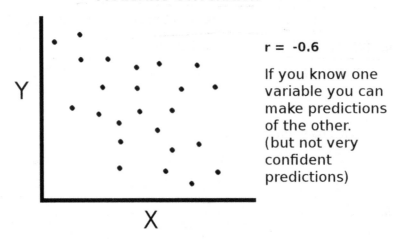

r = -0.6

If you know one variable you can make predictions of the other. (but not very confident predictions)

No Correlation

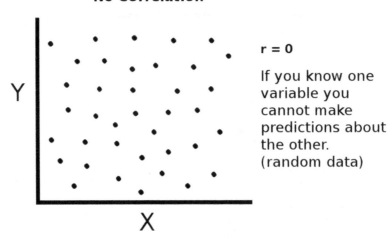

r = 0

If you know one variable you cannot make predictions about the other. (random data)

Even when we find a strong correlation, we have to remember that this is not evidence for causation. While correlations tell us that two variables are related, they can't tell us the *type* of relationship. If I were to measure my students' study time in hours and then measure their exam scores, I may find a positive correlation, meaning that longer study time is related to higher scores.

But simply knowing that long study time and high scores are correlated doesn't tell me anything about causation. There are three ways that causation might be working:

1. Longer study time does in fact cause higher scores. *(X causes Y)*

2. Earning higher scores encourages students to spend more time studying. *(Y causes X)*

3. Some other variable that wasn't in my study influences both study time and scores. *(Z causes X and Y)*

Correlational data has no way of indicating which causation is occurring. While we may sometimes be able to eliminate one of the first two directions of causation, the third option always remains a possibility. This other variable influencing both is referred to as a ***third variable***.

The Third-Variable Problem

The possibility of a third variable makes things difficult, because the third variable could be anything. This is known as the ***third-variable problem***, because there's always a possibility that some variable we never thought of is responsible for the correlation. For example, in the case above, it could be parenting style causing both high study time and higher scores. Or it could be interest in the class material. Or it could be teaching style, or peer competition, or caffeine intake, or something else in the diet, or hormones, or just about anything we could possibly imagine, and then anything we couldn't possibly imagine. We can never eliminate the third variable problem because ***the number of possible third variables is infinite***. If we haven't actually measured the third-variable in question, we can't eliminate it from consideration, even if it seems ridiculous.

If we suspect a particular third variable, we can try to eliminate it by measuring it and comparing participants who are matched for that variable. For example, if I'm concerned that caffeine intake might be increasing both study time and scores, I would want to compare students with equal amounts of caffeine intake. If my sample reports drinking an average of 3 cups of coffee per day, I might want to collect another sample with the same 3 cup average to compare. If this second group drinks the same amount of caffeine but has different study times or scores, this indicates that caffeine is not the main cause of the variation. This approach would be called a ***matched sample***.

If I want to get more specific with my matching, I might compare individuals directly. So if I have a participant who drinks one coffee per day, I want to compare him to another individual who also drinks one coffee per day. If another participant drinks 8 coffees a day, I would want to compare her results to someone who also drinks 8 coffees per day. Each individual in my study would have a partner with the same coffee intake. This would be known as ***matched pairs***.

While matched samples and matched pairs help us rule out particular third variables, they can't help us eliminate them all, because third variables are infinite. So we will never able to match for all of them. Instead, we turn to another solution to the third-variable problem; experimentation.

Experimentation

The best method we have for trying to get around the third variable problem is to perform controlled experiments. An experiment manages to minimize the third-variable problem by manipulating one (and only one) of the variables in the study, rather than simply measuring it, then seeing if this manipulation causes a change in another variable. To use our example above, if I forced some students to study longer but I didn't change anything else, and then I found that their scores increased, I could be more confident that it was the study time that was causing the higher scores. In this case, I don't need to wonder whether parenting style, motivation, or coffee was causing them to study more because *I know* that the experiment was what was causing them to study more. This reduces the possible influence of *all* other third-variables.

Before we go through all the detailed steps of designing an experiment, let's first consider how we come up with ideas for experiments in the first place. In order to conduct an experiment, I first need to have some idea of the type of relationship I'm looking for. I don't simply change any variable at random and then measure another random variable and hope for a pattern to emerge. Instead, I begin with a ***theory***. A theory is a general explanation of how something works or how a phenomenon occurs. For instance, I may theorize that exercise improves problem-solving ability.

A theory is about general properties, so I can't test it directly. I can, however, come up with specific definitions based on my theory that will be testable. This is how a ***hypothesis*** is generated, and it allows us to make a specific prediction about how something will happen, then see if that prediction was accurate.

For example, if I start with the general theory that "exercise" improves "problem solving ability", I need to come up with testable definitions for each of these properties. I may decide that one session of 15 minutes of walking at 65% of maximum heart-rate will be my operational definition of "exercise" and that "problem-solving ability" will be measured by how many Sudoku puzzles a participant can correctly solve in 30 minutes. These certainly aren't the only possible definitions, but they allow me to create a specific prediction. Now I have a hypothesis based on a general theory.

Theory: Exercise improves problem-solving ability.

Hypothesis: Participants who engage in the specified exercise will solve significantly more Sudoku puzzles than participants who do not engage in the specified exercise.

With a testable hypothesis, I'm now able to collect quantitative data which will either support or contradict my prediction. Depending on whether my hypothesis is supported or refuted, I may decide to refine, revise, or reject my general theory. I may decide that the theory is still appropriate, but that my operational definitions were poorly chosen and therefore I should try again with new operational definitions. Maybe I need to change the exercise session, or maybe I need to change the problem-solving task. Or I may decide that the operational definitions were valid and the theory itself should be questioned.

An important point is that *a theory can never be proven.* When we find data which support our hypothesis, we have evidence that the theory is accurate, but no amount of evidence can conclusively determine that a theory will always be true. Even after collecting mountains of data it's always possible that tomorrow we will find subjects for whom exercise has no effect on problem-solving, or for whom it even has the reverse effect.

Until we have tested every possible subject in every possible way (which will never happen) we can't be 100% confident that a theory will always be true. While this may seem like scientists are all being sticklers, we should think of it as an exciting example of infinite possibilities. Each single study's evidence offers a world of opportunity for greater study and new knowledge. If 15 minutes of walking does have an effect, what about 14 minutes? How about jogging for 10 minutes or sprinting for 30 seconds? If Sudoku-solving is improved, what else might be? Is reaction time improved? How about overall IQ? Do these results continue to grow with long-term commitment to exercise? Could this type of exercise be used to help patients with cognitive impairments? We'll never reach the end of these possible questions, and that should serve to excite us and keep us endlessly fascinated with even the simplest of theories.

But before we get too hung up on the types of conclusions we can draw from research, let's take a closer look at exactly how we go about testing a hypothesis and how we need to design an experiment in order to get accurate data.

Manipulation of the Independent Variable

The most important aspect of experimental design is the *manipulation* of one of the variables. In the case above, the manipulation would be the exercise session. By having some participants perform the exercise while other participants don't, I can compare their performance and look for a difference. This is the essence of an experiment.

The participants who are assigned to receive the treatment (in this case, exercise) are referred to as the *experimental group*, while the participants who do not receive the treatment (no exercise) are referred to as the *control group*. In drug studies, the control group often receives a placebo pill, an inert substance with no medicinal properties, that they believe is actually a treatment. This is because simply receiving a treatment (such as taking a pill) can cause patients to feel better (known as the *placebo effect*), and we want to be sure that the real treatment's effects are even stronger than the placebo effect. In our exercise/problem-solving study, participants will know if they exercised or not, so we might give the control group some other neutral task (instead of exercise) so they don't realize they are the control group.

The variable which is manipulated is known as the *independent variable*, because whether someone receives the treatment or not is independent from anything else. It doesn't matter if they wouldn't choose it when given a choice, whether they enjoy it or not, whether they drank coffee or tea that morning or any other possible variable.

In order to be sure that the manipulated variable is truly independent of all other factors, I must use *random assignment*, which is to say that placement of a participant in the experimental group or control group is determined randomly. I need to avoid *self-selection*, where some existing difference between the participants determines which group they are in (such as allowing them to choose whether they want to exercise). I can't even trust my own judgment in assigning groups, because perhaps I will unconsciously assign the more fit individuals to the exercise group, or the more attractive individuals to the no-exercise group, or the people who arrived first to the exercise group because any of these differences might be having an influence on their later cognitive performance and I want to be sure that this isn't the case.

So, random assignment (also called *random allocation*) is a must. Even with random assignment, however, I must remember that demand characteristics may still be influencing the results (perhaps participants in the exercise group suspect the purpose of my study and then devote more effort to their problem-solving in order to be "good" participants).

Once I've randomly assigned my participants to the experimental and control groups and then manipulated my independent variable, I need to assess possible effects on the *dependent variable*. The dependent variable is what is measured following the manipulation. If the treatment has had an effect, then I should see a pattern of variation in the dependent variable. If the treatment has not had an effect, then I won't see a difference in the dependent variable. Recall Rosenthal and Fode's rat experiment and you'll remember that I also need to be careful that my own expectations and biases don't affect my measurement of the dependent variable.

I may wonder if certain differences between my participants are affecting the dependent variable. For instance, what if members of the control group are exercising outside the lab? The idea behind randomization is that if people are exercising outside the lab, some of them will end up in the experimental group and some will end up in the control group, so the effect should balance out, provided that I have a large enough sample *(see note below)*. But for some variables that might be affecting my results, (known as **confounding variables**) I may also want to create some **controls**. I may request that participants refrain from outside exercise for the duration of the study. This would help control for outside exercise. If I'm concerned that different meal times are influencing problem-solving ability, I could control this by asking all participants to fast for 8 hours prior to the experiment. While I won't be able to control all possible confounding variables, I may implement controls for the ones I believe are most likely to affect my data, and assume that randomization will balance out the impact of others. This combination of controls and randomization can help ensure that any effect on the dependent variable is actually being caused by the manipulation of the independent variable. *(Note: it is also possible to use matching techniques in an experimental design rather than using randomization, especially in smaller samples, but for the sake of keeping this guide simpler we will be ignoring these designs).*

Descriptive Statistics

Once I've collected my data, I need to figure out what it means. In order to do this, I'll probably start with some descriptive statistics. Descriptive statistics simply describe the data and give us an idea of how scores are distributed in each group.

First, I'll probably want to know about my experimental and control groups in general. For this, I will look at **measures of central tendency**. There are 3 main measures of central tendency, each with their own strengths and weaknesses, depending on the situation. First is **the mean** (or the average). This is calculated by finding the sum of all the scores, then dividing this by the number of scores.

$$\textbf{Mean} = \frac{\textbf{sum of scores}}{\textbf{\# of scores}}$$

The mean can be useful, but it doesn't tell the whole story. Imagine that I give an exam to a class of 10 students. 9 of the students score a 90 on the exam, and the remaining student scores a 0. In this case, the average score will be 81 (810/10). When I tell my students this, 9 students will think their performance was "above average" even though they each actually just performed better than 1 student. What has happened is that the one extreme score has had a strong effect on the mean. This is the main problem with the mean; it is sensitive to extreme scores or outliers. Just one extreme score can heavily distort the average, especially in small samples.

When we have extreme scores, we may not want to use the mean and instead look to another measure of central tendency: ***the median***. The median is calculated by simply lining up the scores in order, then finding the middle score. For example, in the following distribution, the median would be 5.

2, 4, **5**, 7, 8

In a distribution with an even number of scores, the median will be the average of the two middle scores. So in the following:

2, 4, **5**, **6**, 7, 8

the median would be [5+6] / 2 = 5.5

Back to my exam example above, the scores would line up as follows:

0, 90, 90, 90, 90, 90, 90, 90, 90, 90

And the median in this case would be 90. The distorting effect of the extreme score (the 0) has been reduced. In this case the median gives the students a more accurate picture of how their performance compares with their classmates.

The final measure of central tendency is ***the mode***. The mode looks at the frequency of each score and then tells us which score occurs most frequently. In the example above, the mode would be 90. It should be noted that it's possible to have more than one mode, known as a *multimodal distribution*, where multiple scores are equally high frequency. It's also possible that we have a *uniform distribution*, meaning that all scores are equally frequent and there is no most common score.

Measures of Variance

In addition to wanting to know about the central tendency of my distribution, I also want to know how the scores compare to one another. To consider this, I need to look at ***measures of variance***. The simplest way to measure variance is to calculate ***the range***. The range is the distance between the highest score and the lowest score. This tells me how spread out my distribution is overall, but it doesn't tell me much else. It also suffers from being sensitive to extreme scores, since the range is all about the extremes. Just one very high or very low score can have a dramatic impact on the range.

So we also want to look at another measure of variance. ***The standard deviation*** tells us how each score compares to the mean. In general, are scores gathered closely around the mean, or are they spread widely from the mean? The standard deviation is calculated by comparing each score to the mean, then taking the average of all those comparisons.

The standard deviation gives us a much better idea of how all the scores relate to one another. We know if the distribution is close together or spread out. The larger the standard deviation, the more the scores are spread out from the mean. A small standard deviation means that scores are all clustered together near the mean.

The Normal Distribution

In graphing our data, we may create a *frequency distribution*: showing possible scores on the X-axis and the frequency of each score on the Y-axis. In measuring some traits, we will find that the frequency distribution creates what is known as a *normal distribution* or a bell curve. This means that the mean, median, and mode are all in the center of the distribution, and frequency drops off symmetrically in both directions, with half of the scores on each side of the mean.

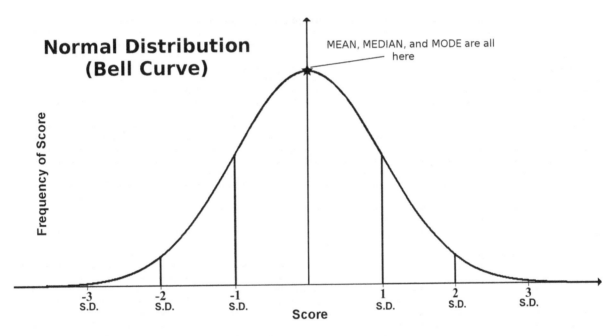

Knowing that we have a normal distribution also allows us to quickly estimate the percentage of scores that will fall within a given range: about 68% of scores will fall within one standard deviation from the mean (in both directions), about 95% of scores will be within 2 standard deviations of the mean, and about 99.7% of scores will be within 3 standard deviations of the mean (we'll see this in more detail when we look at intelligence testing).

Significance

You may be wondering how large the effect of a manipulation needs to be in order to be meaningful. To return to our exercise/problem-solving example, how much better does the exercise group have to perform for us to take notice? How much is enough to conclude that exercise is having an effect? In order to determine this, we need to use *inferential statistics*. Inferential statistics allows us to make judgments about the data we have collected and make inferences about what conclusions might be appropriate.

Significance can be calculated in a number of different ways depending on the type of data we have collected, and calculations are based on the number of participants in our sample, as well as the *effect size*, or how large the difference was between our experimental group and our control group. For example, if I claimed to have developed a smart drug, then I randomly gave one student the drug and one student a placebo, then told you that the student who took the drug scored 95 on an exam while the placebo student scored 80, you might be intrigued, but you would also realize that the odds that the better student just happened to receive the drug are too high because there were only two students. For this reason, we generally want to have as many participants as possible in order to reduce these kinds of coincidences and be more confident in our conclusions. This idea that having more data points is always better is known as the *Law of Large Numbers*.

Similarly, if I randomly assigned 100 students to take the drug, and 100 students to take a placebo, then I found that the experimental group's average exam score was 87 while the control group's average was 86, you should still be skeptical, even though technically I found a difference. The problem here is that the *effect size* is too small. It's probably just a coincidence, because if we take the average score of 100 random students and compare it to the average of another random 100 students, we won't get exactly the same average every time. The fact that the difference is only 1 point means it's not convincing evidence that the drug is having an effect.

In calculating significance we come up with a *p-value*. You can think of a p-value as telling you how likely your data is to occur. We want to collect data that is unlikely to "just happen" on its own. For example, imagine I told you that I could mentally control a fair coin so it always land on heads, and so you want to test this. In testing me, you wouldn't be satisfied with a single coin flip landing on heads, because you know that a single heads is fairly likely to happen anyway, so the p-value would be high. If you flipped the coin 1,000 times and every time was heads, this would be very unlikely to occur on its own, so you might start thinking that this wasn't just chance, and in this case the p-value would be low.

Data that is unlikely to have occurred by random chance suggests that we probably have a real effect, and so a low p-value is a good thing. Usually we want a p-value less than 0.05. When a p-value is 0.05 or lower we say that the results are ***statistically significant***. Because we can never completely eliminate the possibility of our data being a chance occurrence (even 1000 identical flips *could* happen by chance), we will never have a p-value of 0.

If our p-value is 0.05, this means that the probability that there wasn't a real effect (but we happened to get data that looks like one anyway) is 5%. To be clear, the p-value doesn't tell us the probability that our hypothesis is correct, it tells us the odds of randomly observing the data we have observed. In the above example, a p-value wouldn't tell us *how* or *why* this event is occurring, but it would tell us that it's a very, very unlikely event.

Drawing Conclusions from Research

Before drawing conclusions from a study, we need to check that everything has been done correctly. This is known as assessing the ***internal validity*** of a study. Think of internal validity as a checklist that we can mentally go through in order to decide whether the conclusions of a study are appropriate. Here are the questions that we should ask when considering the internal validity of a study:

- Was the independent variable effectively manipulated?

- Were participants randomly assigned to experimental/control groups?

- Was the dependent variable measured in an unbiased way?

- Was a reliable pattern found between the manipulation of the independent variable and the measurement of the dependent variable?

As you should guess from reading all of the preceding material in this chapter, these questions may not always be answered with a simple yes or no. These can be sources of contentious debate, and this is a good thing. The presentation of data should be followed by spirited argument, alternative explanations, and critique of the process by which the data was collected and analyzed. The truth is that there is no perfect study. There is no one way to define a property, manipulate a variable, or measure an effect. We must humbly recognize the potential for flaws in all studies, and remain skeptical of all conclusions as we gather more data, consider new operational definitions, novel manipulations, and better measurements.

We need to remember that every study will always be limited in the conclusions that can be drawn. We cannot conclude causality based on a single result, or even a pile of results. Each study's conclusions must be limited to the variables as defined in the study and also limited to the sample studied.

If I defined happiness as smiling behavior, my conclusions must only be about smiling. If I only studied teenagers at a public school, I must limit my conclusions to teenagers. I can't draw conclusions about happiness in general or how the data might reflect all people. While the journalistic accounts of research may do this with flashy stories and click-bait headlines, scientists must restrict their writing to the specific evidence collected.

Since every study has its limitations, we shouldn't settle for a single study as conclusive evidence. Instead, we may use *triangulation*, a technique of examining a subject from multiple angles in order to get a more complete picture.

Another important part of the process of drawing conclusions is *replication*, which involves repeating an experimental design. Generally this would be done using the same operational definitions and manipulation, but with a new sample of participants. Using the same techniques allows researchers to compare results directly. This is also why precise operational definitions are so important for collecting data. We want to be able to repeat the process as closely as possible, which will also allow us to assess the reliability of a particular claim.

Even when we accept the internal validity of a study, we may wonder whether the results are actually applicable to real-life. This is known as *external validity* or *ecological validity*. This considers whether the variables or manipulation in a study represent normal or typical ways we might see them in everyday life. Quite often we can criticize a study for *artificiality*, or a lack of external validity, because the lab environment doesn't recreate a realistic situation. *Naturalistic observation* (surreptitiously observing and measuring real-life behaviors) and *field experiments* (manipulating a variable and observing responses in a real-life setting) can be great approaches for high external validity, but both of these reduce the researcher's ability to control possible confounding variables. The laboratory environment can be more carefully controlled, but this control may reduce the realistic nature of the tasks involved.

The Ethics of Research

In addition to all of our concerns about reliability and validity, we also need to consider ethical guidelines that determine how we collect our data. The **APA** (American Psychological Association) has established ethical guidelines that must be followed for all studies. Before being conducted, proposed studies must go through an Institutional Review Board (**IRB**) which will assess any ethical considerations before approval. It's worth noting, however, that a great deal of private research, especially consumer research, is not overseen by ethics committees. So these guidelines may not apply to focus groups, a survey you found on facebook, or other reports which are conducted outside of the university research environment.

In general, the following guidelines must be followed:

Informed Consent

Freedom from Coercion

Protection from Harm

Risk/Benefit Analysis

Anonymity and/or Confidentiality

Debriefing

Informed consent means that potential participants are given enough information about the study to determine whether or not they want to participate. Informed consent does not, however, mean that the participant must remain in the study. Studies should be voluntary at all times and participants should have the freedom to stop at any point. Studies using children as participants must get informed consent from their legal guardians.

Freedom from coercion means that researchers cannot force participants to be in a study. While this obviously would apply to physical coercion, it also applies to other types of coercion. Offering higher grades, large sums of money, or other rewards for participation may cause participants to agree to tasks that they would otherwise reject. While researchers can offer to pay participants for their time, they cannot offer rewards or payments that might be considered coercive or else participation wouldn't be truly voluntary.

Protection from harm applies to both physical harm and mental harm. Participants should not be placed in situations of extreme stress or have to deal with situations that may have lasting psychological effects. Researchers may ask participants to take small risks, such as answering potentially embarrassing questions, performing cognitively demanding tasks, or even braving minor pain (such as a mild electric shock or submerging a hand in ice water). In order for these risks to be approved, however, there must be a clear benefit. Researchers can't just run around giving out electric shocks for no particular reason. The risks must be balanced with the benefits and improved knowledge the results can potentially uncover.

Ideally, the data collected from participants will be *anonymous*, meaning that responses will not be connected to the participant's name or identity. This can easily be done for some tasks, especially those involving computer data collection and surveys. In some situations, however, such as face-to-face interviews, it's not possible to have true anonymity. In these cases, it's important for the data to be *confidential*, meaning that researchers will not share a participant's responses with others.

Finally, researchers must give a ***debriefing*** to all participants. A debriefing is a summary of the purpose of the study and it should reveal any deception that was used. It should also attempt to undo any changes in the participant (if a study intentionally did something to make you frustrated, the debriefing should attempt to restore you to your previous emotional state).

A Note About Animal Studies

When it comes to collecting data from animal studies, not all of these guidelines can be followed. Naturally, animals cannot give consent to participate, and as a result, they can be forced to participate in research. Protection from harm, however, is still an important feature. The risk of harm allowed in animal studies is greater than in human studies, however, this risk must have a clear possible benefit. So while it may be acceptable for a study to risk animal harm or even death, the researchers must first demonstrate that the results of the study will have a clear benefit to humans. In addition, the harm must be the minimal amount necessary to receive the benefit and there are still strict standards of care for the animals which must be followed.

While it may be unpleasant to consider these types of animal studies, it's important to remember that these represent a very small number of studies. We should also remember the great advances and benefits of this type of research. Knowledge gained from animal studies has helped to save the lives of millions of people and has also served to improve the lives of other animals. Better understanding of disease, injury, and genetics can help to reduce the overall suffering in the world but sometimes this understanding comes at a cost. We should also be careful to avoid hypocrisy, as most of us implicitly accept the notion that some other organisms may occasionally suffer for human benefit whenever we eat meat, destroy habitats for human use (including farmland), or simply apply antibacterial gel to our hands.

Chapter Summary – Research Methods

- Conducting research in psychology requires careful methods for collecting and analyzing data due to the complexity, reactivity, and variability of responses from human subjects.

- Psychologists must create clear *operational definitions* in order to investigate *properties* which cannot be directly measured. Care must be taken in designing research to avoid potential *bias* and *demand characteristics*.

- Data can be collected in a variety of ways including *correlational studies*, *surveys*, *case studies*, and *experiments*.

- Experiments can provide evidence for cause-and-effect relationships by using *random assignment*, manipulating an *independent variable,* and measuring effects on a *dependent variable*.

- Data collected from studies can be analyzed using *descriptive statistics* such as *measures of central tendency* and *standard deviation*, and *inferential statistics* such as tests for *significance* which help us to draw conclusions about the data collected.

- Psychology has also adopted standards of *ethics* and approval is required before studies can be conducted. These standards include *informed consent, freedom from coercion, protection from harm, awareness of risks, anonymity/confidentiality*, and *debriefing*.

Notes

Chapter 3
Biological Bases of Behavior

Narrowing Our Approach

You'll recall from Chapter 1 that a monist approach assumes that the mind and body are one. In other words, if we want to understand the mind, we can do so by studying the physiological structure and processes of the body. The biological approach to psychology follows this assumption, whether we are trying to understand a relatively simple process like moving your arm, or a complex process like treating depression. While this approach to psychology can be criticized as **reductionist** (i.e. thinking of a complex problem like depression only in terms of neurotransmitter function) the preference towards **parsimony** (looking for the simplest explanation of a complex problem) allows psychologists to study underlying processes and identify reliable and predictable physiological interactions. With this approach in mind, we'll begin by looking at the fundamental building blocks of most organisms: neurons. Neurons are the individual nerve cells which help make up the entire nervous system and understanding how neurons communicate is a key to understanding thought and behavior.

In order to understand how approximately 85 billion neurons in the human brain communicate with one another, we first need to know the parts of a neuron and the function each part serves.

Neuron Structure

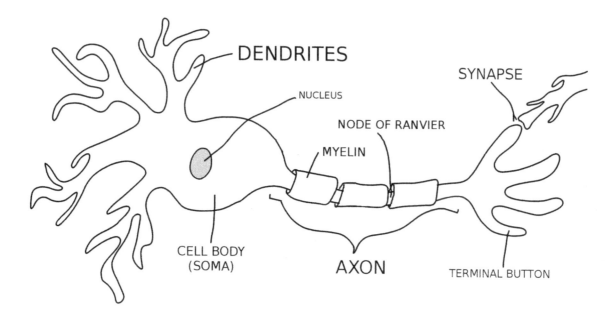

The **Dendrites**– Derived from the Greek word for "tree", dendrites are the parts of a neuron that reach out like branches to receive messages from other neurons. Dendrites are able to receive messages via chemical signals which interact with receptor sites on the dendrites. These receptor sites can be stimulated by messages from other neurons or by other chemical messengers which are traveling in the body.

The **Cell Body** – all of the dendrites lead to the cell body, or **soma**, which collects and aggregates the messages that are being received by the dendrites and it is also where you will find the nucleus of the cell.

The **Axon** – When a certain threshold of stimulation is reached by the dendrites, an electrical signal is sent down the axon, which is the long section of the neuron that leads away from the cell body and out to other neurons (or in some cases to a muscle or organ).

The axon of most (but not all) neurons is covered with a layer of fatty material called **myelin**, which helps to insulate the axon and allows it to send messages faster and more efficiently. You can think of the myelin coating just like the rubber insulation on an electrical wire. A difference, however, is that the myelin is broken up into sections with small gaps between them. These gaps are known as **nodes of Ranvier** (pronounced *Ran-vee-ay*, named after Louis-Antoine Ranvier, the French anatomist who discovered them). These nodes allow the message to travel more quickly by "jumping" along the axon. Each node essentially re-sends the message, preventing its strength from being dissipated along the way. This "jumping" is known as **saltatory conduction**, derived from the Latin word *saltare* - "to jump".

Imagine you and a friend are each standing at either end of a very long hallway. If you wanted to say something, the sound would dissipate and wouldn't reach your friend, so you would need to yell extremely loudly. Now imagine, instead, that many other people were spaced throughout the hallway, and each could repeat your message to pass it along. Now you wouldn't need to shout so loudly, and the message could still reach your friend. This is comparable to how myelin improves the efficiency of neural communication.

The *Terminal Button* – At the end of the axon, the neuron has swelling terminal buttons, which are simply the endpoints of the neuron. These terminal buttons allow the neuron to connect to other nearby neurons. Rather than connecting electrically, most neurons communicate with one another chemically. Inside each terminal button are *vesicles*; special bags which contain chemical messengers known as *neurotransmitters*. These neurotransmitters are released into the space between neurons, known as the *synapse*, where they can float across and interact with the next neuron.

"Protoplasmic Kisses"

Camillo Golgi (1843-1926) developed a silver staining technique (which he called "black reaction" but became known as *Golgi staining*) which showed the dendrites and axons of individual neurons. Golgi incorrectly believed that neurons were all connected to one another, creating a mesh network of neurons (known as *reticular theory*). Ironically, Santiago Ramón y Cajal (1852-1934) adapted Golgi's staining method in order to demonstrate that Golgi was wrong, and that neurons, in fact, did not touch. Ramón y Cajal argued that neurons were actually separated by tiny gaps, which he romantically referred to as "protoplasmic kisses". These tiny gaps between neurons are more formally known as *synapses* (from the Greek for "conjunction"), and they allow neurons to communicate chemically. Ramón y Cajal and Golgi shared the Nobel Prize for Physiology in 1906 (despite their conflicting views – in fact in their Nobel addresses they gave contradictory explanations for the structure of neural networks) and it wasn't until the 1950s that electron microscopes were able to confirm that Ramon y Cajal's *neuron doctrine* was indeed correct, and that neurons were separated by tiny gaps.

Neural Transmission

Now that we know the general structure of the neuron, let's examine in more detail at how it sends messages to communicate with other neurons around it. The communication process for neurons consists of two main types of messages; an electrical message, which carries information within a neuron, and a chemical message, which carries information between neurons.

The Action Potential

When the dendrites of a neuron are stimulated enough to reach a certain threshold, an electric signal travels down the axon of the neuron. This signal is known as an ***action potential***. An important point here is that neuron firing is "***all-or-none***". A neuron either fires an action potential (if a threshold is reached) or it doesn't. There is no in-between. In this way, a neuron is like a gun. It can't be fired a little bit by pulling the trigger more softly and it doesn't fire any harder by pulling the trigger firmly. It simply fires, or it doesn't. Neuron firing is the same, and once the threshold for firing is reached, the action potential generated is always the same. To continue the analogy, after firing an action potential, there is a brief period before the neuron is ready to fire again, which is similar to a machine gun. Holding down the trigger (i.e. continuous stimulation) doesn't generate a solid beam out of the gun barrel, but rather a series of individual firings with brief spaces of time between them. This is also true of neurons. Continuous stimulation doesn't cause a neuron to stay "turned on", but instead causes the neuron to fire repeatedly, with a brief pause between each firing.

To better understand this firing process, let's take a closer look at what actually happens when a neuron is stimulated. The cell membrane is covered with channels (which can be open or closed) that allow for the movement of charged particles (***ions***) in or out of the cell. Stimulation of dendrites causes the movement of charged ions (particularly sodium and potassium) in or out of this semipermeable cell membrane.

This ion movement changes the electrical charge inside the neuron. When a neuron is not firing, the balance of ions inside and outside the cell gives it an electrical charge of about -70millivolts. This is known as the ***resting potential***. Stimulation opens channels for positively-charged sodium ions (Na+) to move into the neuron. When enough sodium moves in and the threshold is reached, many more sodium channels open, allowing even more sodium in. This sudden rush of sodium creates a brief positive electrical charge of about +40millivolts. This positive charge moves along the axon like a wave, traveling from the cell body (soma) to the end of the neuron (terminal button), as sodium channels open sequentially, like a falling line of dominoes. Each sodium channel is open only briefly before closing again while sodium-removing pumps and other ion channels help to restore the neuron to the resting state. The neuron must return to the resting state before it can fire again, and this time delay between firings is known as the ***refractory period***. This process of firing an action potential then returning to resting potential happens quickly, allowing some neurons to fire hundreds of times per second.

It's important to remember that when an action potential travels down the axon, the individual ions themselves aren't actually moving down the axon. This would be far too slow. They are each simply moving in, then back out of the cell membrane in roughly the same place. It's like a baseball stadium doing "the wave". Each person simply stands, then sits, and this triggers the next person to do the same. In this way, the message travels across the entire stadium without the individual people needing to travel the entire distance. You can imagine an action potential the same way; a wave of ion movement that carries a message all the way to the end of the axon.

The Magic of Myelin

I mentioned earlier that myelin helps to insulate axons and improve the efficiency of messages. While we can think of the previous hallway example as demonstrating greater efficiency (you don't need to use as much energy yelling so hard), we can use the baseball stadium analogy to understand the improvement in speed provided by myelin. Imagine that instead of every person in the crowd needing to stand, then sit, we decided that only the first person in each section would stand, then sit. This would trigger the next "section leader" to stand, then sit. In this way, the message could travel the distance of the stadium even more quickly. This is essentially what happens at the **nodes of Ranvier**. The message traveling down the axon jumps along each section, allowing it to reach the terminal button more quickly. As mentioned before, this is known as **saltatory conduction** – from the Latin *saltare* - "to jump".

This improved speed and efficiency makes **myelin** essential, and unfortunately, we can see this importance in diseases which damage myelin (known as *demyelinating diseases*) such as **multiple sclerosis**. In the case of multiple sclerosis, patients' immune systems erroneously attack and destroy their myelin cells. This breakdown of myelin affects the ability to send and receive messages, resulting in problems in movement, coordination, and balance, as well as problems in sensation and cognition.

It's also worth noting that while we are primarily going to focus on neurons in this chapter, we shouldn't completely ignore all the other cells (including myelin) that provide support, insulation, nutrition, and waste removal for neurons. The understanding of these different types of **glial cells** (from the Greek for "glue") has improved greatly in the last few years and researchers are beginning to find that glial cells are involved in more processes than previously thought. They are more than just the glue of the nervous system, and there's evidence that besides the maintenance functions listed above, glial cells may play a role in helping neurons to form new connections.

The Synapse

When the action potential reaches the terminal buttons at the end of the neuron, chemical messengers called **neurotransmitters** are released from containers called **vesicles**. These neurotransmitters then float across the gap between neurons – **the synapse** - and interact with **receptor sites** on the next neurons. When a neurotransmitter binds with a receptor site, it influences the flow of ions into the postsynaptic neuron. The neurotransmitter released by the initial (or **presynaptic**) neuron can either make it more likely that the next (or **postsynaptic**) neuron will fire (**excitatory**) or make it less likely that the next neuron will fire (**inhibitory**).

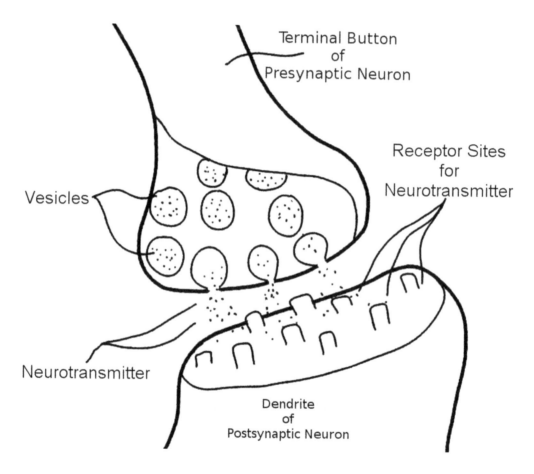

After Release

You may be wondering what happens to the neurotransmitter after it has been released. There are essentially 3 main ways of clearing out the neurotransmitter after a message has been sent.

Reuptake (the vacuum cleaner)

In reuptake, neurotransmitter is sucked back into the presynaptic neuron, where it can be recycled into vesicles and used again.

Enzyme Deactivation (the Pac-man)

Enzymes break the remaining neurotransmitter down into parts which are either recycled or become waste products.

Autoreception (the Thermostat)

The presynaptic neuron also detects levels of neurotransmitter in the synapse, and if the level is high, may prevent more release of neurotransmitter from flooding the synapse.

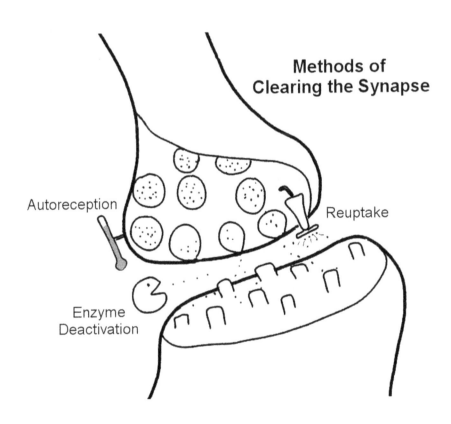

Methods of Clearing the Synapse

Autoreception

Reuptake

Enzyme Deactivation

Types of Neurotransmitters

There are many different neurotransmitters used throughout the body and brain, but let's take a look at a few key examples of neurotransmitters and their related functions. It's important to note that the same neurotransmitter can influence many different behaviors by being used in different areas of the brain. Given the complexity of behavior and the multiple functions of each neurotransmitter, the examples below will, of course, be simplifications of these interactions.

Acetylcholine (ACh) (*ah-see-tyl-koh-leen*) is one of the main excitatory neurotransmitters used in the body and brain. ACh is used throughout the body to control muscle contractions and is also used in brain areas associated with learning, memory, and attention. ***Alzheimer's Disease*** involves deterioration of ACh-producing neurons which causes deficits in memory, learning, and attention. When these neurons cannot produce adequate amounts of ACh, the postsynaptic neurons no longer receive enough stimulation to fire properly. To remember the association between Acetylcholine and Alzheimer's, notice both start with the letter A.

Dopamine is a key neurotransmitter in areas of the brain relating to control of movement and also in areas relating to the experience of pleasure and motivation (the "Reward Area" of the brain). ***Parkinson's Disease*** involves a deterioration of dopamine-producing neurons in an area of the midbrain known as the *substantia nigra*, resulting in problems with coordinating movements. This causes shakes and tremors, one of the main symptoms of this disease. Noticing that a "P" is an upside-down "d" may help you remember the relationship between **P**arkinson's and **d**opamine. In the section on drugs, we'll look at how addictive recreational drugs influence the dopamine-rich "reward area" of the brain.

Gamma-aminobutyric acid, or ***GABA***, is one of the main inhibitory neurotransmitters used in the brain. GABA binds to receptor sites and prevents the flow of positive ions into the neuron, reducing the likelihood that the neuron will reach its threshold and fire an action potential.

Serotonin is a neurotransmitter that is used in pathways related to mood and well-being and is also involved in the regulation of sleep and dreaming. ***Major depressive disorder*** is believed to be associated with reduced activity of serotonin in some brain areas. Lower levels of serotonin affect the functioning of certain neurons, which leads to decreases in mood. The most commonly prescribed type of medication for depression is an ***SSRI*** (Selective Serotonin Reuptake Inhibitor), which increases the level of serotonin available in the synapse by blocking reuptake. This is like clogging up the vacuum cleaner so that it can no longer pull away any of that precious serotonin. This results in serotonin staying in the synapse longer and being better able to influence subsequent neurons, which may help elevate mood.

Norepinephrine (also known as *noradrenaline*) - Norepinephrine is an excitatory neurotransmitter which is involved in physiological arousal and the regulation of heart rate. In a stressful situation, more norepinephrine is released, which then stimulates the heart to beat more quickly.

How Drugs Influence Neurotransmitter Function

Because neurons rely on chemicals to communicate, their communication can be altered by the introduction of certain chemicals in the form of psychoactive drugs. One of the main ways that drugs affect the body and brain is by influencing the communication between neurons. By increasing or decreasing the activity of different neurotransmitters in different areas of the brain, drugs are able to have a variety of effects on behavior. Most drugs have multiple effects on the body and brain, but we'll be simplifying the following examples to focus on relationships with particular neurotransmitters.

When it comes to influence over a particular neurotransmitter's activity, drugs are often classified as being either **agonists** or **antagonists**. Substances which are **agonists** for a neurotransmitter increase the activity of the neurotransmitter. Drugs which are **antagonists**, however, reduce the activity or effectiveness of a particular neurotransmitter. Let's take a look at a few specific drug/neurotransmitter interactions in order to see how some well-known drugs influence neural communication.

Nicotine is an example of an agonist for the neurotransmitter Acetylcholine (ACh). Nicotine's structure resembles that of ACh, allowing it to bind to the same receptor sites on neurons, opening ion channels and increasing the likelihood that certain neurons will fire, particularly those in brain areas associated with attention and learning. While this may sound like a good thing, over time this repeated stimulation of neurons from nicotine reduces the sensitivity of those neurons. As a result, greater amounts of nicotine are required for the same effect. In addition, ACh production is reduced because there appears to be a surplus of ACh with all the increased neuron activity. When nicotine is not available to assist the reduced level of ACh, smokers experience difficulty concentrating, as well as other symptoms of withdrawal.

Alcohol (more specifically *ethanol*) is technically not an agonist, but it does enhance the effects of the neurotransmitter GABA (gamma-aminobutyric acid). You may recall that GABA is an inhibitory neurotransmitter, meaning that its presence reduces the likelihood that postsynaptic neurons will fire. Ethanol increasing the effects of GABA means that it is less likely certain neurons will fire when alcohol is consumed (which is why it is known as a *depressant*). As consumption increases, this inhibition affects different areas of the brain. This can be seen in the progressive deficits that alcohol consumption causes; initially there is a reduction of activity in neurons which regulate and monitor behavior for appropriateness (Should I make a sexually suggestive remark to this person I just met? Should I take my shirt off and dance on the bar?), followed by reduced firing of neurons coordinating movements (stumbling) and speech production (slurring) and eventually inhibiting enough function to cause unconsciousness or even death.

In understanding any kind of substance addiction, remember that the body is always working to compensate for the changes that drugs bring about, in order to restore balance and maintain normal functioning. In the case of alcohol, the nervous system attempts to counteract the inhibition that alcohol causes by increasing the strength of excitatory messages.

It does this by increasing levels of the excitatory neurotransmitter glutamate. This is how a tolerance for alcohol's effects builds up with regular consumption, but with chronic excessive consumption this tolerance can become a dangerous dependency. In this case, the body relies on the inhibitory effect of alcohol to maintain functioning, and without it experiences excessive stimulation. This *excitotoxicity* causes withdrawal symptoms which can include anxiety, shakes, tremors, heart palpitations, and in extreme cases, even death. Similar types of withdrawal can occur with sudden cessation of other depressant drugs like benzodiazepines or barbiturates.

Methamphetamine and Cocaine each have a number of different effects on the brain, but one they share is that they are both agonists for the neurotransmitter dopamine. In the *nucleus accumbens*, the "reward area" of the brain, dopamine stimulates neurons which trigger feelings of pleasure, well-being, and euphoria. While these neurons are normally triggered by behaviors like eating or sex, drugs like meth and cocaine (and to a lesser extent, nicotine) also activate these neurons by influencing the release of dopamine. It is this activation of the reward area that makes these drugs particularly addictive. With repeated drug consumption, these dopamine areas can become damaged, which can lead to reduced ability to experience pleasure (known as *anhedonia*). Meth and coke both stimulate norepinephrine release, causing an increase in heart rate. In the case of overdose, the heart contracts so rapidly that blood cannot properly flow in and out of it, which can lead to unconsciousness or even death.

Caffeine is an example of an antagonist drug for the neurotransmitter adenosine (in addition to other effects on the brain and body). Adenosine is an inhibitory neurotransmitter which is mostly produced as a result of ATP metabolism. The adenosine produced inhibits activity of some neurons, and is partially responsible for feelings of tiredness. Caffeine binds to the receptor sites for adenosine, blocking it from being detected but not actually inhibiting the neurons. As a result, we don't experience the same level of tiredness. Once the caffeine has been broken down, however, the receptors are flooded with the adenosine that has been accumulating, leading to sudden inhibition of the neurons and the feeling of a "crash" we're probably all familiar with.

The Structure of the Nervous System

Now that we've got a general understanding of neural communication, let's take a broader view and look at the nervous system as a whole. The nervous system can be broadly divided into two major sections, the central nervous system and the peripheral nervous system.

The Central Nervous System (*CNS*) includes the brain and the spinal cord, and these vital structures are "armored" by being encased in bone (the skull and the vertebrae).

The Peripheral Nervous System (*PNS*) includes all the other nerves, blood vessels, organs, and glands outside of the brain and spinal cord. Since this includes a wide variety of systems, it is further divided into sections.

One section is the *somatic division* of the peripheral nervous system. This includes skeletal muscles and their nerves, which are generally under voluntary control. You can decide when and how to move your arms, legs, facial muscles, etc.

The second division of the peripheral nervous system is the *autonomic division*. The autonomic division contains nerves, muscles, organs, and glands which are not under voluntary control. This would include systems regulating your breathing, heart rate, perspiration, sweating, and digestion, all of which are generally outside of conscious control. Our bodies have automated these essential processes in order to free up resources for other tasks (you can remember the word autonomic sounds similar to automatic). You can imagine how difficult life would be if we didn't relinquish control and instead had to consciously remember to take each breath, pace our heart's rhythm, or command the processes of digesting our dinner. If these processes weren't on auto-pilot we simply wouldn't have the cognitive resources left for more complex behaviors like moving gracefully, reading great literature, or contemplating the meaning of our existence.

Control of these autonomic processes can be further subdivided into two main systems. The *sympathetic nervous system* works to excite the autonomic division and can be most clearly seen in the face of acute stress which triggers the "fight or flight" response. In the face of a sudden threat, our survival may depend on escaping or fighting off this threat. Despite this name, "fight" and "flight" aren't the only possible reactions to a threat, and there is also a "freeze" response.

The sympathetic nervous system is activated through a combination of processes, including the release of **hormones**, which are chemical messengers carried throughout the body via the bloodstream. Hormones like adrenaline prime our bodies for action. Activation of the sympathetic nervous system increases our level of arousal, our heart rate, blood pressure, respiration, muscle tension, and sweating, while simultaneously decreasing less essential processes like digestion, salivation, and immune response. Escaping from a predator may require all the energy you have available, so for the moment, using energy to digest your lunch or fight germs may not be the best use of your resources.

While we may not be fleeing from tigers very often in the modern age, we still experience the same sympathetic activation in response to threats and stress, which may help explain those knots in your stomach, dry mouth, rapid heart rate, and profuse sweating as you prepare to make a presentation in class. You may wish you had greater conscious control over your autonomic nervous system to command your body to "stop sweating" or "slow heart rate" as easily as you move your arms, but as mentioned above, it's generally a good trade-off that we don't have this kind of conscious control (and thus responsibility) for these systems.

In contrast to the sympathetic nervous response, the ***parasympathetic nervous system*** relaxes the autonomic division, helping us to recover from stress. We cannot always be on high alert, so after escaping from that fierce tiger, we need to put the brakes on the stress response and restore our body to a resting state. Activation of the parasympathetic system causes a decrease in arousal, lowered heart rate, respiration, and muscle tension, reduced levels of stress hormones, and increases in digestion and immune function. Sitting quietly, breathing deeply, or practicing meditation are ways to help activate the parasympathetic nervous system and these behaviors can induce what Herbert Benson calls the "relaxation response". Engaging in these behaviors can be seen as a way of taking greater control over your autonomic nervous system, particularly if you are plagued by chronic stress. So while you can't readily command your heart rate to slow or your immune system to step things up, you can engage in behaviors that will help to accomplish these feats.

Now that we've covered the general organization of the nervous system, let's look in greater detail at its crowning structure; the brain.

Ways of Studying the Brain

In the past, the ability to study structures in the brain was mostly limited to studying the brains of the deceased. Technologies for looking at brain function in living humans didn't exist, and the closest approximation was to study cases of brain damage to particular areas and attempt to relate these to impaired functions. Noticing that a blow to the back of the head was associated with subsequent visual problems would indicate that the back of the brain may be related to vision. One could also study the effects of stroke damage on patients' subsequent behavior. A stroke is a blockage of blood flow in the brain which can cause brain tissue in that particular area to die. By analyzing changes in behavior before and after a stroke, and analyzing the location of brain damage in autopsy, one could make inferences about the role of those areas.

One of the most famous examples of brain damage and clues to function is the unfortunate case of Phineas Gage. Gage was a 25 year-old foreman working on a railroad in Vermont in 1848. While he was working, a charge accidentally detonated and sent a 3-foot iron tamping rod into his left cheek and clear through the top of his head. Along the way, it damaged his left eye, but more importantly, took out a piece of the left frontal lobe of his brain. Miraculously, Gage remained conscious immediately following the accident, even explaining the event to a local doctor (though Gage was later comatose and his recovery was slow). He survived this experience, though there were claims his personality changed following the ordeal. While he was described as previously being a dependable worker and polite young man, following his accident he was described as fitful and profane and his ability to regulate his behavior was questioned.

We can't be too sure of the exact changes in Gage as details are scant. Just how long-lasting any changes were has been called into question, as later Gage was able to work successfully as a stagecoach driver in Chile, a job which would require social skills, planning, and behavioral control. Despite distortions and unsubstantiated claims about the extent of personality change in Gage, his case still demonstrates a way to study brain function and consider what role certain brain structures may play in behavior and personality.

Another famous analysis of brain damage was carried out by physician Paul Broca in the 1860s. Broca saw one patient who was referred to as "Tan" (real name Louis Victor Leborgne). Leborgne's comprehension of language was intact, but he was only able to produce the syllable "tan" when he spoke. Following Leborgne's death, Broca performed an autopsy and found damage to a region in the left frontal lobe. He correctly surmised that this area of the brain must be involved in speech production, and he then collected confirming evidence from autopsies of other patients with the same speech production problem (known as *aphasia*) and similar damage to the left frontal lobe. This is considered to be one of the first cases of direct evidence for localization of brain function and we now know that this area (called ***Broca's area***) helps send messages to the motor cortex to coordinate the muscle movements necessary for speech production.

While these attempts at understanding the brain were crucial milestones of discovery, they pale in comparison to the modern brain imaging techniques that have been developed in the last few decades. One of the oldest methods for analyzing living brain function is the **EEG** or **electroencephalogram**, first used on humans in 1924. The activity of neurons firing produces tiny surges of electrical activity, which can be detected through the skull. By placing electrodes on the scalp, an EEG picks up on these electrical impulses and graphs them as waves of activity, which are referred to as **brain waves**. As we'll see in chapter 8, different states of consciousness have differing brain wave patterns.

A **CAT scan** (also called a **CT scan**) uses X-rays to reveal the structure of the brain. Short for **Computerized Axial Tomography** (*tomography* refers to making a 2D image "slice" of a 3D object), a CT scan sends a series of X-rays through the skull at a variety of angles. A computer then combines how the X-rays pass through varying densities of different brain structures and creates a 2D image of a "slice" of the brain, allowing us to see structural abnormalities or physical damage.

An even more detailed way of looking at brain structure is **Magnetic Resonance Imaging** (**MRI**). An MRI machine sends a magnetic pulse through the brain, causing molecules to temporarily twist, then relax in response to the magnetic field. This slight movement releases energy, and by recording the pattern of energy, an MRI is able to create a detailed image of the brain's structure.

A **PET** scan (**Positron Emission Tomography**) is a **functional imaging** technique, meaning that it is able to show regions of activation in a living brain. In a PET scan, the patient first ingests a small amount of a harmless radioactive substance. This substance travels in the bloodstream to the brain. Brain areas which are working harder will require more oxygen (and thus greater blood flow) so by looking at concentrations of the radioactive substance we can see which brain areas have greater blood flow, and thus more activation. While a PET scan can show us general levels of activation, it isn't able to provide clear images of specific regions of activation over short periods of time. For this, we turn to fMRI.

fMRI (functional magnetic resonance imaging) is similar to MRI in that it uses a magnetic pulse to briefly twist molecules, but in this case, an fMRI machine acts on molecules of hemoglobin. This allows it to reveal levels of blood flow in specific areas of the brain over much shorter periods of time, without the patient needing to ingest a radioactive substance. For now, this is the closest we can get to seeing real-time brain function. Participants in an fMRI machine can carry out cognitive tasks while researchers watch areas of the brain change their levels of activation, allowing us to see localization of brain function in action.

Brain Structures

The brain has a lot of responsibilities spread across a number of different areas and structures, so it's often divided up into categories to simplify things a bit. Generally it's broken up into three main areas, the **hindbrain**, the **midbrain**, and the *forebrain.*

You may also sometimes hear of the "**old brain**" and the "**new brain**", which has nothing to do with a person's age or development. This is a way of categorizing brain areas in terms of evolutionary time, with the structures that have been around the longest being referred to as the "old brain" (generally areas that are crucial for survival – the hindbrain and midbrain), while structures that appeared later in human evolutionary history are referred to as the "new brain" (areas that are useful but less essential – the forebrain).

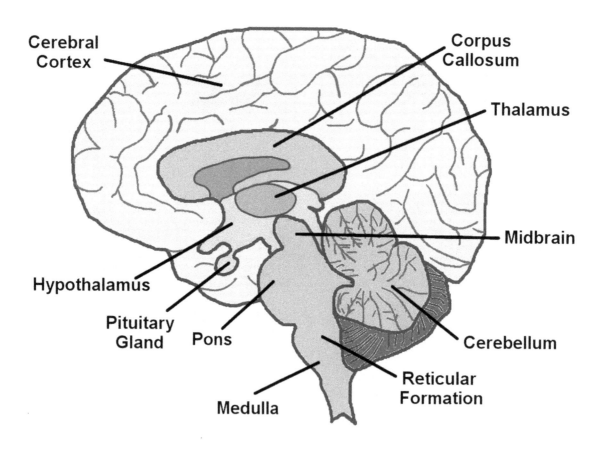

The Hindbrain

The structures of the hindbrain control the most basic elements of survival, giving us a pulse and allowing us to be alert and mobile. The *medulla* regulates several activities which are absolutely essential for survival; heart rate and respiration. The *reticular formation* is involved in the regulation of wakefulness and states of vigilance. The *cerebellum* (from the Latin for "little brain" – based on its appearance) helps to coordinate and fine-tune motor activity, allowing for smooth and graceful movements. The cerebellum is connected to the rest of the brain via the *pons* (Latin for "bridge") which helps relay messages back and forth between the brain, cerebellum, and spinal cord.

The Midbrain

The two areas of the mid-brain, the *tectum* and the *tegmentum*, are primarily involved in orientation and coordination of movement. The *substantia nigra*, an area of the tegmentum which uses dopamine as a neurotransmitter, can be affected by Parkinson's disease, resulting in problems with motor control and tremors.

The Forebrain

Life is about more than just having a pulse and moving around, and this is where the structures of the forebrain really come into play. The forebrain is divided into two categories; the *cerebral cortex*, which is the thin outer layer of the brain, and the *subcortical structures* underneath (literally "under-cortex").

We'll start with the subcortical structures and work our way up.

The *thalamus* is a relay station for information. Information from our senses comes to the thalamus first and is then sent to appropriate areas of the cortex. You can think of the thalamus like an old-timey telephone switchboard operator, receiving calls and then redirecting them out to the appropriate connections.

The *hypothalamus* (literally the "under-thalamus") is the area underneath the thalamus which is involved in regulating hunger, thirst, and body temperature, and it plays a key role in hormone release for the fight-or-flight response. This area is where you'll find the *nucleus accumbens*, the "reward area" of the brain, which is associated with motivation for behaviors like eating or having sex, and as mentioned previously, is involved in drug addiction. A useful bad joke for remembering the four main functions of the hypothalamus is to refer to the four **F**s: feeding, fighting, fleeing, and mating.

The *limbic system* is a group of structures (including the *hypothalamus*) related to emotion and memory. The *amygdala* (Latin for "almond") attaches emotional significance to events and triggers the neighboring *hippocampus* to form memories, allowing us to keep track of emotionally-charged events and stimuli (hippocampus is Greek for "sea-horse"; obviously there were some imaginative early anatomists).

The **pituitary gland** is the "master gland" because it releases hormones which can stimulate other glands to release their hormones.

The **basal ganglia** is involved in voluntary motor control and the initiation of movements.

Finally we reach the **cerebral cortex**, the wrinkled outer layer of the brain (about 2-4 millimeters thick) where the most complex processing occurs. The reason for all the wrinkling and folding of the cortex is that this allows a greater surface area to fit inside our already over-sized heads. If it were smoothed out, the cortex would cover an area about the size of an open sheet of newspaper. Fortunately we don't need to have giant, flat newspaper heads, and crumpling the cortex allows us to fit more brain into a smaller skull.

The Hemispheres

The cortex is divided into different areas that handle different tasks. The first general division is that of the left side of the brain and the right side. These two hemispheres are connected by a band of nerve fibers called the **corpus callosum**, which allows each half-brain to know what the other half is up to. Each of these hemispheres specializes in different types of tasks and is able to function independently.

When it comes to sensations and movement of the body, the hemispheres have **contralateral control**, which means that the left hemisphere controls the right side of the body and the right hemisphere controls the left side of the body. Other tasks are specialized as well, such as language and speech production occurring mostly in the left hemisphere, while the recognition of faces and musical patterns generally occurs in the right hemisphere. These differences in task management may vary slightly from person to person, particularly when someone is left-handed (like myself). In the next section of this chapter, we'll see some examples of patients with split brains who initially helped give us these insights into the specialized functions of each hemisphere.

The Lobes of the Brain

Each hemisphere of the brain can be divided up into 4 distinct lobes, each of which is specialized for particular tasks.

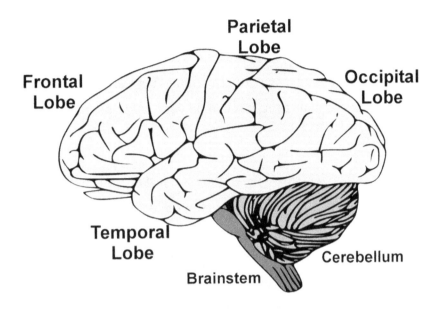

The Occipital Lobes

The occipital lobes are located at the very back of each hemisphere. The main task of the occipital lobe is to process visual information. Information originating from the optic nerves goes to the thalamus and from there is passed on to the primary visual cortex (known as V1) in the occipital lobe. To help you remember that the occipital lobe processes visual information, just imagine the O of **O**ccipital is an eyeball located on the back of your head.

The Parietal Lobes

The parietal lobes are located just under the top of your head in each hemisphere. One of the functions of the parietal lobe is to process touch information coming from the body. Each hemisphere's parietal lobe contains an area known as the ***somatosensory cortex***. The somatosensory cortex is like a map of your skin surface, where body parts are represented according to their sensitivity. Greater sensitivity requires a greater amount of space in the cortex. If we were to make a representation of a person based on the amount of brain area in the cortex, this person (known as a ***homunculus*** – "little man" in Latin) would have giant-sized hands, lips, and other ummm... how should I put it...particularly sensitive areas. Less sensitive areas of the skin surface, such as your legs or torso, require less area in the somatosensory cortex.

The Temporal Lobes

The temporal lobes are located on either side of your head. One of the main functions of the temporal lobes is to process auditory information. Just like with vision, information coming from the auditory nerves goes to the thalamus and is then passed to the primary auditory cortex in the temporal lobe (an area known as A1 – not to be confused with the delicious steak sauce). Auditory input is not strictly contralateral, and both hemispheres receive information from each ear. How each hemisphere processes the information is somewhat specialized, and in general, the left temporal lobe specializes in processing speech, while the right temporal lobe is specialized for processing music. You can remember the temporal lobes relate to hearing by considering that they are located near your ears (just behind your *temp*les).

The Frontal Lobes

Lastly we come to the frontal lobes, which are the brain areas just behind your forehead. Near the border with the parietal lobes, adjacent to the somatosensory cortex, the frontal lobes contain the ***motor cortices*** (cortices is the plural of cortex) which control voluntary movement of different areas of the body. These are arranged contralaterally (left hemisphere controls the right side of the body, and vice versa). These are laid out in a similar manner to the somatosensory cortices, in that movements involving greater dexterity require larger amounts of cortex. So again, the hands and mouth (consider the intricacy of producing speech) take up large amounts of space, while areas corresponding to simpler movements (knee, elbow, etc.) require less space.

More importantly, the frontal lobes can be seen as being the "executives" of the brain which can control and regulate our behaviors. In many ways the frontal lobes set us apart from other primates (notice their sloping foreheads in comparison to ours – they have considerably smaller frontal lobes) and these lobes give us those traits that make us most human. The frontal lobes carry out tasks relating to planning and reasoning, thinking about the future, regulating emotions and making decisions. When a harsh comment and low score on a paper has you ready to physically assault your teacher, the frontal lobes (hopefully) step in and allow you to consider the consequences of your actions, imagine your future life in a prison cell, and come up with an alternative (and more reasonable) course of action.

Splitting the Cortex

One way of seeing differences between the two hemispheres comes from cases of patients with "split-brains". These patients have had their corpus callosum severed in order to prevent the spread of epileptic seizures. While this process effectively stops the seizures, it also creates a few interesting side effects of having two hemispheres which are no longer able to communicate with one another.

This doesn't have a major effect on the patients' lives, as most visual and auditory information is received by both hemispheres, but Roger Sperry and colleague Michael Gazzaniga devised a number of clever experiments to demonstrate some of the specializations of each hemisphere, for which Sperry was awarded the Nobel Prize in 1981. As mentioned when discussing Broca's work on aphasia, speech production is predominantly located in the left hemisphere. This means that split-brain patients are able to talk about information that is in their left hemisphere, but they are unable to verbalize information that is solely in the right hemisphere.

If a split-brain patient were blindfolded and a key were placed in her right hand, she would be able to recognize it and verbally identify it because that sensory information would be in her left hemisphere (remember contralateral control). If, on the other hand (literally), the key were placed in her left hand, she would not be able to say what it was. She would, however, be able to point to the object or even draw it using the left hand. This shows that the right hemisphere is able to have knowledge that cannot be verbally expressed without the help of the left hemisphere.

If a split-brain patient focuses his vision on the center of a screen, anything to the left of the focal point (left visual field) goes to the right hemisphere, while anything in the right visual field goes to the left hemisphere. Note that this division is by visual field not by eye; each eye sends information to both hemispheres, with the left half of what that eye sees going to the right hemisphere and the right half going to the left hemisphere. By selectively presenting images to a particular hemisphere and then assessing the patient's response, we can clearly see how some tasks are localized to that hemisphere.

saw   **+**   **hammer**

For instance, if the words above were flashed on a screen (with the cross as the center focal point), the split-brain patient would say that he saw the word "hammer", yet if he were asked to draw what he saw with the left hand (right hemisphere) he would draw a picture of a saw. In a similar study, Michael Gazzaniga presented images of faces made out of objects and showed that split-brain patients are only able to recognize the faces when they are presented to the right hemisphere, indicating that this hemisphere is specialized for face recognition.

Unfortunately, the popular press frequently exaggerates the importance of these hemispheric differences as though we had to choose which hemisphere to use for each task. It's certainly not the case that artists are "right-brained" or that mathematicians are more "left-brained". These differences in skills and preferences cannot be so easily explained by which hemisphere they use. The truth is that we all use both hemispheres all the time, as most of our behaviors are complex enough to require many areas of brain activation in both hemispheres simultaneously. So while it is true that some processes (like speech production or face recognition) are generally confined to particular hemispheres, this doesn't mean that your left hemisphere is twiddling its thumbs while you look at a face or that your right hemisphere shuts down while you're speaking. Both hemispheres are constantly working and processing information, and assuming that you have an intact corpus callosum, they're also constantly letting each other know what's happening on the other side.

An Introduction to Genes and Heritability

Another one of the main assumptions of the biological approach to psychology is that traits and behaviors are **heritable**, meaning that they can be passed from one generation to the next via biological means. Here's a basic look at how this happens.

We've all heard of genes, but what are they exactly? A **gene** is the name used for a single unit of hereditary information passed from parent to offspring. This information contains instructions used to code for proteins and build the cells of the offspring. All of our genetic information is known as our **genome**. You may be surprised to learn that we share a great number of genes with other species, in fact, humans share about 96% of our genes with chimpanzees. This may seem like a lot, but when we consider the role of genes in building all of our cells, we realize the many commonalities with chimps. Our genes need to tell our bodies how to make hair cells, skin, eyes, ears, a heart, blood vessels, neurons, and so on, and chimps also need to make many very similar structures. With this in mind, we shouldn't be quite so shocked that so many of the instructions are similar.

Our genes are located on our **DNA** (*deoxyribonucleic acid*) which is organized into strands called **chromosomes**. These chromosomes are arranged in pairs, and abnormalities aside, we each have 23 pairs of chromosomes. For each chromosome pair, one half came from your dad's DNA, and the other half came from your mom's DNA. This means that overall, you will share half of your genes with your father and half of your genes with your mother. Exactly which genes you get from mom and which you get from dad, however, is randomly determined.

If you have siblings, they will also randomly receive half of their genes from mom and half from dad, so, on average, you'll share about half of your genes with each of your siblings. Identical twins, or more formally, **monozygotic twins** will share 100% of their genes because they result when a single fertilized egg or *zygote* splits to become two individuals. Since both twins come from the same sperm cell and same egg, their genes are identical (For the nit-pickers, technically it isn't 100% shared genes because development can result in mutations and copy number variation but for our purposes we will ignore these).

Fraternal, or **dizygotic**, twins, however, result from 2 separately fertilized *zygotes*, (two different eggs and two different sperm cells) and so they are just like any other siblings, and will share about 50% of their genes. It's worth noting that when we talk about shared genes among family members, the 50% refers to the percent of genes that may possibly vary among all humans, not the overall difference (as in the chimp example above). In other words, you share somewhere around 99.9% of your genes with all humans, but of the remaining 0.1% that can vary, 50% will be identical with your mom, dad, or siblings, (or 100% of it if you have an identical twin).

Behavioral Genetics

Since these different types of twins have different amounts of shared genes, we can use them to estimate the amount of genetic influence on a particular trait. For example, we might look at a trait like IQ and see if monozygotic twins tend to have more similar IQs than dizygotic twins have. If monozygotic twins are more similar, this would indicate that genes play a role in determining IQ because these twins share more genes. Twin studies like these, along with studies of family histories and adoption studies, attempt to estimate the heritability of certain traits or behaviors. A **_heritability score_** (usually denoted with the coefficient h^2) is a number ranging from 0 to 1 which represents how much of the variance of a trait is due to genetic influence. A heritability score of 0 means that genes have no influence on the differences between people, while a score of 1 would indicate the sole influence of genes in explaining why people differ.

For example, in the case of IQ, the heritability score is generally estimated to be around 0.5, meaning that about half of the reason for people's differences in IQ is genetic, and the other half is explained by their different environments and experiences (like nutrition, parenting, school, access to books, etc).

It's important to remember that heritability scores are always about *groups* of people, not individuals, and that estimated heritability scores will vary in different places, time periods, and populations. A heritability score of 0.5 for IQ doesn't mean that half of your individual IQ score comes from your genes. It means that in comparing IQ scores to each other, the reason for differences is partly explained by the fact that people have different genes and partly explained by the fact that people have different environments. It's also important to note that while heritability indicates the relative strength of these forces, it doesn't tell us which genes or which aspects of the environment are influencing a particular trait.

Molecular Genetics

While the behavioral genetics techniques above can identify relationships between genes and traits, they aren't able to isolate the individual genes responsible. In some cases, however, we are able to specify individual genes that are connected to particular behaviors, traits, problems, or illnesses, and this type of genetic research is known as *molecular genetics*.

Molecular genetics includes the study of *chromosomal abnormalities* that have certain characteristic features. In copying the genetic material from parent to offspring, occasionally an entire half of a chromosome pair is duplicated or missing. Having a particular chromosomal abnormality then predicts a number of symptoms that you may experience. Here are a few examples of possible chromosomal abnormalities and their effects.

Down Syndrome occurs when an extra chromosome is copied on the 21st chromosome pair. This results in the characteristic symptoms of Down Syndrome, including a rounded face, thin lips, and moderate mental retardation.

With the following chromosomal abnormalities, occurring on the 23rd chromosome pair, we can see how sex isn't always an either/or distinction of male/female. Generally, the 23rd pair for females contains 2 X chromosomes (XX), while males have an X chromosome and a Y chromosome (XY).

Turner Syndrome – Turner Syndrome occurs when a female child only has a single X chromosome and is missing the other half of the chromosome pair. The physical characteristics of Turner Syndrome include a webbed neck, swollen feet, widely spread nipples, and abnormal genital development. Girls with Turner Syndrome will not menstruate and will not be able to bear children.

Klinefelter Syndrome occurs when there is an extra X chromosome present in a male child. In this case, the child is XXY, with physical characteristics including above average height, breast development, and smaller testicles. Some males with Klinefelter Syndrome are able to produce sperm (and thus have offspring) but not all.

Individual Gene Mutations

In addition to understanding chromosomal abnormalities, molecular genetics can reveal the structures and functions of individual genes. Genes code for proteins and amino acids and particular versions of some genes will create anomalies in the amino acids they code for. By looking at a person's genetic profile and also identifying the presence or absence of a particular version of a protein, enzyme, or amino acid, we can establish a link between particular genes and certain physiological outcomes.

One such case is the disease **PKU** or **phenylketonuria**. PKU results from the mutation of just one of the 3 billion base pairs that make up the human genome. In this case, the body's ability to create *phenylalanine hydroxylase* (PAH), an enzyme that breaks down phenylalanine, is impaired. Phenylalanine is a toxic amino acid found in certain foods like meat, cheese, and fish that is broken down by PAH into tyrosine, rendering it harmless. Without the correct form of the PAH enzyme, however, people with PKU are unable to break down phenylalanine. As consumption continues, phenylalanine builds up in the body, hindering brain development and resulting in seizures and cognitive deficits.

Fortunately, PKU can be detected early, and a diet which strictly avoids phenylalanine can be adopted. By following a strict diet and also supplementing with some amino acids, people born with PKU can avoid the damaging effects of phenylalanine and live normal, healthy lives.

While these are just a few examples of possible mutations and abnormalities, they can get us started in exploring exactly how our genes make us who we are. We will return to these genetic approaches in future chapters to look for clues in understanding complex subjects like intelligence or personality traits or disorders like depression and schizophrenia.

Chapter Summary – Biological Bases of Behavior

- *Neurons* are the building blocks of the nervous system which can communicate with one another. This communication consists of two main parts: *action potentials* within a neuron, and chemical messages passed in the *synapses* between neurons by *neurotransmitters*.

- The nervous system can be broadly divided into the *Central Nervous System* (CNS) and the *Peripheral Nervous System* (PNS). The PNS is further divided into the *somatic division* under voluntary control and the *autonomic division* which is involuntary. The autonomic division can then be separated into the *sympathetic nervous system* which responds to threats and the *parasympathetic nervous system* which enables relaxation and recovery.

- The brain is composed of a number of underlying structures covered by the *cerebral cortex*, which is divided into two main *hemispheres*, connected by the corpus callosum. Each hemisphere contains 4 *lobes* which process different types of information.

- Studies of *heritability* assess the extent of genetic influence in explaining why people differ. *Behavioral genetics* investigates the overall role of genes on certain traits and behaviors, while *molecular genetics* seeks to identify specific gene interactions.

Notes

Chapter 4
Sensation & Perception

Stimulation and Interpretation

Sensation refers to the actual stimulation of the sensory organs. Light hitting your eyes, sound waves vibrating your eardrums, things touching your skin, or chemical molecules finding their way into your nose and mouth are all sensory experiences that can be sent to your brain. The process of converting these physical signals in the world into neural activity in the brain is known as *transduction*.

Perception refers to the interpretation and organization of the information that is coming in from the sense organs. Most of the time, this processing occurs so quickly and seamlessly that we tend to forget that it is a separate step from sensation. It seems that we immediately recognize objects in our visual field (that's a coffee mug, that's a pen, etc.) or identify the sounds around us (those are footsteps, that's a bird chirping, etc.) but this perception of the sensory information is actually a complex process that is also influenced by our experience with the world. On rare occasions we may be reminded of this separation between sensation and perception when we can't quite make out what we're looking at or what we're hearing. When this occurs, our problem is not in *sensing* the stimulus (we know it's there), but in *perceiving* it (we don't know how to correctly interpret it).

One of the simplest ways to demonstrate this separation of sensation and perception is to find a stimulus that is intentionally ambiguous, such as the "Necker Cube" below:

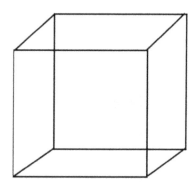

Which panel of the cube is closest to you? There are 2 possible answers. You may perceive the panel starting at the bottom left corner as closest, or you may perceive the panel starting at the top right corner as closest. In fact, you can probably switch which appears closer at will. When we mentally flip our view of the cube, the sensation isn't changing at all, but our interpretation and organization of that sensation (our perception) is changing.

Psychophysics

My apologies to those of you hoping to read about physics gone mad; the truth is that psychophysics is actually the study of our sensitivity to stimuli of different strengths. This is generally done by attempting to measure different types of thresholds.

Absolute threshold refers to the minimum amount of stimulation necessary for a stimulus to be detected. For example, the absolute threshold for vision would be the dimmest light that we could possibly see or for hearing it would be the softest tone that we're able to hear.

Measuring absolute threshold is difficult because it's often hard to know if a participant is actually detecting a stimulus or just guessing. As we approach the minimal intensity, even the participant will have a hard time knowing if he really saw or heard something. In order to accommodate for this, psychophysicists (who may or may not be mad scientists) generally consider the absolute threshold to be the point at which accuracy for detecting a stimulus reaches 50% and higher. Once a participant is able to achieve 50% accuracy, it can be assumed that the participant is actually detecting the stimulus.

In addition to knowing about the minimum intensity necessary for perception, psychophysics also investigates how well we can differentiate between two stimuli that are both above the absolute threshold. In other words, how much change is necessary (in the brightness of a light, the volume of a sound, etc.) for us to detect that a change has occurred? While many psychological concepts have wonderfully creative names, this is not one of them. The minimum amount of change that we can actually detect is referred to as the ***just-noticeable difference (JND)***.

In attempting to measure just-noticeable differences, we run into the following question: Why is it that people can tell the difference between the brightness of 1 versus 2 candles, but not the difference between 100 and 101 candles? Similarly, when I'm at the gym, I can easily feel the difference between a 1lb weight and a 2lb weight (I'm really hitting those biceps hard), but I can't detect the difference between 100lbs and 101lbs. The reason for this is that just-noticeable differences aren't constant amounts of change, they are constant *proportions* of change. This concept is known as ***Weber's Law*** (Ernst Weber was German so it's pronounced Vay-ber, not Web-er).

For example, in the case of detecting changes in weight, people generally need a change of about 2% in order to detect the difference. This explains why an envelope with 2 sheets of paper inside feels noticeably heavier than an envelope with only one sheet, but why a 500 page textbook feels the same as a textbook with 505 pages.

Signal Detection Theory

I mentioned above that a 50% accuracy rate is needed to assume that a participant is actually detecting a stimulus. With this in mind, we should consider that our ability to detect stimuli is not as predictable and dependable as we might like. In fact, our senses are constantly dealing with the problem of "**noise**", both internal and external, which clouds our perception. This term "noise" doesn't just refer to sounds, but anything that might interfere with our ability to detect a stimulus.

If you've had a hearing test you've experienced an excellent demonstration of signal detection theory. Imagine your hearing test is just about to begin. Even in a soundproof room, there may be some unintentional sounds affecting your ability to hear the tones being tested. From vibrations in the floor to the movement of air molecules hitting your eardrums, there really is no "perfectly quiet". Even if these potential distractions could be completely eliminated, you may then become aware of the sound of your breathing, your heart beating, or even the movement of blood in your body, in addition to the noise of your internal thoughts, imagined sounds, and spontaneous neural activity that occurs quite regularly.

Now, let's say the tester is going to either present a stimulus tone (yes), or not (no), and you're going to respond that you detected the stimulus (yes), or not (no). This gives us a matrix of 4 possible scenarios, illustrated below:

	Response: **YES**	Response: **NO**
Signal Present? YES	**HIT**	*MISS*
Signal Present? NO	*FALSE ALARM*	**CORRECT REJECTION**

When a tone is loud and clear, you may not have any doubts, but what do you do when you're unsure? Was that a tone being played or not? Should you err on the side of saying yes? If so, you'll probably get more hits, but you'll also end up getting more false alarms. Similarly, if you tend towards saying no in times of uncertainty, you'll end up with more correct rejections but also more misses.

Your tendency towards saying yes or saying no when you aren't sure is known as your **response criteria** and it may range from liberal (unsure – say yes) to conservative (unsure - say no). Now imagine that the person taking the test after you experiences exactly the same auditory stimulation that you experienced for every single tone (in other words, the two of you have ears which function identically well). Even though your hearing is technically identical, if this person has different response criteria, results on the hearing test will not be the same.

Signal detection theory is not just for hearing tests or attempts to measure absolute thresholds. If you consider just how often we must make decisions without complete information, you'll see that signal detection theory has numerous applications to our daily lives. Is an enemy nation hiding dangerous weapons? Pre-emptive strike or detente? Is that an innocent and injured civilian or an enemy combatant? Send a drone or a first aid kit? Is that person reaching for a weapon or a wallet? Unfortunately, poor decisions in these scenarios can carry tragic consequences and determining how liberal or conservative our response criteria should be is no simple task.

Or consider a doctor who notices an unusual spot on an otherwise routine X-ray; could it be a tumor? How liberal or conservative should the judgment be? Recommend expensive and traumatic preventive surgery that may not be necessary? Or risk allowing the tumor (if that's indeed what it is) to grow or spread? These are not easy choices.

Less seriously, but perhaps still important in terms of major life decisions, imagine that you are an attractive woman being approached repeatedly by men asking for dates. Which potential suitors should you agree to see? If you decide to default to saying No to a first date, you may inadvertently turn down your Prince Charming. Be too liberal saying Yes, however, and you'll find yourself stuck on many boring dates that turn out to be false alarms. (In case you're wondering, my attempts at charm are generally met with "correct rejections" – keep up those excellent signal detection skills ladies!)

Now that we've had an overview of sensation and perception, we'll spend some time looking at the details of our senses in order to better understand the process of transduction for each. And we'll start with the one that we practice using about 16 hours a day nearly every day of our lives.

Vision

In order to understand how vision works, we need to begin at the eye, examining the structures and how they function.

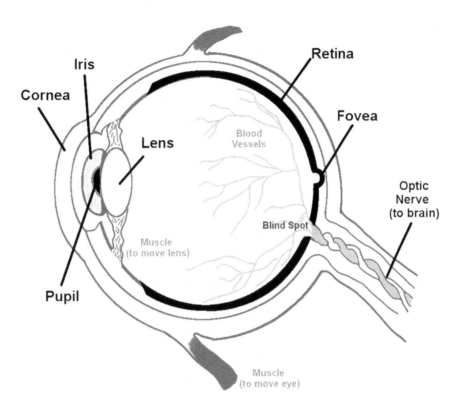

The outer surface of the eye is covered by a translucent layer called the *cornea*. This layer helps to focus light coming into the eye, and it also serves to protect the eye. The cornea is especially touch-sensitive and stimulation of the cornea invokes a reflexive closing of the eyelid. This high level of sensitivity also explains why a tiny speck of dirt in your eye can feel like a boulder.

Underneath the cornea, we reach the *iris*. This is the part of the eye that appears colored (brown, blue, hazel, etc). The iris is able to change shape, modifying the size of the *pupil*, the dark spot in the center of our eyes. The pupil is actually just an opening in the iris, which allows light to enter the eye.

The reason that the pupil appears black is that light can enter the eye, but once inside the eye the light is absorbed, meaning that very little light comes back out of the eye. An exception to this that you're probably familiar with is the "red-eye" effect that can occur in photographs. What's happening is that light from the camera flash is being reflected off the interior surface of the eye and coming back out the pupil. This happens fast enough that the pupil doesn't have time to change size and the camera catches this brief reflected light in the photograph. Because this light is reflecting off the blood-rich interior surface of the eye (known as the *fundus*), the light appears red. As you've probably seen, having another light before the actual flash for the photograph reduces the occurrence of red-eye, because the first light gives the iris time to change the size of the pupil, reducing the amount of light that is reflected back by the flash.

Now, let's get back to the steps of vision. After light passes through the pupil, it hits the **lens**, a disc-like structure surrounded by muscle that focuses the light. The lens directs light to the **retina**, the back surface of the eye. Changing the shape of the lens changes how it directs the light reaching the retina, allowing us to focus on objects at different distances. This focusing ability of the lens, together with the ability to adjust the iris mentioned above and the fact we have two eyes that adjust at different angles to focus on the same point (known as **convergence**) gives us the ability to see a variety of distances with fairly high acuity. Taken together, these three adjustments make up a process called **accommodation**.

As we age, the lens has a tendency to become stiff, reducing our ability to adjust its focus, resulting in impairments in our vision. This is why you may see your parents or grandparents moving a book or paper a certain distance from their faces in order to read it. Because they cannot adjust the lens to bring the text into focus, they are forced to move the object until it reaches the distance where the lens is already focused. The lens may also become cloudy or develop spots (*cataracts*) which may obstruct or otherwise impair vision. The marvels of modern medicine now mean that your lens can be surgically replaced and a quick YouTube search (for the not-too-squeamish) can show you exactly what that process looks like.

The **retina** contains about 125 million **photoreceptors**; specialized cells which are able to respond to stimulation by light. We have 2 main types of photoreceptors; **rods** and **cones**, named after their shapes. Rods are more sensitive to light than cones, but are only able to detect light and dark. Cones are able to detect color and fine detail, though they are less sensitive to low levels of light. This explains why colors appear rather gray in very dim lighting. Dim light is sufficient to stimulate our rods but not our cones, resulting in vision that is gray and not as detailed. In normal light conditions, however, both our rods and cones are stimulated, allowing us to see vivid colors and fine detail.

The area of the retina with the greatest density of cones is the *fovea* (in fact the fovea is composed entirely of cones), a bowl-shaped dent in the retina which provides our highest level of visual acuity. When you look closely at something, you are directing its image onto the fovea (via accommodation), allowing you to see it most clearly.

You'll notice in the image of the eye structure that there is a point where all of the blood vessels and other nerves exit the eye. This means that there is a spot on the retina that lacks rods and cones, and is therefore a *blindspot*. We don't notice the blindspot in each eye for two reasons. The first is that we have two eyes (most of us anyway, sorry pirates) and our two blindspots are in different locations, each eye covering for the other. Even so, you'll notice that if you close one eye, you still can't see your blindspot. This is because the brain automatically "fills in" the blindspot based on whatever information is stimulating the cells around it.

If we look closely at the retina, we'll see more than just rods and cones. In fact, before light stimulates the rods and cones it must first pass through retinal ganglion cells and bipolar cells. Rods and cones are grouped together into areas known as *receptive fields*, where many rods and cones connect to several *bipolar cells*. Several of these bipolar cells then join together to a single *retinal ganglion cell (RGC)*, which carries messages to the optic nerve and then out to the brain. You may be wondering, if a group of rods or cones all connect to a single cell, how can that single cell send different types of messages from many photoreceptors to the brain?

As we learned in chapter 3, the only method that single neurons have for conveying different messages is to change their firing rate. As it happens, a single RGC cell fires at different rates based on the pattern of light on the receptive field, in a process known as *lateral inhibition*. Some receptive fields are known as "on-center", meaning that the retinal ganglion cell responds most intensely when light is in the center of the receptive field, surrounded by darkness. Other retinal ganglion cells are classified as "off-center" because they respond most intensely to patterns of dark spots surrounded by light. In both cases, these cells fire differently than they would in all-light or all-dark situations.

When we see areas of contrast, such as black lines on a whiteboard, this contrast is emphasized, because some of the receptive fields along that border will be partially lit and partially dark, causing those retinal ganglion cells to fire at different rates. This signals that something more interesting than simply light/dark is happening and this exaggerates the line, helping us to see greater contrast.

This can be demonstrated in a simple illusion known as ***Mach Bands***. In the image above, all the bars are solid colors. What you will probably perceive, however, is that each individual bar appears slightly lighter on the left side and darker on the right side. This is occurring because lateral inhibition is causing greater activity in the RGCs along each line where the color changes, emphasizing the contrast so it stands out. As a result, the light gray to the right of each change appears lighter than it actually is, while the darker gray to its left appears darker than it actually is.

We should note from lateral inhibition that some of the process of perception is actually happening before messages even get to the brain. This is happening in the retina itself, and no matter how much we know about this illusion, the process of lateral inhibition, and the processes of receptive fields, we will still experience the effect.

Color Vision and Colorblindness

As mentioned, rods respond to light and dark, while cones allow us to see in color. Color isn't actually in light, but rather light comes in different wavelengths and our brains are able to perceive these differing wavelengths as different colors. Long wavelengths correspond to red, medium to green, and short to blue.

Young-Helmholtz Trichromatic Theory is that we have 3 different types of cones which respond to different wavelengths of light. These three cone types are L-cones, M-cones, and S-cones, corresponding to greater sensitivity to long (red), medium (green), and short (blue) wavelengths. Each cone type actually sees a fairly large portion of the visible spectrum. The wavelengths that cone types can see overlap but each cone type responds more intensely to certain wavelengths. The combination and comparison of different levels of stimulation from all cone types allows us to see an estimated 10 million possible colors. Trichromatic theory also allows us to explain colorblindness, which results when a person has a defect in one (or more than one) type of cone. Most people with colorblindness do see in color, they just can't see all the hues that people with three functioning cone types can see.

The *Opponent Process Theory of Color* is that perception of color depends on comparisons between colors which work in pairs to inhibit one another. These opposing pairs are red/green, blue/yellow, and light/dark. When one half of a pair is stimulated, the other half is inhibited. This may explain why we never describe colors as reddish-green or bluish-yellow because we don't perceive these antagonistic pairs mixing in that way. We can also demonstrate this opponent process with a *color afterimage*. If you stare at a red circle without moving your eyes for an extended period of time (30 seconds or so) then you look at a plain white background, you'll see an afterimage of a green circle.

What's happening is that when you stare at the red circle long enough, the "red" signal to the brain is decreased. When you switch to a white background the white light stimulates red and green equally, but since the red signal has been decreased, the green stimulation seems relatively stronger and you perceive green.

Hearing

In order to understand how we can get from physical sound waves to neurons firing in the brain, let's take a look at the major structures of the ear and what they do.

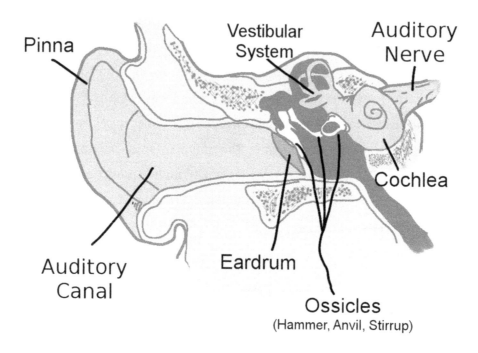

The **pinna** or *auricle* is the visible outer ear. It basically acts as a funnel, helping to direct sound waves into the auditory canal. At the end of the auditory canal is the **eardrum** (or *tympanic membrane* if you want to sound fancy). The eardrum vibrates in response to sound waves. This vibration of the eardrum causes movements of the **ossicles** (Latin for "little bones" – they are the smallest bones in your body) in the middle ear. The three ossicles are (in order) the hammer (*malleus*), the anvil (*incus*), and the stirrup(*stapes*).

The vibrations of the stirrup are passed on to the **cochlea** (Latin for "snail") in the inner ear. The cochlea is a spiral structure filled with fluid. Inside this fluid sits the **basilar membrane**. The basilar membrane contains tiny hair cells (**stereocilia**) which move in response to the vibration of fluid in the cochlea. When moved, these hair cells trigger the firing of neurons. Different wavelengths of sound trigger different hair cells along the basilar membrane, allowing different pitches to trigger different neurons (this is known as **place code**). Messages from the cochlea are carried away from the ear to the thalamus via the **auditory nerve**. From the thalamus, the messages are relayed to the primary auditory cortex (A1) in the temporal lobes for processing.

The Vestibular System

One section of the inner ear doesn't have to do with hearing at all. This is the vestibular system. The vestibular system is used to help us balance and orient ourselves. The vestibular system sits above the cochlea and consists of two **vestibular sacs** (the *utricle* and *saccule*) and three **semi-circular canals**. These structures are filled with fluid which moves in response to head movements, triggering hair cells which help give us information about the body's position in space.

If you've ever spun around too quickly or played "dizzy bat", you've experienced what happens when the vestibular system is disrupted. By spinning in circles quickly you cause the fluid in the vestibular system to move. When you stop suddenly, the momentum generated causes the fluid to continue moving, creating a state of disorientation as other body senses indicate that you aren't moving. Similarly, astronauts often experience "space sickness" due to the disruptions of the vestibular system caused by a lack of gravity (and for which they wear anti-nausea skin patches – vomiting into your space suit is not a good idea).

Touch

Exploring the world by touching and grasping (known as **haptic perception**) is one of our most important senses, and the sense organ responsible, our skin, is our body's largest organ. The skin is more than just a fleshy bag that separates our innards from the outer world; it's a remarkable organ that constantly transmits several types of information to the brain.

Our skin contains a variety of receptors which allow us to detect different properties of the physical world around us. Using these **mechanoreceptors**, we're able to detect **pressure**, **texture**, **pattern**, and **vibration**, as well as temperature (via **thermoreceptors**) and pain (via **nocireceptors**).

As we learned when looking at the brain, our sense of touch is **contralateral**, meaning that the left hemisphere of the brain processes information from the right side of the body, while the right hemisphere processes signals from the left side of the body. When learning about the **somatosensory cortex** in the parietal lobe (which processes touch messages from the body), we also learned that greater sensitivity requires greater amounts of brain cortex. The representation of our hands and face in the cortex is considerably larger than that of our torso, legs, or arms.

Pain

As just about all of us are acutely aware, our skin (along with other parts of the body) has the ability to sense pain, though there are actually rare cases of congenital insensitivity to pain. While you might think this would grant you amazing superhero status, the truth is that a life without pain is far from ideal.

Pain provides crucial messages to quickly change our behavior or escape harmful situations. People who are unable to detect pain are constantly at risk of doing serious harm to their bodies without even being aware of it. Noticing that your skin is melting on a burning stove, recognizing that you're stretching a muscle a little too far, or feeling the dull throbbing of an infection are all important cues to change your behavior or seek medical assistance to prevent further damage. Unfortunately people with a congenital insensitivity to pain miss these cues, and as a result their pain-free lives tend to be rather short as injuries and damage accumulate.

Our experience of pain comes from two different types of pain receptors. Receptors that provide us with information for fast, intense, sharp pains are known as **A-delta fibers**. For longer-lasting, dull, throbbing pain, messages are carried on **C-fibers.** A good mnemonic for remembering which pain types are carried by which fibers is to imagine yourself being stabbed by the sharp point of the letter A (resulting in sudden, sharp, and intense pain). You can also imagine a bunch of **C**s radiating out of your body to represent a dull, sore, throbbing pain. In addition to traveling to the somatosensory cortex (via the thalamus), pain messages also travel to the limbic system (the hypothalamus, hippocampus, and amygdala), which isn't surprising if you recall that these are important areas for emotion, motivation, and memory. Pain, emotion, and memory are closely linked, such as when we learn to experience fear for objects or situations that have previously caused us pain.

A-delta fibers
(sharp, stabbing pain)

C-fibers
(dull, throbbing pain)

It's not only our skin that contains pain receptors. We also have receptors that can signal pain from our bones, our muscles, and our internal organs. In some areas, receptors from both internal and external (meaning skin) sources converge on the same spinal cord nerves. This can cause an experience of ***referred pain***, where internal pain signals feel like they are coming from elsewhere in the body. A well-known example of this occurs when a person is suffering from a heart-attack, as a common symptom is feeling sharp shooting pains in the left arm, even though the actual source of the pain is inside the chest.

Smell

Like taste, smell (or **olfaction**) is a chemical sense, because our sensation comes from direct interaction with chemical molecules. In this case, **odorant molecules** from whatever we are smelling waft up our nasal passages, where they bind with special receptors called **olfactory receptor neurons** (**ORN**). The ORN pass these messages on to the **glomeruli**, which connect to the **olfactory bulb** inside the skull. From the olfactory bulb, these messages are passed directly to areas of the temporal lobes, bypassing the thalamus (the relay station all other senses pass through). It may be the case that the strong ties between scent and emotional memories are due to these direct connections with the brain and their proximity to the limbic system (which processes emotions and encodes memories).

Humans have a total of about 10 million olfactory receptor neurons, which come in about 350 different types. The stimulation of different combinations of these ORN types allows us to detect a wide variety of possible smells. The unique pattern of stimulation that a particular combination of chemicals causes is experienced as a unique scent.

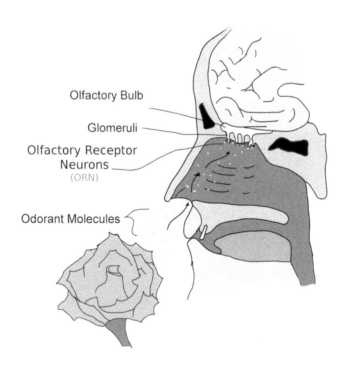

Olfactory Bulb

Glomeruli

Olfactory Receptor
Neurons
(ORN)

Odorant Molecules

While it may be rather pleasant to realize that the scent of a warm apple pie means molecules are actually coming off that pie and going inside your body, it's decidedly unpleasant to consider what this means when you encounter a particularly foul restroom.

You may also note from the illustration that it's possible for odorant molecules to waft up the back entrance to the ORNs via the throat (provided the mouth is open). Food in our mouths sends odorant molecules up the back of the throat to the ORNs, especially as we chew, making smell and taste two very closely linked senses. If you're curious to try tasting without smelling, pinching the nose works fairly well, as it blocks entrance from the nasal passages and also stops air flow from up the back of the throat, preventing much of a food's smell from being detected. I don't recommend trying this in a posh restaurant, as you probably don't want to offend a chef who sees you pinching your nose while eating. And of course for foods like stinky tofu, durian, or Camembert cheese, the powerful smell of the food may just be the most enjoyable part. There are some people (like one of my sisters) who lack the ability to detect scent at all; a condition known as *anosmia*.

Taste Perception

As you've probably noticed, your tongue is covered with small bumps, which are known as **papillae**. There are 4 different kinds of papillae on your tongue which are all named for their shape; *fungiform* (mushroom-shaped), *filiform* (thread-shaped), *circumvallate* (dome-shaped), and *foliate* (leaf-shaped).

With the exception of filiform papillae (which serve mechanical functions), papillae are lined with **taste buds**, which detect taste by interacting with the **tastant molecules** in food. In total, humans have around 5,000-10,000 taste buds. You have more taste buds when you are young, and by age 20 you will have lost around 50% of them. Molecules from food interact with hair-like receptors called **microvilli**, which stick out from the taste bud at taste pores, and this interaction triggers activity in **gustatory cells** inside the taste bud.

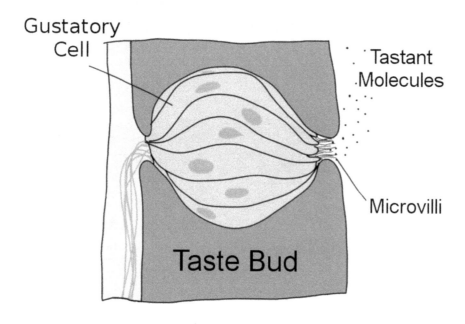

We also have some taste buds on the sides and roof of the mouth (the palate), as well as some parts of the throat. This explains why we can also detect taste in these areas, though not as intensely as on our tongues.

If you ever learned about different taste areas being mapped out on your tongue, I regret to inform you that what you were told is a complete and utter lie! There is no "salty area" or "sweet area" of the tongue (though unfortunately this is still taught in many places). So while this did make for some fun coloring assignments in primary school, the bitter truth is that each taste bud contains receptor cells for all tastes, so each taste is distributed throughout the mouth, not localized. This error comes from the misinterpretation of research showing small differences in sensitivity to certain tastes in some areas – or maybe people were trying to make the topic more exciting, since confusion seems to have originated from a paper by a Harvard psychologist named Professor Boring. So clear your mind of that myth while we consider the types of tastes that humans can sense.

When it comes to detecting taste, different receptors respond to different molecules. Some **gustatory cells** will respond to certain molecules but not others, meaning they are specialized for different "tastes". There are 5 main tastes: **salty**, **sweet**, **bitter**, **sour**, and **umami** (Japanese for "savory" – one your elementary school science class may have been missing). Each of these tastes is associated with different types of molecules. The different combinations of interactions with these 5 receptor types (in addition to information from scent receptors in the nose) gives us all the varied tastes that we can experience.

We also use other nerves in our mouths to tell us about the food we're eating, so our experience of taste is not limited to what happens at the taste buds. Other qualities like spiciness (*pungency* or *piquancy*), temperature, texture, and astringency play crucial roles in our perception of the foods we taste. A great deal of our taste perception also happens outside the mouth (and nose), as we "eat with our eyes". The colors of foods can influence our experience of their taste. When I was a kid, a box of popsicles often included a "mystery flavor" – colored white – that was difficult to pin down. Without the reference point of color (purple=grape, red=berry, yellow = banana, etc.), it's easy to make mistakes in identifying flavors. In addition, our beliefs and expectations about food can also influence our perceptions. In season 3 of Penn & Teller's *Bullshit!*, the comedy/magic duo demonstrated this by duping restaurant customers into eating cheap canned tomatoes, instant potatoes, and meat from microwave dinners. These were all presented as gourmet specialties, leading customers to believe, and perceive, that they were really eating "the best" in taste and quality.

Mingling the Senses

Now that we've looked at each of the senses in detail, we have to remember that they aren't so neatly boxed in real-life. We've seen how we "eat with our eyes", but this concept applies to a mingling of our other senses as well. As a number of perceptual illusions can demonstrate, what we hear influences what we see (and vice versa), what we hear can influence our experience of taste, and what we see can even influence what we feel. Our overall sensory experience of the world is a rich tapestry which synthesizes information from all of our senses. This is true for all of us, but there is also a group of people for whom this is especially apparent. These people are **synesthetes**, or people with **synesthesia**. Synesthesia is a more dramatic mingling of the senses, in which one sense automatically stimulates another, such as sounds causing colorful visions or even triggering tastes. One of the most common types of synesthesia is the experience of seeing certain shapes as colored, even when they are not. For example, a synesthete may see letters or numbers as always having particular colors, like seeing As as red, or 6s as green. This isn't a delusion, as the synesthete knows that the letter or number is printed in black ink, but still has the visual experience of color.

You may ask how we could ever know if a synesthete were lying about this experience. Couldn't someone just claim that an A appears red and we would never be able to get inside his mind to know if this was true? For a long time synesthesia was regarded this way, as if synesthetes were delusional or making things up.

Fortunately, some clever perceptual psychologists came up with ways of testing the experience of synesthetes. When shown an array of letters, they wondered whether synesthetes might recognize patterns more quickly than non-synesthetes. Look at the image here and see how quickly you can find all the Ps mixed in with Qs.

In this case minding your Ps and Qs can be a difficult task, but if you were able to see the letters as having different colors (grapheme-color synesthesia), it would be considerably easier. In fact, this is what happens when some synesthetes are asked to do this task, and researchers have found evidence that they are able to recognize the patterns more quickly. This demonstrates that synesthetes don't just make things up or have overactive imaginations; their perception of the world really differs from that of other people. On the following page you'll see a simulation of how this task might appear for a synesthete who sees Ps and Qs as different colors.

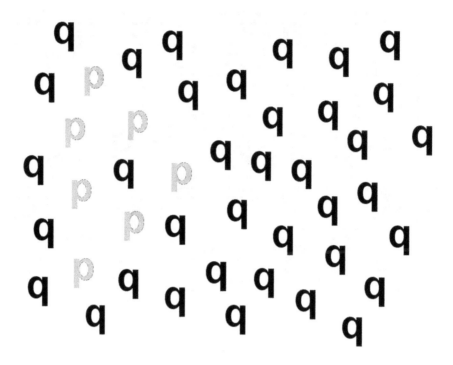

Gestalt Laws

Early perceptual researchers focused on identifying the laws of perception that dictate how we organize and interpret information. The emphasis of gestalt psychology is often summarized as "the whole is different than the sum of the parts" meaning that in order to understand perception, we shouldn't think in terms of isolated pieces, but in terms of how those pieces come together. The following *Gestalt laws* were identified as predictable patterns for how our brains tend to perceive the world.

Closure – Parts of a recognizable image are put together and the mind "closes off" or fills in any gaps.

Proximity – Objects which are closer together are more likely to be perceived as a group.

Similarity – Objects that are more similar are more likely to be perceived as a group.

Continuity – Objects that make up a continuous form are perceived as a group.

Simplicity – Simple explanations are preferred over equally plausible but more complex explanations.

Common Fate – Objects which move in unison are more likely to be perceived as a group.

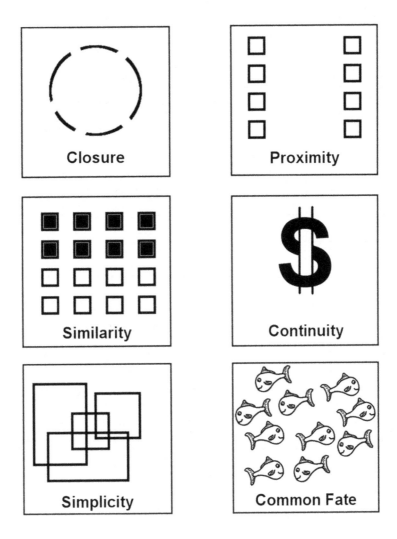

While these Gestalt laws are most frequently demonstrated visually, remember that they apply to all types of perception. For example, we tend to group similar pitches together, while pitches that are far apart can be perceived as coming from separate sources. A great example of this can be heard when a single instrument jumps quickly back and forth between high and low pitches, resulting in an auditory illusion that two separate instruments are playing. An excellent example of this can be heard in J.B. Arban's arrangement of *The Carnival of Venice*, where, in the final variation on the theme, the trumpet soloist moves quickly between low notes playing the familiar melody, and trilled higher notes providing an accompaniment. Played properly, the solo sounds like two trumpet players playing together.

Perceptual Constancy

To consider perceptual constancy, let's imagine a rather routine occurrence. You are standing in a hallway somewhere, and a friend walks down the hall toward you, then begins having a conversation with you. While this may seem trivial, your brain's ability to correctly interpret what is going on is actually quite impressive. In order to do so, your brain must figure out that even though many things are changing, they are actually remaining the same.

Size Constancy – When you see your friend walking toward you, you don't perceive that she is growing rapidly in size even though the image on your retina is indeed growing larger and larger. Instead you are able to determine that your friend is simply moving closer to you.

Brightness Constancy – As your friend is walking toward you, she passes underneath a light fixture on the ceiling. As she approaches, then passes this light source, the hue and brightness of her face changes, shadows appear in new places, and light is reflected off different surfaces. Yet, you don't feel that your friend's complexion is changing in any way.

Shape Constancy – Now, as you're talking to your friend, and she nods her head, its shape on your retina changes drastically. But here again, you don't perceive that her head is actually morphing into new shapes. Instead, your brain perceives it as maintaining a single, normal shape.

Depth Cues

The surface of the retina is 2D, so how are we able to experience a 3D world that has depth? This experience of depth is created from a combination of cues. **Monocular cues** are cues that each eye uses individually, meaning that the appearance of depth from each of these cues still occurs even if you close one eye.

Linear perspective – Parallel lines appear to converge as they get farther away from us and as any artist knows, this can be used to give the impression of depth.

Relative size – We also judge how far away things are from us based on their familiar size. If I see a small image of a person on my retina, I will probably conclude that this is a normal-sized person who is far away from me, rather than an extremely small person who is close to me.

Texture gradient – Texture gradient relies on the fact that our visual acuity is generally better for objects that are closer to us. As things get farther away, their textures appear smoother.

Interposition – Objects block our view of the objects behind them, and this aids us in knowing which objects are closer. If our view of an object is partially blocked, the object must be farther away from us than whatever is blocking it.

Shading – How light falls on objects can also help us to determine their size as well as their distances from us. This is something that you unconsciously use each time you correctly judge the height of a step based on the shadow that it casts.

Binocular Cues

While the monocular cues above all work with only one eye, having two eyes improves our depth perception considerably (sorry again, pirates). You can test this yourself by playing catch with a friend, then trying again with one eye closed. You'll probably find this more difficult, because even if you can still see the object clearly, it becomes harder to judge its distance from you and the speed of its approach.

Binocular disparity – We have two eyes in slightly different locations, so the brain is actually receiving two slightly different views of the world and, rather amazingly, combining these images into one coherent whole. If you hold a pencil at arm's length and focus on it with one eye, then switch eyes, you'll notice that the image of the pencil shifts back and forth a bit. Now hold the pencil closer to your face and repeat the process. Now it appears to shift even more. When objects are close to us, our two eyes see different versions of the object, but when objects are far away, the views are more similar. The brain takes this into account as it combines the two viewpoints into one, improving our ability to judge depth. 3D glasses take advantage of this by showing each eye a slightly different version of a movie (which used to be accomplished with red/blue tints but now uses polarized lenses), allowing the brain to combine these two versions into one that appears to have depth.

Convergence – Using the same pencil viewing task above, as you move the pencil closer to your face, muscles around your eyes are moving your eyeballs to different angles to focus on it. When you focus on something far away, both eyes are positioned to look relatively straight forward. As an object gets closer, your eyes must point progressively closer and closer together to focus on it, and this also provides you with information about how far away the object is.

Motion-based Cues

We also use the motion of objects across our retina to judge depth. For example, if you look out a window on a train passing through the countryside, you'll notice that trees along the tracks seem to move past the window very quickly. The trees in the distance, however, take much longer to travel across the window. The mountain even farther away seems to move at a crawl. This difference in how quickly objects appear to move also gives us clues about depth and is known as ***motion parallax***.

While motion parallax tells us about distances for objects moving perpendicular to us, ***optic flow*** tells us about objects moving toward or away from us. Imagine you are looking out the front windshield of a car speeding down the highway. As an object gets closer, its image grows on your retinas and the speed of this enlargement helps to tell you how far the object is from you and how quickly it is moving towards you, adding to a sense of depth. As we move forward, we can see that objects at similar distances will "grow" on our retinas at similar rates. Closer objects will all grow more quickly, while distant objects will all grow more slowly.

Culture and Perception

While it often seems like perception just happens, remember that it's actually the result of a great deal of experience. We must learn how to organize and interpret the information coming into our senses. We may take for granted the effortlessness of vision because we forget just how many years we spent learning how to make sense of the messages we get from our eyes. This can be seen dramatically in cases where congenitally blind people are able to see, thanks to modern surgical techniques. When the surgery is complete, the process of seeing has only just begun.

These patients must learn to see, and this is actually a slow and difficult process. Their brains have no experience interpreting visual messages and must establish millions of neuronal connections in order to organize the onslaught of visual information. Things we don't give a second thought, such as correctly judging the size and distance of numerous objects as we walk across a room, must be slowly and painstakingly learned by the newly-sighted. The same learning process is true for our other senses, as experience has taught us how to identify the timbre of a piano or a violin, recognize the voice of a friend, or identify an object by touch.

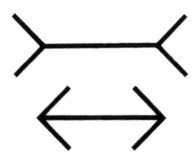

The fact that we must learn how to perceive also opens the possibility that our environmental experiences shape our perception of reality. For instance, our susceptibility to the famous ***Müller-Lyer illusion*** above (which you have probably seen before) has been shown to be influenced by our cultural background. Research by Marshall Segall and colleagues found that European and American subjects experienced the illusion of the top horizontal line appearing longer more often than subjects from other cultures (the horizontal segments are identical). They hypothesized that differing amounts of experience viewing 2D pictures combined with differences in exposure to straight lines and right angles influenced participants' susceptibility to the illusion. This idea that living in an environment filled with straight lines and right angles affects our perceptual inferences is known as the ***carpentered-world hypothesis***. While researchers still disagree on interpretations of the Müller-Lyer illusion and the carpentered-world hypothesis, there is general agreement that culture shapes our perceptual experience of the world.

Chapter Summary – Sensation & Perception

- *Psychophysics* is the study of thresholds for detecting stimuli or changes in stimuli. *Signal Detection Theory* considers how our response criteria influences our detection of stimuli.

- Lightwaves are focused onto the retina where *photoreceptors* convert them into neural activity which is processed in the occipital lobes of the brain.

- Soundwaves vibrate *ossicles* in the ears and the subsequent movement of hair cells in the *cochlea* converts these vibrations into neural signals which are processed in the temporal lobes.

- The skin contains several types of receptors which can respond to stimuli including vibration, pressure, temperature, and pain and these messages are processed in the *somatosensory cortex* in the parietal lobe. Messages from pain fibers are also sent to the *limbic system*, a key area for processing emotion and memory.

- Smell and taste both involve the interaction of chemical molecules with special receptors; *olfactory receptor neurons* in the nose and *gustatory cells* in *taste buds* on the tongue.

- All our senses are combined in the brain, meaning that senses influence one another. This is seen more dramatically in *synesthetes* who experience uncontrollable cross-overs among senses.

- Perception follows some general rules (*Gestalt Laws*) for how we process sensory information. Correctly interpreting stimuli requires practice and as a result perception involves learning from experience.

Notes

Chapter 5
Learning

Learning

On a common-sense level we all know what learning is, but how can we come up with a precise definition of learning? How can we measure learning? As a teacher, I wonder every day whether my students have learned something because I can't really get inside their heads to find out. In school situations, we generally depend on observation to determine whether learning has occurred. We don't just take your word that you've learned something, we want to see evidence. This is actually very similar to how behavioral psychologists of the 1920s to 1950s thought about learning. They believed that the inner workings of the mind weren't important; what mattered was observable behavior. With this emphasis on behavior, we can say that *learning* is a relatively long-lasting change in behavior that results from our experience with the world. Because of this emphasis on behavior in assessing learning, the conditioning theories we'll learn about in this chapter are often collectively referred to as *behaviorism*. Behavior is not the only way of assessing learning, and as we'll see at the end of this chapter, research eventually moved away from a strict emphasis on behavior. But before we get ahead of ourselves, let's look to the start of behaviorist psychology with the work of Ivan Pavlov.

Classical Conditioning

Chances are you've heard someone mention "Pavlov's dog" or something being a "Pavlovian response", so let's take a look at the details of some of Pavlov's work and the key terms for discussing what is known as *classical conditioning*.

Ivan Pavlov was a Russian physiologist studying digestion in dogs (for which he won the Nobel prize in 1904) who noticed an interesting phenomenon. Pavlov had been collecting saliva samples from dogs when food was presented to them, but he noticed that the dogs began salivating even before the food was presented (like while the researcher was preparing the food). It was as if the dogs knew that food was on the way.

Pavlov then wanted to see if dogs could also learn to expect food (shown by their salivation) following a particular stimulus like a bell, a metronome, a light, etc. In the most well-known version of his experiments, he rang a bell prior to the presentation of food. Initially the bell was a meaningless sound, but by repeatedly following that sound with food, Pavlov was able to teach the dogs to salivate whenever the bell rang.

In this case, the bell started as a ***neutral stimulus (NS)***, meaning that it didn't elicit a response on its own. If you go up to a random dog on the street and ring a bell, there isn't a specific response that will occur. The food, however, would be an ***unconditioned stimulus (US)***, because it doesn't need to be conditioned, or taught to the dog. If you give food to any random dog, a predictable response will occur: salivation. This response, salivating to food, hasn't been taught so it's called an ***unconditioned response (UR)***. Conditioning consists of repeatedly presenting the neutral stimulus followed by the unconditioned stimulus, which will automatically cause the unconditioned response.

After enough training, the neutral stimulus will be able to elicit a predictable response all by itself. The previously neutral stimulus can now be called a ***conditioned stimulus (CS)***. The response that has been taught, salivating to the sound of a bell, is now called a ***conditioned response (CR)***. When the dog has learned to salivate to the sound of the bell, we can say that ***acquisition*** has occurred. Here's a summary of the steps in classical conditioning:

Before Conditioning

Neutral Stimulus (bell) alone : no response

Unconditioned Stimulus (food) alone : Unconditioned Response (salivate)

The Conditioning Process

Neutral Stimulus (bell) then Unconditioned Stimulus (food): Unconditioned Response (salivate)

After repeating this several times, the Neutral Stimulus becomes a Conditioned Stimulus, which means...

After Conditioning

Conditioned Stimulus (bell): Conditioned Response (salivate to the bell)

If we stop pairing the bell with food, this conditioned response won't continue on forever. Eventually, the dog will stop responding to the stimulus, and we can say that ***extinction*** has occurred. But just because the dog has stopped responding to the stimulus doesn't necessarily mean that the dog has completely forgotten the learning. In fact, Pavlov found that after extinction the conditioned response would reappear after a rest period of about a day. This was referred to as ***spontaneous recovery*** and shows us that the dog hasn't forgotten the association, he has just temporarily stopped responding. In addition, if this dog were to be trained with bell/food pairings again in the future, he would relearn the association more quickly than a dog without any prior conditioning.

After teaching the dogs to salivate to the sound of a bell, Pavlov found that they also salivated to the sound of a similar bell (playing a slightly different tone). This became known as *stimulus generalization*. After conditioning, the conditioned response can occur in the presence of stimuli which are similar to the conditioned stimulus. As an interesting side note, Pavlov found that the response to other tones weakened as the tone frequencies got farther and farther from the original stimulus, but then increased when reaching an octave, indicating that dogs also perceive octaves as sounding like the "same" note just as we do.

With more conditioning, Pavlov discovered that he could teach the dogs to respond only to a particular stimulus. For example, by always presenting the food in the presence of a particular tone but never in the presence of a second (different) tone, Pavlov could eventually condition the dogs to only salivate to the first tone. This ability to differentiate two similar stimuli is known as *stimulus discrimination.*

Pavlov also found that after dogs had been conditioned to salivate to a bell, he could get them to salivate to a light by turning it on before the bell, even though the light was never directly paired with food. This is known as *second-order conditioning* or *higher-order conditioning*. Because the dogs had learned that the bell meant food was coming, then learned that the light meant that the bell was coming, they would salivate to the light.

Pavlov wasn't the only one conducting experiments in classical conditioning. *John B. Watson* and *Rosalie Rayner* conducted a study in 1920 showing that classical conditioning could be used to teach fear. In an ethically-questionable procedure, Watson and Rayner presented a white rat to an 8-month old baby (known as "Little Albert"), then hit a metal bar with a hammer, creating a loud, startling noise which made Albert cry. After repeated pairings of the rat with the loud noise, they found that Albert would show distress when the rat was presented, suggesting that fears could develop via classical conditioning, known as *aversive conditioning*. Albert also showed *stimulus generalization* because he showed distress not only to rats, but also to other furry objects like a rabbit and a white-bearded mask that Watson wore.

Biological Aspects of Conditioning

There are biological constraints on which types of associations can be learned via classical conditioning. While studying the effects of radiation on rats, John Garcia and colleagues noticed that the rats refused to drink water from the dishes in their cages following radiation exposure. The radiation was making the rats sick, and apparently the rats were automatically associating this illness with the water they had drank prior to exposure. This suggested that the rats had a biological predisposition to learn relationships between food and illness. Garcia and Robert Koelling conducted later studies teaching rats to associate a noise with an electric shock which followed and to associate flavored water with subsequent nausea, but they discovered that they couldn't teach rats to associate noise with nausea or drinking flavored water with an electric shock. This demonstrates that we have a **biological preparedness** for certain types of learning and some pairings will be learned more easily than others. If we consider an evolutionary approach to understanding this, it makes sense that we should be able to quickly learn to associate illness with food (so we can avoid that food in the future) while associating nausea with noise would be less practical. This **learned taste aversion** doesn't quite follow the rules of classical conditioning because there may only be a single pairing of a food with illness as well as a long delay between the two, and yet the learning can still occur.

If you've seen Stanley Kubrick's *A Clockwork Orange* (based on the novel by Anthony Burgess), you might recall the scene in which Alex is taught to avoid violence via classical conditioning. He's given an injection that makes him feel sick (though he was told it was a vitamin supplement) and is then forced to watch violent films. The goal is for him to be conditioned to associate violence with illness, thus avoiding violence in the future. While it may sound like a good idea in theory, in practice Alex would have a biological predisposition to associate his illness with whatever food had been served to him hours earlier and not with the violent films he was forced to watch.

Operant Conditioning

Though classical conditioning provided some explanation for the formation of associations between stimuli and automatic responses, it didn't provide much insight on the development of voluntary behaviors. In studies of classical conditioning, the organism being studied is rather passive. Pavlov's dogs simply stood around waiting for bells to ring, food to be presented, etc. They weren't exploring the environment, searching for food, or interacting with stimuli. In order to understand these real-life behaviors, we need to look to another type of conditioning, in which the organism operates on the environment and experiences the consequences of its behavior.

To begin, we'll look to one of the first researchers in this area, **Edward Thorndike**. Thorndike placed a hungry cat in a box, then placed food outside the box. Inside the box was a lever which, when pressed, would cause the door to open, allowing the cat access to the food dish. Thorndike would repeatedly place cats in this "puzzle box", and observe how long they took to escape. Thorndike found that the cats learned that pressing the lever opened the door and they became successively faster with each trial. Initially they may have stumbled upon the lever accidentally, but after repeated placement in the box, the cats had learned how to escape.

After observing his cats escaping from these puzzle boxes, Thorndike postulated the simple *Law of Effect*, stating that behavior which is followed by positive consequences is more likely to be repeated. In this case, pressing the lever gave the hungry cats access to food, so this lever pressing would be more likely to be repeated. Thorndike referred to this as *instrumental learning*: learning to perform behaviors which bring positive consequences.

Thorndike's research examining the relationship between behavior and consequences laid the groundwork for **B.F. Skinner**'s research (if your name was Burrhus Frederic, you'd prefer to go by B.F. as well). Skinner examined behaviors and their outcomes in greater detail, believing that nearly all behaviors could be explained by their associations with rewards or punishments.

Skinner referred to a desirable consequence of a behavior as **reinforcement**, because it reinforced to the animal that this was a behavior that should be repeated in the future. Reinforcement could come in many forms, from things which satisfy basic biological drives like food or warmth (known as *primary reinforcers*), to things like grades, stickers, or money (known as *secondary reinforcers*), which are rewarding due to learned associations (using money to buy food, being praised for good grades, etc.).

Skinner differentiated between *positive reinforcement*, in which an organism receives something desirable (like food), and *negative reinforcement*, in which an organism has something undesirable removed (like turning off electric shocks or loud noises). Imagine you have a terrible headache. You perform the behavior of taking a pill and your headache goes away. This will make it more likely that you'll take a pill in the future (whenever you have a headache) and so the behavior of pill-taking is being reinforced. It's important to note that both types of reinforcement (positive and negative) are used to encourage a behavior so that it will be repeated. This is a commonly-confused concept of conditioning, particularly in popular culture, as films and television shows have often mistakenly referred to negative reinforcement when they should have referred to punishment.

Some consequences reduce the likelihood of a behavior being performed in the future. This is **punishment**. There are also two main types of punishment. **Positive punishment** is receiving something unpleasant. So when you touch a button and receive a painful electric shock, you'll be less likely to touch that button in the future. **Negative punishment** (also known as **omission training**) is when something desirable is taken away as a result of a behavior. So a police officer issuing a fine (taking away money) for speeding is a negative punishment designed to reduce the behavior of speeding in the future.

While punishment can be effective in quickly stopping behavior (like if you press a button and receive a shock), one of the problems it has is that it doesn't provide any information about which behaviors are desirable. In addition, punishments often don't follow immediately after the undesirable behaviors, and therefore may not actually be associated with those behaviors. From the example above, rather than reducing speed, in the future a driver may simply drive on other roads in an attempt to avoid police (associating the fine with getting caught, not with speeding).

The "Skinner Box"

Skinner studied the different effects of reinforcement by placing animals like rats or pigeons inside what he called "**operant boxes**" (often referred to by others as "Skinner boxes") which offered food rewards for behaviors like lever pressing or disc pecking. These boxes tracked how often the animal performed the behavior, and this data could clearly demonstrate increases in behavior based on reinforcement.

Skinner also found that behaviors could be successfully linked together in what is known as **chaining**. For instance, a pigeon might be reinforced for pushing a lever and also reinforced for pecking a disc, and then these two behaviors could be chained together so the pigeon is only rewarded for pecking the disc and then pressing the lever.

For teaching more complex behaviors, Skinner would reinforce successive approximations of the desired behavior; a process known as **shaping**. If you want to teach a rat how to play basketball you can't simply wait around for the rat to pick up a ball and place it into a hoop then reinforce this behavior. A behavior this complex won't just suddenly occur on its own (like pecking a disc or pressing a lever might) and therefore it needs to be gradually developed. In this particular case, a rat might first be reinforced just for touching a ball. Then this wouldn't be good enough, and the rat would only be rewarded for actually picking up the ball, then only for carrying it to one side of the cage, then only for placing it inside a basket, and so on until the rat is only rewarded for completing the full behavior (picking up the ball, carrying it to the raised hoop, and dropping the ball in).

This process of shaping applies to human behaviors as well. If we want kids to learn calculus, we don't sit around just waiting for them to solve an integral equation so we can reward them. First we reward counting, then addition, subtraction, multiplication, algebra, etc. until finally we only reward the complex behavior (Mom probably doesn't praise you for adding 3+4 like she used to, now it seems you've got to bring home an A in multivariate calculus to get any rewards).

By closely monitoring the occurrence of behaviors and the frequency of rewards, Skinner was able to look for patterns. Receiving a reward each time the lever is pressed would be an example of ***continuous reinforcement***. But Skinner also wanted to know how behavior might change if the reward wasn't always present. This is known as ***intermittent reinforcement*** (or partial reinforcement). By tracking the accumulated behavioral responses of animals in his operant boxes over time, Skinner could see how different reward schedules influenced the timing and frequency of behavior. Though each of these approaches could be varied in countless ways, there were 4 general types of schedules that Skinner tested.

Schedules of Reinforcement

Fixed-Ratio (The Vending Machine)

A fixed-ratio schedule follows a consistent pattern of reinforcing a certain number of behaviors. This may come in the form of rewarding every behavior (1:1) or only rewarding every 5th response (5:1), according to some set rule. Just as nobody continuously feeds coins to a broken vending machine, when the set ratio is violated (like when each level press no longer delivers food), animals quickly learn to reduce their behavior.

Variable-Ratio (The Slot Machine)

A variable-ratio schedule rewards a particular behavior but does so in an unpredictable fashion. The reinforcement may come after the 1st level press or the 15th, and then may follow immediately with the next press or perhaps not follow for another 10 presses. The unpredictable nature of a variable-ratio schedule can lead to a high frequency of behavior, as the animal (or human) may believe that the next press will "be the one" that delivers the reward.

This is the type of reinforcement seen in gambling, as each next play could provide the big payoff. Skinner found that behaviors rewarded with a variable-ratio schedule were most resistant to extinction. To illustrate this, consider a broken vending machine (fixed ratio) versus a broken slot machine (variable-ratio). How long would you keep putting money into a broken vending machine? You'd probably give up after your first or maybe second try didn't result in a delicious Snickers bar. But now imagine playing a slot machine that is broken and unable to pay out (though everything else appears to be working). You might play 15 times or more before you cease your coin-inserting and button-pressing behavior.

Fixed-Interval (The Paycheck)

In a fixed-interval schedule, reinforcement for a behavior is provided only at fixed time intervals. The reward may be given after 1 minute, every 5 minutes, once an hour, etc. What Skinner found when implementing this schedule was that the frequency of behavior would increase as the time for the reward approached (ensuring that the animal gets the reward), but would then decrease immediately following the reward, as if the animal knew that another reward wouldn't be arriving any time soon.

This may be of concern for human fixed-interval situations like biweekly or monthly paychecks, as work effort may be reduced immediately after a paycheck has been received (just as most students reduce studying effort in the days immediately following exams, because the next exams aren't coming for a while).

Variable-Interval (The Pop-Quiz)

In a variable-interval schedule, reinforcement of a behavior is provided at a varying time interval since the last reinforcement. This means a pigeon might be rewarded for pecking after 10 seconds, or it might be rewarded after 1 minute, then after 5 minutes, then 5 seconds and the time interval between reinforcements is always changing. This schedule produces a slow and steady rate of response. The pigeon pecks steadily so it doesn't miss any opportunities for reinforcement but there's no need to rush, since that won't influence the length of delays.

A human comparison might be a class with pop-quizzes for extra credit given at varying and unpredictable times. These would encourage students to study a little each day to always be prepared to earn some points, though they probably wouldn't cram for hours and hours every night.

Superstitious Minds

Skinner also tried rewarding the animals at random, dropping food into the box at unpredictable times that didn't correspond to any particular desired behavior. Rather than doing nothing and just waiting for the food to arrive, the animals who were rewarded randomly developed bizarre "superstitious" behaviors.

If the animal was lifting a leg or turning his head in the moment preceding the reward, this behavior would be reinforced, making it more likely to be repeated. If, by chance, this behavior was repeated as the reward was delivered again (randomly), this would further serve to reinforce the behavior. As a result, Skinner found pigeons turning in circles or hopping on one leg, simply as a result of this random reinforcement. From this we may view all sorts of superstitious human behaviors, from rain dances to lucky charms to salt thrown over the shoulder, as the result of chance occurrences of reinforcement.

Behavior Reinforcing Behavior

David Premack did research with monkeys which suggested that some behaviors are naturally more desirable than others, and they could therefore be considered to be *high-probability behaviors*. This is known as the *relativity theory of reinforcement* or the **Premack Principle**. In essence it means that we can use preferences for one behavior as reinforcement for another behavior, such as letting a child play video games (presumably a high-probability behavior) only after finishing a number of math problems (presumably a low-probability behavior).

So if your mom ever insisted that you could only play after you finished your homework, now you know she was actually applying this Premack principle, attempting to use a desirable behavior (game playing) to reinforce a less desirable behavior (doing homework). Of course, preferences for some behaviors may vary between individuals, which will influence which behaviors can be used as reinforcement. Some children may love solving math problems and hate playing video games, so our strategy above wouldn't work well for them.

Biological Limits to Learning

Earlier we saw Garcia and Koelling's research on food aversions demonstrating that biological drives influence the associations that can be formed in classical conditioning. Keller and Marian Breland also found that they weren't able to train animals to perform certain tasks which conflicted with biological instincts. For instance, rather than carrying coins to a piggy bank, they found that pigs would repeatedly "root" the coins, pushing them around with their snouts as if the coins were food. Similarly, raccoons would repeatedly rub coins together and attempt to wash them with their paws, something that they usually do with food prior to eating. Both of these demonstrate *instinctual drift*, which is when a behavior being conditioned is similar to an instinctual behavior, and as a result, the instinct takes over and prevents the conditioning from being acquired properly.

Cognitive Learning

The strict focus on observable behavior couldn't last forever and eventually psychologists began considering the cognitive elements of learning more closely. Over time, evidence began to accumulate that we could actually study cognitive elements in a scientific manner, and as a result, psychology shifted away from its emphasis on behavior and started on what is often referred to as the "cognitive revolution". In the following two chapters we'll look at cognition more closely, but before we do so, let's look at some of the theories that shifted the tide away from the behaviorist view and towards a cognitive approach.

Beyond Associations: The Contingency Model of Classical Conditioning

You might wonder, if Pavlov's dogs knew to expect food during his bell experiments, why didn't they always salivate to Pavlov's mere presence? Why weren't they just salivating as soon as he walked into the room and started setting up his bells, lights, and metronomes? There were innumerable things that the dogs could have associated with food (the presence of Pavlov, the dog happening to wag his tail before food arrived, the clock on the wall, the clipboard on the table for Pavlov to record data, etc, etc, etc.). This suggests that while the dogs may have been learning that all of these other stimuli are associated with food, this mere association wasn't enough to cause salivation.

The **Rescorla-Wagner model** suggests that a dog in Pavlov's experiment wasn't just learning an association between the bell and the food, but was really learning that the bell is a **reliable predictor** of food. Part of the reason the bell is a reliable predictor is because the bell is **salient**. Pavlov may be standing there the whole time, so the dog may look at him without food arriving, or may not be looking at him just before food arrives, but we can be sure that the bell will at least temporarily capture the dog's attention just before the food. Rescorla and Wagner's contingency model of conditioning emphasizes that we don't just want to learn associations, we want to know what these associations mean and how accurate our predictions about the world will be.

Observational Learning

Imagine that you watch me walk up to a strange device you've never seen before. I press a button and immediately scream out in pain as I receive an electric shock. Are you willing to try pressing the button? Or perhaps I press a different button; a slot opens, and cash pours out into my hands. How likely is it that you would press this button?

According to strict theories of behaviorism, the probability of a behavior should only change when you are reinforced or punished. In this scenario, however, this view doesn't quite work, as you haven't actually been rewarded or punished, and in fact, you haven't really even performed a behavior. Yet we see that your probability of performing a particular behavior has in fact been modified by your experience of watching me. You've learned something about the button-pressing behavior without needing to do it yourself. The idea that we can learn without actually doing led Albert Bandura to investigate whether something like aggressive behavior might be learned simply through observation. To study this, Bandura had children observe an adult playing with a "Bobo doll", a large inflatable toy.

Some of the children saw an adult's behavior that was "aggressive"; punching, kicking, throwing, and beating the doll, while other children were not exposed to this aggressive play (instead the adult quietly played with tinker toys). Bandura wanted to see if observing this behavior had an effect on how the children later played with the toys. After observing the adult, the children were allowed to play with the toys in the room including the Bobo doll. Bandura then observed and recorded the children's actions, looking for mimicry of the behaviors, as well as novel "aggressive" behaviors.

It may not be surprising to learn that Bandura found children directly mimicking behaviors they had observed. Children exposed to the "aggressive" adult play were more likely to perform the "aggressive" behaviors themselves, suggesting that they had learned aggression via what Bandura called **modeling**.

In later versions of the study, Bandura rewarded (with candy) or punished (via scolding) the adult models, to see if this influenced the children's subsequent behavior. He referred to the consequences the children observed as **vicarious reinforcement**. Bandura found that children could demonstrate the effects of reinforcement (or punishment) on behavior simply by watching another person be rewarded (or punished) for performing that behavior. This has important implications for understanding how children can learn so many behaviors so quickly, as they don't necessarily need to experience all the consequences through trial-and-error in order to learn appropriate behavior.

While it may seem obvious that children learn by observing and mimicking behavior, Bandura's study demonstrated that direct reinforcement wasn't necessary for learning, which also implies that there were cognitive elements at play while children were watching the adult's behavior.

Latent Learning

Edward Tolman conducted research in the 1930s and 40s, though the dominance of a behaviorist approach to understanding learning at that time meant that his work was largely ignored until the 1960s. In one classic study, Tolman and Charles Honzik (1930) divided rats into 3 different conditions and had them complete the same maze repeatedly over the course of 17 days. They monitored each rat and counted the number of errors it made in completing the maze.

For the first group of rats, there was a food reward at the end of the maze. As we would expect from operant conditioning, these rats quickly learned to run to the end of the maze to get their reward, and they gradually made fewer and fewer errors over the course of the 17 days. For the next group of rats, there was no food reward at the end of the maze. Again, without reinforcement, behaviorist theory would suggest that the rats wouldn't learn anything, and not surprisingly, these rats wandered around the maze day after day, and the number of errors they made didn't decrease much over the 17 days.

So far you may be wondering why Tolman's work is still remembered today. As you might guess, the interesting part of the study comes with the third group of rats. This group did not have a food reward at the end of the maze for the first 10 days, then for the last 7 days a food reward was added. A behaviorist might predict that these rats would wander for 10 days, then gradually start learning beginning on the 11th day. But this is not what happened! While these rats did wander aimlessly for the first 10 days, once the food reward was available they rapidly reduced the number of errors they made, and in the last few days these rats actually performed better than the rats in the first group, who had been rewarded all along.

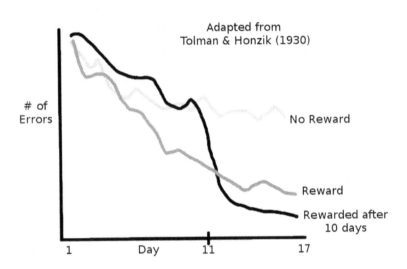

This suggests that the rats in the third group actually were learning during those first 10 days, they just weren't demonstrating their learning yet because there was no incentive to do so. Tolman referred to this as *latent learning*. This is learning that occurs without reinforcement, and isn't demonstrated until there is an incentive or reward.

This type of learning isn't just for rats in mazes, and in fact you probably do it all the time. Teachers rely on the fact that students engage in latent learning during classes and lectures. We assume that between when class started and when class ended you actually learned something, even though we may not have provided any way for you to demonstrate this learning. Just like the rats who waited 10 days before showing how well they knew the maze, you probably have waited weeks in order to demonstrate all the learning leading up to that midterm or final exam.

In another study, Tolman repeatedly placed a rat into a simple maze with only one route available and other routes blocked. The rat would run straight, turn left, then right, then turn right again, then run down a long hallway which ended with a food reward. After learning this maze, the rat was then placed in a similar maze, except the first straight path was blocked and several hallways were available in other directions. A behaviorist would expect the rat to either choose the most similar hall (almost straight) or perhaps to turn left, since that was the first turn it usually made. Instead, the rats showed that they actually knew the general location of the food in relation to the starting point, and correctly turned down the path angling off to the right and leading to the food, even though this angled right turn had never been rewarded in the past. This suggests that the rats had learned a *cognitive map*, a mental representation of the food's location, rather than just the behaviors (i.e. turn left, turn right, turn right) which had been rewarded in the past.

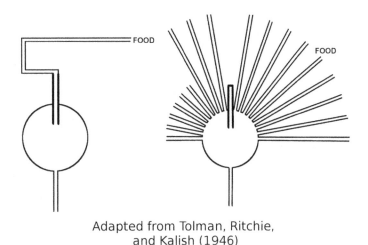

Adapted from Tolman, Ritchie, and Kalish (1946)

Humans also use cognitive maps and this is easily demonstrated if you imagine arriving at a restaurant. While you wait to be seated, you ask to use the restroom and are instructed to walk straight, turn left, turn right, then go to the end of the hallway. Later in the evening, after being seated at your table, you need to use the restroom again. Instead of following the specific previous behaviors (turn left, turn right) you now need to perform new behaviors to get to the restroom (walk straight, turn left) because you are starting from your table. Rather than becoming hopelessly lost and soiling your pants, you use a cognitive map of your position in relation the location of the bathroom to figure out a new route with relatively little effort.

Abstract Learning

We don't only learn specific behaviors tied to specific situations or stimuli. We also learn more complex concepts like what a tree is (we can understand that a willow is a tree and a palm tree is a tree, even though they look quite different). Similarly, we're capable of learning other abstract concepts like love, humility, or pride and these influence our thoughts and behavior even though they may not be readily observable.

While we may excel at it, this ability to learn concepts may not be limited to humans. In fact, research has shown that even pigeons can demonstrate this type of abstract learning. After being taught to peck a picture of a chair, pigeons could also peck at pictures of chairs that they hadn't seen before. While this may seem like just stimulus generalization, their ability to correctly respond to a novel stimulus suggests the possibility that pigeons actually have a cognitive understanding of the concept of chair. In a study by Shigeru Watanabe, Junko Sakamoto, and Masumi Wakita (1995), pigeons were taught to differentiate between Picasso and Monet paintings and later could do so with paintings from these artists they had not seen before. This implies that there are important cognitive elements in their learning process that can't be fully understood through simple behavioral observation.

Insight Learning

Wolfgang Köhler studied learning in chimps and presented them with puzzles to solve in order to obtain bananas. Bananas were suspended high above the ground or placed out of reach behind a fence, and chimps needed to stack boxes to stand on or use sticks to drag the bananas closer. Once the chimps had figured out what to do, they worked at that solution (such as stacking boxes) until they were able to perform it successfully. Köhler observed that the behavior of the chimps differed from that of Thorndike's cats, who discovered the solution to the puzzlebox by simple trial-and-error. It wasn't the case that the chimps simply stumbled onto the solution, but instead that they mentally worked out a solution then acted in a purposeful way.

Rather than a gradual strengthening of a stimulus-response association, the learning in this case seemed to appear in the form of a sudden realization, which Köhler considered to be an example of *insight*. After their initial failures to reach the bananas, the chimps seemed to contemplate solutions, rather than constantly trying new behaviors. This suggests an internal cognitive learning process that is occurring without the need for repeated trial-and-error behavior.

End of an Era

The accumulating evidence of biological and cognitive aspects of learning gradually led to the decline of behaviorism as the dominant approach in psychology. In the following two chapters on memory, language, and cognition, we'll attempt to better understand the internal workings of the mind and how our mental representations of the world influence our thoughts, emotions, and behaviors.

Chapter Summary – Learning

- *Classical conditioning* refers to learning which results from the repeated pairing of stimuli. A neutral stimulus is followed by an unconditioned stimulus (which generates an unconditioned response) repeatedly until the neutral stimulus alone causes a response (called a conditioned response) at which point the neutral stimulus is referred to as a conditioned stimulus.

- In *operant conditioning* an organism learns to associate rewards and punishments with particular behaviors. Positive and negative reinforcement both encourage a behavior either by giving something desirable or taking away something undesirable, while positive and negative punishment discourage a behavior by giving something undesirable or taking away something desirable.

- Reinforcement in operant conditioning can be given according to different schedules including *fixed-ratio*, *variable-ratio*, *fixed-interval*, and *variable-interval*.

- We have *biological predispositions* for some types of learning such as associating taste with nausea. *Instinctual drift* can also prevent some behaviors from being learned properly.

- Increasing evidence for cognitive components of learning from studies of *latent learning*, *observational learning*, *abstract learning*, and *insight learning* eventually led researchers away from a strict emphasis on behavior for understanding learning.

Notes

Chapter 6
Memory

Memory

Why do we remember some things and not others? How much can we remember and how long can our memories last? What processes shape our memory of the world? Memories are a fundamental part of who we are, so it's natural that we should have so many questions about why some memories persist while others fade, or how it is that we can win a game of Trivial Pursuit and on the same night forget where we left our keys.

We can think of the memory process as having three distinct phases: encoding, storage, and retrieval. You'll notice that these words are shared with computer terminology and this is a result of a shift in thinking during the 1950s and 1960s as psychology began to think of the mind as being similar to a computer in how it processes information.

Encoding refers to the process of transforming information into a memory or creating a new memory.

Storage refers to maintaining the memory over time, whether that means holding onto it for a few minutes or for a lifetime.

Retrieval refers to getting access to a memory that has been stored.

As we'll see throughout this chapter, failures are possible at any of these steps in the memory process. These different types of memory failures will have different characteristics, depending on whether encoding, storage, or retrieval has been affected. We'll also look at how mnemonic techniques can be used to help reduce memory failure and how knowing more about how your memory works can help you to use it more effectively.

Let's begin with a fairly simple model for our different types of memory. The **3-Box information processing model** proposed by Richard Atkinson and Richard Shiffrin divides memory into 3 types: sensory memory, short-term memory, and long-term memory. While the latter two types may be familiar to you in everyday use, you may not be familiar with the first type.

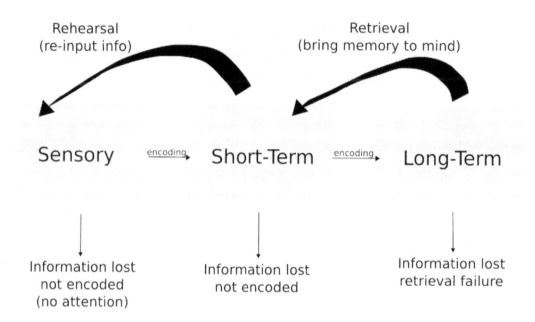

Sensory Memory

Sensory memory is the first "box" in this model. Sensory memory is a highly detailed and accurate representation of information from our senses, which only lasts for about a second. Because it lasts so briefly, it's difficult to study sensory memory, but *George Sperling* devised a clever way to investigate it. Sperling showed participants a slide containing 3 rows of 4 letters (such as below) for only 1/20 of a second.

J B W F

R W M L

N Q D G

He then immediately asked the participants to recite what they saw on either the top, middle, or bottom row. He found that participants were generally able to recall any row he asked for with near perfect accuracy, provided that he asked immediately (errors quickly increased if the delay was 1 second or longer). Participants were essentially "reading" the letters off of a fleeting mental image and this short-lived visual information store is known as *iconic memory* (while auditory sensory memory is referred to as *echoic memory*). This research indicates that the sensory memory store actually contains all of the letters, but that this storage lasts very briefly. Despite their ability to recall **any** row requested, the participants weren't able to recall **all** of the rows. The sensory memory store dissipates so quickly that in the time it took to recite one row, the others had disappeared from memory and could no longer be recalled accurately.

By focusing their attention on one of the rows (the one requested) participants were able to store that information a bit longer. This also demonstrates the role of *selective attention* in memory storage. We can only pay attention to a small amount of the information in our sensory memory at once, and this dictates which information will make its way to the next "box" of the 3-box model: short-term memory.

Short-Term Memory

Research by **George Miller** has estimated that short-term memory can hold somewhere between 5 to 9 items (described in a classic paper titled: *The Magical Number 7 Plus or Minus 2*). When asked to recall a list of words, a string of digits, or a sequence of colors, most people do fine up to about 7 items, after which accuracy drops off sharply. This "**magical number 7**" can be extended through the use of mnemonic techniques such as looking for relationships and patterns among items or creating stories. These techniques are known as **organizational encoding**. One particular type of organizational encoding, known as **chunking**, consists of placing multiple items into groups. For example, if you wanted to remember the number 2317761945007 rather than think of individual digits you might create chunks you recognize such as "Michael Jordan's jersey #", "Declaration of Independence signed", "End of WWII", and "James Bond's agent number" allowing you to recall all 13 digits while only needing to remember 4 items.

Short-term memory only lasts for about 10-30 seconds, but this can be extended by **rehearsal**; mentally repeating the items to keep them from fading. This is essentially a way of re-inputting the information into sensory memory, allowing us to repeat the cycle. If attention is divided or distracted, however, rehearsal will no longer be effective. You may have experienced this if you've ever been interrupted while mentally trying to repeat a phone number. Since Atkinson and Shiffrin first proposed the 3 box model, some changes have been made, including the addition of the term **working memory**. Working memory refers to information in short-term memory that is currently being manipulated. For example, when you are attempting to add several numbers, like solving 478 plus 23, you need to hold each of these numbers in your mind, but you also need to be able to work with them and keep track of changes.

Long-Term Memory

The final memory store in the 3-box model is **long-term memory**. There isn't a known capacity limit for human long-term memory, so there isn't a point at which your memory can be considered "full" and you can no longer encode any new memories. The duration of long-term memory varies greatly; some items may be held for a matter of hours, others for a lifetime.

Long-term memories can be divided into 3 main types: episodic, semantic, and procedural. **Episodic memories** are sequential events and narrative stories that make up your own personal history. These might include memories of your third-grade class, a first date, or a vacation. These are generally remembered as a "gist" of the story and not as a list of specific facts. So when I ask you about your vacation, your episodic memory allows you to give a general description of the overall experience.

Semantic memory consists of factual knowledge of the world; names, dates, word meanings, categories, etc. Both episodic and semantic memories are examples of *explicit* (or *declarative*) memories because they can be consciously recalled and described.

Procedural memory is a memory for skills and how to perform them. These memories can be demonstrated but may be rather difficult to put into words or be consciously described. For this reason, procedural memory is often considered a type of *implicit* (or *non-declarative*) memory because you may not need to consciously recall it in order to perform the behavior. In fact, you may not even be consciously aware that the memory exists. For instance, you can probably effortlessly tie your shoes, but if you were asked to consciously describe each step of tying your shoes, you might find it difficult. You may even need to perform the behavior and then narrate what you see your hands doing. This divide between our memory of how to do things and how to consciously describe how we do those things can provide insight into the complexity of teaching physical tasks. These different types of memory explain why someone may be able to perfectly execute a complex maneuver, but find themselves at a complete loss for words when it comes to describing exactly what they are doing.

Schacter's Seven Sins of Memory

Despite the shared terminology with computers, our memory doesn't work like a hard drive, neatly and accurately storing information to be called up later. Our memory is subject to error, either at the level of encoding, storage, or retrieval, resulting in several different types of failures, which Harvard professor *Daniel Schacter* refers to as the *"Seven Sins of Memory"* : Transience, Absentmindedness, Blocking, Misattribution, Suggestibility, Bias, and Persistence.

Transience is a failure of retrieval that results from the passage of time. The German researcher *Hermann Ebbinghaus* worked to quantify how much memory faded (and how quickly it faded) by repeatedly testing himself with lists of nonsense syllables made by placing a vowel between two consonants (creating "words" like DEK, PUV, DUT, etc.). Based on his data, he described a "*forgetting curve*" which showed that a great deal of information is lost rather quickly, and then the rate of information loss slows and the curve gradually flattens.

The inevitably transient nature of our memory highlights the importance of regular review for memories we wish to maintain. By repeatedly reviewing information, we can gradually raise the curve and increase our retention. In the Improve Your Memory section at the end of this chapter we'll go into more detail on how to maximize the effectiveness of your review to reduce transience.

Absentmindedness is a type of forgetting that occurs due to a lapse in attention. If you've ever forgotten an umbrella in a restaurant or a bag in a taxi, you've experienced absentmindedness. It generally isn't the case that the memory has been completely forgotten (since it is often recalled just moments later) but rather that our attention is momentarily placed elsewhere and so we fail to bring the memory to mind when we need it. We can think of this as a type of retrieval error, because even though the memory has been encoded and stored accurately (as evidenced by our later recall) we fail to retrieve the memory at the appropriate time.

Knowing that our future self may fail to remember something at the appropriate time and then making plans to prevent this from occurring is referred to as ***prospective memory***; memory for the future. This is planning a reminder for something that will force our attention to retrieve the memory at the appropriate time. For instance, if you're worried about forgetting to bring an important bag with you tomorrow morning, you might place the bag in front of the door tonight. This will ensure that you see the bag as you are leaving in the morning, directing your attention to retrieve the appropriate memory (bring this with me) at the appropriate time (and not 20 minutes later when you are half-way to your destination).

Blocking occurs when we have a memory but are temporarily unable to successfully retrieve it. This may cause a "***tip-of-the-tongue***" ***experience***; the frustrating condition in which we know that the memory is there even though we can't bring it to mind. We know that we have encoded and stored the memory, so the error is at the level of retrieval. This tip-of-the-tongue experience can be triggered when we attempt to retrieve memories that are infrequently accessed, such as when trying to recall the word for a person who makes maps, or when trying to remember the name of a former classmate.

Misattribution occurs when we incorrectly identify where a memory came from. We have the memory, but we think it came from somewhere else. If you start telling a juicy story to a friend and are interrupted by "I'm the one who told you that yesterday", misattribution is to blame. Misattribution reveals that our brains aren't particularly good at ***source memory***, or memory for where information came from. So while we may correctly encode an interesting fact, we may have trouble recalling whether a friend told us, we read it on a blog, or saw it in a YouTube video. This memory error can be particularly troublesome in the courtroom, as eyewitnesses may incorrectly identify innocent bystanders as perpetrators (because they recognize their faces) or even falsely accuse others they recognize from completely different circumstances.

A famous (and somewhat ironic) example of this occurred when a woman accused Donald Thomson of rape. Thomson's alibi was sound, as he was at a television studio filming a live broadcast when the crime occurred. The woman had actually been watching the program prior to her attack, and she misattributed her memory of Thomson's face to that of her attacker. The irony is that in his television appearance, Thomson, a psychologist, was discussing eyewitness memory for faces.

Advertisers use our poor source memory to their advantage, as they blatantly sing the praises of their own products. While this type of blow-hard bravado may seem in poor taste, later we may recall hearing positive messages about a product, though we've forgotten that we heard those good things from the very company selling the product.

Misattribution can also occur in the form of ***false recognition***, when a novel stimulus is similar enough to a previously-seen stimulus that we think they are the same. So we may believe that we recognize someone or something that we haven't actually seen before. This false recognition has been proposed as one possible explanation for the phenomenon of *déjà vu*, as a new experience may trigger feelings of familiarity because it resembles a previous experience. In contrast, we may occasionally suffer from ***cryptomnesia***, when we believe that a thought is new, when actually it is a memory of an old thought. This can lead to inadvertent plagiarism; we think an idea came from our own creative processes, but in fact it is a memory of someone else's work. Authors and musicians may be heartbroken (and legally liable) upon the realization that a wonderful turn of phrase or catchy riff is not a sign of their genius and creativity, but rather, a sign of their source memory's fallibility.

Suggestibility is the idea that external information can infiltrate and modify our memories, even implanting memories that weren't there in the first place. In a number of studies, ***Elizabeth Loftus*** and colleagues have demonstrated that leading questions can change existing memories and false memories can be successfully created via suggestion. In one study, Loftus and John Palmer found that participants' estimates of vehicle speed in a video of a car accident were influenced by the use of "smashed" vs. "hit" in the question (speed estimates rose significantly when participants were asked about cars that "smashed into each other").

In another study, Loftus was able to successfully implant the false memory of being lost in a shopping mall as a child into the minds of several of her participants. These studies on suggestibility cast doubt on how much we can trust our own memories. We should remember that our memories are not recordings of events, but rather, ***reconstructions*** of events and we are always prone to the possibility of error each time we try to mentally put the pieces together.

Our memory is also subject to ***bias***. We tend to reconstruct our past so that it seems more like our present (known as ***consistency bias***) and we also tend to selectively recall memories that make us look better (known as ***egocentric bias***), such as when college students who were asked to recall their high school transcripts tended to successfully recall the high grades but forgot more of the low grades they had received. This may be a bias that's not so bad, as there might be practical implications for our self-esteem. Egocentric bias may help ensure we recall our previous successes and minimize our failures, helping us feel more capable and motivated.

The final "sin" of memory from Schacter's list is when intrusive memories are brought to mind repeatedly and without conscious control, known as **persistence**. Flashbacks of negative events and traumatic experiences can repeatedly disrupt the minds of victims, interfering with their lives. Persistence demonstrates the powerful and sometimes painful connection between emotion and memory. We may consider the role of persistence in syndromes such as Post-Traumatic Stress Disorder (**PTSD**) in which patients feel trapped reliving the same traumatic event over and over again.

Those with PTSD may represent the extreme of persistence but for all of us, emotional events tend to be remembered better than non-emotional events. This can be seen in **flash-bulb memories**; detailed memories of emotionally-charged events. I can recall exactly where I was on the morning of September 11, 2001, and that's an example of a flash-bulb memory. I can remember more details of that morning than some other non-emotionally-charged morning of say October 7, 2007. This isn't to say that my memories of September 11th aren't still subject to all of the other potential errors and biases above, but rather that the emotional intensity of that particular morning partially explains why it is more memorable and why memories of that particular morning may be brought to mind more often.

Our physical and emotional state plays a role not just in encoding memories, but also in their retrieval, as our current state prepares us to recall events from similar physical and emotional states. This is known as **state-dependent memory**. For example, when we're brimming with enthusiasm and motivation, we're more likely to recall memories filled with optimism and excitement, but when we're feeling down it's easier to recall past experiences of sadness and disappointment. This has important implications for the treatment of disorders like depression because it may contribute to a downward spiral as depressed patients are more likely to recall negative memories and experiences, further reducing their mood.

The Biology of Memory

One major breakthrough in understanding brain structures and memory came from the case of H.M., a patient who had the hippocampus surgically removed from both sides of his brain to reduce epileptic seizures. Following his surgery, which was successful in reducing seizures, H.M. was unable to form new memories, a condition known as **anterograde amnesia**. While hippocampectomy is rare, other patients with hippocampal damage from injury or infection have provided similar case studies. These cases also provide evidence that long-term memory is a separate store of memory in the 3-box model, since these patients have intact sensory and short-term memory. They can repeat lists of words, copy diagrams, and answer questions, but they cannot move this information to long-term memory. Just moments later they won't remember the words in the list, the fact that they had been drawing, or even what question they are in the middle of answering.

There is some evidence, however, that they are able to retain some long-term memory in the form of **procedural memories**. H.M. was able to improve his ability in certain types of physical tasks (such as drawing while looking in a mirror) even though he couldn't consciously remember practicing the tasks. It appears that the cerebellum, basal ganglia, and striatum are crucial structures in the formation and storage of these types of procedural memories, which is why H.M. was still able to learn them despite lacking functioning hippocampi.

The case of Clive Wearing, a British musicologist who received damage from a brain infection, is even more severe, because in addition to anterograde amnesia he suffers extensive **retrograde amnesia**, or loss of existing memories. He has almost no prior declarative memories, and, being unable to form new memories, this leaves him with only the present moment. He has functioning sensory memory and short-term memory, but no ability to create new long-term memories and very little ability to retrieve old long-term memories. This means that he is mentally living in a brief window of time, lasting only a matter of seconds. He does have procedural memories intact, as he can still speak and use language correctly, walk and move normally, and even play the piano. As with the cases above, this suggests that procedural memories must be stored and organized differently than other types of long-term memory.

Neural Mechanisms of Memory

Synaptic activity between two neurons can lead to a strengthened connection between those two neurons, known as **Long-Term Potentiation (LTP)**. This is often summarized with the expression "neurons that fire together wire together". Even though these neurons don't actually "wire together" in terms of physically touching, the strength of their connection is increased via chemical interactions when they repeatedly fire synchronously. While the exact mechanisms of this process are not yet fully understood, there are several factors that are believed to be important. One possible signaling pathway is **NMDA,** for **N-methyl-D-aspartate,** a receptor for the neurotransmitter glutamate.

Repeated firing of a synapse causes the postsynaptic neuron to increase its number of glutamate receptors and this changes the postsynaptic neuron's sensitivity to future stimulation. Mice who have had an NMDA antagonist injected into their hippocampus have shown impaired spatial learning in a maze task (Morris, 1986). Ketamine, an anesthetic frequently used as a recreational drug, is an NMDA antagonist, explaining why one of its many effects is memory loss.

Understanding the neural aspects of memory formation also opens the possibility for the development of drugs to improve our memories. Mice given boosts to their NMDA levels show improved performance in learning tasks, so we may wonder whether human memory drugs will be hitting pharmacy shelves in the not-too-distant future. Until that day arrives, however, we'll need to rely on other methods of improving our memory, and fortunately humans actually have thousands of years of experience in this department.

How to Improve Your Memory

My hope is that this section of the book is the most valuable and will help you to recall and apply the material from all of the other chapters. I think that it's best to have background understanding of the preceding material in this chapter first, so if you haven't already read the first half of this chapter, I highly recommend you do so before reading this section, as much of the terminology used here is explained there. Now let's look at how we can leverage our knowledge of memory to improve our ability to retain information. Along the way we'll learn a few more terms for some memory concepts, but with a focus on how they can be applied to mastering our own memory.

I want to keep this section practical and applicable, so I'm going to step back from explaining the details of the research supporting these principles. That said, if you are interested in more of the technicalities of this type of memory research, I encourage you to check the references section, where I've listed supporting studies for these concepts.

The Importance of Organization

One of the first steps to improving memory is to organize the information that we want to recall. If I need to buy 15 items from the grocery store, rather trying to remember all items in a haphazard manner, organizing them by category would immediately improve my chances of recalling them correctly. Chunking these items into groups like vegetables, prepackaged foods, beverages, etc. provides a hierarchical structure that has been demonstrated to improve recall. Waiters and waitresses often use the same technique, organizing items by category, rather than blindly sticking to the mismatched sequence of items as customers placed their orders.

This may seem fairly obvious when it comes to grocery lists and entrees, but this organizational encoding can and should be applied to just about anything you want to remember. If you're looking to learn a bunch of SAT words you might start by organizing them into categories of nouns, verbs, and adjectives or maybe you'd prefer to break them into groups based on positive and negative connotations. There are any number of groupings that might make sense, you just want to avoid a chaotic jumble of terms.

While I've tried to organize terms in this book by related concepts, you might find that you remember them better by focusing on key individuals and the terms necessary for talking about their work. The type of organization you prefer is personal, but the key point is that you should have a structure in place. Later, once you have a good grasp of most of the information, you can shuffle your flashcards or pick out random terms to mix things up but this should be during review, not initial learning.

Breaking it Down with Ebbinghaus

In the section on transience, we learned about the forgetting curve that Hermann Ebbinghaus created, but what wasn't mentioned is that Ebbinghaus also found recall tended to be better for certain items based on their location in his lists. He found that he was better able to recall the items at the beginning and the end of a list, known as the ***serial position effect***. Improved recall for the initial items on a list is known as ***primacy***, while the improvement for the final items of the list (which are most recent) is referred to as ***recency***.

Imagine that you had a list of 20 items you wanted to recall. Serial position effects mean that you might recall the first few and last few terms better, but what about the 15 or so in the middle? Simply by breaking this list into 2 groups of 10 items, you'd be doubling your primacy and recency effects. And if you were to break those two lists down into smaller lists of just 5 items, you'd probably find your recall substantially improved without spending more time reviewing.

This is why it's important to take frequent breaks and to study material in small sections. Not only is it easier to stay focused and maintain your attention, but you also get the benefit of having more first items and more last items. Keep this in mind when you make your overly-ambitious study plans which include marathon cramming sessions. Rather than planning to slog your way through an entire book at once, plan to read just one section, then break, then return for the next section, etc. Provided that you keep returning (and those breaks don't turn into 4 hours of video games) you'll probably find that you're able to recall more of the material even after just one reading.

Testing Yourself

Students around the world may groan when they hear this, but testing does actually have benefits for memory, provided that you get a chance to see the answers and get feedback on your responses. This type of testing + feedback has been shown to improve recall more than simply having another review session and the resulting memory boost is known as the ***testing effect***. We should take advantage of this by making all our review a type of test. This is why flashcards can be so much more effective than simply re-reading definitions. By forcing yourself to come up with an answer every time and then getting immediate feedback, you're able to get the testing effect many times over.

It's also a good idea to review often and in short sessions. This is known as ***distributed review*** and it has been shown to be more effective than long sessions or ***massed practice***. Each time we review we raise that forgetting curve and slow the rate of its decline. There are a number of programs available which can schedule your review for you, known as ***spaced-repetition software*** or ***SRS*** (I personally use Anki and can recommend it). These programs calculate your next review based on your ranking of how well you remembered an item.

If you're sure that you've really learned everything, don't stop just yet. There's actually good reason to continue to review. Ebbinghaus found that transience decreased when he continued to review material that he already knew. This is known as **overlearning** and it should actually be a part of your study plans. Hopefully this will help you to pass your exams, but more importantly, help you to recall the material long after the exams have passed.

Go Deep

Information which is more deeply processed tends to be remembered better, known as **levels of processing theory**. This deeper processing refers to considering the information, and reflecting or analyzing how it may fit in with other memories and experiences. This is something that I've tried to naturally incorporate throughout this text.

Rather than simply listing terms and definitions, I've tried to connect ideas and explain why particular concepts are so important. This technique is strengthened when information can be made more personal. This is known as the **self-referential effect**. Connecting something to your own personal sense of self strengthens your ability to recall it. For instance, if you were trying to remember a random list of words and one was *chihuahua*, and you have many fond memories with your pet chihuahua, chances are good that you would remember this word better than the others on the list. Thinking of ways you've personally experienced classical conditioning, vicarious reinforcement, or memory failures will strengthen your ability to recall and apply these concepts.

Create Retrieval Cues

Retrieval cues are related memories that can help us to retrieve a particular memory. You probably use these quite often when you are having trouble recalling something. Imagine that someone has asked you the name of an actor who starred in a particular movie. You know the actor, but you're experiencing **blocking** and can't come up with his name. You may begin searching your memory for retrieval cues such as other movies that he has starred in. These other movie titles, though they don't feature the actor's name, can serve as retrieval cues because they may be mentally connected to the actor's name. Our related memories tend to form networks of connections to one another, so recalling one can help to activate another.

Similarly, I might ask you to read the following list:

hospital, nurse, sick, bed, stethoscope, physician, medicine, exam, gown

Now if tomorrow I were to ask you to recall as many words from the list as possible, there's a high likelihood that you would recall the word "doctor", even though it wasn't on the list. Because I activated many words related to "doctor", it may feel as if doctor itself was activated. This ***spreading activation*** of memory can be used to our advantage by activating as many related memories as possible for something that we want to recall. While in the case above recalling "doctor" would be an error, if we really wanted to recall the word doctor tomorrow then reading this list would be an excellent way to help make that happen.

Sleep and Memory Consolidation

As we'll see in chapter 8, there is a strong relationship between sleep and memory. Sleep seems to play a key role in consolidating our memories while sleep deprivation has clearly been shown to wreak havoc on our ability to form new memories. We'll look at some of the evidence in chapter 8, but for now, suffice to say that getting enough sleep is fundamental to maximizing your memory powers. Long, late nights of cramming might not be nearly as effective as shorter sessions followed by plenty of sleeping time.

The Method of Loci

This technique is perhaps the most important concept in this book and it has the potential to truly transform your ability to remember. The beauty of this mnemonic technique is that it is incredibly simple and requires only minimal preparation to implement.

The method of loci (sometimes called the ***Journey Method***, or the ***Roman Room method***) has been used for thousands of years and consists of mentally traveling along a familiar route and placing mental images at different locations (*loci* in Latin) as you go. These mental images represent the information to be remembered, and by using a familiar route, the order of the information will naturally be preserved.

This technique can truly revolutionize your memory abilities. While entire books have been written on the subject of memory improvement, I believe that the method of loci is the most efficient and practical technique that can be taught, and it can be learned in minutes. Of course, practice is necessary to really unlock the potential power of this technique.

First, you need a journey that you know well, such as your home or apartment. Now, let's say that you wanted to remember the 12 animals of the Chinese zodiac, in order. They are:

Rat, Ox, Tiger, Rabbit, Dragon, Snake, Horse, Goat, Monkey, Rooster, Dog, Pig

In order to quickly memorize this list, you could use your home or apartment and come up with 12 locations (in order) to place each animal. Perhaps you start at your bed, imagining it covered with rats (certainly a memorable, if unpleasant, image), then you'd move to the next location, perhaps a table next to your bed. Imagine a giant ox carefully balanced on the table, trying not to fall off and wake you. Then perhaps you move to the closet where you part the clothes to find a tiger staring you in the face, ready to pounce. As you continue through the natural sequence of your home, you use your imagination to create vivid images.

When you've finished, you'll find that simply mentally traveling through your house will bring each animal to mind. It won't feel like you're "studying" the list at all, but you'll be able to bring it to mind nearly effortlessly. The order of the list will naturally be preserved because the order of rooms won't suddenly change. Now the only limit to how many items you can recall is how many locations your journey has (and how much time you want to spend creating images). This method has been used by world champion memorizers to recall tens of thousands of items.

If you want to remember something permanently you'll still need to review it, and this means you give it a dedicated journey that isn't used for anything else. So if I had 20 products I want to always have mentally ready for work, I might use 20 locations around my workplace for those items and those items only. Then I could effortlessly rattle off all 20 products in order without worrying about leaving any out.

For other information that you only need to remember for a short time, you can use a journey, then reuse that journey later for new information. This multi-purpose journey is like a mental USB drive that you might keep documents on for short periods, constantly swapping things in and out. Just mentally clearing out a journey (by imagining the locations empty) is generally enough to allow you to refill it with new images.

I personally use my childhood home frequently for information that I want to remember short-term but don't need long-term. I use this journey to do memory demonstrations in my classes, in which case I may only need to remember the information (such as a random list of words) for an hour or so. After the demonstration is over and I don't need to remember the info, I simply don't review it. Next time I do a demonstration, I can use the same journey locations again because the old associations have faded.

I believe that when used effectively, the method of loci can incorporate many mnemonic techniques in one and this is what gives it tremendous power. I'd like to briefly outline how all the factors we've learned already can apply to the Method of Loci and why it's the first mnemonic technique I'd recommend to anyone looking to improve memory.

Creating a journey immediately imposes a structure (***organizational encoding***) and it relies on mental images (known as ***visual imagery encoding***). The Method of Loci forces you to consider the information and connect it to something that you already know (in this case, a familiar journey). This means that you are processing the information more deeply, and this in itself should help to make it more memorable (***levels of processing theory***). You can add to this effect by considering any emotional response for the image you have created. What other senses and emotions does it evoke (***state-dependent memory***)? Regardless of emotional impact, the images and relationships you create will be personal (***self-referential effect***). Even when we struggle to recall something in a journey, the location serves as a vivid starting point to help us (***retrieval cue***). In addition, this method allows us to review materially mentally by going through our journey so we can review often (***spaced repetition***) and each time we mentally reach a location and try to recall the image we are testing ourselves (***the testing effect***).

All of these factors have me convinced that the Method of Loci is the most versatile and effective mnemonic tool for improving memory. But you may not be convinced just yet.

What about things that aren't easily visualized?

This might appear to be the Achilles' Heel for this technique, but fortunately it is a weakness that can be overcome. When faced with items that are hard to visualize (like foreign words, numbers, or abstract ideas) we need to apply additional systems in order to place mental images along our journey. This isn't as hard as it might seem, though creating images will require some creativity.

Sound-alikes - This is sometimes referred to as the ***Link Method*** or the ***Keyword method*** and it's useful for things that don't have mental images associated with them, such as the sounds of a foreign word. In this case, a mental image is created based on similar sounds that will help link the original word with its definition. For example, if you were learning that the Spanish word for beer is cerveza, you might realize that *cerveza* sounds a bit like "survey sir" (not exactly, but close enough to cue your memory). You might imagine someone sitting in a bar, and rather than bringing a nice cold beer, the waiter brings a survey to complete, saying "survey, sir". This mental image might be just enough to remind you that the word for beer is *cerveza*.

While this technique isn't going to work for every new word you encounter, it can help if you've got a lot of terms to learn. You may even find that just trying to create the sound-alikes will force you to engage with the words and consider self-referential images for remembering them, which certainly won't hurt your chances of correct recall. While this method is often touted as a stand-alone technique, I find it combines quite well with the method of loci because placing the images you create along a journey will help to ensure that you review them and will also provide additional structure to help you retrieve them.

Number Systems

One way to visualize numbers is to use a shape system that creates a visual image for each digit. 0 could be an egg, 1 a baseball bat, 2 a swan, 3 a pair of breasts(!), 4 a sailboat, 5 a hook, 6 a golf club, 7 an axe, 8 a snowman, and 9 a balloon on a string. Now, rather than trying to remember whether a digit was a 4 or a 5, you'll have very different mental images that are less likely to be confused. When confronted with the task of remembering a number you can place a mental image of each digit along a mental journey, just as you did for the animals in the zodiac. Then when you recall the images, just translate back into numbers.

If there were a number that I wanted to permanently commit to memory, I would give it its own journey which is not used for any other information. I've memorized my passport number by using a journey through an airport security check, placing images in the little plastic bin, the x-ray machine, the metal detector, the "wand area", the end of the conveyor belt, etc. For memorizing a friend's telephone number, you might use their apartment as the journey for the images.

If you're more ambitious, you can try tackling a more complex number system, creating a mental image for every two-digit number. So you'll have a visual image you can bring to mind for all numbers from 00 to 99. This cuts the number of images that you need in half (though it does take a little more time to create and practice with) and adds the advantage of *chunking*, allowing you to remember numbers in groups rather than single digits. This is a system that I use to memorize numbers and I have a "character" that I bring to mind for each pair of digits. Rather than randomly selecting a person for each number, I populated my list by using a system of name initials shown below.

0=O 1=A 2=B 3=C 4=D 5=E 6=S 7=G 8=H 9=N

This is known as the Dominic System, after Dominic O'Brien, world memory champion and author of several excellent books on memory training. I first learned this system many years ago from one of O'Brien's books on mnemonic systems and methods for memorizing numbers, cards, dates, and more.

So in my list, each two-digit number becomes a set of initials, which then becomes a visual image of a person. If I wanted to recall 341630, the number 34 (CD) becomes Cameron Diaz. 16 (AS) becomes Arnold Schwarzenegger, while 30 (CO) calls up an image of Conan O'Brien. Now when faced with the task of memorizing a long string of digits, I just need to convert each pair to a person and place it along my mental journey. When faced with an odd number of digits, I combine this pair-system with the shape system above, which is only used for the final (single) digit.

If you want to really get extreme, you can also add an action for each character, and then an object as well, so that now each single mental image can store 6 digits (first two digits – person, next two digits – action of second person, next two digits – associated object of third person). So 341630 would become a single image of Cameron Diaz (*person)*, flexing her muscles (*action* for Arnold), while holding an Eisenhower coffee mug (*object* for Conan).

This advanced person-action-object technique is mostly for the hardcore mnemonists looking to compete, but it can be used by anyone who has reason or inclination to memorize long strings of digits on a regular basis. The people, actions, and objects are highly personal, and as a result, the above may not make much sense to anyone but me so the biggest time commitment comes in creating your own personalized people, actions, and objects.

Even if you aren't looking to get this deep into the bizarre world of mnemonic techniques, I encourage you to learn the basics of the Method of Loci and apply it whenever you need to memorize something. You might be surprised at just how well your memory works.

A Memorable Example

Let's end with a more practical example and say that you wanted to memorize Schacter's Seven Sins of Memory from earlier in this chapter. All you would need to do is create a mental image for each sin, then place each image along a 7-location journey. Here's some ideas for visual images for each: **Transience** (a transient hobo), **Absentmindedness** (Fred McMurray as the absent-minded professor – or Robin Williams in the remake *Flubber*), **Blocking** (a large block of wood), **Misattribution** (a blurry-faced mugshot), **Suggestibility** (a smashed-up car from Loftus and Palmer's study), **Bias** (a scale of justice heavily tipped to one side), and **Persistence** (a melting watch from Salvador Dali's *The Persistence of Memory*). It takes a bit of work and imagination to create these images, but once you have done it the time you'll save on mindless studying will be more than worth it.

Now if you placed these images along a short journey, you could review these seven sins any time you wanted, without needing to carry around flashcards or a bulky textbook. With enough practice, eventually you'd easily recall them without even needing to think of the journey at all.

Chapter Summary – Memory

- The *3-Box Information Processing Model* divides memory storage into *sensory memory*, *short-term memory*, and *long-term memory*.

- Daniel Schacter has described memory failures as the 7 "sins" of memory: *Transience*, *Absentmindedness*, *Blocking*, *Misattribution*, *Suggestibility*, *Bias*, and *Persistence*.

- Memories can be categorized as *explicit* or *implicit*, depending on our level of conscious awareness. Within these categories, memories can also be labeled as *episodic*, *semantic*, or *procedural*.

- Emotion and memory are closely linked, and this link can be seen in *persistence*, *flash-bulb memory* and *state-dependent memory*.

- Evidence from case studies of patients like H.M. and Clive Wearing highlights the role of the *hippocampus* in memory formation. At the neural level, *long-term potentiation* refers to strengthening of synaptic connections between neurons after they repeatedly fire together.

- Memory can be improved through the use of mnemonic strategies such as the *method of loci*, *visual imagery encoding*, *chunking*, and *spaced-repetition*.

Notes

Chapter 7
Language & Cognition

How Do We Acquire Language?

In 1957, B. F. Skinner published *Verbal Behavior*, an explanation of language acquisition according to behaviorist principles of reinforcement and punishment. Skinner believed that language acquisition could be understood in the same way that lever pressing and disc pecking was understood. Children were reinforced for proper language use, and ignored or punished for improper use, and the buildup of all these consequences eventually led to their full development of linguistic capabilities.

Noam Chomsky, a young linguist at MIT, was not convinced by Skinner's explanations and in 1959 wrote a scathing review which argued that Skinner's claims about language acquisition were unsupported speculations. While Chomsky's review was not without critics of its own, this fiery attack of an icon of behaviorism has been suggested to have played a role in the cognitive revolution that followed. Beginning in the 1960s psychologists shifted their focus away from observable behaviors and onto internal mental processes.

In considering internal processes in language acquisition, Chomsky argued that humans must have a "*Language Acquisition Device*" (*LAD*). This isn't necessarily a brain structure or particular gene sequence, but rather a term for some device, system, or network in the human brain that allows language ability to emerge as long as there is sufficient input. Chomsky claimed that humans have this LAD and other animals don't, which explains why nearly all human children develop linguistic abilities almost effortlessly, while even years of intensive training is not able to effectively condition complex language use in animals.

The Building Blocks of Language

In order to better understood critiques of the behaviorist approach, we need to know a little bit more about *linguistics*, the study of language.

All spoken languages are made up of individual sounds, though the sounds used in each language may vary. Some sounds (like the rolled Rs in Spanish or clicking sounds in Xhosa) may be somewhat unique, while other sounds may be shared among many languages. These small units of sounds that are used in a language are called *phonemes*. Examples of phonemes in English would be sounds like the f sound in **f**at or the c sound in **c**at. English uses about 40 phonemes in total, while other languages may have twice this amount, or may manage to get by with just over a dozen.

While phonemes like **f** and **c** don't mean anything on their own, language also contains small units that are meaningful. These meaningful units are referred to as ***morphemes***. (You can remember that morpheme starts with **m**, and **m**orphemes have **m**eaning). Morphemes can be as small as one letter like **a**, or they can be short words that cannot be further broken down into smaller meaningful parts, like **bat**. Morphemes also include suffixes and prefixes that affect meaning, like **pre-**, **post-**, **-ism**, or even just an **-s** at the end of a word to make it plural. So we might have one word composed of multiple morphemes, like **bats** (two morphemes: bat and -s), or **batman** (two morphemes: bat and man). Just as a limited number of phonemes can create thousands of morphemes, these morphemes can be combined to create many more thousands of different words (as evidenced by the 616,500+ word-forms you can find in the Oxford-English Dictionary).

When combining multiple sounds from phonemes and morphemes to create words there are certain rules. Each language has different rules for how its phonemes and morphemes can be combined and how these combinations are spoken. These rules are known as ***phonological rules***. Violation of these rules in a particular language results in an ***accent***, which may be characteristic of a particular region. For example, a regional Boston accent, often demonstrated with the sentence "Park the car in Harvard Yard", is known for dropping **r** sounds when they follow vowels, resulting in something like "Pahk the cah in Hahvahd Yahd". In this case, a Bostonian is combining phonemes in a manner that doesn't follow the phonological rules of standard English.

Accents that arise when learning a new language may occur because people are carrying over phonological rules from their native language, or because they have difficulty recognizing or producing the combinations of phonemes of the new language. For example, native Mandarin speakers may have trouble pronouncing English words that end in "L", because Mandarin doesn't use this phoneme in this way (L sounds are always followed by a vowel – like in *la, le, li, lu*). If you've seen the show *An Idiot Abroad*, now you can better understand the difficulty that Karl Pilkington had with Chinese speakers always calling him "Karl**a**".

Now that we have phonemes and morphemes and rules for combining them to make words, we need to have a set of rules for how to combine these words into meaningful phrases and sentences. These are ***syntactical rules***. These aren't the nit-picking grammatical rules from your English class, but the more general rules for the order of words and using tenses to communicate meaning.

Universal Grammar

Chomsky proposed a theory of "***universal grammar***" which suggests that the overall brain mechanisms for understanding and processing human language are the same for any language and therefore must be an innate human characteristic. Since children everywhere seem to automatically learn the language around them, regardless of what that language is, it seems that understanding of the general rules of how language works will naturally arise in any child exposed to language. In this respect, language seems different from the acquisition of other concepts like mathematical understanding. For example, intuitive understanding of concepts of grammar will emerge naturally starting around age 2 in just about everyone given language exposure. We don't see similarly rapid and near-universal understanding in other areas, suggesting a unique biological predisposition for concepts of grammar.

Many people misunderstand the concept of universal grammar. It's not saying that languages all share the same grammatical rules. It's saying that human languages all follow similar types of rules in their overall structure because all human languages are created and used by human brains. All those brains innately conceive of language working in the same way.

So while languages may differ in where they place subjects and objects, whether they conjugate verbs or not, or how they structure the future tense, these are just minor details compared to the overall structure of how language works. The concept of universal grammar points out that although languages differ in the details, they all have ways of indicating the concepts of nouns, verbs, and adjectives because these are the structures necessary for human brains to communicate linguistically. Unlike other animals, we seem to be born prepared for language, and this innate predisposition allows us to learn language rapidly.

Language Development

The rate of vocabulary growth in children is truly phenomenal. Between the ages of 1 and 5, children will acquire a vocabulary of thousands of words, at an average rate of around 10 words per day; far too quickly for reinforcement to effectively condition in such a short time. Part of this explosion of vocabulary growth comes from ***fast-mapping***; the ability to connect a word with a meaning after only a single exposure. So when Mom is in the grocery store and says "this is an *apple*", the child is able connect these new sounds "*apple*" with this new object. Without any further reinforcement, the child may see an apple a week later, and correctly name it.

Children also develop an understanding of syntax quite rapidly. Children begin babbling at around 4 months old, and by the age of about 1 year children generally begin speaking single words, usually nouns. This is actually quite impressive because it demonstrates their understanding of the concept of nouns from all the other words and sounds they have heard.

Around age 2, children begin stringing words together into short sentences of just 2 words, known as **telegraphic speech**. These mini-sentences leave out function words like *the, an, a*, etc. and only include the most important words for communicating (like a telegraph message). This indicates that children are already able to identify which words really matter and which words are just grammatical fluff. These two word sentences show further evidence of grammatical understanding because they tend to follow the syntax of the child's native language.

Young English speakers, for instance, will say things like "want cookie" rather than "cookie want", following the general rule of placing an object after a verb in English. They will also say things like "big dog", placing the adjective before the noun, while their Spanish-speaking counterparts are saying "*perro grande*", reversing the order to follow the syntax of Spanish. Even these tiny fragments reveal that children are already picking up the rules of the language around them.

Around age 4 or 5, children begin making grammatical errors. These errors actually provide evidence that children are learning the rules of language rather than simply imitating others. At this age, children make errors such as saying "She *hitted* him" or "He *runned* to school". These errors reveal two important things. The first is that children have acquired an understanding of how the language works without necessarily having explicit grammar instruction. This **overgeneralization** of a rule reveals that the children actually understand the "-ed makes the past tense" rule, even though they are misapplying it.

Secondly, overgeneralization (also sometimes referred to as **overregularization**) supports the idea that language isn't learned by conditioning because these new errors have not been reinforced in the past (or even heard, since Mom and Dad never say things like "goed" or "bringed").

Another well-known demonstration that children are discovering the rules of language is known as **The Wug Test**, created by Jean Berko Gleason. In this test, children are introduced to a novel word by being shown a picture or toy called a "wug". Then when another wug is presented, the children complete the sentence "Here are two ___". The fact that young children can correctly complete the sentence with "wugs" means that they understand the concept of pluralization of nouns, even though they haven't been explicitly taught this rule and they've never heard anyone else say "wugs". Overgeneralization and the Wug Test demonstrate that a child is actively working out the rules of language, not simply parroting back phrases. This process of working out the rules seems to occur naturally with exposure to language.

There is, however, a clock ticking on this natural process of figuring out the grammatical rules of a language. In order for this to occur, it seems that a child must have exposure to a language before some time around age 7. Without exposure before this time, a ***critical period*** has passed and the development of full fluency in language is no longer possible.

This can be seen in the tragic cases of children deprived of language exposure for many years. Genie was a girl who was kept in isolation by her father, who didn't speak to her at all, from when she was 20 months old until she was rescued at the age of 13. Despite intensive efforts to teach Genie language, she was never able to develop a high level of competency. A similar case involved a girl named Isabelle who was kept in silent isolation until she was 6 years old. Following her rescue, however, Isabelle was able to make a full recovery and in fact within 1 year of instruction her language abilities were within a normal range.

It's important to remember that this critical period refers to ability for language and grammar in someone's first language, not a second (or third or fourth) language. It's not stating that if you haven't learned a particular language before age 7 that you can't learn it. But you have to have learned your **first** language by this point in order for your brain to develop the ability to process the rules of any language.

It seems that if children have had sufficient exposure to any language, this equips their mind to understand the concepts of grammatical rules, which in turn allows them to learn other languages in the future, even if the specific grammatical rules of the next language are completely different. While it is true that younger age in starting a second language is associated with the attainment of higher levels of fluency, it is still possible for people to achieve high levels of proficiency and fluency in another language, even if they begin learning at a later age.

There are some people, however, for whom naturally understanding the rules of grammar just doesn't seem to happen. These are people with ***genetic dysphasia***, a rare condition in which a person is unable to learn the rules of grammar in his or her native tongue. Despite being able to learn complex ideas and use advanced vocabulary, these people are seemingly unable to work out the rules of grammar and repeatedly make errors. This suggests that language is a specialized module, unrelated to other types of learning and cognitive skills. In this way, the fact that people with genetic dysphasia can't seem to learn grammar provides further evidence that, for most people, acquiring language is an innate and near-automatic process.

The Importance of the Social Environment

The evidence for critical periods and the importance of exposure to language at a young age both suggest that the social environment is a crucial component of the language acquisition process. With this in mind, we shouldn't adopt a strictly nativist approach, but should instead adopt an ***interactionist approach*** to consider how our genetic predisposition for language interacts with our environment to allow for the complete development of linguistic fluency.

One of the most startling cases of how our social environment allows language to develop comes from Nicaragua. Following a revolution in 1980, the government in Nicaragua created schools for the deaf in the capital city of Managua. For the first time, deaf children from remote areas all over the country were brought together and given instruction in sign language. Previously, many deaf children had been deprived of a full language environment in their hometowns and had only learned to communicate with family and friends via simple gestures. Without a formal sign language in place and deprived of a social environment which would allow them to communicate with others, these children never developed full linguistic fluency and concepts of syntax. With the new school, however, the hope was that deaf children could be taught an existing sign language, learn vocational skills, and become more independent members of society. Hopes for these lofty goals were questioned, however, as initial attempts to teach a formal sign language failed.

What happened instead was even more exciting. By placing all these young children together in the same environment, with a strong desire to communicate with one another, a new language began to emerge. While these gestures were initially dismissed as mere miming and mimicry, this turned out to be more than just playground slang. It was a fully functional language that naturally emerged, complete with all the syntactical rules, tenses, and other grammatical features you would find in any other language. This case shows us that the human mind has a natural drive to communicate and create structured language. So while you may think that grammatical rules were created to punish you in English class, the truth is that grammar is a naturally-emerging phenomenon that allows us to communicate more fully with others.

Does Language Influence How You Think?

One puzzling question that arises when thinking about language is how language and thought are related. When we see deaf adults from Nicaragua who were too late for the development of full language abilities, we may wonder just what their thoughts are like. Our own thoughts are so intertwined with our language that it may seem impossible to separate the two. For most of us, it often seems that all the thoughts we have occur in the form of words and we may wonder how those words influence our ways of thinking about the world.

The notion that our native language influences how we perceive the world is known as the ***linguistic relativity hypothesis***. It is also referred to as the ***Whorf-Sapir hypothesis***, based on the work of Benjamin Whorf and his mentor Edward Sapir. Whorf proposed that due to the grammatical structures of their language, speakers of the Hopi language conceptualized time differently than English speakers.

Whorf's views (published in the late 1930s and early 1940s) were heavily criticized throughout the 1960s (likely due to the dominance of the view of universal grammar) but have recently been re-examined and some psychologists are reconsidering the possible role of language on how we think about the world. While few would suggest that our language determines our thought, researchers have studied how the language we speak may influence our perception and memory for colors, objects, and time, though results have been mixed.

We also see the question of how language and thought are related in the form of popular articles listing "untranslatable" foreign words, often suggesting that speakers of these languages conceptualize the world in ways that other speakers don't. We may wonder, however, if this is actually the case, since while these terms cannot be reduced down to single words in other languages, they can most certainly be described (or else the article couldn't be written). This would suggest that even if we don't speak the language we can still have the same types of thought. Just because English doesn't have a single word for *schadenfreude* doesn't mean that I can't conceptualize (or even experience) taking joy in the suffering of others.

One of the problems with analyzing how language influences thought is that language is such an integral part of culture. We may readily admit that culture influences how we think, but it can be difficult or impossible to determine exactly how language fits in to this interaction. One way of attempting to separate language from culture is to look at people who live in similar cultures but speak different languages. For instance, I could look to a country like Switzerland and find native speakers of French, German, Italian, and Romansh who, apart from language, arguably have rather similar cultural environments.

In addition to considering how language influences thought between individuals, we can consider how language may influence thought *within* individuals. In bilingual individuals who speak both languages fluently, perhaps their thinking varies when using one language or another. Several studies have investigated this, with some surprising results. Research by Michael Ross, Elaine Xun, and Anne Wilson in 2002 found that bilingual Chinese/English speakers described their personality traits quite differently depending on the language they used for the description. Similarly, Nairán Ramírez-Esparza and colleagues published a study in 2006 looking at bilingual Americans and Mexicans and found variation in their personality scores for extraversion, agreeableness, and conscientiousness depending on whether they were assessed in English or Spanish.

While the linguistic relativity hypothesis considers thought across languages, we may also wonder how language influences thought within a particular language. Does Orwellian "newspeak" really influence how people think about important issues? Does the fact that Beijing media refers to the city's pollution as 雾霾 *wu mai* (literally "fog-haze") rather than using the general term for pollution 污染 *wu ran* (literally "dirty contamination") influence how the city's residents perceive their environment? As we've already seen in memory experiments by Elizabeth Loftus, and as we'll see in framing studies by Amos Tversky and Daniel Kahneman in the next section, it does seem to be the case that particular wording has the potential to influence thought and decision-making, though the extent of this influence is still up for debate.

Concepts and Categories

Language provides us with ways of organizing thought, and one way that we see this organization is the creation of **concepts** and **categories**. These are mental groupings of objects or ideas which are similar. Rather than creating a completely new word for every possible shape of a chair, we can use the generic word "chair" both to represent a particular chair, and the concept of a chair in general. The question is, how do our brains go about this organizational process? When we walk into IKEA, how do we immediately recognize that a stimulus we've never seen before is in fact a chair?

If we try to come up with the rules our brains are using to decide on "chair-ness", we find that it's no simple task. Must it have 4 legs? Well, some chairs don't have legs at all but have solid bases instead and we recognize those just the same. A soft or hard surface? Again, both seem acceptable, so that doesn't help us to create a rule. Sharp or rounded corners? None of these rules seem to work in helping us recognize chairs, and yet, we can almost always recognize any chair immediately upon seeing it. So if we aren't following specific rules, how are we doing this?

What seems to be happening is that we have some guidelines rather than rules. These guidelines are the features that are common to chairs, and when we think of a chair, we generally think of these characteristics. We seem to think of an idea of a chair that has most of these features, but we also recognize that there are exceptions and variations. In considering a new object, these guidelines come to mind, but we don't use them as hard-and-fast rules for making a judgment.

To demonstrate this, take a moment and quickly doodle a picture of a bird.

Do so now, before looking ahead ;)

Now, if my magical powers of intuition are correct, you may have drawn something like this:

Chances are that you didn't draw a penguin, or an ostrich, or a peacock. While all of these are fine examples of birds, they probably aren't the first birds that came to mind. What probably came to mind is a "most-typical" version of a bird. This most-typical or best example is known as a **prototype**. A prototype has many or all of the characteristic features that we associate with a particular category.

So for birds, your prototype is probably small, feathered, winged, able to fly, and has twig-like legs and a small beak. If, when walking in a park, you encounter a new stimulus that might be a bird, you mentally compare it to your prototype to see how well it fits this category. A bird that is a close match to your prototype would probably be recognized more quickly than one that differs drastically. The same would be true for recognizing chairs. You have a mental prototype of a chair with all the "most chair-like" features, and you compare new possible chairs to this mental image.

In attempting to explain category recognition, **exemplar theory** considers that we aren't limited to thinking just about prototypes, and we may also mentally compare a stimulus to other examples in memory (though this may take us a little longer). For chairs, this may allow you to recognize a soft lumpy mass as a chair, because you have a memory of beanbag chairs as a less-common but still acceptable type of chair. Or if you were to encounter a large, flightless animal, you could still consider the possibility that it is a bird, even though several features don't match your prototypical bird.

How Do We Solve Problems?

Our minds do quite a lot of problem solving on a regular basis, but how do we go about solving problems? For some problems, it turns out, we don't actually have to do much solving. If I were to ask you to solve 3 + 4, chances are that you don't actually need to solve it. Instead, you simply need to remember the answer that you figured out long ago. But when you were younger and still learning addition, you may have had to actually work out the solution, perhaps by counting on your fingers.

So our memory of solutions that have worked in the past can help us to solve problems that appear again, but the downside to this approach is that it makes us vulnerable to applying a solution that has worked in the past that won't necessarily work in the present. This tendency to think only of what has worked in the past is known as our *mental set*. As Abraham Maslow wrote: "I suppose it is tempting, if the only tool you have is a hammer, to treat everything as if it were a nail" (Maslow, 1966, p.15). Perhaps, like me, you've wasted a great deal of time trying old solutions on new problems because you were unable to think of the problems from a new perspective.

There's also a tendency to view tools as only being useful in the ways that we usually use them. This is known as *functional fixedness*. Let's say that you want to hang a picture on your wall but when you check your toolbox you realize you lent your hammer to a friend. You might not immediately realize that you could probably drive in the nail using the side of the wrench sitting in front of you. You might not immediately realize this solution because of the tendency to think of wrenches as being used for wrenching things, not for hammering them.

I'm not suggesting that functional fixedness is always a bad thing. In fact, this tendency to concentrate on the normal functions of objects and tools is probably a good thing. Sure you could also use your cell phone to drive in that nail, but in the process you'd probably ruin its ability to perform the functions that it was specifically designed for. Nevertheless, we should be aware of this tendency and consider when novel uses for tools might be beneficial.

A related concept here is the difference between convergent and divergent thinking. In *convergent thinking*, we move towards one single solution to a problem. So if you're solving an algebra equation, often there is only one solution and each step should move you towards that single solution. In our hammer example, convergent thinking answers the question "how do I hammer in a nail?" by pointing towards one solution: a hammer.

Divergent thinking, on the other hand, is for situations with many possible solutions, and one solution may not be at all related to the other solutions. For example, if I asked you to imagine all the possible uses of a hammer, you may think of using it as a paperweight, and a moment later you may think of using it to get an object that's just out-of-reach, even though these solutions don't have much in common.

Obstacles to Problem Solving

As we begin considering solutions to problems, we should be aware of our tendency towards *overconfidence*. We tend to think that our views and judgments are correct, even when they aren't and we can be more confident than correct. For instance, when attempting to spell difficult words participants who felt 100% sure they were correct were actually only correct about 80% of the time.

Of course, even now that we know about overconfidence, we might feel that this error only applies to other people, not us. If you believe that you're never overconfident, then you are probably both wrong and overconfident. This tendency to think that errors and biases are just other people's problems relates to another type of bias. If you ask people to estimate how their own traits and abilities compare to others (e.g. attractiveness, IQ, driving ability, etc.) what you will find is that most people believe themselves to be above average. This is, of course, a statistical impossibility, but that doesn't always factor in to people's self-assessments. This tendency to feel above-average is known as *illusory superiority* or *The Wobegon Effect*, named after the fictional town of Lake Wobegon from Garrison Keillor's *A Prairie Home Companion;* a place "where all the women are strong, all the men are good-looking, and all the children are above average."

The Wobegon Effect may actually be a part of our "psychological immune system". Perhaps the tendency to exaggerate our estimates of our own positive traits helps to keep us motivated and upbeat, and when combined with a sense of overconfidence, makes it easier to make decisions and more likely we take action toward our goals.

Belief Bias

It's not surprising that our beliefs can cloud our judgment, but we may not realize just how easily our pre-existing beliefs can disrupt our ability to think logically. Research by Jonathan Evans, Julie Barston, and Paul Pollard found that previously existing beliefs influenced subjects' ability to determine whether statements were logically valid or invalid. It seems that we have difficulty separating our beliefs from our analysis of logic and we may not be aware of this influence.

Not only are we unaware of how our beliefs can influence our reasoning, our beliefs are resistant to change. This is known as *belief perseverance*. Even when we are confronted with contradictory evidence, it generally does little to change our beliefs. Lee Ross, Mark Lepper, and Michael Hubbard (1975) gave participants false feedback on their performance (to create a belief about their abilities) then revealed that the feedback was unrelated to their actual performance (contradictory evidence). They then asked participants to assess their own performance and found ratings which still matched the false feedback previously received. Participants who had been told they performed well stuck to the belief that they were good at the task, even though they knew the feedback hadn't been accurate.

I'd like to offer a personal example that many students will relate to and illustrates several of the ideas above. Just as students tend to be overconfident in how quickly they can complete assignments, I was overconfident in how quickly I could write this book. Each chapter took me much longer than I had expected. Nevertheless, as I began a new chapter, I once again believed that I would be able to finish rapidly, ignoring the contradictory evidence and maintaining my belief.

This tendency to cling to our existing beliefs can be dangerous when making important decisions like determining the innocence or guilt of criminal defendants. While we may hope to uphold the notion that everyone is innocent until proven guilty, once a person has been viewed as a prime suspect it may be difficult for judges, jurors, or witnesses to overcome an initial belief of guilt.

If you're looking for a way to avoid this potential trap, research by Charles Lord and colleagues may be able to help. Their research suggests that considering opposite findings may have a stronger corrective effect than simply trying to be unbiased. When evaluating studies on the death penalty, some participants were told to "ask yourself at each step whether you would have made the same high or low evaluations had exactly the same study produced results on the other side of the issue." Other participants were simply told to be as unbiased as possible. The "consider the opposite" participants showed less bias in their critical evaluations of the studies and their attitudes toward the death penalty did not become as polarized.

Problem Solving Approaches

When it comes to solving problems, there are different approaches that we can take. One way to solve a problem is to use an *algorithm*. An algorithm is a step-by-step procedure that guarantees you will reach a solution. Imagine that I'm getting ready to go out, but I can't find my apartment keys. I know they must be somewhere in my apartment, because I previously used them to get inside. An algorithm which would guarantee finding the keys would be to start in one corner of my apartment and systematically move through every square inch of the apartment until the keys were found.

Even though this approach would guarantee finding my keys, it's probably not the approach I would actually use. Instead of using an algorithm, I would probably use a *heuristic*. A heuristic is a mental shortcut that doesn't guarantee a solution, but works most of the time. In searching for my keys, a heuristic I might use is to look where I last remember having them. Now they may not actually be where I last remember having them, but it's still a good place to start, rather than beginning in a corner of the room and slowly moving inch-by-inch through the apartment.

Heuristics and Decision-Making

It turns out that our minds love using heuristics. We're generally willing to accept the trade-off of occasionally being wrong in order to get the benefit of being fast. Amos Tversky and Daniel Kahneman spent decades uncovering the heuristics we use by creating ingenious demonstrations of how these heuristics can lead us astray. Here are just a few of the questions that Tversky and Kahneman have posed to participants, along with descriptions of the heuristics they reveal. These studies show us the consistent pattern of errors we make, which can be likened to the way that visual illusions consistently fool our perception. Dan Ariely refers to these as "decision illusions", and unlike visual illusions, it can be difficult for us to realize when we are being fooled.

The Availability Heuristic

In their first study of the availability heuristic, Tversky and Kahneman asked participants to estimate whether English had more words that started with the letter **k** or more words that had **k** as the third letter. What do you think?

If you're like most participants in their study, you might guess that there are more words that start with k than words that have k as the third letter, when in fact this is not the case. The reason you might have misjudged is that you were probably able to bring to mind more examples of words that start with k. We don't usually bring words to mind based on their third letter, so naturally it was harder to think of those examples. Thinking of words that start with k probably seemed much easier, and as a result you may have felt that these words are more common. The ***availability heuristic*** says that we tend to estimate the frequency of events based on how easily we can come up with examples, or how "available" they are to our mind.

This tendency to assume that things which are more easily recalled are more frequent can be seen when we attempt to estimate the likelihood of events like terrorist attacks or plane crashes. Examples of these unfortunate events tend to spring to mind rather easily, and this may cause us to assume that these events occur more frequently than they actually do.

On the other hand, events and dangers which actually are more frequent may not come to mind quite so readily. So parents may fear letting their children walk to school because of highly-memorable news stories of child abductions, even though the risks posed by choking, drowning, or car accidents are far greater. Often it seems that the things we fear might kill us are not the things that are actually likely to kill us. As comedian Norm Macdonald noted, you spend time thinking "gee, I hope a terrorist doesn't attack and kill me", when it's far more likely that your own heart is what will attack and kill you.

That Sounds Like A ….

In another study, Tversky and Kahneman asked participants to read randomly selected assessments from 100 interviews with 70 engineers and 30 lawyers. Participants were then asked to guess the likelihood that the person in question was an engineer or a lawyer. So I might randomly pull out an assessment and tell you that Adam was described as particularly outgoing, interested in politics, and displayed skill in argument. Then you would guess the odds that Adam was a lawyer or an engineer. What do you think? Here's another example from one of Tversky and Kahneman's descriptions:

"Dick is a 30 year old man. He is married with no children. A man of high ability and high motivation, he promises to be quite successful in his field. He is well-liked by his colleagues." (Tversky and Kahneman, 1973)

What do you think about Adam and Dick? What do you think the odds are that Dick is an engineer?

You probably immediately thought of Adam as a lawyer but found Dick a little harder to pin down. Most people in the study figured there was equal chance that Dick was an engineer or a lawyer, and so they estimated the odds of him being an engineer at around 50%. If you thought the same way, you relied on the **Representativeness Heuristic** – estimating likelihood by using information from prototypes and ignoring more useful information about base rates. In this case you tried to match these profiles to your prototypes of engineers and lawyers, and in doing so, you ignored information that was more relevant. If 70 interviewees were engineers and the assessments were randomly selected, there is a 70% chance any selected profile is an engineer regardless of personality traits. So if you were betting on accuracy in this task, the smart money would always be on engineer.

The Framing Effect

Tversky and Kahneman also investigated how the framing of questions can influence our decision-making by giving two groups of participants the same decision to make, but with a slight change in wording. Participants were asked to imagine the outbreak of a rare virus in a village of 600 people. They were then asked to adopt a program to combat this threat.

One group of participants was told that Program A would save 200 lives, while Program B had a 1/3 chance of saving everyone, and a 2/3 chance of saving no one.

The other group was told that with Program A, 400 people would die, while Program B had a 1/3 chance no one would die and a 2/3 chance everyone would die.

As you can see, choices are mathematically-identical for both groups and the difference is how the options are framed: lives saved vs. deaths. When the choices were framed as "saving", Program A was popular, but when those same numbers were framed as how many would die, the riskier Program B was widely adopted. Tversky and Kahneman proposed that when we consider benefits we like certainty, but when we consider losses we're more likely to take risks.

We see the use of framing in everyday life as well. Medications and interventions emphasize their 70% effectiveness rate, rather than frame it as a 30% failure rate. Customers find it more appealing when gas stations offer a "cash discount" rather than a "credit card fee" and government agencies may find more popular support for programs that aim to "help the needy" rather than "provide welfare".

How we define options can have an effect on the decisions that are made and which choices seem preferable. Eric Johnson and Daniel Goldstein analyzed data on organ donation in countries across Europe and found that the major factor in how many people were willing to participate in the organ donation program was whether the sign-up form was an automatic opt-in or opt-out. If the default option was joining, membership in the program was high, nearly 100% in many countries, but when not joining was the default, membership rates were low. We may not like the realization that we are so easily influenced by default options and the choices that form-designers make for us, but the evidence certainly points us toward that conclusion.

The Sunk-Cost Fallacy

The final decision-making error that we'll address may be familiar to you already and is known as the *sunk-cost fallacy*. This is the tendency to make present decisions based on previous investments. These previous investments may no longer have any actual bearing on the decision being made, but we seem to have a hard time letting them go. So gamblers and stock speculators may make increasingly risky bets in attempts to make up for past losses even though those past losses don't have any effect on their odds of winning the present bets.

Perhaps this shouldn't always be considered a fallacy, as there are certainly times that our previous investments rightly influence our present decisions but we should consider how we frame past events and how they may become a part of our decision-making. Abandoning relationships or quitting jobs on a whim may be situations in which we can be glad that our previous investments constrain our decisions and allow us to keep a cool head.

Part of the explanation for the sunk-cost fallacy is that we seem to have a tendency to keep a sort of mental accounting of costs that we've occurred for specific circumstances. Tversky and Kahneman (1981) demonstrated how different frames of our past experiences can influence our decisions by asking participants to consider the scenario below.

"Imagine that you have decided to see a play where admission is $10 per ticket. As you enter the theater you discover that you have lost a $10 bill. Would you still pay $10 for a ticket for the play?"

When given this question, 88% of participants said yes they would purchase the ticket. Other participants saw this version of events:

"Imagine that you have decided to see a play and paid the admission price of $10 per ticket. As you enter the theater you discover that you have lost the ticket. The seat was not marked and the ticket cannot be recovered. Would you pay $10 for another ticket?"

In this second case, only 46% of participants were willing to purchase the ticket. In both cases, the loss of $10 is identical. The difference is that in the second case people feel that they have already invested $10 in the play, so they are unwilling to pay twice for the same show. Tversky and Kahneman suggested that rather than a purely rational single mental account of gains and losses, we tend to keep separate mental accounts. In the second case, the mental "theater-cost account" is already at -$10, so purchasing a new ticket would put the account at -$20, which is deemed too expensive for the show. In the first case, however, the lost $10 was not considered as part of the theater cost, and as a result did not come to bear on the decision.

Is There a Silver Lining?

If all this discussion of our biases and errors is upsetting, it shouldn't be. Gerd Gigerenzer has suggested that rather than thinking of these heuristics as biases, we should consider them as tools. We should take a moment to consider just how amazing our information-processing abilities are. Our capabilities are truly astonishing, and the very fact that our brains can contemplate their own shortcomings should be enough to inspire hope. The better we understand our failures and biases, the better able we will be to create systems that will help us to overcome them. And for all the failures that heuristics bring, we shouldn't ignore just how helpful they are.

There are even situations in which having little information can actually be more helpful in guiding us to the right answer. Daniel Goldstein and Gerd Gigerenzer asked American and German participants to estimate whether San Diego or San Antonio had a higher population. 62% of Americans were able to correctly identify San Diego as more populous. Interestingly, 100% of the German participants answered correctly. Were these Germans more knowledgeable about the population of American cities? Nope. These Germans reported that they had never heard of San Antonio, but were at least familiar with the name of San Diego. Without any information about the population of San Antonio, they relied on the assumption that the city they had heard of was probably a larger one, and as a result they were guided to the correct answer. This ***recognition heuristic*** shows how our minds are able to make decisions based on very little information. Rather than being crippled by indecision, our minds gladly take shortcuts whenever possible and some of these shortcuts turn out to be rather effective.

It also seems that we can create these shortcuts for our decision-making with extensive practice. This allows us to effectively automate decisions and conserve valuable mental energy. Our constant search for mental shortcuts combined with extensive experience can create expertise that allows people to make lightning-fast decisions while still maintaining high levels of accuracy. Chess masters can quickly size up the correct move with just a brief glance at a game board, baseball players can tell a good pitch from a bad one and decide to swing in an instant, and chicken-sexers can identify male or female chicks based on ambiguous genitals in less than a second, without even knowing exactly how they do it.

So while heuristics do cause us to make errors in judgment, we shouldn't ignore their usefulness. These shortcuts help make the world more manageable and allow us to make thousands of decisions each day, and for the most part, the decisions we make are good ones. Instead of being overwhelmed by the constant influx of irrelevant information, we somehow manage to move along, and even with these flaws, the history of human existence has been a story of increasing knowledge and unceasing improvement. So in our quest for greater cognitive efficiency we may occasionally stumble, but we shouldn't ignore the times when these shortcuts allow us to leap.

Chapter Summary – Language & Cognition

- With exposure, language seems to emerge naturally in children, suggesting humans have a biological predisposition for **language acquisition**.

- **Telegraphic speech**, errors of **overgeneralization** and **The Wug Test** all indicate that young children begin to understand and apply grammatical rules without explicit instruction.

- Acquisition of one's first language depends on early exposure and a **critical period** for proper language development means that exposure must happen before some time around age 7.

- While language doesn't determine thought (the **linguistic relativity hypothesis**), there is some evidence for ways that language may shape thought and perception.

- We are all subject to a number of **biases** which can distort our thinking including **overconfidence**, the **Wobegon Effect**, and **belief perseverance**.

- Rather than always using **algorithms** to solve problems, our brains seem to prefer using **heuristics**; mental shortcuts which allow us to make decisions quickly, though they also increase our risk of making errors.

Notes

Chapter 8
States of Consciousness

What is Consciousness?

Before we can consider different states of consciousness, we have to attempt an answer to a rather prickly question – What is consciousness? As we consider this question, we'll see a number of problems with even attempting to come up with answers.

The Mind-Body Problem

In chapter 1 we looked at Descartes' notion that the mind and body were separate entities. Descartes suggested that the non-material mind controlled the material body via the pineal gland, but as we'll see later in this chapter, the pineal gland is now known to serve other functions.

We may admit, however, that the mind does feel separate from the body. When we imagine ourselves looking out into the world, we may have a tendency to think in terms of the *Cartesian Theater*. This is the feeling that the mind is like a person inside of the head looking out at the world and controlling the body. This little person in the head doesn't really exist, of course, and if it were to exist, we would have to wonder what was inside of the head of that person inside the head, ad infinitum. This difficulty in understanding the relationship between the mind and the body is known as the *mind-body problem of consciousness*.

Zombie Apocalypse?

If I begin by at least accepting the notion that I'm conscious, how do I know that you are conscious? How can I be sure that I am not the only conscious one? In imagining a world in which no one else is actually conscious, you may realize that it might not be all that different from the world you currently experience. People move around, talk, and go to work and school, but what if they were all just automatons? What if they were just mindless zombies going about tasks with no internal mental experience at all? Sure, they could tell you they have internal experiences, but how could you be certain that their words weren't just for show, a clever ruse to throw you off track?

Certainly I could program a computer to say things that would make it sound like the computer has internal experience, but that wouldn't mean that it feels like something to be that computer. It seems that we naturally assume that other humans all have an internal mental experience, but can we ever really know?

This *problem of other minds* may make us wonder about the experience of other non-human organisms as well. In a famous essay, "What is it like to be a bat?" philosopher Thomas Nagel pondered this question. When we observe a bat's behavior, we might think there is "something it is like to be that organism" and then wonder what that something is actually like.

Nagel theorized, however, that it would be impossible for us to ever truly understand the experience of being a bat, because we are trapped in the viewpoint of being human. Nagel wrote that when he considers the experience of being a bat, "it tells me only what it would be like for me to behave as a bat does". Our assumptions and expectations of what it's like to be another animal probably reveal more about what it's like to be a human. So when you try to see the world through your dog's eyes, you reveal how you think dogs experience the world, which may not represent how dogs actually experience it. In attempting to imagine the experience of other minds, we cannot escape the experience of our own minds.

Perhaps even our tendency to imagine that others have internal mental experience is unique to our human minds. We seem to automatically assume internal intentions, characteristics, and traits simply by observing behavior. We do this when we observe other humans (which is why movies are more engrossing than just patterns of light on a screen) and also when we observe other animals and even objects. This was demonstrated in a classic study by Fritz Heider and Marianne Simmel in which participants observed a brief animation of two circles and a triangle moving around a square. After viewing the video, participants felt that the shapes had distinct personalities, motivations, and emotions. While this film certainly wouldn't win any Academy Awards, it demonstrates our human tendency to assume internal experience based solely on observation of behavior.

A Spectrum of Consciousness

In considering the consciousness of others, we might think of being conscious as being able to react to stimuli in the environment. This can be referred to as *minimal consciousness*. Of course, this minimal consciousness doesn't necessarily imply an experience of being that organism. Plants respond to light in their environment (and many even move toward it) but we may still doubt whether it feels like something to be a tree or a vine. On the other end of the spectrum, we might consider the rich and varied experience of full human consciousness, which includes responding to our environment as well as our own internal thoughts.

Part of the richness of this experience includes the ability to be aware of our own conscious processes and reflect on our own experience, known as *self-consciousness*. In this way, we're able to make ourselves the object of our conscious focus (rather than just being the subject that is experiencing consciousness). We can consider how others view us and even reflect on our own thoughts and reflections.

Speaking of reflecting, one way of attempting to determine whether other animals have a sense of self-awareness is the *mark test* used by Gordon Gallup in 1970. After giving chimps some experience with mirrors, Gallup secretly placed a spot of dye on their faces, then had those chimps interact with a mirror again. If, upon seeing the spot, they reached toward their own faces, Gallup believed this indicated that they understood how mirrors worked and could view themselves as objects.

Other research has indicated that human children are able to pass this test by the age of about 18 months. This test has been repeated in a number of animal designs, revealing that humans are in select company when it comes to being able to recognize ourselves in mirrors. Other primates like chimps and orangutans are able to pass the test (along with elephants, dolphins, and perhaps some bird species) while most other animals fail. This may not come as a surprise to dog or cat owners who see their pets repeatedly flummoxed by mirrors, never learning that they are looking at their own reflections.

Of course, while it's certainly interesting to consider which animals seem to be able to recognize themselves, we still can't be sure that passing this test really reflects some special type of self-awareness.

What Purpose Does Consciousness Serve?

Even if I put aside the possibility that everyone else is a philosophical zombie and instead I assume that they do indeed have conscious experience, one large problem remains. If we aren't all zombies, why not? Why aren't we simply automatons? Why is there a subjective component to our experiences? And if we adopt a monist approach, how is it that this subjective experience arises from physical processes in the brain? This is known as the *hard problem of consciousness*. And given just how hard a problem it is, we don't quite have a good answer for it. We may assume that there must be some sort of evolutionary advantages to developing consciousness, but it's hard to say for sure why those advantages couldn't arise in non-conscious zombies who were simply programmed to behave as we do.

Levels of Consciousness

Information in our minds may fall into a number of different categories of consciousness, depending on our level of access to the information. The *conscious* level contains information that we are presently aware of. This would include all the thoughts and sensations that we are currently thinking about. Thoughts that aren't in our conscious mind at the moment but can be brought into consciousness rather easily are considered to be at the *preconscious* level.

The *subconscious* level consists of influences and mental processes that we are generally unaware of, though we can see their effects on our behavior. We may not be aware of these in the moment, but we can clearly see how they have influenced behavior after the fact. This level would also include the subtle influence of priming and mere-exposure effects, which will be discussed later in this chapter (you can remember **sub**tle and **sub**conscious).

Things can get murky here because these subconscious influences are frequently described using the term **unconscious**, though this is not meant to imply the Freudian/Psychodynamic unconscious. The Freudian **unconscious** level refers to wishes, desires, and fears which are repressed from the conscious mind in order to reduce anxiety, though the existence of this level of consciousness is disputed and not common in psychological research today.

Finally, the **nonconscious** level would include things that we are almost never aware of. This would include many processes of the autonomic nervous system such as muscle contractions for heart-rate or digestion, or levels of activation in different brain areas. We simply don't have conscious access to these processes in our body even if we try to think about them.

Consciousness During Waking Life

Even if we can't quite address all the philosophical questions that consciousness raises we can still consider what our subjective experience of consciousness is like and try to understand it. So let's consider some of the traits that consciousness seems to have (though there is still disagreement on some of these) as well as some evidence supporting the existence of these traits.

Unity – Consciousness is generally singular. While our precise state of consciousness may change, it tends to be considered a single state, rather than multiple consciousnesses at once. In this way, our consciousness tends toward unity. Consider watching a movie and you'll realize that we automatically incorporate the sights, sounds, and emotions into a single consciousness, rather than experiencing them as separate entities.

Intentionality – Intentionality means that consciousness is always focused on something. Consciousness seems to always be directed toward particular objects, thoughts, or events. Even when we daydream and our minds are wandering, in each moment our consciousness seems to be focused on something, whether that something is an internal thought, a particular sensation, or an external stimulus.

Selectivity – Our consciousness seems to be selective. It is able to pick up some messages and perceptions while ignoring others. This can be seen in what's known as the **Cocktail Party Phenomenon**. Imagine that you are at a cocktail party, in a large room with a few dozen other people. People gather in clusters and there is the constant din of other conversations around you. In this situation, you are able to focus your attention on the particular conversation you are in, and everything else fades into a kind of background static.

It's not simply the case that you can't hear the others; it's that your attention is not directed toward them. In fact, if you were to eavesdrop on the conversation next to you, you might be able to hear it just fine. Now, without anything in the environment changing, your attention has selectively been placed on this other conversation, and the one you were previously in becomes background noise. We don't always have complete control of this selection process, however, as you've experienced if you've ever been in a conversation but then became distracted by hearing your name on the other side of the room. This cue can grab your attention and pull it to the other conversation. Hopefully you'll manage to switch your attention back to your present conversation before your partner asks a question, only to discover that you haven't really been listening.

This selective nature of attention can be tested in the laboratory in what's known as a **dichotic listening task**. In this design, participants attempt to listen to two messages simultaneously, one in each ear. Participants are asked to shadow one message by verbally repeating it. This ensures that their attention is focused on that message. When asked questions about the other message, however, participants show very little knowledge of it. In fact, they may not even notice if the voice of the other message changed or if the message was actually an incoherent jumble of words.

This type of research points out that we are not particularly good multi-taskers. Our attention doesn't divide well. So while you might occasionally manage to eavesdrop without getting caught, if you think you can text and drive you are wrong. You can drive, then text, then switch your attention back to driving, but you can't actually direct your attention to both activities at once. So while you may think you are skilled enough to multi-task (remember *illusory superiority*) the truth is that attention doesn't work that way. If you text and drive you put the safety of yourself and others at risk.

Our tiny spotlight of attention is actually much smaller than we think and anything going on outside of it is barely detected, if it is detected at all. This can be clearly seen in demonstrations of **change blindness**. In these studies, large changes can be made in the environment without people noticing, provided that their attention is directed elsewhere. In one clever study by Daniel Simons and Daniel Levin, a pedestrian asking for directions from a stranger was switched to a completely different person and in half of the trials the stranger didn't seem to notice the change.

A related phenomenon is **inattentional blindness**, where we fail to detect an otherwise-obvious stimulus because our attention is directed elsewhere. This has also been demonstrated in studies by Simons and Christopher Chabris including a particularly well-known example involving basketball players. I don't want to give it away here (though perhaps I've said too much already) so I encourage you to check YouTube now for "the awareness test" and see just how well you can track the basketball players passing the ball.

SPOILER ALERT

Don't keep reading if you want to check your awareness in the Simons and Chabris demonstration. If you're already seen it or just watched it now, you may have missed (like more than half of the participants) the gorilla walking into the scene, beating his chest, then walking off. While your spotlight of attention was focused on the ball-passing by the white-shirted players, your mind filtered out the black-shirted players and as a result, inadvertently filtered out the gorilla costume as well. **END SPOILER**

Transience – Finally, our minds love to wander. William James compared consciousness to a stream, because it was always moving and flowing. Our minds are constantly flitting about, moving from sights to sounds and feelings to thoughts, sampling widely from the surfeit of possible stimulation.

To remember these 4 traits of consciousness – *unity, intentionality, selectivity*, and *transience*, imagine that you are moving through a cave in the dark with a single flashlight. Now imagine that the spot of light from this flashlight represents your consciousness. There is only one spot of light (*unity*) it is always shining on something (*intentionality*), you have some control over where you point it (*selectivity*) and you'll have a tendency to keep moving it as you explore the cave (*transience*).

How Much Control Do We Have?

We may wonder just how much we control our own consciousness. For a brief demonstration of the problem of mental control, I can simply challenge you not to think of a white bear for the next 5 minutes. In a study by Daniel Wegner, participants given this thought-suppression challenge thought of white bears far more frequently than participants who were not told to suppress thoughts of white bears. This as an example of an *ironic process of mental control*, in which our attempt to control our thoughts creates a counterintentional effect.

In addition to failures of conscious control, we may not realize that we've already ceded a great deal of control to unconscious processes. Even though our conscious attention tends toward unity, we also have subconscious processing that is occurring in parallel. This idea of simultaneous conscious and unconscious processing is known as *Dual-Process Theory* and it is often said we have a two-track mind: one track following our conscious experience, while the other track discreetly collects and processes information beneath our awareness. These tracks are also sometimes referred to as *System 1* (unconscious) and *System 2* (conscious). One way of getting a glimpse at the unconscious processing of System 1 is a technique known as *priming*.

Priming refers to how subtle cues in our environment can activate certain mental concepts which are then capable of influencing behavior. For a simple example, I could prime you by talking about sports, then ask you to quickly fill in the blanks below to create a word:

_ _ L L

You might come up with "ball", but if I had previously mentioned shopping you might be more likely to fill in the blanks to create "mall".

One of the most famous studies of priming, conducted by John Bargh and colleagues in 1996, involved priming participants for the concept of "elderly" by having them create sentences from scrambled words. For the experimental group, some sentences included terms like "Florida", "wrinkle", and "bingo", while controls completed the same task with non-age related terms. Bargh and colleagues then secretly recorded the time it took participants to walk to the elevator after the task and found that the elderly-primed participants walked more slowly than the controls. This suggests that subtle cues in our environment can have measurable impact on our behavior, though this influence may be outside of our conscious awareness.

Another unconscious influence on our behavior is the **mere-exposure effect**, which is that we have a tendency to like things more when they are more familiar to us. While this relationship between familiarity and fondness isn't exactly shocking, it may surprise you that this relationship holds even when people aren't aware of being exposed to the stimulus. Research by Robert Zajonc (pronounced like "science" but starting with a "z") and colleagues found that Chinese characters repeatedly flashed on a screen too quickly for conscious awareness were later rated as more likeable than other characters by participants who couldn't read Chinese. Similar effects of repeated exposure have been found for nonsense words, tones, and even people's faces.

Advertisers are acutely aware of the effect of familiarity, and as a result they spend millions of dollars getting products in front of our faces. Most people insist that ads don't affect their behavior, but this is probably because some of the effects are occurring unconsciously. It's not that you see an advertisement and immediately run to the store, but rather that you may unconsciously develop greater fondness for that particular brand because you have seen it before.

Of course, the effects of priming and mere-exposure are subtle and it seems that environments must be carefully controlled in order to observe them. They certainly shouldn't be seen as magical brain-washing or powerful subliminal mind-control techniques. Nevertheless, they should make us question just how much we control our conscious behavior and how much influence is exerted outside of our conscious awareness.

Consciousness During Sleeping Life

You may think, as many people do, that sleeping is a type of unconsciousness, but this isn't accurate. Despite expressions like "dead to the world", sleepers do have some awareness of their surroundings. They manage to keep their bodies in their beds, and in the case of dreaming, they certainly have a vivid experience of being asleep. In fact, stimuli from a sleeper's environment may even be seamlessly incorporated into dreams, which you may have experienced if the sound of your alarm clock has ever found its way into your dreams as a blaring fire alarm, a ringing phone, or a singing banana.

So rather than unconsciousness, we should think of sleeping as another state of consciousness that differs from waking life. Instead of sleep and wakefulness as an on/off switch for consciousness, we should think of a dimmer switch, which allows us to slide back and forth between different levels of awareness.

The Rhythm of the Night

Our sleeping pattern follows a *circadian rhythm*, which is really just a way of saying a daily pattern of wakefulness and sleepiness (circadian derived from Latin: *circa* - "about" and *diem* - "day"). Our circadian rhythm is influenced by environmental factors, known as *zeitgebers* (German for "time-givers") which help to set this internal clock.

One of the most most powerful zeitgebers is light. When light hits your retina, messages are not only sent to the occipital lobe for visual processing, they are also sent to the *suprachiasmatic nucleus*, an area of the hypothalamus. In the presence of light (especially wavelengths corresponding to blue light), the suprachiasmatic nucleus inhibits the *pineal gland* from releasing melatonin into the bloodstream. *Melatonin* is a hormone which, when released into the bloodstream, causes us to feel drowsy. Through this process of inhibiting melatonin release, light helps to keep us feeling alert, while darkness helps bring drowsiness.

This process probably worked quite well in setting our circadian rhythm for millions of years of our evolutionary history, but the ubiquity of artificial light in most of our lives today may be interrupting this system. While our ancestors only really had bright light from the sun, we can have bright light any time we want. The darkness of dusk that told our ancestors to unwind and stay in the safety of shelter now simply signals us to turn on the lights.

If you have trouble falling asleep at night, light may be part of the problem and limiting your exposure to it in the evening may help you to fall asleep more easily. You may even consider using blue-light blocking glasses in the evening or downloading programs like f.lux which reduce the amount of blue-light emitted by your laptop or phone screen after sunset.

Light is not the only zeitgeber that influences our level of alertness. The timing of our meals, the ambient temperature, and our social interactions also play a role in the circadian rhythm. This may explain how you managed to stay awake all night at slumber parties and why it's so easy to fall asleep in a warm room while a lecturer drones on and on without any chance of interaction.

The settings of this internal clock also vary with age, as teenagers tend to be "night-owls" whose concentration and attention peak later in the day or evening, while older adults tend to be "larks" who perform best in early morning, then decline as the hours go by. This is clearly seen in the classic class-time conundrum, as adults (parents and teachers) set the times that work best for them, while teenagers are alert at 11pm but stumbling and slumbering through early morning classes.

The Sleep Cycle

As we sleep through any given night, we move through a number of different stages of sleep. These different stages can be identified by their differing patterns of brain activity, as recorded by an **EEG** (*electroencephalogram*). These measurements of electrical activity in the brain are recorded in the form of waves, with peak and valleys, and the resulting patterns are where we get the term "brain waves". In an awake but relaxed, drowsy, or meditative state, the brain produces "*alpha waves*", while a state of vigilance produces "*beta waves*".

When we first fall asleep, we move through the following stages of sleep. The first 3 stages are referred to as NREM, for Non-Rapid-Eye-Movement sleep.

NREM Stage 1 – Stage 1 is characterized by de-synchronized *theta waves*; slow irregular waves of activity. In this stage, sleepers may experience brief dream-like visions, known as *hypnagogic imagery*, and occasionally experience sudden twitches and falling sensations, known as *hypnic jerks*. This stage may last for only a few minutes before moving to stage 2.

NREM Stage 2 – Theta waves continue, though occasionally interrupted by sudden bursts of activity, known as *sleep spindles*. In this stage we also see high amplitude spikes known as *K-complexes*, which are hypothesized to reduce cortical arousal and help maintain sleep. When you first fall asleep, this stage will generally last for around 15-20 minutes. Throughout the course of a night, about 50% of sleep time will be spent in Stage 2 sleep.

NREM Stage 3 – By stage 3 we see more obvious changes in brain activity as the waves increase their amplitude and decrease their frequency while also becoming more synchronized, resulting in "***delta waves***". This stage is considered to be the stage of deepest sleep and lowest awareness of surroundings. If you're groggy and confused when someone wakes you (known as *sleep inertia*), there's a good chance that you were in this "slow-wave" sleep at the time. Note: you may see reference to Stage 4 sleep in some texts; the American Academy of Sleep Medicine reclassified the stages in 2007, combining stage 3 and 4 into a single stage.

So far this probably seems as you'd expect; the longer you've been asleep, the deeper the level of sleep. But after about an hour, something bizarre happens. The depth of your sleep lessens as you rise back up to stage 2, and then you enter the most interesting stage of all.

REM Sleep

REM sleep or ***rapid-eye-movement sleep***, is sometimes referred to as ***paradoxical sleep***, and with good reason. In contrast to the other stages, in REM heart rate, blood pressure, and respiration increase, along with physical signs of sexual arousal. Every 30 seconds or so your eyes begin moving around under your eyelids (hence the name). Your brain activity closely resembles that of a waking state, and yet your body becomes paralyzed. People who are awakened from Non-REM stages may report some dreamlike imagery, but those awakened from REM report vivid dreaming.

Who Needs Sleep?

Although the processes of sleep are not yet fully understood, REM seems to be particularly important for the consolidation of memory. The importance of REM can be seen in the fact that people (and animals) who are temporarily deprived of REM sleep for a night will experience a ***rebound effect***; spending more time in REM than usual during subsequent sleep. Babies spend more time in REM than adults, and people who are experiencing higher levels of stress will also spend more time in REM when they sleep.

For most people, an entire sleep cycle from Stage 1 to a completed period of REM will last about 90 minutes. At this point the cycle is repeated, though in subsequent cycles we spend less time in deep sleep (by the end of the night skipping slow-wave sleep completely) and spend more time in REM sleep. While initial REM stages may last for 15 or 20 minutes, later cycles may have REM sessions lasting 45 minutes to an hour.

One way of assessing the importance of sleep is to consider what happens when we don't get it. This can be considered either by examining the effects of ***chronic sleep deprivation***, in which people are repeatedly not getting enough sleep, or by ***acute sleep deprivation***, in which people stay awake continuously.

Physical effects of Sleep Deprivation

Sleep deprivation causes a number of physical changes in the body. Physical symptoms of sleep deprivation include fatigue, dark circles and/or bags under the eyes (caused by the very thin layers of skin in this area becoming more pale and allowing blood vessels to become more visible), fluctuations in hormone levels, and reduced performance on physical tasks.

Chronic sleep deprivation is associated with obesity, which may be a result of several hormonal changes which occur during sleep deprivation. Going without enough sleep increases levels of the hormone ghrelin, which increases feelings of hunger, and deprivation decreases the hormone leptin, which helps to signal satiety. As a result, sleep-deprived people are more likely to have cravings for food and also likely to eat more before feeling full. Sleep deprivation also reduces willpower, which means that when those cravings hit they may be even harder to resist.

Sleep deprivation also increases levels of the stress hormone cortisol, which can trigger the body to store fat. This stress response also means that sleep deprivation suppresses the activity of the immune system. This means that people who don't get enough sleep are more likely to get sick, and also explains why when we do get sick we tend to spend more time asleep (in order to activate the immune system).

Cognitive Effects of Sleep Deprivation

Sleep deprivation has profound effects on cognition and attention. Both chronic and acute sleep deprivation impair concentration, memory, judgment, coordination, and reaction time. These cognitive deficits shouldn't just concern you when it comes to your exam performance after an all-nighter. The potential for serious injury and death from sleep deprivation is high. Studies of "drowsy driving" have found impairments similar to drunk driving and driver fatigue has been estimated to be responsible for 100,000 crashes, 1,550 deaths and 71,000 injuries every year in the United States alone. So even if you join Edgar Allan Poe in loathing sleep as "little slices of death", remember that trying to do without sleep may lead to a death far more permanent.

Sleep Disorders

The most common sleep disorder is ***insomnia***, and it is estimated that about 10% of adults will suffer from insomnia at some point in their lifetime. Insomnia is a persistent difficulty or inability to enter the sleep state, or to remain asleep, often despite feeling tired. So while we all occasionally have difficulty getting to sleep at night, in most cases this wouldn't be considered to be clinical insomnia.

While you may think that sleeping pills (or an alcoholic "night-cap") would help those with insomnia, these aren't recommended. While sleeping pills may aid muscle relaxation or reduce anxiety to help patients enter the sleep state, unfortunately they reduce the quality of REM sleep. This means that while patients may spend more time sleeping, they end up getting less REM sleep and as a result still feel tired.

Insomnia sufferers also have a tendency to underestimate how much sleep they are getting, often believing they are sleeping half as much as they actually are. This may occur because they enter the sleep state and reawaken without realizing they were asleep. If they repeatedly check the clock throughout the night they may think that they were awake until 2 or 3am, when some of that time was spent asleep. They may also recall waking during the night and believe that they stayed awake much longer than they actually did.

Another common sleep disorder affecting about 5% of people (though more common in males) is **sleep apnea**. In this disorder, when muscles in the throat relax during sleep, the tongue and epiglottis obstruct the flow of air. This is also what causes those strange sounds of snoring, except in sleep apnea airflow is completely blocked. This blockage of airflow causes the patient to awaken in order to breathe. Patients with sleep apnea may not remember awakening throughout the night, but report feeling tired and lethargic despite what appears to be adequate sleeping time.

Obesity increases the risk of sleep apnea, though as we've seen already, sleep deprivation (which would be a side effect of sleep apnea) also increases the risk of obesity, so this interaction could be working both ways. A common treatment for sleep apnea is to use a CPAP (continuous positive airway pressure) machine. This device consists of a mask, worn at night, which slightly increases air pressure on the throat, helping to keep the airway open and allowing the patient to remain breathing (and sleeping).

Sleep walking (or *somnambulism*) occurs during the deep stages of slow-wave sleep. The sleeper may get out of bed, wander around, and even eat or perform other behaviors while still in the sleep state. Sleep walking is more common in young children, especially males, and often goes away on its own by adolescence. Episodes of sleepwalking and behaviors performed are rarely recalled the next morning.

Children are also more likely than adults to suffer from **night terrors**. In night terrors, the person wakes up in the middle of the night and may scream, feeling an overwhelming sense of fear, and usually doesn't remember the experience in the morning. Like sleepwalking, night terrors also tend to fade by the end of childhood.

REM Sleep Behavior disorder is a rare disorder in which the usual paralysis and loss of muscle tone (*muscle atonia*) of REM sleep does not occur. This means that sufferers are able to engage in "dream enactment", which can have dangerous consequences. They may kick, punch, scream, or jump out of bed, potentially injuring themselves or their bed partner. REM sleep behavior disorder can be treated with muscle relaxants to reduce activity, in addition to creating a safer environment for the sleeper which may even include a special sleeping bag that helps to restrict movements.

Narcolepsy is a rare sleep disorder affecting about 1 in 2000 people (0.05%), in which patients suffer from an irrepressible need to sleep, even though they are spending adequate amounts of time sleeping at night. They repeatedly lapse into sleep and often also experience *cataplexy*, a sudden loss of muscle tone. The sudden attacks of sleep generally only last for a few minutes and may occur at any time, making it difficult for sufferers of narcolepsy to live a normal life. Narcolepsy sufferers tend to enter the REM state very quickly after falling asleep, meaning that they spend less time in slow-wave stages of sleep, which may relate to their feelings of drowsiness during the day.

Narcolepsy can be treated with stimulants (such as *Modafinil)* which promote wakefulness, though these do not cure the disorder. Some sufferers remain awake and aware of their surroundings during *cataplexy* but are unable to move. People nearby may attempt to "awaken" the person with pinches or shouting. The sufferer can feel and hear these attempts but is unable to respond.

Polyphasic Sleep Schedules

You may have heard of polyphasic sleeping schedules, which involve splitting sleep time up into several separate chunks throughout a 24 hour period. Attempts to adopt these schedules seem to be spurred by claims from Thomas Edison that sleep is a "complete waste of time" and they are encouraged by life-hackers seeking to supposedly maximize sleep efficiency. These schedules are often claimed to derive from the odd sleeping habits of eminent thinkers like Leonardo DaVinci and Nikola Tesla, though evidence that these figures actually followed these types of schedules for extended periods is scant to nonexistent.

We should note that much of the initial research on polyphasic schedules conducted by Claudio Stampi was intended to determine sleep efficiency in a particular subset of people: solo-sailors during lengthy competitions in which full periods of sleep were not possible. Stampi tested a number of possible ways of dividing sleep in order to assess which allowed for greater physical performance over a relatively short period of time. Life-hackers tend to ignore that these schedules weren't intended to be adopted as routine sleeping habits, but were for specific short-term situations which necessitated some level of chronic sleep deprivation.

We should also avoid thinking that just because there are names for these schedules this means they are actually viable ways of organizing quality sleep. Unfortunately creating names like the "Everyman" and "Uberman" schedule may give a false sense of credibility to these schedules. This is related to a cognitive error known as the *nominal fallacy*, which is the flaw of thinking that because we have a name for something we actually understand it. So if I were to invent the "Deca-doze Distribution" of sleeping for 10 minutes every 2 hours the mere fact that I've given it a scientific-sounding name might make people more likely to believe it's something that can be done.

You should also note that in evolutionary terms these schedules don't make much sense. We have evolved to be alert and awake during the day (when we can hunt and gather) and sleep during the night (when it's dark and we are more vulnerable). This rhythm indicates that we are best suited to a single long session of sleep (*monophasic*) or perhaps a *biphasic schedule*, which is a large chunk of sleep at night, with the addition of an early afternoon siesta. Attempting to drastically deviate from the circadian rhythm which has developed over millions of years seems unlikely to create benefits, and as we've already seen, the risks of sleep deprivation are great.

So if you've been tempted to try adopting one of these polyphasic schedules, remember that sleeping less in exchange for more grogginess, irritability, cognitive deficits, and a higher risk of fatality from accidents doesn't seem like a particularly wise trade-off. There's a certain irony to the belief that if you want to be successful and productive you need to learn how to sleep less. In actuality, achieving high levels of performance, in both cognitive and physical tasks, seems to necessitate spending more time in sleep. Sleep helps to consolidate new memories, enhance concentration, and improve reaction time, endurance, mood, and energy levels. So ignore those admonitions from Edison and help uncover your potential by spending more time under the covers.

Theories of Dreaming

Freud's approach to understanding dreaming was based on the assumption that dreams were representations of unconscious desires. Because these desires are too anxiety-producing for us to consciously consider, they are not directly revealed. One way they emerge, according to Freud, is when we are dreaming.

He believed that dreams consisted of two features, the manifest content and the latent content. The **manifest content** is what we are shown, meaning what we actually dream about. So if we dream about riding a train, arguing with a talking dolphin, or watching a burning tree, these would be the manifest content.

The **latent content**, however, is the hidden message behind the dream. It's those anxiety-producing unconscious fears and desires that our conscious mind needs to be shielded from. So our dream about a train may be about sex, the dolphin might represent conflict with our mother, or the burning tree the death of a friend. Freud believed that a therapist could analyze the manifest content of a patient's dreams and, over time, uncover clues about the unconscious forces shaping the patient's personality.

There are two main problems with this approach to understanding dreams. The first is that we frequently dream explicitly about our desires and fears. These often manifest themselves quite directly in dreams and we have conscious access to these themes. We actually do dream of having sex, fighting with a parent, losing a friend, or any number of other stressful and anxiety-producing events. If these desires must be hidden from consciousness, why would they sometimes appear in the manifest content?

Secondly, there are infinite possible interpretations of the manifest content, so we can never be sure which interpretation is correct. What your therapist thinks a train or a dolphin means may actually reveal more about the therapist's mind than it reveals about your own.

So while Freud's notion that there are hidden clues to the unconscious in dreams gained some popularity, it ultimately failed to provide a satisfying answer to why exactly we dream what we dream. It may be true that dreams reveal some aspects of our thoughts as well as our hopes, fears, and desires. What doesn't seem to be true is that these elements are revealed through predictable patterns and symbols.

A Brain-Based Approach

In 1977, J. Allan Hobson and Robert McCarley proposed a new theory of dreaming, **the activation-synthesis model**. The activation-synthesis model suggests that during sleep, brain activation occurs somewhat randomly, and these patterns of random activation are combined and interpreted (synthesis) by the brain. This results in the bizarre (and characteristic) features of dreams. In this model, dreams are seen as the brain's flailing attempt to make sense of these unusual patterns of activation.

This approach attempts to explain the apparently inexplicable nature of dreams by suggesting that often our brains are dealing with patterns of activation that simply don't occur in waking life. The brain is being forced to come up with explanations for bizarre patterns of activity and we're just left watching the show (and scratching our heads as to what the director was thinking). If, for instance, you find yourself dreaming that you are now vacationing with your 3rd grade art teacher, it's probably not because of some repressed sexual desire (as a Freudian might suggest), but rather that your memory for that teacher just happened to be stimulated at the same time as your memory for last year's travels. In a valiant attempt to reconcile this new pattern, your ever-explaining brain creates a storyline in which the two coexist.

Information-Processing

Since the activation-synthesis model was first proposed, there has been considerably more research on the patterns of activation that occur during REM sleep, suggesting that perhaps the activation isn't quite random. This ***information-processing dream theory*** considers that the activation patterns that occur during REM serve other purposes and are not simply random noise. Neural activation in dreaming may allow our brains to sift through new experiences, revisit old memories, and maintain neural connections and networks.

One way that this can be seen is in how our dreams often incorporate "day residue" of our present situations and experiences, combined with memories from years or even decades before. If we spend hours playing a video game during the day, imagery from the game tends to show up in dreams that night but may be combined with other memories or situations. If, as Robert Stickgold has suggested, one role of sleep is to consolidate memories and integrate our experiences into a cohesive sense of self, it may no longer come as a surprise that dreams combine our recent experiences and learning with other memories. Rather than random activation, this may reflect sleep's role in reorganizing information and considering alternatives in order to inform our future responses.

This might also account for common themes in dreams, as we all share many similar problems, fears (predators or exams), sources of embarrassment (oops I forgot my pants), or worries for the future (I've lost my teeth and hair) that our minds are simulating and working out responses to. At the same time, it accounts for individual differences, as how our brains choose to interpret, explain, and react to these simulations may reflect something of our own unique experiences and viewpoints.

Finally, a section on dreaming wouldn't be complete without mentioning ***lucid dreaming***. Lucid dreaming is when a dreamer becomes aware of the dream state, but remains asleep. The dreamer may then be able to take conscious control of the dream and direct the course of events. This raises some questions about the nature of consciousness during dreaming and how awareness that one is dreaming may be separated from the dream experience itself. Stephen LaBerge has spent decades studying lucid dreaming and believes that anyone can learn to lucid dream on a regular basis. He has written several books on learning to lucid dream and believes that lucid dreaming can help to foster greater creativity, insight, and new perspectives and interpretations of events and behaviors.

Drugs and Consciousness

In chapter 3 we looked at several drug and neurotransmitter interactions such as nicotine and acetylcholine, and alcohol and GABA, to understand how chemical interactions in the brain influence behavior. What we didn't address, however, is how these might influence our consciousness. In this section, we'll look at how ***psychoactive drugs***, substances which alter the chemistry of the brain, are capable of altering our state of consciousness.

Getting Into the Brain

Generally speaking, the brain doesn't want to be messed with, so to keep things under control, the ***blood-brain barrier*** prevents most things in the bloodstream from getting into the brain. This blood-brain barrier works by only allowing certain molecules, like vital nutrients, through its special channels. This is generally a good thing, and why brain viruses and infections are so rare. Even if an infection is in your body and traveling in your bloodstream, the tight-knit endothelial cells of the blood-brain barrier can usually provide an adequate security network. The downside is that when you do have an infection in your brain, it's especially difficult to get medication in to fight it.

Some chemicals, however, are able to sneak through this barrier, gain access to the brain, and influence its functioning. Once inside the brain, these chemicals can travel to synapses and affect neural communication. Some chemicals boost the message of a neurotransmitter, either by mimicking the action of the neurotransmitter, blocking its removal from the synapse, or stimulating its release. These drugs are considered to be ***agonists*** for the neurotransmitter they influence. Other drugs, however, do the opposite and decrease the effects of a neurotransmitter by blocking its receptor sites, increasing its removal, or decreasing its release. These drugs are ***antagonists*** for the neurotransmitter affected.

This agonist/antagonist categorization doesn't address the effects the drugs have on behavior or cognition. Based on their effects, drugs can be roughly categorized into 3 main groups: ***depressants***, ***stimulants***, or ***hallucinogens***. Of course, because it's possible to influence more than one neurotransmitter or more than one brain area or body function, some drugs may fit into more than one category.

In considering the effects of these different types of drugs, we should remember that the body is constantly trying to maintain a state of ***homeostasis***, the balance needed to maintain normal functioning. Repeated introduction of drugs into the brain causes changes, known as ***neuroadaptation***. This is how ***tolerance*** to a drug builds over time. After repeated exposure, the brain builds a resistance to the effects of the drug, so a greater dosage is required to achieve the same effects, perhaps explaining why just one cup of coffee doesn't get you going like it used to.

After a tolerance has developed, neuroadaptation also explains why going without the drug can be difficult. This is known as **withdrawal**. Essentially the brain has adapted to having the drug around, and has developed a **dependence** on the drug's effects. In the case of caffeine, sudden cessation may result in a minor headache, but for more powerful drugs, withdrawal can be an overwhelmingly painful experience. Intense cravings combined with physical pain can drive a user back to the drug, even though he may rationally know that it is destroying his life.

This **physical addiction** to the chemical reactions a drug causes is not the only type of addiction, and users may also experience **psychological addiction** to a substance. In this case, people believe they need the drug, or find using it to be a way of coping. Alcohol is a good example of a drug that is physically addictive but also has strong psychological components of addiction. People may feel a desire for alcohol in order to function in particular social situations or in order to deal with disappointment, stress, or anxiety. Even after the physical symptoms of withdrawal have faded, a former alcoholic may still have difficulty dealing with the psychological components of addiction in certain situations.

Stimulants

Stimulants are drugs which speed up processes in the body and stimulate the autonomic nervous system. These drugs increase heart rate, blood pressure, and breathing, and may increase our state of vigilance while decreasing feelings of tiredness. In addition to this stimulation, some stimulants activate the reward area of the hypothalamus, triggering a rush of dopamine that causes short-lived feelings of euphoria and well-being. Common stimulant drugs include caffeine (which is the world's most commonly used psychoactive drug), cocaine, amphetamines, methamphetamine, and ecstasy (MDMA – *methylenedioxymethamphetamine*).

Depressants

Depressants have the opposite effect on the nervous system, slowing processes and inhibiting activation. This causes slowed heart rate and breathing, and reduced muscle tension. Depressants include alcohol (specifically *ethanol*) and tranquilizers (also known as *anxiolytics* or anti-anxiety drugs) which include barbiturates and benzodiazepines (like Valium and Xanax).

Overdose of depressant drugs can lead to enough inhibition of function to induce a coma or even cause death. Withdrawal can also be dangerous, as the body's dependence on the inhibiting effects of regular use mean that sudden cessation can cause *excitotoxicity*. Dependency causes the nervous system to be overstimulated when the depressant drug is no longer suppressing function, causing anxiety, seizures, and in extreme cases, death.

Narcotics (including *Opiates*) are sometimes classified as a separate category of drugs but can be considered depressants because of their inhibiting effects on the nervous system. The word narcotics comes from the Greek root *narko* meaning "numbness" or "stupor". The term *narcotics* can be misleading though, as legal definitions differ from medical definitions. In the United States any prohibited drug may be referred to as a narcotic, so the term can refer to cocaine (a stimulant) and marijuana (a hallucinogen) even though in medical terms neither would be considered a narcotic.

In medical terms, narcotics are pain-relievers that mimic the body's own natural painkillers (*endorphins*) and include morphine, heroin, methadone, oxycodone, codeine, and opium (from which *opiates* and *opioids* get their name). These drugs block pain messages and provide a sense of euphoric, drowsy bliss for the user. Unfortunately, neuroadaptation occurs rapidly with opiates, causing the body to reduce endorphin production, thus leaving it unable to manage pain well on its own. Without natural endorphins to block their pain, recovering addicts face an agonizing withdrawal process where it can seem the only thing to stop their pain is the very drug they are trying to avoid. This torturous withdrawal process explains why these drugs can exert such a powerful influence over users.

Hallucinogens

The last category of psychoactive drugs includes those drugs which alter perception of reality and identity, and have the potential to induce sensory hallucinations. *Hallucinogens* (also known as *psychedelics*) include LSD (*lysergic acid diethylamide*), mescaline, psilocybin mushrooms, marijuana, PCP (*phencyclidine*), ketamine, and ecstasy (which is also a stimulant).

The effects of hallucinogenic drugs are considered to be less predictable than other drugs and seem to be more dependent on psychological factors such as the user's expectations and emotional state. Another difference from stimulants and depressants is that hallucinogens may remain in the body considerably longer. For instance, by-products of THC (*delta-9-tetrahydrocannabinol*) in marijuana may remain in the body as long as a month, and this lingering means that subsequent uses may actually have a stronger effect than the initial use. This may allow regular users to get high using a smaller dose of the drug and is referred to as *reverse tolerance*.

With a few exceptions (like PCP and ketamine) the physical withdrawal and dependency seen in other drug types is not common with hallucinogenic drugs. While animals will press levers thousands of times to get another hit of coke or meth, they generally won't work to get hits of LSD or psilocybin. As a result, these drugs generally aren't considered to be physically addictive in the same way as heroin, cocaine, alcohol, or even caffeine.

This does not mean that addiction isn't possible, however, as psychological addiction may still occur, particularly if these drugs are used to escape negative emotions or stress. The fact that they don't tend to cause withdrawal also doesn't mean that they aren't harmful. There are still a number of negative effects associated with their use including anxiety, paranoia, and problems in learning and memory formation.

While all the drugs mentioned above have physiological effects on the body, expectancy and beliefs also influence how they affect consciousness. While this is especially true of hallucinogens, it's also true of other drug types. People can be duped into believing that decaf coffee has improved their alertness (if they don't know it was decaf) or that non-alcoholic beverages have made them tipsy. These effects of beliefs and expectations mean that drugs aren't the only ways of changing our state of consciousness and it has been suggested that hypnosis and meditation can also create altered states of consciousness.

Hypnosis

In considering what hypnosis is, perhaps we should start by considering what hypnosis is not. Despite what you may have seen in a stage show, on television, or in movies, hypnosis is not a magical state of mind-control in which a hypnotized subject obeys the every whim of the hypnotist. Instead, we can think of a hypnotic state as a state of relaxation, focused attention, and increased imagination. This state is generally entered via hypnotic induction, in which the hypnotist encourages the subject to become relaxed, then gradually makes suggestions to the subject (your eyelids are becoming heavier, your eyes are closing, etc.). People vary in how strongly they respond to these suggestions, and this is referred to as their **hypnotic suggestibility**. Some people are considered to be "highly hypnotizable" and become absorbed in the suggestions of the hypnotist.

We shouldn't equate hypnotic suggestibility with mere gullibility, however, and when subjects are given this negative connotation their hypnotic suggestibility sharply decreases. We might think of hypnotic suggestibility as an ability to focus attention and imagination on the suggestions of the hypnotist. A sense of will remains, however, and subjects who have been hypnotized will not perform tasks that they would not otherwise do.

Therapeutic Uses of Hypnosis

The increased state of imagination and attention does allow some therapeutic use for hypnosis, the most prominent of which is pain reduction (*analgesia*). Subjects who are hypnotized may also have greater access to their own healing powers, which may be similar to the placebo effect. Hypnosis has been used to successfully treat stress-related skin problems, asthma, and obesity. Its use in treating addictions to alcohol, nicotine, and other drugs, however, has not been shown to be as successful.

Despite the popular perception, hypnosis is not able to increase accuracy of past memories. As we saw in Chapter 6, our memory is subject to failures and biases, and unfortunately hypnosis is unable to overcome these. One thing it is able to do, however, is make subjects more confident in the accuracy of their memories, even though the memories are not actually more accurate. This can be a dangerous combination, particularly when these supposed recovered memories involve allegations of crime or abuse.

While it can't successfully recover repressed memories, hypnosis does seem to be able to reduce memories of the hypnotic session itself, known as *posthypnotic amnesia*. Subjects can also engage in directed forgetting, in which they respond to suggestions that certain information or experiences will not be remembered following the session.

How does Hypnosis Happen?

One theory for explaining the behavior of hypnotized subjects is that they are like actors on a stage. They are obeying the hypnotist, who acts as a director and manages their perceptions. This is known as *Role Theory of Hypnosis*, and if we accept this explanation, we might think that hypnosis is not in fact an altered state of consciousness.

Another theory, however, suggests that hypnosis really is a different state from normal wakefulness and involves a division of consciousness. This *Dissociation Theory*, proposed by Ernest Hilgard, notes that hypnotized subjects may continue to follow suggestions even when they believe they are not being observed. This would indicate that hypnosis is more than just playing along. The fact the hypnosis can also effectively be used to manage pain suggests that it may actually be altering the perceptual experiences of subjects. Hilgard demonstrated this by asking hypnotized subjects to hold their hands in icy water. These subjects were then asked about whether they were experiencing pain. While subjects said they weren't experiencing pain, they still showed awareness that the icy water was actually painful. This suggested to Hilgard that the subjects were splitting their consciousness between awareness of the pain (which they had) and the experience of the pain (which was reduced).

Meditation

Another possible altered state of consciousness can be seen in meditation. In many ways, hypnosis and meditation are quite similar, as they both are a state of relaxed awareness, though meditation does not necessarily focus on particular suggestions. While there are many varieties and traditions of meditation, we will briefly focus on two types: focused awareness meditation and mindfulness meditation. Both of these practices involve cultivating a relaxed and calm state of mind.

In **focused attention meditation** the meditator chooses a single focus of attention and attempts to maintain this focus. The sole focus of attention may be one's breathing or it may be a **mantra**; a word or phrase that is repeated (mentally or chanted). While you may have heard of some of the familiar mantras like "Om" or "Hare Krishna" that are used by some groups, any word at all can be used. The importance of the mantra is to track one's awareness and notice when it has deviated.

Another type of meditation is **mindfulness meditation**. The main difference here is that rather than maintaining a single focus, the meditator attends to all the sights, sounds, feelings, and thoughts that occur, but without becoming attached to any of them. Jon Kabat-Zinn describes mindfulness as "paying attention in a particular way: on purpose, in the present moment, and nonjudgmentally".

There may be similarities here to the dissociation theory of hypnosis, where subjects seem to separate their awareness of sensations from their experience of those sensations. Experienced meditators engaging in mindfulness meditation have shown similar types of analgesia, having awareness of pain but having reduced experience and emotional reactivity to the pain.

Herbert Benson has researched how the practice of meditation elicits the "**relaxation response**" a metabolic change that activates the parasympathetic nervous system. This is essentially the opposite of the "fight or flight response". This relaxation response reduces activation of the sympathetic nervous system, decreasing heart rate, blood pressure, and stress hormones, while increasing relaxation, digestion, and immune function.

How to Start Practicing Meditation

While this isn't intended to be a comprehensive guide to meditation, I thought I would give readers a few pointers if they are interested in how to begin. Meditation isn't all that complicated, and all that you really need to do is set aside some time to sit quietly and calm your mind.

The first point that beginners may struggle with is the widespread misconception that meditation is some sort of esoteric and mystical experience. You don't need to understand how to balance your *qi*, align your *chakras*, or look out your third eye in order to meditate properly. You don't need to travel to Tibetan mountaintops or gaze at Ganesh under the guidance of a guru in order to get the calming benefits that meditation can give. While understanding these cultural traditions and practices can be fascinating, it's not a prerequisite for getting started.

Another problem that plagues people who want to start meditating is the feeling that they just can't do it. Their mind wanders, they feel uncomfortable or restless, and they give up, thinking that meditation is not for them. If you're looking to start regular meditation, remember that trying to maintain a single focus, getting distracted, then bringing your mind back to focus is what meditation is. It doesn't mean that you're doing it wrong or that it's not for you. Focus, distraction, and refocus are supposed to happen, so accept this cycle. Continuing to sit quietly and face down distraction and discomfort is a challenge, and that's exactly the point.

Choose a comfortable sitting posture (lying down usually leads to falling asleep, which is not what we want), choose something to focus on (your breathing, a mantra, or your present sensations), and you've begun to meditate. If you can embrace the fact that you aren't waiting for anything miraculous to happen and you recognize that catching your mind wandering is what meditation is, then you're on the right path toward cultivating this practice. Realizing that this is a practice that needs to be cultivated means you don't need to start with 45 minutes or an hour all at once. Start with a small goal that is attainable (maybe just 5 minutes per day) then gradually build as you get more comfortable with the practice.

While this is all you really need to get started, if you want to read more about meditation, I highly recommend the writing of Jon Kabat-Zinn, especially "Wherever You Go, There You Are" which was quoted above. His writing is clear, accessible, and inspiring, and is what has helped me most with meditation. I hope that you'll consider creating the habit of regular meditation and I wish you the best on this journey!

Chapter Summary – States of Consciousness

- The study of consciousness is wrought with problems including the **mind-body problem**, the **problem of other minds**, and the **hard problem of consciousness**. Four characteristics that generally describe consciousness are **unity**, **intentionality**, **selectivity**, and **transience**.

- Our level of awareness of information can be classified as **conscious**, **preconscious**, **subconscious** (also **unconscious**), or **nonconscious**. Studies on **priming** and the **mere-exposure effect** support the existence of a separate track of subconscious processing, referred to as **System 1** in **Dual-Process Theory**.

- The **circadian rhythm** refers to our "internal clock" or pattern of alertness throughout the day and is influenced by **zeitgebers** such as exposure to light, meal times, and social interaction.

- The sleep cycle is divided into 4 stages; NREM 1, NREM 2, NREM 3, and REM sleep. Proper sleep may be disrupted by a number of disorders including **insomnia**, **sleep apnea**, **sleepwalking**, **night terrors**, **REM sleep behavior disorder**, and **narcolepsy**.

- Depending on how they alter the nervous system and consciousness, **psychoactive drugs** can be categorized as **stimulants**, **depressants**, or **hallucinogens**.

- **Hypnosis** is a state of increased imagination and suggestibility which can be used to treat some illnesses and reduce pain. **Meditation** is a state of relaxed awareness which can also reduce the experience of pain and activate the parasympathetic nervous system.

Notes

Chapter 9
Intelligence

What is Intelligence?

Intelligence is something we all think is important, but what exactly does this term refer to? We might all hope to have intelligence, but what are we hoping for? Always knowing the right answer? Making better decisions? Earning higher grades or more income? Being more successful in reaching our goals? Having a greater sense of control over our lives?

In this chapter we'll be examining the concept of intelligence in three main ways. First, we'll consider how to define intelligence. What does it mean to have intelligence (or not) and how have definitions of intelligence changed over time? Second, once we have some ideas about how to define intelligence, we'll look at attempts to measure it. How can we assess someone's intelligence? Finally, once we have assessments of intelligence, what do these results really mean? What causes differences in scores and how should we interpret these differences?

The first thing that we should remember when considering the idea of intelligence is that it is just that; an idea. Like many properties that psychologists attempt to investigate, intelligence is a hypothetical construct. We need to avoid the temptation for **reification**: treating an idea as if it were a real, concrete object that can be objectively measured. When we consider someone's IQ score there can be a tendency to think of that score as a measurement of some fixed entity, but we should try to avoid thinking this way.

Since intelligence isn't a concrete object we can directly observe, we need to agree on some terms in order to make sure that we're all talking about the same thing. What should we consider intelligence to be? Let's take a look at some historical precedents for the concept of intelligence, along with some newer approaches that have attempted to clarify this potentially vague notion.

Charles Spearman (1863- 1945) is considered to be one of the first researchers to provide evidence that intelligence is a single underlying trait which affects a number of abilities. While looking at relationships between performance in different areas, Spearman found that high performance seemed to be linked across domains. People who did well on one task also tended to do well on other tasks. Spearman collected results for performance on many tasks, then used ***factor analysis***; a statistical technique for examining whether a large number of correlations can be explained using a small number of factors. Spearman identified one underlying factor influencing many cognitive abilities and he called this ***g-factor***, for ***general intelligence***. Spearman recognized that people also have specialized skills but he believed that these were influenced by an individual's *g*-factor. A helpful mnemonic for remembering Spearman's association with g-factor is to imagine a *spear* with one point – pointing to the single factor of *g*.

Louis Leon Thurstone (1887-1955) challenged Spearman's concept of *g* and proposed a different organization of mental abilities. Thurstone proposed a multi-factor theory of ***7 primary mental abilities*** which each influenced particular sets of skills. Despite Thurstone's evidence for these domains, further analysis has supported the idea that there is still a general intelligence factor which influences several primary mental abilities at once. You could visualize this as a sort of pyramid: a single g-factor (at the top) influences several different domains of mental ability (the middle), which each then influence the development of many specific skills (at the base).

We still see echos of this debate today and definitions of intelligence are never satisfactory for everyone. Similar to Thurstone's primary mental abilities, **Howard Gardner** has proposed a theory of ***multiple intelligences***, believing that our mental abilities should be considered as separate modules. It is possible for an individual to flourish in one area of intelligence independent of others. Gardner has suggested there is evidence for the existence of at least 8 separate intelligences including ***verbal***, ***mathematical***, ***musical***, ***spatial***, ***bodily-kinesthetic***, ***interpersonal***, ***intrapersonal***, and ***naturalistic*** intelligences.

Possible evidence for these separate intelligences can be seen in ***prodigies***, children with high ability in a single area but normal development in other areas, and ***savants***, individuals with extremely high proficiency in one area, accompanied by low ability or disability in other areas. The existence of prodigies and savants suggests that intelligences are (or at least can be) separate domains.

Perhaps the most famous savant in recent times was Kim Peek (1951-2009), the inspiration for Dustin Hoffman's character Raymond Babbitt in the film *Rain Man* (note: in the film, Babbitt was portrayed as autistic though Peek did not have autism). Peek's prodigious memory for facts and figures was accompanied by disabilities in other areas such as difficulties with reasoning and metaphorical thinking along with physical coordination problems.

Cases of patients with brain damage resulting in specific types of deficits also provide some support for a modular view of multiple intelligences. If a person is in an accident and subsequently loses the ability to perform a specific set of skills without loss of ability in other areas, this might indicate those skills are a separate module of intelligence. Similar evidence that intelligences are separated comes from cases of ***acquired savant syndrome***. In these cases, brain damage actually causes a sudden heightening of ability in a particular area, which may mean that inhibition of some brain regions (via injury) has the potential to boost performance in other areas. This doesn't mean that you should start bashing your head against a wall in hopes of boosting your math scores, but perhaps there is a way to harness this inhibition on a temporary basis. At the end of this chapter we'll look at transcranial stimulation, which may allow us to temporarily knock out specific brain regions in order to allow others to shine.

While these cases of damage suggest a separation of skills, they don't necessarily suggest that overall development is not still influenced by some single underlying factor (like g). Specific damage demonstrates that some types of intelligence may be isolated in their localization in the brain but this doesn't provide conclusive evidence that these types of intelligence develop separately.

Even if we accept that there are separate multiple intelligences this still doesn't necessarily provide us with clear definitions of what intelligence is. For instance, if we were to agree on some definition of intelligence which included bodily-kinesthetic abilities, we would still have the problem of how to define this particular area and then how to assess it. Should bodily-kinesthetic intelligence include reaction time, muscle fiber types, balance, endurance, or hand-eye coordination? Should we assess Michael Jordan's bodily-kinesthetic intelligence based on his basketball playing or his baseball playing? How do we separate this intelligence from specific skills developed through extensive practice? If I practice free-throws for hours each day, I will probably improve at least a little bit, but has my bodily-kinesthetic intelligence improved, or just this specific skill? Is there a difference?

Robert Sternberg has suggested that our definitions of intelligence should really be focused on those abilities which bring us overall success in living. Excellent performance on math or reasoning questions may not accurately predict success in dealing with real-life problems, and a practical measure of intelligence should reflect this. In real life, problems aren't clearly defined and almost never have single solutions. We're often on our own in defining the problems we face, generating multiple solutions for these problems, and then weighing a number of factors in determining which courses of action we should implement and how we should adjust those courses along the way.

Sternberg's *triarchic theory of intelligence* proposes 3 main types of intelligence: *analytical* intelligence; the ability to generate solutions to specific problems, *creative* intelligence; the ability to generate novel solutions, and *practical* intelligence; the ability to choose the most appropriate solutions based on the situation and context. Practical intelligence means recognizing that the "best" answer isn't always the same as the "correct" answer, such as knowing when to accept your boss's flawed decision, when to tell your friend a new outfit looks great (when it doesn't), or when to give up fighting an argument even though logic is on your side.

This brings us to consider the possible role of emotional intelligence, first proposed by Peter Salovey and John Mayer (no, not that John Mayer), though perhaps most associated with Daniel Goleman, who has written several popular books on the subject. *Emotional intelligence* emphasizes the importance of recognizing, expressing, managing, and using emotions. The ability to console a friend, conceal contempt for a co-worker, or deliver a rousing speech can influence our likelihood of success and therefore could be considered a fundamental part of behaving intelligently.

A final idea for defining intelligence comes from Raymond Cattell, who used factor analysis to distinguish between fluid intelligence and crystallized intelligence. **Fluid intelligence** refers to the capacity to solve new problems and incorporate new information effectively. **Crystallized intelligence**, on the other hand, refers to specific knowledge and skills that have been accumulated through experience.

Imagine that you're an avid video gamer who has logged many, many (perhaps too many) hours playing Call of Duty. Now you purchase a new first-person shooter game. You are delighted to find that the controls for this new game are identical to those for Call of Duty. Your immediate success in the early levels of this new game could be attributed to your *crystallized intelligence*. You have previously accumulated specific skills in using this controller layout, and these existing skills can be applied directly to the new game. In later levels, however, you find that none of your old strategies from Call of Duty seem to be working, and you are forced to use your *fluid intelligence* to adapt to these new circumstances and come up with novel solutions in order to beat these levels.

Assessing Intelligence

Even if psychologists can't quite agree on the perfect definition of what intelligence is or should be, this hasn't stopped them from attempting to measure it. This desire to measure first and ask questions later is true for many other psychological traits, abilities, and processes. The study and design of testing for abilities and traits, including personality traits (which will be addressed in the next chapter), is known as **psychometrics**, and a person doing the investigating would be a **psychometrician**.

Test Types

In designing an intelligence assessment, I may want to know the level of difficulty that someone is capable of solving. In this case, I would probably look at whether a person is able to solve a particularly difficult puzzle or not. This would be considered a **power test**. In this context *power* refers to how well a measurement can differentiate results.

A question that everyone can solve has low power because it doesn't tell us anything about how people differ. A question that some people can solve and others can't solve allows us to make finer distinctions between people and therefore would have higher power.

Designing tests isn't just about the questions but also includes other factors like time. Questions with low power may still be useful if you want to see how quickly someone can solve a number of simple puzzles. You could measure how many puzzles a person is able to solve in some set amount of time. This would be considered a **speed test** rather than a power test. In this case, it's ok if you use questions that everyone can solve (low power) because you're differentiating people based on their speed, not on whether they can answer the question.

Most tests you take in school measure knowledge or skills that you have learned, so they would be considered **achievement tests**. IQ tests are generally intended to be **aptitude tests**; tests that predict potential ability. Predicting ability is far more challenging than simply measuring achievement, which is why the design and implementation of intelligence tests can be controversial. While a low score on an achievement test may simply indicate someone hasn't learned something *yet*, a low score on an aptitude test could be interpreted as meaning the person is incapable of ever learning something. This interpretation may have major implications for a person's future, so we have to be particularly cautious when it comes to designing aptitude tests and drawing conclusions from them.

Whenever we consider some hypothetical construct or property like "intelligence" there are three points we should examine closely: The **property** (which we think exists), the **behaviors** we associate with this property (the observable behaviors that make us think it exists in the first place), and finally, **responses to assessments** aimed at measuring this property.

As we consider these three points, we can question the relationships between them. Do those behaviors really represent the property? Does this assessment actually relate to the property? If the answer to both of those questions seems to be yes, then we should find a clear relationship between the assessment and the actual behaviors. In other words, if grades truly reflect intelligence, and an IQ test is actually assessing intelligence, then we should find a relationship between grades and IQ scores. Ideally this relationship would always hold, but of course, we can imagine exceptions; the brilliant prodigy so bored in class she doesn't bother doing assignments (high IQ score but low grades) or the charming student whose charisma earns him higher grades than his IQ score might otherwise predict (low IQ score but high grades).

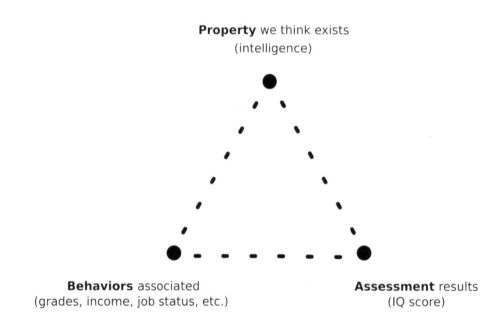

Validity

As with any variable we investigate, we want to reduce the possibility of bias and error in our assessment of intelligence. When it comes to intelligence tests, there are a number of techniques we can use to try to ensure validity and reliability.

Validity refers to making sure that the test actually measures what we want to measure. It's tough to determine how to define intelligence, but once we've decided upon a possible definition, we want to design a test which will actually measure it. While there are a lot of terms for different types of validity, this is not to torture you with a laundry list of definitions. Once learned, these terms will make it easier to talk about potential flaws in a test. Ideally we could satisfy all the types of validity below, but in practice, most tests can be criticized in at least one of these areas.

Construct validity refers to ensuring that there is actually a relationship between what we measure on a test and the property (or construct) of intelligence. We want to be sure that there is a relationship between what we're measuring and what we're claiming to assess. This is probably the most essential of the types of validity discussed here, because without a clear relationship to the property, even the most carefully-collected data is useless for drawing conclusions.

Face validity refers to a surface-level assessment that a test relates to what it is intended to measure. For instance, if I wanted to assess an artist's skill, I might create a test of different brush techniques. It would be easy to see that this test is inappropriate for assessing the skill of a chef, but for an artist it seems to make sense. This doesn't mean my test is a detailed assessment of artistic skill, just that it looks like it is related to the property I'm interested in.

To consider the validity of a test more carefully, ***content validity*** (also referred to as *logical validity*) asks whether the test is comprehensive enough to cover all the aspects needed to assess the property in question. In the case of artistic skill, I'm going to need to assess more than just brush strokes, because we all know that there is more to artistic skill than brush technique. Content validity can be problematic for assessing intelligence because concepts of what should be considered intelligence can be quite broad. An intelligence test which only assessed verbal abilities could have face validity (those abilities appear to be related to intelligence) but this test would be lacking in content validity because it fails to assess many other abilities which are also related to the concept of intelligence. Even fairly comprehensive IQ tests available today could be argued to lack content validity for their failures to fully assess creativity, divergent thinking, emotional intelligence or practical intelligence.

Finally, we may wonder how well a test compares to other assessments and how well it predicts future events, known as **criterion-related validity**. This can be divided into two main components. **Concurrent validity** refers to whether a test's results match up with other related results at the same time. For instance, if you took an IQ test today, I might want to know how your score relates to your current grades in school (just remember that *concurrent* means existing simultaneously). **Predictive validity**, however, assesses how well a test can predict future outcomes, like whether your childhood IQ score can predict your later SAT results, or whether your SAT results can predict your later college performance, etc. (remember it is about *predicting* future outcomes).

Reliability

Reliability refers to the idea that if I measure the same object with the same measure, I should get the same result. There are a few ways to assess this for intelligence. One way would be to look at the test questions themselves.

Split-half reliability consists of randomly splitting a test into two halves, then calculating two separate scores. If the questions are randomly divided, on average test-takers should receive about the same score on each half. If the two half-scores are drastically different for many test-takers, this would indicate a possible lack of reliability.

Test-retest reliability refers to a single participant completing an entire test on more than one occasion, then comparing the scores. If you're measuring the same person, you should get roughly the same result each time. This technique can also help to identify the possible presence of bias in test administration. For instance, if many people receive lower scores when retesting with a particular examiner, that might indicate bias on the part of the examiner, rather than an actual drop in all participant IQs.

If people will take the same exam more than once, we need to have different versions of the test. Otherwise, there's a chance that scores could improve simply as a result of some participants already knowing the answers. Naturally, we need to ensure that alternate versions of the test are still assessing the same thing in the same way. We need to ensure that we have **equivalent form reliability**. The SAT provides a great example of this. The test needs to be different each time, since students can take the exam more than once, but each version needs to be the same level of difficulty in order to compare scores among many students.

This brings us to a related point. In considering the validity and reliability of a test, we need to consider more than just the test itself, we need to consider who is taking the test and how it is being scored. We want a test to be **standardized**, meaning that the rules for administering and scoring the test are clearly dictated. The SAT, SAT II, ACT, and Advanced Placement Exams are well-known examples of tests that are standardized.

We also want to ensure that a test is appropriate for the people it is intended for. For a test like the SAT, we want to know how actual high school students will respond to the questions. We need to test these questions with a sample of high school students, who would be the **standardization sample**. This is something that the SAT does regularly, in fact it does so with a very **representative sample**; actual SAT test-takers. New experimental questions are added to the tests students take, but these have no influence on scores. Instead, these questions are assessed for possible use on future exams. In scoring, **norms** are established for which questions are of the appropriate difficulty and how scores will be calculated and compared.

A Brief History of Intelligence Testing

Now that's we've got the vocabulary for discussing assessment and psychometrics, let's take a brief tour through the history of different attempts to assess intelligence, followed by an overview of the main intelligence tests used by psychometricians today.

We'll begin with **Sir Francis Galton**, a half-cousin of Charles Darwin and a man obsessed with the measurement of man. Spurred by his relative's idea of natural selection, Galton believed that high intelligence was inherited and he spent years studying the genealogical histories of eminent minds (detailed in his book *Hereditary Genius* in 1869). Galton thought that in order to be passed down, intelligence must offer survival advantages and these advantages might be seen in physiological measurements. Galton invented the technique for calculating correlation, then measured reaction times, sensory acuity, muscular power, and even the body proportions and head sizes of thousands of people in an attempt to connect these physical traits to intelligence (which is why Galton is generally considered the founder of psychometrics). Despite his best efforts, however, Galton was unable to provide convincing evidence that any of these traits were strongly correlated with mental ability.

As the 19th century drew to a close, the French education system was dealing with a great difficulty. Education reforms meant that thousands of French children would receive mandatory free schooling, but a lack of previous education meant that many of these students were quite far behind. The wide variety of education levels meant that students couldn't simply be lumped together by age. Schools needed to identify which students would be able to catch up through remedial classes and determine how to place students appropriately. In order to identify and help those children who could benefit most, **Alfred Binet** (pronounced *Bih-nay*) worked to design assessments. This goal led to collaboration with **Theodore Simon** (try your best French accent – *See-mohn*) to create a multi-faceted examination. This **Binet-Simon test** compared a child's skills to the performance of children of different ages. This allowed Binet and Simon to compare children based on **mental age**. For instance, a precocious child of 8 who was able to perform as well as children aged 12 was said to have a mental age of 12. If, on the other hand, a 12 year-old only performed as well as most 10 year-old children, he would have a mental age of 10.

This concept of mental age was adopted by the German psychologist **William Stern**, who used it to calculate an **Intelligence Quotient**, or **IQ**. Stern divided mental age by chronological age, then multiplied that result by 100. If a child had a mental age of 5 and was actually five years old (chronological age), this would give a value of 1 (5/5), which, multiplied by 100, would give an IQ of 100. A five-year old performing at a mental age of 6, however, would end up with an IQ of (6/5) * 100 = 120.

This type of calculation, known as a **ratio IQ score**, worked pretty well for comparing children. After all, a 5 year-old who can perform as well as most 8 year-olds certainly would seem to be highly intelligent, while a 9 year-old performing at a 6 year-old level could indicate low intelligence. The problem arises once ages pass a certain point. At younger ages, just one year of mental age can mean a great deal of difference in abilities. But what's the difference between a mental age of 18 and 19? What would it mean for a 60 year-old to perform at the level of most 30 year-olds? Wouldn't that be a good thing? In this equation the denominator (chronological age) is always increasing at a steady rate, while the numerator may not be, meaning that scores would appear to continuously drop with age. One way around this was to use a chronological age of 20 for all adults in order to compare them, but this wasn't an ideal solution.

Psychometricians no longer rely on ratio IQ. Standard IQ tests today calculate what's known as a **deviation IQ score**. A deviation IQ score is calculated by dividing an individual's score by the average score of all test-takers within that age range, then multiplying the result by 100. This is why the average IQ score will always be 100; if your score matches the average for your group, this will divide to give you 1, which, multiplied by 100, gives you a deviation IQ score of 100. If you perform better than the group average, your IQ will be above 100, and if you score worse then it will be below 100. Even if everyone's raw test scores improved by 10 points, the average IQ would still be 100 (though as we'll see later, this makes comparing scores over time more difficult).

Because your IQ score is only compared to those within your age group, IQ scores aren't meant to be assessments of intellectual ability across age ranges. In other words, a 5 year-old child with an IQ of 130 might not be able to solve problems that an 18 year-old with an IQ of only 90 can solve. Remember that IQ is meant to be about aptitude, so a high score at a young age doesn't mean that the child actually has more skills, but rather, the child is believed to have a greater potential to develop skills in the future.

In the United States, Alfred Binet's work in creating assessments was taken up by ***Lewis Terman*** at Stanford University. Drawing on the Binet-Simon test, combined with Stern's calculation of ratio IQ, Terman created the ***Stanford-Binet Intelligence Scale*** in 1916, and it is still in use today (though now in its 5th edition and calculating deviation IQ scores, not ratio IQ scores). Terman is perhaps best known for initiating a longitudinal study in 1921 which aimed to identify the long-term predictive ability of IQ assessment. Terman believed that while educational environment did play a role in reaching one's fullest IQ potential, intelligence was mostly determined by heredity and thus could be identified at an early age.

Terman assessed 168,000 children, then followed 1,500 with exceptionally high scores (above 135 on the Stanford-Binet test) throughout their lives. This was a change from previous methods of considering the relationship between intelligence and success, which were mostly done by studying successful adults and attempting to retrace their childhood experiences and family histories (such as Galton's genealogical studies).

Terman tracked the educational outcomes, occupational status, income levels, and achievements of his high-IQ children (who were affectionately referred to as his "Termites") compared to average-scoring children to determine just how much childhood IQ mattered to later life (in fact the study is ongoing with the remaining survivors). Terman hoped results would dispel the notion that childhood geniuses were socially inept or tended to burn out and he believed that early high IQ could predict later success. Terman did find that these children tended to do better in life than their peers; they published more academic papers and novels, registered more patents, received higher educations, job status, and earned higher incomes, though their high IQ wasn't a guarantee of success and not all of his Termites lived happily ever after. IQ also wasn't a guarantee of truly world-class scholarship and Terman didn't find any Nobel prize winners among his 1,500 child geniuses. Ironically, William Shockley was a young child tested by Terman who didn't score high enough to become a "Termite", though he did go on to win a Nobel prize in Physics.

While the Stanford-Binet test developed by Terman is still in use, the most commonly administered intelligence test today is the ***Wechsler Adult Intelligence Scale*** (WAIS), first developed by David Wechsler in 1939 (as the *Wechsler-Bellevue Intelligence Scale*) and currently in its 4th edition. In addition to the WAIS, there are two other versions designed for younger children: the ***Wechsler Intelligence Scale for Children*** (WISC), and the ***Wechsler Preschool and Primary Scale of Intelligence*** (WPPSI). The Wechsler scales all test multiple abilities and include verbal and performance-based assessments. Despite what you might see in popular depictions of IQ testing, these tests are not predominantly pencil-and-paper exams and they are administered in person by a trained psychologist. The WAIS-IV consists of 10 core sub-tests (and 5 supplemental sub-tests) assessing areas such as general knowledge, word meanings, memory, and rule application. The majority of these sub-tests do not involve any writing, and none involve writing words.

IQ Differences

IQ scores differ and this is what makes IQ worth studying. Intelligence tests are all about differentiation. If everyone got all the questions correct, or everyone got all the questions wrong, everyone would have the same IQ score, and as a result, IQ scores would be meaningless. We want IQ scores to be as different as possible, because that means we're able to generate finer distinctions between people.

This push for differentiation may create a problem when it comes to interpreting IQ scores. Perhaps the tendency to emphasize differences leads test-creators to create artificial distinctions between people whose intelligences aren't really that different (though their IQ scores may be). In other words, the difference in intelligence between two people, one who scores 100 and one who scores 104 may actually be negligible. While it's great that a test can discriminate between these two people's abilities, this doesn't necessarily imply any practical difference in their intelligences.

This is not to suggest that IQ scores don't provide information about individuals, but rather that there are a number of caveats to keep in mind when it comes to interpreting score differences. That said, let's look at how scores are usually analyzed, and then we can consider what differences in scores may mean for understanding individuals.

Individual Variation

When we look at the frequency of different scores on IQ tests, as well as many other traits, ranging from height or weight to personality traits, they tend to be distributed in something close to a **normal curve** or **bell curve**. This means that scores in the middle of the range are the most frequent, and the frequency of extreme scores falls off symmetrically in both directions. Very low scores are rare and very high scores are rare, so most scores are clustered around the mean. As we saw in the calculation of deviation IQ, the average IQ score is 100. The standard deviation for IQ tends to be about 15 points. This means that most people have an IQ score close to 100, and about 68% of people will be within 15 points of 100 in either direction (from 85 to 115).

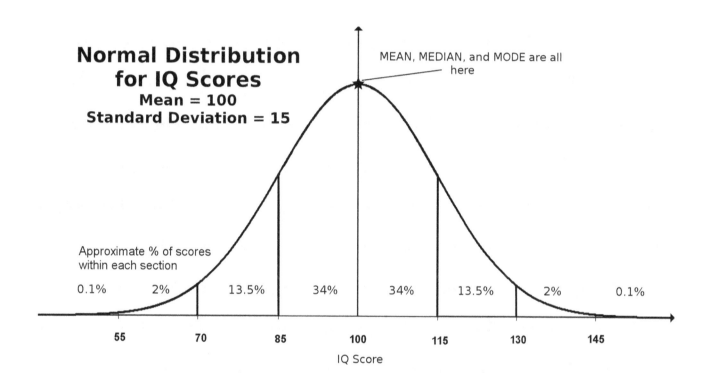

Knowing that IQ follows a normal distribution with a standard deviation of about 15 means that one can also estimate a **percentile score**. A percentile score lets an individual know how his or her score compares to everyone else who took the test by telling what percentage of people received lower scores. An IQ score of 100 would be in the 50th percentile, because half of the test-takers scored below this point (which means that half also scored above). An IQ score of 115 would be around the 84th percentile, because about 84% of test-takers would score below this level. Just remember that higher percentile scores indicate better performance, while lower percentile scores indicate worse performance compared to other test-takers. You may be familiar with percentile scores if you've taken the SAT, as the College Board includes a percentile score in your score report.

So what can be said about individuals who score above, below, or at the mean? What predictions can we make about other behaviors? What real-life outcomes are associated with IQ scores?

It turns out that an IQ score can act as a fairly good predictor of future success. Higher IQ is associated with a number of positive outcomes ranging from education level, job status, income, and job performance. While it could be argued that many of the above consequences are too closely related (higher IQ leads to higher grades which lead to better college acceptances which lead to better job opportunities and higher pay), higher IQ is also related to somewhat unexpected consequences such as greater longevity. Perhaps we could see this as the ultimate measure of "success in living" as those with higher IQ generally manage to live longer. Whether this increased longevity is a result of better "system integrity", health management, accident and disease prevention, or access to greater resources is still open to debate, though we may expect that all of these factors (and perhaps others) play a role.

IQ is also correlated with other more directly observable phenomena and individuals with higher IQ are able to correctly judge line lengths and differentiate colors and tones with shorter "inspection time" than others and these individuals also show faster and less variable reaction times to a number of different stimuli. These results suggest that despite flaws and controversies around what intelligence is and how it can be tested, IQ scores actually reveal some ways in which individuals differ and scores do allow some behavioral predictions.

IQ Extremes

IQ extremes can be defined in a statistical manner, according to the normal curve. Once a score is more than 2 standard deviations (30 points) away from the mean, it can be considered to be exceptional, as only about 2-3% of scores will fall into these ranges in either direction.

High levels of intelligence are referred to as ***intellectual giftedness***. While this is often considered to be IQs over 130 (2 standard deviations above the mean) there is no precise score value that defines *giftedness*, and as the rest of this chapter has already indicated, conceptions of intelligence can vary widely. So what does giftedness mean? Despite some popular misconceptions, intellectual giftedness does not necessarily imply introversion, poor social skills, or depression. In fact, most people with high IQ seem to be well-adjusted and have fulfilling work, family, and social lives. Giftedness generally refers to children who have the ability to learn material quickly, with fewer repetitions, and in more broad areas compared to their peers.

People with IQs below 70 are considered to have an ***intellectual disability*** (**ID**). This was previously regarded as the cutoff point for *mental retardation*, but this term is no longer used. The farther below 70 an individual's score, the more severe the disability tends to be, though extremely low scores (more than 3 standard deviations below the mean) are difficult to assess reliably.

What Causes IQ Differences?

When we think about IQ differences, we inevitably wonder what causes these differences. You probably already know that the answer won't be as simple as "genes" or "environment", but rather a complex interaction of these forces.

Evidence for genetic influence on intelligence comes from twin and family studies which have demonstrated that identical twins tend to have more similar intelligence scores than fraternal twins, who in turn are more similar than random unrelated individuals. It seems that the more genes people share, the more similar their IQ scores are. Twin studies can also tell us about the importance of the environment by comparing shared vs. nonshared environments. Will identical twins raised in different homes still have similar IQ scores? Will two non-related adoptive children have more similar IQ scores when they are raised in the same home environment?

Studies of monozygotic (identical) twins raised in the same home have found an IQ score correlation of 0.85 but a correlation of 0.6 for dizygotic (fraternal) twins raised together. Nonbiological siblings raised in the same home show an IQ score correlation of only 0.25 in childhood and this correlation drops to zero by adulthood, suggesting that an early shared environment does not have a powerful long-lasting effect on general cognitive ability (Plomin et al, 2013 p.30, p.97).

From these types of studies, researchers calculate a heritability score to represent the strength of genetic and environmental influences. Heritability scores can range from 0 to 1 and tell us how much of the variance in a particular trait can be explained by genetic forces. The heritability score for IQ is generally estimated to be somewhere around 0.5 which means that about half of the variance in IQ scores in the population is due to genetic factors. Remember that the concept of heritability is not about individuals; heritability only tells us about groups. It doesn't explain the scores themselves, it explains why the scores differ. Saying that heritability is 0.5 doesn't mean that half of your IQ score comes from your genes, or even that your genes account for half of your intelligence. A heritability score of 0.5 means that when we attempt to answer the question of why people have different IQs, the fact that people have different genes provides about 50 percent of the explanation, while differences in environments account for the other half.

We should also remember that heritability scores vary. When environments are more similar, genes may matter more. For example, if all students had equal nutrition, identical educational opportunities, the same parenting, etc. then any differences in their IQ scores would mostly come from their differing genes (so heritability would be high). If students had very different environments (some went to school, others didn't, some were malnourished, others weren't) then these environmental differences would contribute more to explaining any IQ differences, and thus the heritability score for this population would be lower. Heritability for intelligence has been shown to increase with age and heritability scores as high as 0.8 have been calculated in older populations, suggesting that genes may have a snowball effect of increasing influence over time.

A heritability score doesn't identify which genes or which aspects of the environment are involved. At this point, other than identifying genes for specific disorders which affect cognitive development (discussed below), we don't have particularly precise ideas of which individual genes are "responsible" for IQ and it seems exceedingly unlikely that there is a single intelligence gene. Intelligence is likely the result of the complex interactions between *many* genes and *many* environmental factors.

The role of genes can be seen in genetic and chromosomal abnormalities which are known to affect intelligence and cognitive development. **Down Syndrome** is a disorder that results from an extra copy of the 21st chromosome (known as *trisomy*) and causes cognitive impairments and other symptoms. Down Syndrome is one of the most common causes of intellectual disability, affecting about 1 in 1,000 births. Down Syndrome is the result of a mutation, and thus is genetic but not actually *inherited* and does not run in families (sufferers of Down Syndrome are infertile and thus do not pass on the disorder; each case represents a new incidence of the mutation).

Fragile X syndrome, resulting from repeated triplets of base pairs on the X chromosome, is the second most common cause of cognitive disability, affecting approximately 1 in 5,000 males (and 1 in 10,000 females). It is the most common *inherited* cause of cognitive impairment (repeated triplets can build up over successive generations, meaning that incidence increases over time).

Another case of genetic influence on IQ is **Williams Syndrome**, a disorder caused by the deletion of a number of genes on chromosome 7, affecting about 1 in 10,000 births. Williams Syndrome is an intriguing example because it highlights the difficulties of defining what "intelligence" means. People with Williams Syndrome tend to score below 70 on IQ tests and have difficulty with everyday tasks such as counting, tying their shoes, or determining left from right. Yet, these same people often show exceptional gifts in areas of language and music which defy our usual expectations for people with low IQ scores and raise questions about how genes may influence different areas of cognitive development.

Another example highlights the importance of the interaction between genes and environment in understanding intellectual development. **Phenylketonuria** (PKU) is a genetic mutation which prevents the body from making *phenylalanine hydroxylase* (*PAH*), an enzyme that breaks down phenylalanine, a common substance found in many foods which can be toxic to neurons. Most people naturally produce this enzyme and as a result, consuming phenylalanine is harmless. Those with PKU, however, accumulate toxic levels of phenylalanine, destroying neurons and stunting their intellectual development. While this sounds entirely genetic, the key idea here is that by controlling the environment (avoiding foods with phenylalanine), the risk of cognitive impairment is greatly reduced. Despite obvious genetic factors, environmental interaction is still fundamental for understanding PKU's influence on development.

Now imagine that instead of a single gene, we had hundreds of genes that each might be involved in intelligence in different ways. Each gene may help or hinder cognitive development, depending on interaction with hundreds of other environmental factors. The same environmental factor could trigger the expression of one gene while inhibiting another. The "best" environment could depend on one's genes, or the "best" genes could depend on features of one's environment. Now we begin to see the mind-boggling level of complexity involved in understanding the role of genes on something as broad as intelligence.

There is not necessarily a single way that genes operate and the environment is almost always fundamental for understanding traits and behaviors, even when specific genes are known to be involved. This applies whether we are trying to understand the role of genes on intelligence, a personality trait, or a mental disorder.

Interpreting Group Differences

We've already seen that individual IQ scores vary. If we were to collect IQ scores from many different people, we might not be surprised to find that some groups of people (such as neurosurgeons) outscore other groups of people (such as janitors). We might even use this information to estimate someone's IQ based on their group membership (so without any other information, I might guess that a neurosurgeon's IQ is fairly high). But we may find ourselves more hesitant when we consider the possibility of group variation in IQ scores according to gender, nationality, or ethnicity. How do these groups differ when it comes to average IQ scores, and how can we interpret these differences?

Potential group differences also complicate the question of exam design, even before we begin to consider the social and political implications of research on this sensitive topic. Our social ideals and our scientific objectivity may occasionally appear at odds with one another. Addressing our scientific curiosity to understand how people differ has the potential to uncover differences we might prefer not to discover. We may also wonder whether we are really uncovering fundamental ways that humans can vary or if our current methods for collecting or analyzing data are flawed.

While we don't want hindsight to reveal that we were blinded by an overly-idealist preconception of complete equality, we also don't want to jump to hasty conclusions that could potentially marginalize entire groups of people or limit their opportunities. Perhaps the best we can do is admit the complexity of the questions we face and proceed with caution.

What do we do when tests reveal differences between groups of people? A big part of this question is tied to atrocities that have been committed by those who have used flawed intelligence research to rationalize racism and legitimize discrimination. The history of group differences in intelligence testing is a dark one, as early researchers combined views of heredity with a distorted interpretation of natural selection in order to promote the concept of **eugenics**; a belief in the inherent racial superiority of certain groups (this term was actually coined by Sir Francis Galton himself, the Greek prefix *eu* added to *genic* to refer to "good genes").

The eugenics movement suggested that the human gene pool could be improved by only allowing the reproduction of those believed to be superior. This was sometimes also referred to as *social Darwinism* – a disgrace to Darwin's good name. To be clear, Darwin's notion of natural selection doesn't necessarily suggest inherent superiority or inferiority and the oft-used expression "survival of the fittest" (not coined by Darwin) should refer to organisms best suited to their living environment with the "fittest" referring to the "best fit" not the "most fit". A particular trait may be advantageous in some environments but not others, so a "best fit" at a particular time isn't necessarily a sign of inherent superiority of that trait.

While eugenicists used early IQ results as evidence of racial inferiority, it's quite likely that bias was to blame for the group differences observed. **Robert M. Yerkes** (pronounced *Yer-keys*) formed a committee including Lewis Terman and Henry Goddard to create intelligence tests that were eventually used on over 1.75 million army recruits during the first world war. Many of these recruits were recent immigrants to the United States, and their results were used to place them in ranks and determine their suitability for officer training. There were two tests designed by Yerkes, the Army Alpha test, for literate soldiers, and the Army Beta test, for those who were illiterate.

Ideally, these tests would have been administered in a standardized way, but this was not the case. In "A Nation of Morons" Stephen Jay Gould suggested that incorrect test forms were often used (giving the Alpha test to those who probably should have taken the Beta) and that procedures weren't standardized for instructions, timing of sections, or even scoring. For the Beta test, Gould noted "The Beta examination contained only pictures, numbers and symbols. But it still required pencil work and, on three of its seven parts, a knowledge of numbers and how to write them." As a result, scores were inaccurate and the average mental age of an army recruit was about 13. In this first mass-produced intelligence test, there were really two types of bias occurring. There was bias in the administration of the exams, and there was also cultural bias in the formation of test questions.

Those who had been living in the United States longer performed better on the Alpha Test, while more recent immigrants struggled with questions that had nothing to do with innate intelligence, such as "*Cornell University* is at: *Ithaca Cambridge Annapolis New Haven*" and " *'There's a reason'* is an "ad" for a: *drink revolver flour cleanser*".

In retrospect, the obvious cultural bias in these questions seems almost comical but the implications were far from funny. Unfortunately, the eugenics movement developed powerful political influence in the United States, and played a role in the adoption of the Immigration Act of 1924, which restricted the immigration of people from southern and eastern European countries. This immigration policy prevented millions of people from escaping the later rise of fascism and its adoption was also seen as endorsement of the "science" of eugenics.

It's tempting to look back and think that the eugenics movement must have been the result of second-rate scientists, but this isn't the case. Eugenics provided a way to rationalize racism and warped the views of some of the most eminent minds, including Nobel Laureate William Shockley, who supported sterilization, and fellow Nobel Laureate Konrad Lorenz, who wrote:

"Usually, a man of high value is disgusted with special intensity by slight symptoms of degeneracy in men of the other race...The selection for toughness, heroism, social utility...must be accomplished by some human institution if mankind, in default of selective factors, is not to be ruined by domestication-induced degeneracy. The racial idea as the basis of our state has already accomplished much in this respect..." Lorenz (1940), quoted in Lerner (1992) p. 63-64

This "human institution" referred to **artificial selection** to refine the gene pool and remove the "bad" genes believed to be holding the human species back. This was done by controlling the reproduction of those believed to be inferior, resulting in tens of thousands of sterilizations in the United States. The mentally ill, those on the fringes of society (such as prostitutes and criminals), members of ethnic minorities, and people with disabilities believed to be of genetic origin had their reproductive rights taken from them forcibly and sometimes without their knowledge.

The widespread adoption of eugenic policies by Nazis during the 1930s is common knowledge, but the early precedents set by American eugenicists and the fact that some sterilization practices continued into the 1970s is less well-known. It's not a pleasant part of the past to ponder, but it should provide us an important warning of the possible ramifications when discriminatory beliefs are allowed to masquerade as science. We should never forget that psychometric tests have been used as justification for discrimination and violation of basic human rights.

While early group differences can be mostly attributed to bias in the administration, scoring, and interpretation of tests, bias doesn't seem to account for group differences found in modern test results. Bias in testing design has been greatly reduced in the past few decades (some might say eliminated) and yet we still find performance gaps on the basis of race and gender. Are modern tests really providing an accurate depiction of differing abilities? What might be causing these performance gaps and how should we interpret them?

Gender Gaps

When we compare male and female performance on IQ tests, we don't find a difference in general intelligence and average scores are comparable. That said, studies have found that each gender has a tendency to do better on certain types of tasks. In a summary of this research, Diane Halpern noted that males tend to outperform females on tasks involving visual and spatial transformations, some motor skills, fluid reasoning, and abstract scientific reasoning while females tend to perform better than males on tasks involving semantic information, complex prose, fine motor skills, and perceptual speed of verbal information. Another interesting gender difference is that males tend to be overrepresented in extreme scores and males are more frequently diagnosed with learning disabilities than females (Halpern, 1997). This may be partly explained by the prevalence of disorders such as Fragile X syndrome (discussed above), which is more common in males.

So what do these gender differences mean? Well, first we must remember that these differences are only about group tendencies, not individuals. There are millions of females who can outperform most males in abstract reasoning and millions of males who outperform most females in production and comprehension of complex language. Even so, we may wonder what is causing these overall group differences.

Addressing this question is complex because being male or female affects a huge number of other variables that may play a role in intelligence development. It's not just that males and females have different genes, different hormones, different levels of risk-taking, or that they spend different amounts of time on different activities; it's also relevant that cultural expectations and preferences exert pressure on the options and opportunities available for males and females. In fact, countries which are more gender-neutral tend to have smaller performance gaps. With all of these factors combined, it's clear that observed differences in task performance are not simply genetic and are the result of a complex biopsychosocial process which is not yet fully understood.

Race Gaps

When comparing the IQ distributions of different racial groups, researchers have found consistent performance gaps. Might these differences in average performance be caused by genetic differences between races?

In their book *The Bell Curve*, Richard Herrnstein and Charles Murray (1994) suggested genetic factors could be responsible for observed racial differences in IQ and suggested using intelligence scores in the formation of social policies. Subsequent critiques challenged many of Murray and Herrnstein's assumptions, as well as their statistics and data analysis. In response to the controversy, a series of statements signed by a group of intelligence researchers was published in the Wall Street Journal which acknowledged that the normal curve for blacks was approximately 15 points lower than whites, with Hispanics somewhere between those two, and the curves for Jewish and Asian groups perhaps higher (Arvey et al, 1994).

This response was criticized for appearing to support some of Herrnstein and Murray's claims and the American Psychological Association created a task force to report on the current state of intelligence research. This report (Neisser et al, 1996) clarified that the causes for group differences are not known and emphasized the possible roles of socioeconomic status and culture, noting that even when some within-group differences are genetic this does not mean that genes explain average differences between groups. In addition, the report noted that disadvantaged groups in caste-like systems tend to have lower scores than dominant groups, even when these groups are not considered racially distinct.

Some evidence indicates that the 15 point Black/White gap has closed somewhat since the publication of *The Bell Curve*. More recent estimates put the gap around 10 points and suggest it may continue to close (Dickens and Flynn, 2006). James Flynn has also suggested that the higher average estimates for Asian populations have been miscalculated due to improperly normed tests and nonrepresentative samples. Nevertheless, at present, performance gaps persist. What should we make of these differences?

What is Race?

A fundamental assumption for considering group differences by race is that race is a category that can be used to group people. But just how useful is a racial category like "black" or "white"? In terms of genetics, skin color certainly can't tell the whole story, especially when we consider that black-skinned Africans have more in common genetically with light-skinned Europeans than they do with similarly-black-skinned Australian aborigines.

While there are genetic differences between people that lead to what we might identify as "race", these differences are far from clear-cut. Ancestries get complicated quickly and the lines between supposedly different races are blurred. Racial categorizations aren't being made by any sort of genetic evaluation, they're often self-selected by an individual checking a box on a form. When it comes to what being "black" means, it's worth noting that "Almost all Americans who identify themselves as black have white ancestors" (Arvey et al, 1994). The same can be said of many other supposedly distinct racial groups. As Sternberg, Grigorenko, Kidd, and Kenneth noted in their review on intelligence, race, and genetics: "Race is a socially constructed concept, not a biological one. It derives from people's desire to classify."

Environmental Forces

As we saw with gender, performance gaps may also be influenced by differing cultural pressures. For example, the fact that Asian students routinely outscore their white American counterparts in mathematics might suggest genetics at first glance, but when we consider that Asian students spend approximately 30% more class and homework time on math, we might be more likely to consider the gap a result of environmental differences.

James Flynn has found that IQ scores have risen dramatically throughout the past decades, with the average score gaining approximately 0.3 points each year, or 3 points per decade, a phenomenon referred to as the *Flynn Effect*. Tests are constantly rescaled so the average has stayed at 100, though questions have become more challenging. This means that a person who scores 100 today would score above average compared to earlier test-takers. If we extrapolate from this increase, however, we might wonder whether we are now a nation of geniuses, or whether our ancestors really were a nation of morons. Are we really getting this much smarter this quickly?

What could account for this increase? It's probably not genes; it's far too rapid for higher IQ to be selected for. More likely, it's a number of other factors. Improvements in nutrition are certainly part of the explanation. This can be seen in developing countries; as nutrition improves and fewer children are malnourished, average IQ rises. It has even been suggested that the introduction of iodine into table salt was responsible for several points of average IQ increase in the United States by preventing cases of iodine deficiency disorder and the intellectual impairment it causes.

Education is another factor. Most people today have far higher levels of education than was common just a few decades ago. Flynn has noted that in addition to more time spent in school, the type of education we receive has also changed. Modern schools place great emphasis on abstract reasoning, and this is something that wasn't as important in the past. Many people in previous generations weren't considering purely hypothetical situations in order to make decisions but now young children are trained to do this day after day, year after year.

When we see how environmental forces can create gaps between groups of people over time, it becomes easier to see how environmental influences could be related to the group performance gaps that we see today. It's probably not the case that the smart are getting smarter but rather that lower scoring individuals who were previously holding the average down (due to factors like poor nutrition, lack of educational opportunity, testing bias, etc.) now have far greater opportunities to demonstrate their true potential. Evidence also suggests that the Flynn Effect has been slowing in recent years, but perhaps this can be seen as a triumph of the greater equalization of opportunity. Those who had previously been held back have made significant gains and we are now closer to a level playing field than ever before.

Expectations Matter

Perhaps gender or race-based expectations may be partially responsible for some observed group differences. Teachers may create **self-fulfilling prophecies** in which expectations actually cause the expected results. In a study published by Robert Rosenthal and Leonore Jacobson titled *"Pygmalion in the Classroom"*, all students at a California elementary school took an IQ test at the beginning of the school year. Teachers were then given a list of the 20% of students who were considered to be "spurters"; children expected to make great progress in the coming year. At the end of the year, all students completed another IQ test, and the 20% "spurters" did show more improvement than the other students.

The twist was that these 20% had actually been randomly selected at the beginning of the year. Just by believing that these students would improve, teachers managed to create this improvement. When teachers believe students are gifted they may raise expectations, call on them in class more often, and encourage them more persistently, all of which may turn that expectation into reality. What if teachers believed that every student would make a breakthrough? Why shouldn't we expect all students to make improvements?

The fact that students experience different environments is also seen in "**tracking**" that many schools practice. Early on, students are placed into tracks based on performance. This might sound appropriate (like what Binet was trying to accomplish), but schools may have a tendency to focus limited resources on the higher tracks, and view the lower tracks as lost causes. When we try to estimate the long-term consequences of high IQ in young children, it can be difficult because we have created situations in which the good get better and the bad get worse. When it comes to consequences like occupational status, educational achievement, or income later in life, it may be that early high-IQ children tend to do better because of additional educational opportunities and resources. Students who struggle initially may get the message that school is not for them, closing doors that could be opened with a little more push.

Programs like the **Head Start Program** seek to improve opportunities for children and enhance their cognitive development. There's evidence that the Head Start program does have a positive effect on child IQ and can indeed boost scores. Critics of the program, however, point out that these boosts in IQ seem to dissipate over time, suggesting that the program isn't able to create permanent change. But maybe we shouldn't expect too much of these programs when it comes to creating lasting improvement. After all, if we remove the enriched environment, perhaps we shouldn't be surprised that the benefits fade. We wouldn't be surprised if a perfectly well-nourished body could not maintain itself indefinitely when faced with later malnutrition or starvation. We shouldn't think of enriched environments as one-shot approaches to boosting IQ, but as long-term interventions that need to be maintained.

This relates to another problem in IQ research, which is the assumption that abilities are fixed and stable. IQ improvements which are only temporary are often dismissed, implying that intelligence is stable and short-term changes represent error rather than actual fluctuation. This message that IQ doesn't change is one that many students receive from an early age, causing them to believe that their IQ is a set number and there's nothing they can do about it. This might seem fine for those who do well, but for students who initially score poorly it may reduce motivation to work hard.

Carol Dweck has contrasted a **Fixed Mindset** and a **Growth Mindset**, based on whether people believe that change is possible or not. She has shown how these two mindsets influence behavior when it comes to effort and problem-solving. Those who have a fixed mindset believe that abilities are stable and innate and they tend to avoid hard work, even if they believe their own ability is high. When ability is believed to be high, it can be accompanied by a fear of failure. People with fixed mindsets who initially perform well may avoid future challenges because failure could indicate that they weren't really "smart" in the first place. With a growth mindset that IQ is malleable and can be improved with effort, the possibility of receiving a lower score is not so frightening. A low score represents a temporary setback rather than a fixed part of one's identity.

Situations Matter

What about gaps that are found even when environments are similar? Before thinking that this must mean genes, we may wonder if subtle differences in testing situations are causing these gaps. Claude Steele and Joshua Aronson had black and white undergraduate students at Stanford answer tough GRE questions. These students were told that the questions would assess their innate intelligence. Results showed that white students outperformed black students by a significant margin, even when adjusted for SAT score. The race gap seemed to be alive and well.

In a second condition, however, students were given the same GRE questions, but were told that this was a problem-solving task (rather than an assessment of intelligence). Now the race gap between SAT-adjusted scores disappeared and black students performed comparably to white students.

Steele and Aronson proposed a theory of **stereotype threat**. Stereotype threat suggests that when people are placed in situations where there is the possibility of confirming a negative stereotype about their group, this creates additional anxiety which affects performance on the task. An IQ test may cause stereotype threat for black students and this means that the experience of taking an IQ test is different for black and white students.

Steele has referred to these circumstances as "*identity contingencies*", suggesting that we all encounter situations where some aspect of our identity matters. Whether we are black students taking an IQ test, females taking a math exam, or older adults visiting a youthful start-up, there are circumstances in which possible negative stereotypes about our identity are relevant and these can influence behavior. Even if we don't believe these stereotypes, our knowledge of their existence can be enough to disrupt focus and impede performance.

This concept of how our identity influences us has direct implications for how we think about the way the world works. Stereotype threat isn't just about our ethnicity or our gender, it's about the fundamental nature of how our minds process social information. It can inform us of how subtle cues in the environment can have surprising effects on behavior and performance, and on the positive side, how minor changes can break down these nearly invisible barriers and help to bring out everyone's best performance.

Steele and Aronson's work also demonstrates that even if there is no bias in the administration of IQ testing, stereotypes and biases could still be influencing results. Neither the white nor black students needed to actually believe stereotypes regarding race and intelligence. The test administrators and instructions were not intentionally or overtly prejudiced. Awareness of possible stereotypes combined with a scenario which makes them relevant can be enough to negatively affect performance. Non-prejudiced people with the best of intentions may inadvertently be creating situations with subtle but powerful identity contingencies. You can have a prejudice-free test administrator giving a reliable and unbiased test to people who do not believe the negative stereotypes associated with their group and yet these stereotypes can still be responsible for negative effects on their scores. For more on this, I highly recommend reading Claude Steele's book, *Whistling Vivaldi: How Stereotypes Affect Us and What We Can Do.*

Smart Shortcuts?

It's inspiring to see environmental interventions that can help to raise group averages overall and reduce performance gaps, but what about your individual score? Are there ways of quickly increasing an individual's intelligence or improving cognitive performance?

Stimulation

One new approach for quickly modifying your brain's abilities is **transcranial direct current stimulation** (**tDCS**) or **transcranial magnetic stimulation** (**TMS**). These technologies have the potential to temporarily influence activity in particular brain regions by altering the flow of ions and making neurons depolarized or hyperpolarized, changing their likelihood of firing. tDCS delivers stimulation using electrodes placed on the scalp, while TMS uses a magnetic coil held over the skull. There's some evidence that stimulating different brain regions can enhance or inhibit certain skills for a short period of time, including possibly improving some cognitive abilities and motor skills, though this research is still in initial stages.

"Cognitive Enhancers"

Another avenue for attempting to alter cognitive performance is pharmaceutical intervention in the form of drugs, most of which were created for the treatment of attention and wakefulness-related disorders like ADHD and narcolepsy. Drugs like methylphenidate (**Ritalin**), **Modafinil**, and **Adderall** are increasingly used by students and workers in an attempt to increase concentration and reduce mental fatigue, allowing them to work or study for longer hours. Off-label and recreational use can be dangerous and it's important to remember that these drugs may be addictive and have potential side effects, particularly when administered without medical supervision.

In addition to the prescription drugs above, there are other supplements known as "**nootropics**" which are claimed by some to offer cognitive benefits. These include a class of drugs known as *racetams*, in addition to nutritional supplements like fish oil, B-vitamins, ginseng, or others, all purportedly providing a cognitive edge. While some of these supplements may have benefits, they are part of an industry where limited regulation means that marketing can overshadow merit and the placebo effect may be convincing users of efficacy that isn't really there.

Training Your Brain

In 2008, a study by Susanne Jaeggi (pronounced *YAH-kee*) and colleagues raised the possibility that fluid intelligence could be improved through training with the ***dual-n-back task,*** a working memory task that involves remembering a sequence of visual and auditory stimuli. If you'd like to try the dual-n-back task, you can play a free version at www.soakyourhead.com. In recent years other "brain training" games and apps have gained tens of millions of users, most notably through subscription sites like Lumosity, BrainHQ and CogMed. Some question whether these sites offer more hype than science and evidence that improved performance transfers to other tasks is weak or nonexistent. Some of these sites have even claimed their games can stave off cognitive decline (leading to fines for deceptive advertising from the FTC) though it's not certain these tasks are any more effective than real-world cognitive challenges like reading, solving puzzles, or learning a new language or musical instrument.

Before you commit yourself to hours of daily dual-n-back in hopes it will raise your grades, you may want to consider a more focused approach. While we don't yet have much evidence brain training improves performance on other tasks, we do know that practicing specific tasks can lead to improvements in those skills. In other words, if you're hoping to boost your intelligence because you think it would make calculus class easier, you're probably better off just spending that time working on calculus problems.

In addition to spending more time on the types of activities you'd like to improve at, there are a few other simple interventions that can help you to maximize your performance on a wide range of tasks. You've undoubtedly heard them all before, probably from your mother. Proper sleep (deprivation is known to reduce performance on cognitive and physical tasks), regular exercise, and a healthy diet are far more likely to help you than any games or nootropic powders. When it comes to reaching your fullest potential, my advice is get your sleep, exercise, and nutrition on track, maintain a growth mindset, and then just put in the time on the tasks you want to improve.

Chapter Summary – Intelligence

- Theorists have considered a single factor (*g*), multiple intelligences, practical intelligence, and emotional intelligence in their definitions of intelligence.

- The most commonly used intelligence assessments today include the ***Wechsler Adult Intelligence Scale*** and the ***Stanford-Binet Intelligence Scale***.

- Scores on intelligence tests tend to follow a ***normal distribution*** with a mean of 100 and a standard deviation of about 15 points. A score below 70 is considered to be a sign of ***intellectual disability***, while a score above 130 is evidence of ***intellectual giftedness***.

- The heritability score for intelligence seems to be around 0.5, though this may vary. Though specific genes for intelligence have not been identified, genetic influence on cognitive ability can be seen in some disorders including ***Down Syndrome***, ***Fragile X syndrome***, and ***Williams Syndrome***.

- Gender and race-based performance gaps in intelligence have been observed. Some interventions have successfully reduced these gaps, which probably result from a complex interaction of biological, environmental, and social forces.

- Average intelligence has risen over the past several decades, though this ***Flynn Effect*** appears to be slowing. The possibility of individual IQ improvement from training, supplements, and brain stimulation has received some attention recently, though the efficacy of any of these approaches remains unclear.

Notes

Chapter 10
Personality

What is Personality?

As you've probably noticed, people differ. But how can we determine and describe the ways that people differ? While you've undoubtedly used the word personality before, we're going to have to dig deeper than just saying someone has a "great" personality. We can think of **personality** as a unique and characteristic pattern of thinking, feeling, and behaving that is consistent across situations. Just as we saw with intelligence testing, it's important that personality testing allows us to distinguish between people. Behavior patterns in which people don't vary can't tell us much, so we want to identify aspects of personality which vary between people but are stable over time and across many situations. These aspects will allow us to make predictions about people's thoughts, feelings, and behaviors.

Modern psychologists aren't the first to consider the ways in which people differ and the analysis of personality goes back thousands of years. In addition to wondering about the ways in which people can differ, some people have wondered how we can measure those differences. We've already seen approaches to measuring one particular trait (intelligence) and much of what we've learned about testing will apply to the measurement of other traits.

There are two main ways to study personality: a **nomothetic approach** (from the Greek *nomos* - "law") focuses on finding universal laws that apply to all people to identify the aspects of personality that everyone has. An **idiographic approach** focuses on studying a person's particular peculiarities or the unique aspects of that single individual (you can think of studying their *idiosyncrasies* to remember *idiographic*).

Hippocrates (460-370 BC) suggested that personality had biological roots and that our physical bodies influenced our ways of thinking, feeling, and behaving. Hippocrates believed that we were influenced by 4 humors; blood, yellow bile, black bile, and phlegm. This idea was applied by Galen (129-216 AD), who suggested 4 main personality types based on high level of a particular humor: *sanguine* (blood), *phlegmatic* (phlegm), *choleric* (yellow bile), and *melancholic* (black bile).

While this way of thinking has faded, the idea that biology can be used to predict personality has remained. When phrenologists like Franz Josef Gall were measuring bumps and dents in the skull, they were hoping that these physiological measurements could be used to assess or even predict something about personality.

Modern ways of approaching physiological measurements no longer focus on humors or skull shapes, but do still consider how biology might influence our behavior, our thinking, and how we respond to the world. Is there something about your genes, your nervous system, or your brain structure that drives your personality? Before we get to these modern approaches, however, let's consider the history of personality psychology in the past 150 years or so, beginning with the theories of psychology's most famous figure, Sigmund Freud.

The Psychoanalytic Approach

Sigmund Freud (1856-1939) was a medical doctor specializing in nerve disorders who began to wonder whether some ailments were connected to psychological factors rather than physiological factors. This line of questioning led Freud to consider the possible causes of mental illness. Much of Freud's work was theoretical and was based on his own experiences, in addition to the experiences of his patients, most of whom were members of the upper-class in Vienna, where Freud lived for most of his life.

Freud believed that our thoughts and behaviors were heavily influenced by the *unconscious*. This was a repository of our hidden desires, wishes, and fears which were kept out of conscious awareness in order to avoid the anxiety these thoughts and feelings would provoke. Freud believed that when these unconscious forces conflicted with our conscious thoughts, feelings, and behaviors, the resulting anxiety could cause mental illness. By collecting clues about the contents of the unconscious, one could better understand conflicts and anxiety could be reduced.

This investigation of the unconscious could be done through a number of methods such as *dream interpretation* and *free association*, a practice in which a patient was encouraged to speak without restraint; no thought was considered too embarrassing or too trivial. Freud also suggested that a *parapraxis* (from Greek *para* - "contrary" and *praxis* - "action") or "slip of the tongue" (also called a *Freudian slip*) could reveal aspects of the unconscious. By analyzing the contents of dreams, thoughts, and errors, Freud believed that a therapist could understand the forces of the patient's unconscious, then work to resolve conflicts.

Freud's Personality Structure

Freud proposed a structural organization of personality with three main components; the *id*, the *ego*, and the *superego*.

The *id* was the raw animal drives of the personality. These included drives for food, sex, and aggression, which were driven by *libido*, the psychic energy of the mind. This psychic energy came in two forms, *Eros* (the life instinct) with drives toward survival (hunger, sex, etc.) and *Thanatos* (the death instinct) with drives toward death (such as aggression). The id operates on the *pleasure principle*, meaning that it is driven solely to maximize pleasure. Essentially, the id follows the rule "if it feels good, do it".

This type of pleasure-maximizing drive might help us to survive and procreate, but it isn't the only rule to live by. We can't just run around eating, fighting, or mating whenever and wherever we please. This is where the *ego* comes in. The ego's role is to restrain the drives of the id in order to maintain relationships and integrate into society. The ego operates on the *reality principle*, which is to balance the id's drives with the realities of social life.

The last structure of Freud's personality construct is the *superego*. The superego contains all of the messages from parents, teachers, and others about who we should be. The superego represents the ideal person who is perfectly moral and virtuous. We can never reach this societal ideal, but the superego urges us to try, though our inevitable failure may cause guilt, shame, and anxiety.

To remember these three personality structures and how they interact, imagine the following scenario. You've arrived at a friend's house where you're planning a surprise birthday party. A rushed and busy day has meant that you haven't had a chance to eat and you're feeling rather ravenous. Before your friend is due to arrive, you find yourself in the kitchen, alone with a pristine chocolate cake.

In this situation, your id is basically saying "EAT IT! You're hungry, it will taste amazing, just do it!" Your ego, on the other hand, is considering the effects of this behavior on your social standing and relationships. After all, what would the consequences be if your friend found you stuffing your face with her birthday cake? Your ego suggests that you manage to wait just a little while longer, then you can have your cake and maintain your friendship too. Rather than relying on the animal drives of the id or the pragmatic propositions of the ego, your superego pushes for the most virtuous of responses. How could you enjoy even the thinnest slice of cake when you know that elsewhere others are truly starving? How could you celebrate when there are people suffering in this world? The superego might suggest you take that cake down to the nearest soup kitchen and give it to those who are most in need.

A Note about Freudian Terms

   This chapter is a bit heavy on Freudian vocabulary, so many students wonder why they have to memorize all these terms that are no longer used in modern psychology or psychiatry. Researchers no longer spend much time talking about *ids* or *egos*, yet these words remain fundamental for discussing early psychoanalysis. While all these terms may seem like a foreign language, it probably wasn't Freud's intention to create a separate lexicon. Bruno Bettelheim (1903-1990) has suggested that a great deal of Freud's legacy has been misinterpreted because of these very terms. We must remember that Freud lived nearly his entire life in Vienna and all of his writing was in German. The psychoanalytic terms we see (which have been translated into Latin or occasionally Greek) feel disconnected from daily life, but this wasn't the case in the original German Freud used. The "ego" was *Ich*, literally "I", the "superego" *Über-Ich* would be the "over-I", while the "id" was *Es*, literally "It", a neuter pronoun used for referring to children. Bettelheim has suggested that these German terms had deeper emotional connections that have been lost in translation, resulting in a version of psychoanalysis which is missing some of its essence.

Personality Development – The Psychosexual Stages

   Freud believed that early childhood experiences were fundamental for the formation of personality and that these effects rippled through to our adult lives. Our different personalities could be explained through the vicissitudes of early life and the ways we adapted to childhood conflict. Freud proposed a theory of personality development based on stages, which we needed to move through in a step-wise fashion. Each stage was based on a focus of pleasure known as an *erogenous zone* and a potential conflict which needed to be resolved. Failure to move through a stage properly could result in a ***fixation***; a sticking point in development which would shape future behavior until it was resolved.

   The first stage in Freud's model is the ***Oral Stage***, lasting from birth until about 12-18 months of age, during which the focus of pleasure is the mouth. Babies explore their world by putting just about anything in their mouths; sucking, biting, or chewing whatever they can. Freud believed this represents the potential anxiety of whether they will be fed adequately or not, and a fixation develops in a child who is either under or over-fed. This ***oral fixation*** could then reveal itself in later behaviors focused on the mouth and pleasure. Cigarette smoking, obsessive gum-chewing, overeating, eating disorders, or talkativeness would indicate to a psychoanalyst that a patient had experienced conflict during the oral stage.

The next stage is the **Anal Stage**, from about 18 months to 3 years of age, during which the focus of pleasure is the anus and the expulsion or retention of feces. During this stage children take pleasure in controlling their bowel movements and conflict has the potential to influence behavior related to cleanliness and order. **Anal-retentive** types (yes, this is where the term comes from) would become excessively neat and orderly in later life, while **anal-expulsive** types took such pleasure in producing feces that they would become disorderly and messy, though also taking more pleasure in creativity and productivity. Freud would have found a perfect example of the anal-expulsive type in the artist Mary Barnes, who suffered from schizophrenia. While institutionalized, she spent her time "painting" with her own feces, until she was given paints as a way to express her creativity.

If things haven't gotten weird enough for you yet, following the Anal Stage is the **Phallic Stage**, lasting from age 3 to about age 5. During this period, the focus is on the penis, or lack thereof. During this stage, a boy develops sexual desire for his mother, but thanks to some guy named "Dad", the boy can't have mom all to himself. So the boy harbors unconscious wishes to murder his father. This is known as the **Oedipus complex**, named after the Greek myth of the tragic hero destined to kill his father and marry his mother. Since dad is bigger and stronger, the boy fears that he will detect this patricidal desire and punish him with castration. This **castration anxiety** keeps the boy from acting on his latent sexual desire and instead he learns to be like dad. If he can't have mom to himself, he can learn from dad and someday find a girl of his own (ideally one just like mom). This process of learning to be like dad was called **identification**, and Freud believed this was how a boy learned his gender role and sexual behavior.

A girl, on the other hand, notices that she lacks a penis, resulting in **penis envy**. She also experiences a latent sexual desire for her father and a wish to kill her mother, who she blames for her apparent castration. This was referred to by Carl Jung as the *Electra Complex*, though Freud disagreed with this label (perhaps rightly so, since Electra's story doesn't involve desire for her father, but rather a desire for revenge after his death). Just as boys resolve their fears and desires by learning to be like dad, Freud believed that girls overcome their anxiety and penis envy by **identifying** with their moms and thus learning proper gender roles and sexual identities. Freud believed that problems and unresolved conflicts during the phallic stage resulted in homosexuality, sexual fetishes, or confused gender identity or gender role behaviors.

Following these torrid affairs of the phallic stage, children move into the rather boring **Latency Period**, lasting from age 6 until puberty. This period is characterized by dormant sexual desires and Freud didn't really think much was happening at this point. During this time children's personalities are setting like a jello mold that has been mixed by early experience, and now is sitting in the fridge solidifying.

After this uneventful latency period, puberty carried children to the final stage of psychosexual development, the *Genital Stage*, where the focus of pleasure is still the genitals but now includes a desire for mutual sexual gratification rather than just personal pleasure. This compels people to seek out sex and intimate relationships, and to show concern for the welfare of others.

Defense Mechanisms

In Freud's approach to understanding personality, anxiety plays a fundamental role. We all experience conflict between the id, ego, and superego, and this conflict necessarily creates anxiety. Freud categorized three main types of anxiety: *reality anxiety* came from objective dangers in the environment, *neurotic anxiety* related to fears of losing control over the id, and *moral anxiety* came from fears of past or future immoral behavior.

Even if this anxiety isn't causing mental illness, Freud believed it's still there for all of us. As a result, we need ways of coping with this ever-present anxiety and so we develop *defense mechanisms*, unconscious strategies for managing and reducing anxiety. Here are a few examples of possible defense mechanisms, some of which you may have heard in everyday use. Many of these come from Freud's writing, though some were later added by his daughter, Anna Freud.

Repression is the process of burying anxiety away in the unconscious. When conflict occurs, it is pushed beneath the surface and out of awareness. "Out of sight, out of mind" would be an apt description, though it's not so much out of mind as in a part of the mind that is inaccessible. Repression is a fundamental strategy because it is the technique that helps to fill the unconscious with all its wishes, desires, and fears.

Regression is a defense mechanism of reverting to a previous stage of development, presumably one in which the person felt comfortable and didn't experience anxiety. Freud believed that this could be seen when anxiety causes an adult to engage in behaviors like thumb-sucking, watching cartoons, or whining and acting childish. Regression was even used as a therapeutic technique in psychoanalysis, as patients were encouraged to regress to the stage that was believed to have formed unconscious conflict so that the therapist and patient could work to resolve it.

Reaction Formation - "Every action has an equal and opposite reaction" might be appropriate here, as this defense mechanism involves behaving in the opposite manner of the behavior causing anxiety. A common example would be the suggestion that strongly homophobic individuals are acting this way because of their own latent feelings of homosexual attraction. Rather than accepting these feelings, reaction formation causes them to condemn the feelings and speak out in hatred of homosexuality.

Rationalization involves creating a logical excuse for one's behavior which ignores the true underlying explanation. So a person who smokes because of an unconscious oral fixation might rationalize her smoking as being a strategy to help her socialize.

Intellectualization involves focusing on academic analysis and study of an area relevant to the person's anxiety. For instance, after Joe is cut from the basketball team he obsesses over studying game strategies and biomechanics in order to distract himself from the emotions he feels.

Displacement refers to redirecting anxiety away from the real threat and onto a less-threatening object or situation. For instance, after being berated by a teacher for unsatisfactory work, John displaces his anger and aggression away from the teacher and onto another child on the playground, pushing him and calling him names.

Denial is an unconscious refusal to admit to the reality of a situation causing anxiety. In the case of a marital relationship, one spouse may unconsciously overlook any evidence of an affair, even though it seems quite obvious to other observers. Or you may choose denial rather than admitting that your parents have a sex life which includes favorite positions and erotic fantasies.

Projection refers to projecting one's own fears and anxieties onto other people. This might be seen when a husband with a roving eye accuses his wife of flirting with other men or if your unconscious dislike of a classmate causes you to insist that the classmate hates you.

Sublimation refers to a redirection of sexual or aggressive energies onto pursuits which are more socially acceptable. So rather than getting into fist fights, a writer sublimates his aggression into violent characters or an artist sublimates his sexual desires into stunning visual displays.

I think that the ready application of these defense mechanisms helps to reveal the appeal of Freud. We can see that it's rather easy and fun to create these ad-hoc explanations for people's behavior. We needn't worry ourselves with statistical analysis, predictive power, or possible gene/environment interactions in shaping behavior. We can create seemingly logical explanations for a wide variety of behaviors, even though we can't really prove that any of this is actually happening at the unconscious level.

This is part of Freud's legacy in that he made psychological issues approachable and applicable for many people. Because these ideas were based on his casual observations of common behaviors, it's not hard to apply them to other commonly-occurring behaviors. Those versed in Freudian terminology are suddenly armed with labels for talking about the intellectualization of their professors, the sublimation of sculptors, and the projection of political pundits.

Other Psychodynamic Theorists

Freud influenced the next generation of psychiatrists, many of whom adopted the notions of unconscious influences and the importance of early experiences on personality development. These *Psychodynamic* or *Neo-Freudian* theorists continued Freud's work in attempting to understand mental illness, though they disagreed with many of Freud's original ideas.

Alfred Adler believed that Freud was overly focused on sexual and aggressive drives and felt that Freud failed to fully incorporate the importance of social tensions on personality development. Adler believed that our early social interactions influenced the development of complexes such as an *inferiority complex* or on the positive side, a strive for superiority.

Karen Horney (before you embarrass yourself in class, it's pronounced *Horn-eye*) found Freud's approach male-centric, particularly the suggestion that all females experienced *penis envy* as a part of their normal psychological development. Horney suggested that males experience *womb envy* because they are unable to bring life into the world, which drives them to compensate by dominating and disparaging women.

Perhaps the most famous of Freud's followers was Swiss psychiatrist *Carl Gustav Jung* (1875-1961) though he eventually split from Freud and disagreed with Freud's emphasis on sexual and aggressive drives. Jung preferred to focus on aims and aspirations and he emphasized conflict within an individual rather than conflict with society or reality. Jung proposed that our personal unconscious also contained a *collective unconscious*, which included the symbols, myths, and memories inherited from our ancestors. Jung believed that this collective unconscious influenced everyone and could be seen in shared mythology, fears, and symbols. These include *archetypes*, which are universal images and motifs that exist in everyone but may vary in form. These would include representations of devils, heroes, tricksters, or sages which can be seen across many cultures, though their specific manifestations may differ. You can probably come up with several examples for particular archetypes by considering characters from Star Wars or your favorite Disney cartoons.

Assessing Personality

How can we assess personality? How can we measure the differences between people, and how can we use these differences to predict behavior?

Projective Techniques

If you ever looked up at the clouds as a child (or even as an adult) and allowed your imagination to run wild with what you were seeing, you've done something similar to a projective test. Projective tests are attempts to tap into a person's characteristic ways of interpreting or assessing ambiguous stimuli, with the assumption that this reveals aspects of personality. These types of assessments can be regarded as *idiographic*, meaning that they attempt to uncover the fine details of a single individual's personality (though it would be impossible to describe all aspects). Idiographic approaches are about individuals and don't necessarily aim to make comparisons between people.

Perhaps the most famous projective test is the *Rorschach Inkblot Test*, developed in 1918 by Swiss psychiatrist (and Brad Pitt doppelgänger) *Hermann Rorschach*. Adapting his childhood hobby of dripping ink onto a blank sheet, folding it in half, then unfolding it to reveal an abstract symmetrical pattern, Rorschach created ambiguous stimuli which were open to interpretation. Rorschach believed that by analyzing responses to these patterns, a psychiatrist could uncover the unconscious influences and elements of a patient's mind. For example, recurrent thoughts of weapons, violence, or harm might serve as an indication of an aggressive personality.

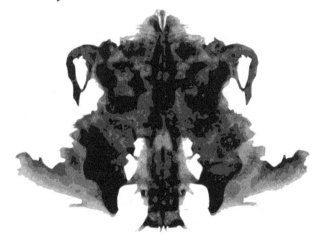

Sample image from Rorschach's test (public domain)

See all 10 original images at www.psychexamreview.com/rorschach

A few decades later, Henry Murray created a similar type of projective assessment, known as the **Thematic Apperception Test** or **TAT**. Rather than having participants identify ambiguous stimuli, Murray's test focused on explaining ambiguous situations. In a set of 10 TAT cards, subjects would see characters in ambiguous situations then explain what was happening, who the characters were and how they were related, and why they were behaving the way they were. Murray believed that the situations and relationships described could reveal motives, concerns, and a characteristic way of viewing the social world. Repeated themes of success, failure, competition, jealousy, aggression, or sexuality could be interpreted as representations of the viewer's personality.

(While it would be nice to show a sample from the TAT here, images from Murray's original test are still under copyright by the Harvard University Press and may not be shared publicly).

While projective techniques may sound promising for understanding how someone views the world, there are a number of problems associated with their use. First and foremost is whether stated views represent wishes, motives, or preferences. Even if we assume they do, it's still unclear whether these reveal how a person *is* or how they *want to be seen*. We may wonder whether some respondents create bizarre narratives because those actually come to mind easily, or whether the respondents are just bored with the task or are trying to be unique or funny.

Given that there are infinite possible narratives, truly standardized scoring for these types of tasks is impossible and the same traits could be expressed in innumerable ways. Likewise, similar answers might be given for different underlying reasons and it's not clear how an examiner might reliably tell the difference or whether another examiner would reach the same conclusion.

This brings us to another major problem, the interpretation of responses by the examiner. Might a consistent pattern of interpretations reveal more about an examiner than it does about her patients? Freud is frequently lampooned for seeing themes of sex and aggression everywhere and this should remind us that these interpretations may speak volumes more about Freud than about any of his patients.

Trait-Based Assessment

Rather than relying on a subjective assessment of projective responses, a trait-based approach to personality attempts to identify characteristics of people in a much more direct manner. These assessments choose particular traits which are deemed to be relevant for understanding personality then questions are aimed at assessing those particular traits.

These assessments tend to be **nomothetic** (rather than *idiographic*) which means that they look for universal trait dimensions that all people have as a way of organizing people into groups or classifications. Nomothetic assessments provide information about where people stand on certain dimensions rather than attempting to describe the nuances of one person's personality.

Given that these assessments have a limited number of questions and limited possible answer choices, many people can receive identical results, but this doesn't imply that their personalities are truly identical. We also have to consider that attempting to measure traits automatically invokes comparison. The results of these assessments aren't really about particular individuals as much as points of comparison for how people can differ. For instance, high extraversion necessarily involves a comparison to other people in order for it be considered "high".

The trait-based approach frequently relies on **self-reports**; asking people to answer questions about themselves. Of course, assessing ourselves can be difficult, since our point of view may be biased or we may not be able to provide an accurate view of ourselves even if we try. The report we give of ourselves may be more of a report on who we think we are, not who we actually are. After all, do conceited people realize they are conceited?

A self-report may have a tough time collecting information for traits with negative connotations. If you recall the concept of *face validity* from the previous chapter, now we see that it's not always something we want to have. Sometimes we don't want a question to look like it's measuring what it actually measures. If I want to measure a negative or potentially embarrassing trait, I don't want to be obvious because then people may give me *socially desirable* answers instead of honest ones. The statement "I frequently mistreat others" might appear to be a good measure of callousness (and thus would have *face validity*), but that doesn't mean that the responses I get will actually be useful, because most people, even callous ones, will probably report that this statement does not describe them.

One way of getting around this problem is to insert questions designed to catch faking. For example, if someone agrees with the statement "I never feel angry" we might question their honesty for other answers, because everyone gets angry at times. This question is there to help us find out about honesty, not anger. For measurement of some traits with negative connotations we can also use an **implicit assessment** which attempts to assess a trait in an indirect way that is difficult for the participant to conceal.

Assessing Accuracy

When it comes to determining the accuracy of a personality assessment, we might think we could just ask people how well the assessment describes them. This straight-forward approach runs into problems, however, because we can't always trust people's subjective perceptions of accuracy.

This was demonstrated in a study published by Bertram Forer in 1949. Forer gave feedback from a personality assessment to participants, who were asked to rate the accuracy of the statements in describing their personalities. Participants rated their assessments as highly accurate, only to discover that they had all received the same generic personality descriptions. This tendency to find personal meaning in vague assessments is known as the **Forer Effect**, though it's also frequently referred to as the **Barnum Effect**. This is a reference to P. T. Barnum saying "we have something for everyone" though perhaps it could apply to another quote frequently attributed to Barnum: "there's a sucker born every minute".

We should keep this effect in mind for all personality assessments, as people may be prone to agree with results regardless of actual accuracy. This effect can also be used to explain how supposed-psychics and fake fortune-tellers are able to use vague descriptions and hazy predictions to swindle victims. People find personal relevance in these stock statements, making them more likely to believe that the "seer" is really seeing something.

The MMPI

One frequently used self-report is the **Minnesota Multiphasic Personality Inventory (MMPI)**, first published in 1943 and most recently updated as the **MMPI-2-RF** in 2008. This inventory lists several hundred statements about the self, to which a subject responds with either *True* or *False*, depending on how well the statement matches his sense of self. Rather than attempting to determine which traits cause people to differ, the MMPI works in reverse. In a technique known as *criterion keying*, this assessment is given to groups of people who are known to differ in some way, then responses are analyzed to show how these groups differ in their self-assessments. By giving the inventory to people who have already been diagnosed with a particular disorder, researchers can look for patterns of responses which can then be associated with that disorder. In this way, usefulness comes not from what the specific response patterns are, but that they differ for different groups of people.

For example, by giving the inventory to a group of people known to be depressed and comparing their responses to a group of people who have not been diagnosed with depression, researchers may be able to find characteristic differences between the groups, which could then be helpful for identifying depression in the future. This approach can be problematic, however, as it assumes that existing diagnoses are accurate and that different disorders have distinct patterns, which may not always be the case. Nevertheless, the MMPI can provide useful points of comparison for how people differ. The inventory contains 338 statements designed to assess 10 main sub-scales such as Masculinity/Femininity, Depression, and Paranoia, in addition to statements designed to assess the likelihood a subject is over- or under-reporting or trying to "fake bad" or "fake good".

Which Traits Should be Assessed?

The number of personality traits that might be assessed is staggering. In 1936 Gordon Allport and Henry Odbert analyzed the dictionaries of the day and found over 18,000 words that could be used to describe someone's personality. Allport and Odbert then worked to sort these terms for synonyms, creating a list of possible traits. Allport proposed that trait terms could represent cardinal dispositions, central traits, or secondary traits. **Cardinal dispositions** characterized just about everything a person did and therefore revealed most about personality. **Central traits** influenced many thoughts or behaviors, while **secondary traits** influenced only a few.

Which traits should we consider important? Answers may vary. For instance, in the 1940s, to understand the rise of fascism, some psychometricians were interested in the possibility of a trait they called **authoritarianism**, which referred to a tendency for obedience to authority, conformity, and political conservatism, though interest in exploring this trait has waned in recent decades. Rather than proposing traits that might be important and then examining those, another approach involves examining many traits and letting statistics tell us the most important ones.

This approach involves **factor analysis**, a statistical technique we saw used by Charles Spearman to investigate intelligence in the previous chapter. Factor analysis involves collecting data for a number of items, then calculating the correlations between each of those items. When a group of items are all highly correlated, this suggests that they can be represented by a single label, called a **factor**.

In the case of personality, many of the terms used to describe people go together. People rated as kind are likely to also be rated as compassionate or loyal but probably not also rated as rude. If we find that scores for kindness, compassion, empathy, and loyalty are all highly correlated, we might consider that these represent a single factor we could label "agreeableness".

Based on this type of factor analysis, Raymond Cattell proposed 16 traits for categorizing people (including intelligence), which he referred to as *source traits*. Cattell created an assessment of these traits known as the *16PF test*, a version of which is still used today for workplace and career guidance, clinical diagnosis, and relationship counseling.

Hans Eysenck took this approach further and believed that personality could be summarized into two main dimensions: ***Introversion/Extraversion*** and ***Neuroticism***, which assesses a person's level of emotional stability or instability (though in 1976 he and his wife Sybil Eysenck proposed a third dimension of ***Psychoticism*** which assessed things like hostility, impulsiveness, and lack of empathy).

Eysenck's initial 2-dimensional model for personality suggested that a large number of traits could be seen as the combination of a person's level of introversion and level of neuroticism. For example, a person with a high level of neuroticism might express this instability in the form of moodiness if introverted but as aggression if extraverted. The combination of these two dimensions creates 4 main quadrants for traits, which can be likened to the 4 personality types of Galen (melancholic as high neuroticism/low extraversion, choleric as high neuroticism/high extraversion, sanguine as low neuroticism/high extraversion and phlegmatic as low neuroticism/low extraversion).

The Big Five

Cattell's analysis reduced thousands of trait terms into 16 factors, though this could be considered a bit too long of a list, while Eysenck's two (or three) dimensions might not be quite enough to describe all the differences between people. Today, most researchers look at 5 traits. These traits are based on the NEO-PI-R assessment developed by Robert McCrae and Paul Costa, and are known as the ***The Big Five*** (or the ***Five Factor Model***).

Each of these traits actually refers to a dimension, with everyone falling somewhere along a continuum from low to high. While there is a great deal of evidence supporting the existence of these five factors, there's still some disagreement over which labels should be used, as the name a factor is given has connotations that may inadvertently emphasize or downplay some measures related to the factor.

The Big Five are:

Openness to Experience – This factor relates to curiosity, willingness to try new things, intelligence, and perhaps imagination.

Conscientiousness – This factor refers to a person's tendency to follow through and get things done, though it also relates to things like organization, sense of responsibility, and carefulness.

Extraversion – As discussed above, extraversion refers to how outgoing a person is, though it may also include things like social dominance, confidence, sociability, and spontaneity.

Agreeableness – This factor refers to how well someone gets along with others as well as a willingness to cooperate or compromise in order to maintain good social relationships.

Neuroticism – As mentioned in Eysenck's dimensions, neuroticism refers to emotional instability and anxiety.

The big five traits can be remembered with the mnemonic **OCEAN** (or if you prefer, **CANOE**). If each person has some score on each of these 5 dimensions, then we could think of an individual's particular combination of these traits and how these combinations interact with one another as that individual's unique *personality profile*. Changes in one trait could influence the expression of other traits, creating a wide variety of personality possibilities.

Despite being considered separate factors, some of these traits may appear to be related to one another. Maybe how socially outgoing someone is indicates how open she is to new social experiences, or maybe this extraversion relates to previous positive experiences which resulted from her agreeableness. This may cause us to wonder whether these traits really could be distilled into just 2 or 3 factors.

We may think that just 5 traits is too few and that something is lost when personality is considered in such limited terms. This is true in the sense that scores on these 5 dimensions can't really be used to tell us about specific behaviors of an individual. This is a tradeoff we make in sacrificing a high level of detail and accuracy in order to create assessments that are easy to use for large numbers of people.

Recall the triangle we drew for the hypothetical construct of intelligence, looking at actual behaviors (grades, income, etc) and then responses to assessments (test scores) and then analyzing whether there was a relationship between these behaviors and assessment results. This same triangle should be considered for any personality trait we measure. We should wonder how well assessments compare with actual behavior. Do people who score as introverted actually spend more time alone, or do they just report that they do?

To address this, Walter Mischel worked to identify correlations between trait assessment results and actual behaviors. In his controversial book *Personality and Assessment*, Mischel reported that the average correlation for traits and behaviors was only about 0.3 (Mischel, 1968). This weak correlation surprised many people and made them wonder whether trait assessments tell us much about an individual's behavior. But perhaps we shouldn't expect too much. Remember that traits aren't really intended to tell us about specific behaviors, and moreover, Mischel's correlations were for single traits. Our behavior is a complex amalgamation of all of the big five (or perhaps more) traits simultaneously, occurring in some situational context. With this in mind, we might not expect to ever find a strong correlation between a single behavior and one single trait.

More recent research on personality traits and behavioral tendencies has used a technique known as **experience sampling**. Participants in these types of studies are given pagers (or more recently, smartphone apps) which randomly buzz several times per day, prompting the participants to record what they are doing. By repeatedly measuring actual behaviors and then comparing them to personality inventories, researchers can get a clearer picture of how well assessments represent actual behavioral tendencies, such as seeing if people who are open to experience actually spend more time trying new things.

There are some other criticisms of the trait perspective and perhaps the most important of these is that traits don't tell us anything about *how* personality works. Traits can describe how people differ, but can't describe what those differences mean in terms of **intrapersonal functioning** or how a person processes information, makes decisions, and chooses behaviors. The trait-based perspective can be accused of using circular logic to evade providing explanation. We can say Jill scores highly on conscientiousness because she is very neat and well-organized but when we ask *why* she is neat and well-organized our only answer is that she is high in conscientiousness. In order to dig deeper on how these traits function and why people differ, we'll have to include other perspectives.

What Causes Differences?

If we accept that there are trait dimensions, where do these traits come from? Why do people differ in their levels of conscientiousness, neuroticism, or agreeableness? Are these differences the result of genes, biological processes, upbringing, or different ways of thinking about the world? As with any topic in psychology, there are different approaches to answering these questions. We should remember that none of these approaches is THE approach to understanding personality and each offers a new perspective. Each of these perspectives is not necessarily intended to be a complete explanation, but another piece of the puzzle.

The Biological Perspective

Earlier we saw that Eysenck's two dimensions of extraversion and neuroticism mapped onto Galen's 4 personality types and while Eysenck certainly didn't believe in humors, he suggested that there may be underlying biological links to personality traits. Rather than humors, we might consider how our modern understanding of hormones and neurotransmitters could be used to understand personality differences. Eysenck suggested a somewhat counter-intuitive notion that introverts had higher levels of cortical arousal, meaning that they were already over-stimulated and therefore didn't need much stimulation from the environment. Extraverts, on the other hand, might have lower levels of cortical arousal, causing them to seek out more stimulation from the environment. This fits with evidence that introverts are better at vigilance tasks and are also less likely to use stimulant drugs and more likely to use depressants, suggesting a kind of self-medication to keep their cortical arousal at a manageable level. Further research has suggested the existence of two opposing systems which may relate to sensation-seeking and emotional stability.

The *Behavioral Approach System* (*BAS*) is a reward-seeking system related to dopamine pathways and greater activity in the left prefrontal cortex in responding to incentives and rewards. The *Behavioral Inhibition System* (*BIS*) represents an opposing force, involving serotonin and GABA pathways and greater activity of the right prefrontal cortex. This system is more reactive to punishments and is related to anxiety, aversion, disgust and fear. Each individual may have different levels of activity and responsiveness for each of these systems and this may be responsible for traits such as extraversion or neuroticism.

Genes

Twin studies can examine whether personality traits are inherited and allow us to estimate heritability for certain traits. Heritabilities for each of the big 5 personality traits tend to range from around 0.3 to 0.6 (Bouchard & Loehlin, 2001) meaning that while genes play a role in personality, environment may play an equal or greater role.

One area of genetic involvement relates to the biology of the nervous system mentioned above, with genes possibly influencing receptors for neurotransmitters like dopamine or levels of hormones like testosterone. Another piece of evidence for the role of genes on personality can be seen in differences between very young children. Infants show immediate differences in their *temperament*, which refers to their activity levels, sociability, and emotionality and the early emergence of these differences suggests that that these traits might be inherited.

Thinking of personality as variations in the nervous system which are inherited like physical traits opens the possibility for questioning whether animals also have personalities. Pet owners often accept that a dog or a cat has its own unique personality, but a trait like extraversion can also be observed in an animal such as a monkey or even an octopus. We can consider the possible evolutionary advantages of certain traits such as how agreeableness or aggression might aid a species' survival. We can also see how evolutionary forces could stabilize traits, as extreme traits in either direction may not be desirable. For example, extremely low sociability would be undesirable because there are times we must interact with others, on the other hand, extremely high sociability would also be undesirable because there are inevitably times when we are forced to be alone.

The Socio-Cognitive Perspective

A socio-cognitive perspective on personality considers how people construct *schema*, or sets of cognitions, which guide behavior. George Kelly suggested that people all have *personal constructs* of how the world works and he emphasized that all events are open to multiple interpretations. The internal cognitive processes for how a person perceives, interprets, and recalls experiences may play an important role in that person's behavior and personality. A cognitive approach considers how schema, memory, information processing, and interpretation of situations all play a role in the personality that is expressed.

Walter Mischel suggested *person variables* including competencies, encoding strategies, personal constructs, expectancies, values, and plans which all play a role in building personality. We use schema to structure our knowledge and inform our decisions and actions, and these schema influence behavior and personality. Our schema are built up from our experience with the world and influence how we see others, our sense of gender roles, social situations, relationships, and emotions.

We also have a *self-schema*, which may be larger and more complex than most other schema. Like any other cognition, our self-schema is subject to bias. We may selectively remember aspects of ourselves that fit our pre-existing schema, and we may show bias in our recall or twist our recollections of events. Most people show a *self-serving bias*, recalling their achievements and successes while forgetting their failures, which may play an important role in the development of self-schema.

If we accept that situations influence behavior and we have scripts or schema we follow in certain situations, we may wonder just how much personality comes from the person and how much comes from the situation the person is in. How do we make sense of the fact that Jim is quiet and withdrawn in class but outgoing and sociable at parties? Is his personality really changing or is this a case where situation dominates? The socio-cognitive approach recognizes this difficulty, acknowledging that we can't assess personality in all situations in order to solve this *person-situation controversy*.

But just because we can't predict behavior in all situations doesn't mean it isn't worth describing personality anyway. Even when we speak non-scientifically about personality, we don't limit ourselves to strict rules. Instead, we have a tendency to use *verbal hedges* because we intuitively recognize that situations matter. Rather than only using blanket statements like "John is shy" or "Jennifer is aggressive", we tend to allow flexibility in our everyday assessments by adding context like "John is shy around new people" or "Jennifer is aggressive when confronted".

Existential Psychology

Another perspective on why people differ has to do with existence itself. Regardless of our own traits, we cannot escape death and our present existence is all we can be sure of. This means that we must each have our own unique way of dealing with existence, often referred to using the German word *dasein*; "being in the world".

How we respond to this existential crisis may create our personality, and how we deal with the *angst* created by the knowledge of certain death may explain some of the differences between us. The awareness of death causes us to engage in **terror management** as we are forced to define the meaning of our lives. This is generally done in the context of our social and cultural environment as we attempt to figure out our own value and how we fit into the larger framework of existence.

Death is unavoidable, and when people are reminded of this fact (known as **mortality salience**), they have a tendency to cling to their cultural values to affirm their own worth within their society. I remember seeing and experiencing this myself, following the 9/11 terrorist attack on the United States. The sudden death of thousands of innocent civilians didn't cause Americans to reflect on America's flaws or consider how their country's values might be perceived negatively elsewhere. Instead this event caused most people to wave flags, affirm their national pride, and sing a declaration that each was "proud to be an American".

This isn't meant as a criticism of these behaviors, but a recognition of how reminders of mortality can pull the knit of a society's fabric tighter and further entrench its views. Rather than searching for the existence of traits like authoritarianism, we could consider how mortality salience may play a role in the escalation of wars, as the greater and greater threat of death causes each side to dig in more deeply and further commit to values which may have initiated the conflict. In a more positive light, this tendency to cling to cultural values in the face of death could encourage bravery, perseverance, and unflinching devotion to a meaningful cause.

The Humanistic Approach

Beginning in the 1950s and 60s psychiatrists began to shift their focus away from the doom and gloom of repressed anxiety as the driving force of human behavior. Instead, humanistic psychiatrists considered the more positive forces that influenced thoughts, feelings, and behaviors. **Abraham Maslow** focused on people's innate drive to satisfy needs and find their potential. Maslow believed that rather than being victims of early childhood experiences, people had personal choice and a drive for **self-actualization**; a longing to reach their fullest potential.

Carl Rogers believed that we struggled with incongruence between the *real self* we actually are and the *ideal self*; the version of the self that we want to be. Reducing this incongruence by working to be the best version of ourselves would allow us to become **fully-functioning**. Rogers felt we could be held back by *conditions of worth*, or certain conditions we thought needed to be met before we could accept ourselves or feel appreciated by others. Rogers suggested that all people needed **unconditional positive regard**, a feeling of acceptance regardless of the specifics of their thoughts and behaviors. He felt that therapists should always strive to provide this positive regard for their patients (whom he referred to as *clients* to reduce stigma) rather than criticizing behaviors. We'll see more of the humanistic approach in the next chapter on motivation and emotion, and then again when considering approaches to the treatment of mental disorders.

The Self

We should also take some time to consider the self itself. How do we view ourselves and how might this reflect or influence our personality traits and our behaviors?

If you recall the section on bias, you might remember the **Wobegon Effect** (also known as **illusory superiority**) which is the tendency for most people to believe they are above average (a statistical impossibility). This also relates to *self-serving bias*, which is to remember times when we succeed and ignore or forget our failures. This may be driving our tendency to see ourselves as capable and may help to keep our self-esteem high. It can be problematic in relationships, however, as we tend to see ourselves as more important and valuable than we actually are. When individuals are asked to estimate their contributions to the completion of a group project or when members of a couple are asked to estimate things like what percentage of the housework they do, totals usually surpass 100% (such as each person claiming to do 60% of the work), meaning that individuals have a tendency to believe they are contributing more than they actually are.

George Kelly proposed **personal constructs**, mentioned previously, which are ways we understand the traits and behaviors of others. By asking people to describe others they know and how these people differ, one can see which traits a person focuses on when trying to understand the social world. This could reveal how the person values certain traits, revealing more about the person than those being described. We also have our own constructs for ourselves; ideas about how we think, feel, or behave, and the sum of all these ideas can be referred to as our **self-concept**.

Albert Bandura, who we previously learned about for his Bobo Doll study on observational learning, proposed that personality could be understood through 3 factors which all influenced each other through a process known as **Reciprocal Determinism**. Bandura suggested that we have an initial biological predisposition for certain traits and behaviors and this predisposition influences which environments we find appealing. These environments then further influence our behaviors and the development of a trait.

Biological disposition (inherent trait)

Behavior and its consequences

Environment (some situations encourage particular traits to emerge or develop)

For example, imagine that Sam is naturally introverted and finds busy environments overstimulating. He would then be driven to seek out solitary situations, such as reading in the library. His preference for the library would then encourage him to be more withdrawn, because he isn't learning how to reach out to others. When placed in a social situation Sam may feel uncomfortable because he doesn't have much experience interacting with others. This discomfort might cause him to retreat back to the familiarity of the book stacks, further entrenching this pattern.

In contrast, imagine that Sam's classmate Charles is naturally predisposed to being extraverted and thus seeks out social stimulation. His early experiences are positive and because others now see him as outgoing, he's more likely to be invited to social situations and parties, further developing his comfort in these environments and the ease with which he can meet new people.

Self-Efficacy

When it comes to getting what we want, it may not be enough to know what we need to do, we also need to believe that we are capable of doing it. Bandura suggested the idea of **self-efficacy** or **efficacy expectancy**, which refers to our own beliefs in our ability to do the things we want to do. We may see ourselves as incapable of certain behaviors (such as getting along well with a group of strangers) and this feeling of competence will influence the environments we seek out and how we interpret the consequences of our behaviors.

A closely related idea to self-efficacy is the notion of *locus of control* proposed by Julian Rotter. Rotter suggested that people tend to either see themselves as having control (*internal locus of control*) or they see things as being outside of their control and dependent on others, the environment, or fate (an *external locus of control*). Perhaps not surprisingly, a strong internal locus of control tends to be associated with higher levels of success and happiness. You can think of the difference between an internal and external locus of control as the difference between a person who believes "I always make things happen" versus one who believes "things always happen to me".

Daryl Bem has suggested that our own *self-perception* is heavily influenced by the behaviors we see ourselves doing. Just as we form opinions of others based on our observations of their behavior, so we also form ideas about ourselves based on observations of our own behaviors. Rather than thinking that our thoughts about ourselves dictate our behaviors, we should consider that our behaviors can influence how we think about ourselves.

For instance, a person repeatedly interacting with others (even while feeling shy) may change her perception that she is shy because her behavior no longer matches this perception. Her behavior is no longer demonstrating shyness, and as a result this trait may no longer be seen as a part of her self-concept. As we'll see in the next chapter on emotion and motivation, there is also evidence that our behaviors can influence our emotional states, rather than our emotional states always dictating our behaviors. There seems to be growing support for the notion that "fake it 'til you make it" is a strategy that can help us to make changes in our personalities and our emotional states.

Lastly, we have an evaluation of the self, known as *self-esteem*. This assesses how positively or negatively people feel about the self. While high self-esteem is associated with higher achievement and lower levels of depression, it's hard to say that self-esteem is causing these relationships, since greater achievements could lead to increases in self-esteem.

Wait, What About the Myers-Briggs?

Chances are that some readers out there are asking this very question. How could I write a chapter on personality psychology without mentioning the **Myers-Briggs Type Indicator** (**MBTI**)? If you've ever expressed your interest in personality or psychology in general, chances are you've had someone tell you their results from the Myers-Briggs Type Indicator or ask you about your type. Given what we've learned about personality in this chapter, perhaps we can more easily dissect the problems with the MBTI and understand why it doesn't receive much attention (other than criticism) from most personality researchers.

Even though the Myers-Briggs Type Indicator is one of the most widely-used personality assessments today (taken by over 2 million people each year), it is not highly-regarded by most researchers and it is mostly used for career and leadership-training purposes. The MBTI was developed by Isabel Briggs Myers and her mother, Katharine Briggs, neither of whom were trained psychometricians, and it is a self-report which consists of *forced-choice* questions, meaning that the respondent must choose only one of two options, not both. Responses are used to label personality type using 8 different letters. These letters correspond to Introversion or Extraversion (I or E), Sensing or iNtuition (S or N), Thinking or Feeling (T or F) and Judgment or Perception (J or P), and a person is either one letter or the other, and cannot be both. This results in a total of 16 possible letter combinations representing 16 personality types.

There's an important reason why a trait-based approach uses dimensions, rather than types. While dimensions place people along a spectrum, a typology such as the MBTI places people into categories. This means that for something like extraversion, the MBTI only identifies two kinds of people; introverts and extraverts, a fairly broad categorization. This means that the difference between two individuals who receive the same letter (highly introverted and slightly introverted) can be greater than the difference between two individuals who fall on either side of the cutoff point and thus receive different letters (slightly introverted and slightly extraverted). This also reduces reliability, as people who score near the middle will frequently receive a different type with each testing (one study has estimated as many as 50% of respondents receive a different type indication on a second test).

The MBTI paints people with rather broad brushstrokes, allowing them to fill in the details themselves. As we've seen, this type of general feedback may encourage the Barnum Effect and may explain why so many people rate MBTI feedback as accurate. If we're feeling especially critical, we may wonder if the MBTI provides a kind of modern-day astrology, bathed in the glimmering light of what appears to be science. Like astrological signs, the MBTI types provide a convenient way of simplifying the world and its people, fitting them into neat boxes that supposedly allow us to understand them.

While it's possible that the MBTI has some useful applications, results are often taken out of context and used to make predictions about skills and behaviors that the test is not designed to make. The appropriateness (and ethical implications) of its widespread use by career-counselors and corporations (for job placements and leadership purposes) should be more carefully considered to ensure that capable individuals are not kept out of certain positions on the basis of their types. We should think of all personality assessments as tools for assessing *personalities*, not people. So while the MBTI provides a way of thinking about how people vary, it certainly can't tell us *all* the ways that people can vary from one another.

The perspectives on personality and the self discussed in this chapter aren't comprehensive and other factors are involved in patterns of behavior. In the following chapter, we'll focus on emotion and motivation and further examine humanistic perspectives. We'll also consider how biological drives, motives, and self-regulation may influence a person's unique pattern of behavior.

In light of each of the perspectives above, we also have ways of thinking about mental illness. Could some disorders be extremes of certain personality traits, disruptions of biological systems, or maladaptive cognitive schema? We'll return to these ideas when we look at mental illness, including personality disorders.

Chapter Summary – Personality

- Freud divided personality into the *id*, *ego*, and *superego*. Childhood development focused on *psychosexual stages* and *defense mechanisms* were ways of coping with anxiety.

- *Projective techniques* for assessing personality include the *Rorschach Inkblot Test* and the *Thematic Apperception Test*, which involve the interpretation of ambiguous stimuli or situations to reveal personality.

- The *Big Five* (or *Five Factor Model*) focuses on identifying where people fall on 5 main trait dimensions: *openness to experience*, *conscientiousness*, *extraversion*, *agreeableness*, and *neuroticism*.

- *Biological approaches* to personality have focused on levels of cortical arousal or genes which influence particular neurotransmitters and hormones, while *socio-cognitive approaches* have emphasized the role of *schema* and situations on behavior.

- *Existential psychology* considers how coping with existence and the inevitability of death plays a role in shaping personality and behavior.

- *Abraham Maslow*, *Carl Rogers*, and other humanistic psychologists emphasized the role of growth and personal development on personality. *Albert Bandura*, *Daryl Bem*, and *Julian Rotter* have each proposed theories related to how *self-efficacy*, *self-perception*, and *locus of control* shape personality.

Notes

Chapter 11
Emotion & Motivation

What is an Emotion?

Even though you've probably experienced a wide range of emotions for as long as you can remember, it still may be tough to say what an emotion is. So while you probably know that an emotion is a feeling, if you're having a hard time defining it, that's ok, you're not alone. It turns out that psychologists also struggle with defining specific emotions. Instead of attempting to carefully define each emotion, psychologists find it easier to talk about emotions by making comparisons. We may struggle to say exactly what happiness is, but we can generally agree that it's better than sadness.

Using a technique called *multidimensional scaling*, we can compare emotions to one another and then map them out on two main dimensions. The first dimension is how strongly an emotion can be considered a positive or negative experience, referred to as *valence*. The second dimension is to consider how an emotion relates to our *physiological arousal*; some emotions like fear, excitement, or surprise have our hearts racing, while others, like boredom, calmness, or depression are characterized by low levels of arousal. While these aren't the only two dimensions we could use to think about emotions and we may not always agree on exactly where emotions fall on these dimensions, this approach gives us a way of organizing and comparing emotional experiences.

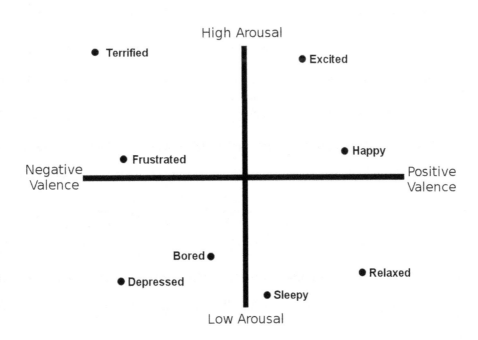

How Do Emotions Happen?

When we consider how emotions differ in terms of physiological arousal, we may begin to wonder how this process gets started. There are several approaches to thinking about the relationship between arousal and emotional experience. The first of these, suggested independently by William James in the United States and Carl Lange (pronounced *lawn-guh*) in Denmark, is referred to as the ***James-Lange Theory of Emotion***. This theory suggests that an emotional experience is the result of physiological arousal. In other words, we see a stimulus, this stimulus influences our level of arousal, and this physiological activity causes us to experience a particular emotion. A classic example is walking in the woods and suddenly seeing a large bear. This stimulus causes your heart to race, and your racing heart tells you that you are afraid.

This may seem fairly logical, but the problem we have is that this theory doesn't address how different emotions might arise from similar physiological states. Your heart may also race while you are exercising, but this doesn't cause you to experience fear.

Later theorists Walter Cannon and his student Philip Bard suggested that instead of a chain-reaction, a stimulus causes both the nervous system activation and the emotional experience at the same time, known as the ***Cannon-Bard Theory of Emotion***. This would mean that the bear causes your heart to race *and* it causes you to feel afraid at the same time. This theory helps explain some scenarios that don't fit the James-Lange Theory, such as blushing. In the case of embarrassment, people often experience the emotion immediately though the tell-tale physiological sign of a flushed face is slightly delayed (taking 15-30 seconds to occur). So if you were to accidentally fart in class you probably wouldn't need to wait until your face was red to feel embarrassed.

Stanley Schachter and ***Jerome Singer*** proposed that the stimulus and our general level of physiological activity are combined and interpreted to give us our emotional experience, and this is known as the ***Two-Factor Theory of Emotion***. In an experiment to demonstrate this, participants were given an injection of epinephrine, which increased their physiological arousal. Some of the participants were told the truth about what the drug would do (increase heart-rate, breathing, etc.) while others were misled (told it would cause numb hands, itchiness, and a headache). The participants then interacted with a confederate in a waiting room who acted either goofy (making paper airplanes, tossing balls of paper, and twirling hula hoops) or enraged (tearing up a survey form and storming out because of questions such as: *With how many men (other than your father) has your mother had extramarital relationships?*).

During and after this interaction, participant behaviors were observed and they completed a self-report of their emotional state. The ones who had been told the true effects of the drug reported feeling relatively normal but the participants who had been misled were more likely to report feeling giddy or angry depending on which confederate they had interacted with. It seems these participants were experiencing strong physiological arousal but since they didn't know where this arousal was coming from (the epinephrine), they incorrectly assumed it was part of their emotional state. By manipulating cognition, Schachter and Singer were able to influence emotional state.

This provides evidence that an emotional experience is not just a physiological response to a stimulus but an active cognitive *appraisal*, in which we assess and ascribe meaning to how our body is feeling. This interpretation isn't always correct and we can be fooled by our physiological arousal and misinterpret our emotional experiences, known as *misattribution of arousal*.

 Our physiological reactions influence our emotional state when we believe they're relevant. Stuart Valins found that men's sense of attraction to women's images could be influenced by hearing a false-heart beat (which they believed was their own) that sped up when viewing the pictures. The effect of hearing heartbeats was also demonstrated at a live podcast recording by WNYC's Radiolab in 2015 when a loud heartbeat sound used in the show caused many listeners to feel dizzy, and even caused some listeners to faint.

Misattribution of arousal was perhaps most famously demonstrated by Donald Dutton and Arthur Aron in 1974 when they found that men were more likely to call the phone number left by a female interviewer if they met her while crossing the shaky Capilano suspension bridge in Vancouver than if they met her on solid ground elsewhere in Capilano park. Dutton and Aron suggested the bridge caused the pounding heart and sweaty palms men experienced but that these signals were misattributed as signs of attraction to the woman.

Emotions in the Brain

In 1936, Heinrich Klüver and Paul Bucy removed the temporal lobes of rhesus monkeys and discovered that the monkeys then tried to eat all sorts of inedible items and also became hypersexual, attempting to mate with just about anything. Another result of the surgery was that the monkeys remained incredibly calm when handled and no longer showed signs of fear, even when faced with snakes. These traits became known as *Klüver-Bucy syndrome*, or temporal lobe syndrome.

Despite this name, it turns out that it wasn't removal of the temporal lobe that was responsible for these changes but damage to subcortical structures in the limbic system. A few decades later, research by James Olds and Peter Milner revealed that an area of the hypothalamus known as the *nucleus accumbens* plays a key role in motivations for hunger and sex. Rats who could self-administer electrical stimulation to this area by pressing a lever would ignore food, sleep, and potential mates, pressing the lever continuously until they collapsed from exhaustion. At the time, Olds and Milner thought they had found the "pleasure area" of the brain, but later research revealed a more appropriate name would be the "***reward area***". It wasn't just that the stimulation was pleasing the rats; it was motivating them to keep pressing the lever.

As for the lack of fear in Klüver and Bucy's monkeys, this was probably the result of damage to another structure of the limbic system: the ***amygdala***. The amygdala seems to be a key area for appraising a stimulus and determining an emotional response. Without properly functioning amygdalae, it seems that these monkeys could not correctly identify the threat posed by a snake, and therefore did not show fear. Their ***emotional appraisal*** was impaired, meaning that they weren't able to assess what was happening or why it mattered.

Joseph LeDoux has proposed that our emotional response to a stimulus occurs via two different pathways: a ***fast pathway*** which quickly jumps to the amygdalae, and a ***slow pathway*** involving the cortex. The fast pathway or "low road" quickly determines if something is good or bad and prepares us for immediate action. The slower pathway, or "high road", involves the cortex of the frontal lobes and takes time to identify the stimulus and consider its importance, at which point we can modify our course of action. You've experienced the time delay between these two pathways if you've ever been startled by something unexpected (fast pathway) and a moment later identified it as harmless (slow pathway). Richard Lazarus has suggested that some of the process of appraisal is occurring unconsciously and Robert Zajonc has suggested that we have no conscious awareness of some of our emotional reactions. This can be seen in studies in which people have shown fear reactions to stimuli even when the stimuli were presented too quickly for conscious awareness (see Whalen et al, 1998).

Unfortunately, improved understanding of emotion in the brain also has a dark history. The prospect of blunting emotions led to attempts to sever connections in the brains of human patients who were prone to emotional outbursts. Egas Moniz, a Portuguese neurologist, developed the *leucotomy* in 1936, a procedure which involved drilling a hole in the skull and inserting an instrument to cut fibers between the frontal lobes and the thalamus. Moniz was later awarded the Nobel Prize in 1949 (though in recent years some have called, unsuccessfully, for the Nobel Committee to rescind this award). This procedure was renamed the **lobotomy** and popularized in the United States by neurologist Walter Freeman and neurosurgeon James Watts. In 1937, Freeman and Watts began performing the procedure and quickly found thousands of patients, the most famous of which was 23-year old Rosemary Kennedy (sister of John F. Kennedy), who spent the rest of her life institutionalized and incapable of speaking after an unsuccessful lobotomy.

Freeman later simplified Moniz's procedure to the *transorbital lobotomy*; chiseling an icepick-like-instrument through the eyesocket rather than drilling a hole in the skull. Watts took issue with Freeman's new procedure and severed ties, though this new technique meant that a surgeon was no longer necessary and Freeman began performing the procedure himself (rendering unconsciousness using electric shocks and shocking physicians by not wearing gloves or a mask while "operating"). Freeman traveled throughout the US, visiting psychiatric institutions and Veteran's Affairs centers in a camper he called the "lobotomobile", promoting use of the procedure by psychiatrists. An estimated 40,000 lobotomies were performed in the United States (Freeman claiming at least 3,500 himself), most during the 1940s and 50s, though the practice continued into the 1970s in some states. As with forced sterilizations, this procedure has been alleged to have been used to silence some members of society, including prisoners and political dissidents.

Lobotomies fell out of favor or were banned in many places, partially due to the advent of new medications, but this wasn't the end of psychosurgery. Decades later some still advocated for procedures involving destruction or removal of parts of the limbic system in attempts to reduce violent behavior and aggression. Other psychosurgeries such as *cingulotomies* have been used in the treatment of Obsessive-Compulsive-Disorder (with mixed results) and similarly controversial procedures are still being carried out for drug addiction and mental illness in China, where a heated needle is sometimes used to destroy brain tissue in the nucleus accumbens.

Emotional Regulation

The involvement of the frontal lobes in the slow pathway suggests their role in cognitive and behavioral strategies to control and regulate our emotional experiences. Understanding emotional regulation can also help us to deal with negative emotions. Research by Richard Lazarus and Elizabeth Alfert found that emotional reactions to watching a video of a circumcision were reduced and rated less distressful when the event was described as a joyous religious ritual. In the chapter on Stress and Health, we'll also look at how we can change our emotional reactions to stressful stimuli by engaging in this type of ***reappraisal***, in which we reconsider possible meanings for stimuli.

We know that regulating emotions is predominantly a job for the frontal lobes. We all adopt cognitive or behavioral strategies to try to influence our emotions, whether to help us feel better or prevent us from feeling worse. Based on our previous chapter, you may now be starting to see some connections between our ability to control and regulate our emotions and what might constitute part of our individual personality (particularly when it comes to traits like conscientiousness or neuroticism). When we start thinking about the ability to regulate emotions and control behavior as a function of particular brain regions, this can also raise some unsettling moral questions. What happens when cortical damage influences a person's ability to regulate and control their emotions?

Questions of accountability and culpability aren't just thought-experiments and represent real problems that the future of psychology may be forced to answer. This may make us wonder just how we assign blame; do we blame the person or blame a faulty brain? Given the accidental nature of his injuries, we might hesitate to place blame on Phineas Gage for any moments of rage. After all, what can we expect from a man missing a chunk of his brain? But what if Gage were to commit a crime? Or what if his accident wasn't quite so severe? What if it were only a concussion, but one which caused damage to the same brain regions? Or what if instead of injury, a genetic defect was impairing prefrontal cortex function? This is where things get murky.

We might consider the case of Charles Whitman, who perched himself in a clocktower and shot dozens of people in Austin, Texas in 1966. How much do we blame the man, and how much do we blame the pecan-sized brain tumor discovered in autopsy? Where do we draw the line when we discover that the prison population has about 7 times the average incidence of traumatic brain injury in the United States? How should we think about punishment for these "bad brains"?

Expressing Emotions

Our emotions are more than just internal feelings and they have several ways of making themselves known to others. Our emotions find their way out through speech, tone of voice, eye gaze, posture, and perhaps most importantly, through facial expressions. More than forty different muscles in the face work together to reliably produce actions which are tied to particular emotional states. But how do we learn these movements and how do we know what they mean?

In line with his ideas on natural selection, Charles Darwin proposed that the expression and recognition of emotions had evolutionary significance. Immediate knowledge of someone's anger or fear could aid your survival, so it would follow that this ability might be inherited. Darwin's ***universality hypothesis*** suggested that humans around the globe expressed certain emotions in the same way, regardless of their culture or upbringing. After weathering the storms of strict behaviorism and cultural relativism in the early-to-mid twentieth century, it appears Darwin's theory was right. The evidence supporting universality comes from a number of sources, from infants who smile just days after birth, to members of isolated tribes and congenitally-blind individuals whose facial expressions all match the emotions we would expect.

Paul Ekman, who conducted early research examining the facial expressions of the Fore tribe in Papua New Guinea, proposed that there are 6 emotions with universally recognized expression: ***joy***, ***sadness***, ***anger***, ***fear***, ***surprise***, and ***disgust***. Chances are that you could easily recognize these expressions on someone's face, regardless of the person's language, culture, or region.

Another point of support for universality is the widespread adoption of emoticons in communication around the world, suggesting that people easily understand the emotions behind these simple images of faces. Emojis (from the Japanese 絵文字 "*picture character*") on the other hand, can be confusing because they may include culturally-specific references which are not universal (such as hand gestures, foods, sports, or celebrations).

Our facial expressions aren't just the consequence of emotions, they are also part of the cause. This idea that how we move our face tells us how we are feeling and influences our mood is known as the ***facial-feedback hypothesis***. This hypothesis suggests that emotions are self-reinforcing, meaning that expressing emotions increases their strength. In one study students who held pencils in their teeth (to simulate smiling without asking them to smile) reported higher moods than those in the control group. It seems that smiling doesn't just show that you're happy, it can make you feel happier too.

Of course, you can't walk around grinning like an idiot all the time, even if it does make you feel good. Expressing and recognizing emotions is fundamental for smooth social interaction, but there are times when we don't want our face giving away our mood. This isn't just for the poker table, but for a wide variety of social interactions, and different cultures have different **display rules** for when certain expressions are acceptable. No matter what's going on in your mind, you probably don't want to be beaming at a funeral or grimacing at a party. At times we may want to *intensify* (smile big as if that gift is really great), *de-intensify* (don't look quite so happy to see your friend's girlfriend), *mask* (force a smile to hide your contempt), or *neutralize* emotional expressions (stay stone-faced despite those pocket aces). But despite our best efforts, our bodies and faces often betray us, sending out signals of how we truly feel which trained observers can learn to detect.

Here's a few tips for spotting whether an emotional expression is likely to be genuine, though remember that these are guidelines, not hard-and-fast rules. Sometimes the form or *morphology* of an expression can reveal the truth, such as a genuine smile, which involves crinkling around the eyes that is tough to fake. Other clues include *symmetry* (genuine expressions tend to be somewhat asymmetrical), *duration* (genuine expressions usually last about 0.5 to 5 seconds, but of course, you already knew that never-ending beauty pageant smile didn't seem right) and *temporal patterning*, which refers to how smoothly an expression appears and fades on someone's face; not surprising if you consider the all-too-sudden and not-too-sincere smile that jerks itself on to some jerk's face.

Deception isn't just in our faces, and other clues can be used to help identify when someone is lying. Despite generally high levels of confidence, it turns out that most people aren't particularly good at detecting liars and don't do much better than chance when put to the test. There are things to look for, however, and trained observers are able to detect liars with about 80% accuracy. What are they noticing? It might not be the things you think.

Many people incorrectly assume that liars can be spotted because they talk too quickly and avert their gaze, but neither of these is strongly associated with lying. In fact, liars tend to talk more slowly, take longer to answer, and include less detail in their responses. Truth-tellers tend to be more engaging, more fluent, and they tend to include imperfections, superfluous details, expressions of self-doubt (I think he was wearing a blue shirt but I'm not really sure) and spontaneous corrections (it was about 5pm, no, 4pm). It's a bit ironic that these types of "errors" are avoided by liars, who seem to think that self-correction or doubt will give them away, when in fact it's a lack of correction and doubt that can indicate lying.

Now you may be wondering about the accuracy of lie-detectors. A **polygraph** (Greek for "many writings") tracks a number of physiological changes in the body, including heart-rate, blood pressure, and galvanic skin-response, which indicates sweating. We should remember that despite their popular name, these machines aren't actually detecting lies but simply measuring physiological changes in the body during questioning. While the assumption is that lying will be revealed through patterns of physiological activity, this will not always be the case. People can be trained to fool a polygraph, and people who aren't lying can give false positives. While polygraphs are a bit better than chance, they aren't good enough to establish certainty as to whether or not someone is lying.

Why Do We Have Emotions?

While you probably aren't running from bears on a daily basis, emotions play a major role in everyday life. When we think about anything that feels good or bad, we're relying on an emotional assessment. The **hedonic principle** is the idea that we want to experience pleasure and avoid pain. From this view, we can see how emotional experiences help us to know what is good (it's *good* because it feels good).

Antonio Damasio studied a patient named Elliot, whose brain damage from an accident reduced his emotional responses. With reduced emotions, we might expect a person like Elliot would be completely rational in his decision-making. Instead, patients like Elliot struggle to make even the most mundane of daily decisions. Choosing an appointment time became an endless consideration of pros and cons because Elliot never found a time that felt right. Without any emotional cues for what was *good*, he could flounder endlessly between equally dull options. He didn't vacillate because he cared about the outcome, his indecision was the result of what we might consider severe apathy. Decision-making relies on emotional responses to help guide behavior.

Other patients with brain damage to their limbic system have suffered from a bizarre condition known as *Capgras Syndrome* in which they believe that a loved one has been replaced by an imposter. William Hirstein and Vilayanur Ramachandran have proposed that this preposterous belief in imposters results from a lack of emotional response when the patient sees the person. Without the emotional response that used to accompany the sight of Mom, the patient infers that this must not be Mom. Once again we see just how much it matters that things feel right.

Motivation

When we ask why we have emotions, our main answer is likely to be that emotions motivate us. Positive emotions motivate us to seek out pleasurable experiences, while negative emotions signal which situations we should avoid.

One early way of thinking about motivation was based on **instincts**, which didn't require any previous experience in order to motivate behavior. Instincts were considered to be inherited tendencies activated by features of the environment which made us seek out certain goals. For example, we would have an inherited tendency to seek out food, not because of anything we learned, but simply because this instinct would help us to survive.

The concept of instincts seemed to be a good way of thinking about motivation, but the problem was that it was hard to tell which behaviors were the result of inherited instincts and which were learned. Early psychologists, including William James, quickly piled up a list of thousands of instincts, which meant that many of these supposed instincts were merely new names for behaviors rather than explanations of behaviors. This unwieldy number of instincts, combined with the rise of behaviorism and its emphasis on learning meant that the study of instincts was soon on the decline.

But despite a heavy emphasis on environment, even behaviorists had to admit that other factors influenced behavior. After all, a well-fed rat in a cage with food may just sit there but wait a few hours and without any change in the environment eventually you'll see a change in behavior and the rat will begin eating. How could this fit into the stimulus-response explanation for behavior if there doesn't appear to be any new stimulus? Rather than falling back to the idea of instincts, behaviorists used a new term which referred to much the same thing: a **drive**. A drive was considered to be a change from an *optimal physiological state* which motivated certain behavior in order to return the organism to that optimal state. In the example above, the hunger drive was what was now compelling the rat to eat.

Drive Reduction Theory

This idea of drives is closely linked to the concept of **homeostasis**, which is that the body wants to maintain a particular state and any departures from that state create drives to modify behavior. Drive reduction theory, developed by Clark Hull, stated that a behavior was rewarding because it reduced a drive, so in our previous example, the reward would not be the food itself, but the reduction of the hunger drive.

Drive theory also distinguishes between primary and secondary drives. A **primary drive** would be for something that aids our survival, like food, water, or warmth, while a **secondary drive** doesn't aid survival directly but is associated with a primary drive. The drive to earn money, which can then be used to buy food, would be a secondary drive, though the theory doesn't adequately explain how a money-earning behavior would actually reduce a drive and thus be rewarding.

The **opponent process theory of motivation**, described by Richard Solomon, suggests that emotions are paired, with each emotional experience having a *primary process* and an *opponent process*. With each successive exposure, the strength of the primary process is reduced, while the opponent process is strengthened. Solomon and J.D. Corbit considered emotional responses in skydivers, finding that first-timers mostly experienced fear, while experienced skydivers showed little fear and higher joy. Similarly, dogs which were given electric shocks initially showed anxiety after the shocks, but with repeated exposure, the end of a shock period seemed to bring relief and contentment.

Another way of thinking about what motivates our behavior is **Arousal Theory**. This is similar to some of the ideas of stimulation we discussed in the previous chapter on personality. In the context of introverts and extraverts, we considered how differing levels of cortical arousal may influence their preferences. Arousal theory considers this as a more general explanation of behavior and proposes that we each have an optimal level of arousal that we want to reach, and so we are motivated to seek out behaviors which will increase or decrease our level of arousal. When arousal is below the optimal level we are motivated to do things to increase it and when arousal is above the optimal level we are motivated to decrease it.

The **Yerkes-Dodson law**, proposed by Robert Yerkes (yes, the same Yerkes from the intelligence chapter, pronounced *yer-keys*) and John Dodson, suggests that peak performance on a task is associated with a particular level of arousal and departures in either direction (arousal too low or too high) will decrease performance, creating a curve similar to an inverted U. Yerkes and Dodson formulated this theory by observing how quickly mice learned a task in the presence of weak, moderate, or strong electric shocks, finding that both low and high shocks reduced performance compared to moderate shocks. You might imagine yourself taking an exam; if you don't care at all about the results you might not do well (not bothering to check answers, etc.) or if you're extremely anxious your performance would also suffer (unable to focus, second-guessing every answer, etc.) while some middle level of arousal would allow you to do your best. A mnemonic you might use is thinking "*Your key* (Yerkes) is to find the optimal level of arousal."

A related notion is the concept of **flow**, proposed by Hungarian psychologist Mihaly Csikszentmihalyi (pronounced *me-high cheek-sent-me-high*). When an activity doesn't challenge us we become bored, and when a task is too demanding for our skills we experience anxiety but when we find an ideal balance of challenge and skill, we experience flow and become deeply absorbed in the task.

Hunger

We all eat, and we've all probably experienced hunger, though hopefully not in the extreme. We've already considered hunger as an example of drive theory, but how exactly does this hunger signal work?

There are two parts to the hunger signal: the **orexigenic** signal is the "on" signal that motivates us to eat (you can remember **O**rexigenic and **O**n), while the **anorexigenic** signal is the "off" signal when we feel full and stop eating. Both of these signals rely on biological cues controlled by hormones, as well as psychological cues like our memory of when we last ate, visual stimuli like an appetizing dessert tray, and cultural preferences for particular tastes.

Hormones involved in the orexigenic signal include **orexin**, which is released by the **lateral hypothalamus** in the brain, and **ghrelin**, which is released by the stomach when it is empty (you can think of your stomach *growling* to remember *ghrelin*). Rats with damage to the lateral hypothalamus never seem to get hungry and will starve to death if they aren't force-fed. Several other hormones are also involved in hunger, including insulin, which is released by the pancreas and helps to regulate blood glucose levels.

The satiety signal indicating that we are full involves another area of the hypothalamus called the **ventromedial hypothalamus**, in addition to involving the hormone **leptin**, which is released by fat cells. Destruction of the ventromedial hypothalamus in rats seems to disrupt their satiety signaling, and they eat significantly larger amounts of food, eventually tipping scales at 2 to 3 times their normal weight. This weight gain may also be related to a faster gastric emptying rate, with food moving out of the stomach so quickly that the "full" signal is impaired.

Eating Disorders

Bulimia Nervosa is an eating disorder in which patients binge eat large quantities of food, then purge by vomiting, using laxatives, or exercising excessively. Bulimia nervosa is associated with negative emotions like sadness, anxiety, and shame, and sufferers can feel trapped in a destructive cycle: bingeing to cope with negative emotions, purging to reduce regret, then experiencing guilt and shame from purging. **Binge-Eating Disorder** was recently added to the official diagnostic list of disorders (the *Diagnostic & Statistical Manual of Mental Disorders - Fifth Edition*, or *DSM-5*) and refers to episodes of binge-eating and feelings of guilt and shame, without any compensatory purging behaviors.

Anorexia Nervosa is an eating disorder characterized by severe food restriction and fear of weight gain, usually accompanied by a distorted sense of one's own body shape and size. Unfortunately it's not the case that patients just need to eat something to solve their problems and popular misconceptions of the disorder can increase the stress that sufferers face.

Eating disorders have high rates of mortality, but they can be successfully overcome with treatment and therapy. There's still a strong social stigma attached to eating disorders and resulting shame or embarrassment can prevent sufferers from seeking the help they need before it is too late. Like most disorders, eating disorders seem to involve complex interactions of genes, family environment, stress, hormones, and cultural pressures.

Obesity

The widespread struggle with obesity demonstrates the evolutionary origins of hunger signaling. The genes our ancestors passed along have given us a preference for calorie-dense foods as uncertain food supplies and lengthy famines were common in our evolutionary past. As a result, our genes have predisposed us to crave calorie-rich foods that would better prepare us to survive lean times. For most people today, however, lean times are few and far between and our evolutionary habit to gorge ourselves in times of plenty means that we are gorging ourselves all the time. We also have a predisposition to gain weight because it is easier for our bodies to store calories than burn them. As we all know, it's easier to finish off those fries in just minutes, while burning those calories off at the gym takes significantly longer.

Obesity is often defined in adults based on their ***Body Mass Index*** (***BMI***). BMI is calculated by dividing one's weight in kilograms by one's squared height in meters. BMI scores from 18.5 to 24.9 are considered normal, while those below 18.5 are considered underweight, 25-29.9 overweight, over 30 obese and over 40 morbidly obese. This calculation isn't ideal, however, because it doesn't consider where the weight comes from, so individuals with large amounts of muscle mass may have BMI scores in the overweight or even obese range despite low levels of bodyfat. In addition, since BMI scores are not differentiated by gender, differences in body composition mean males are more likely to have high BMI scores than females.

Set Point Theory suggests that people have different body weight set points which influence how many calories they are compelled to consume and their ***metabolism*** or how their bodies then burn or store those calories. Set point theory is still an oversimplification, however, because individuals who have had drastic changes to their body weights don't necessarily show corresponding changes to their metabolisms. A person's set point seems to be influenced by genes but early environment may also play a role, as illustrated by the "Dutch Hunger Winter", or *Hongerwinter*, which occurred during the winter of 1944-1945 in Holland.

During this time Nazis successfully blockaded trade routes and millions of Dutch people starved for several months. The ***Dutch Famine Birth Cohort Study*** found that the children of women who were pregnant during the famine were more likely to suffer from type-II diabetes, cardiovascular disease, and obesity later in life. This suggests that this traumatic prenatal experience had lasting repercussions on their metabolisms, making their bodies less responsive to insulin and more likely to store fat. It seems that children of these children have been affected as well, which would be an example of an ***epigenetic*** change, or an environmental influence that causes changes which are then passed on to future generations.

Sexual Motivation

Just as hunger signals provide important motivations to keep individuals alive, sexual motivations help to ensure the survival of the species via reproduction. In humans, sexual motivation is influenced by hormones including testosterone, estrogen, progesterone, oxytocin, and vasopressin. While hormone levels can influence sexual motivation, they don't directly regulate sexual behavior.

In many other species (but not humans), females undergo a period of ***estrus***, or *heat*, during which they become fertile and are receptive to sexual advances from males. This window of sexual availability and fertility varies widely for different species, and may occur as often as once every few days (rats) or perhaps only once per year (pandas). Human females ovulate on a monthly cycle but this is not the sole precursor for sexual activity and women can engage in sexual behavior at any time during their cycle. In addition, human females "hide" their fertility, meaning that males cannot tell if a woman is ovulating by looking at her. Unlike the swollen bottoms of baboons or red chests of gelada monkeys which advertise estrus, human females don't have any obvious displays of when they are most fertile.

One proposed evolutionary explanation for this unpredictable timing of sexual desire combined with hidden fertility is that it encourages males to stick around. If a male can't be sure when a female is capable of becoming pregnant, he has an incentive to be around often to ensure paternity when the opportunity arises. If a male were certain that a female could not become pregnant for long periods of time, then he could leave during that time without the possibility of returning to raise offspring that are not his own. In evolutionary terms, this provides an advantage to the female because it helps to ensure that the male will be around to help provide resources for potential offspring, rather than being able to stray for months at a time.

Of course, if I were to ask people why they have sex, reproduction would not be the only answer. In fact, many people who have sex are hoping *not* to reproduce. So why are they doing it? One reason is that it feels good. Just as our genes encourage us to eat calorie-rich foods by making them taste great, we're driven to sexual behaviors not strictly for the noble cause of continuing the species but because sex just feels good. People also engage in sex for other reasons, including emotional intimacy, satisfying their partner, relieving stress, impressing friends, coping with negative emotions, or feeling more attractive.

The Human Sexual Response Cycle

In the 1960s, ***William Masters*** and ***Virginia Johnson*** set out to better understand sex, and recruited willing (and rather uninhibited) couples and individuals to come to the lab and have orgasms. Based on observation of over 10,000 orgasms, Masters and Johnson identified the stages of the human sexual response cycle, which were the same for males and females.

Masters and Johnson identified four physiologically distinct phases of the human sexual response cycle: excitement, plateau, orgasm, and resolution.

The cycle begins with the ***excitement*** phase, during which sexual arousal occurs. While the increased breathing and heart rate during the excitement stage suggests activation of the sympathetic nervous system, sexual arousal actually involves activation of the parasympathetic nervous system. Excessive stress and anxiety can cause problems with sexual arousal and may be responsible for erectile dysfunction in males or insufficient vaginal lubrication in females.

Arousal doesn't continue to rise indefinitely, and eventually reaches the ***plateau*** stage, where it remains high but relatively stable. As sexual activity continues, it reaches the ***orgasm*** stage, characterized by increased heart rate, involuntary muscle contractions and spasms, and feelings of euphoria.

The orgasm stage is followed by ***resolution***, when heart rate and breathing return to a resting state. This stage is also characterized by a ***refractory period*** in males, during which further stimulation does not result in arousal.

Other Motivations

While some may disagree, there's more to life than just food and sex; people are motivated to perform a wide variety of other behaviors. ***Abraham Maslow*** suggested that our motivations could be organized into a "***hierarchy of needs***", meaning that some needs must be met before others, and we gradually move up the hierarchy. The most basic are ***physiological needs***, for food, water, warmth, and sex. These exert powerful influence on an individual and need to be met before other needs can be considered. Once these are met, needs for ***safety and security*** follow, then needs for ***love and belonging***, which include friendships, family, and intimacy. These are followed by needs for ***esteem***, including self-esteem, freedom, independence, and a sense of self-respect. Finally, at the top of the pyramid, is the need for ***self-actualization***. Self-actualization refers to a need to realize one's full potential as a person.

While Maslow's hierarchy does have an intuitive logic to it, the progression of needs may not be so clear-cut. We may consider hunger strikes and vows of abstinence as defiance of physiological needs in order to satisfy higher needs. Or we might consider altruistic acts where individuals risk their own safety in order to help others, or famines, where individuals who are starving share their food with friends and family, placing the need for community and social bonds before their own physiological needs. Maslow later suggested the possibility of a level higher than self-actualization: *transcendence*, where an individual is no longer concerned with personal needs, which could be used to explain such acts of altruism and self-sacrifice.

Intrinsic vs. Extrinsic Motivation

Motivations can be broadly categorized as intrinsic or extrinsic. ***Intrinsic motivation*** refers to an internal sense of satisfaction and enjoyment from performing a task while ***extrinsic motivation*** refers to motivation driven by external rewards and punishments. In the chapter on learning theory we saw the behaviorist approach to understanding how rewards and punishments can encourage and discourage behavior, but we didn't see some of the ironic effects of rewards and punishments on motivation.

One such ironic effect was demonstrated in a study conducted by Mark Lepper, David Greene, and Richard Nisbett in 1973. Lepper, Greene, and Nisbett initially observed the amount of drawing behavior children engaged in during their free time at several nursery schools. Then children at some schools were told they would receive "Good Player" awards for drawing. Not surprisingly, this expected reward caused an increase in drawing behavior. What was surprising, however, was that when this reward was no longer offered, the increased interest in drawing didn't maintain itself, or even return to its previous baseline. Instead, drawing behavior decreased compared to the period before the reward was ever offered.

This is known as the ***overjustification effect***, in which extrinsic rewards come to replace intrinsic motivation. Essentially the children learned that one draws in order to get rewards, and so when those rewards are no longer available it seems there's no longer any reason to draw. Lepper, Greene, and Nisbett also had judges who were blind to the conditions of the experiment evaluate the quality of the artwork produced by children, and work produced during the "expected reward" period received the lowest ratings. This indicates that children weren't motivated by creativity and a sense of accomplishment, but instead were dashing off their "art" in order to get the reward.

An intuitive understanding of this overjustification effect may explain why many artists, musicians, or writers prefer to view their efforts as passions rather than as jobs for the sole purpose of earning money. A meta-analysis of 128 experiments by Edward Deci, Richard Koestner, and Richard Ryan in 1999 found that external rewards which are tangible (rather than verbal rewards or praise) could reduce intrinsic motivation. We should question rewards-for-grades programs that have been put into place in some school districts, which may cause students to see their learning as work, rather than a process of discovery which is rewarding for its own sake.

We can't rely on intrinsic motivation all the time of course, because sometimes we have to do things that we'd rather not do in order to get rewards later. In these cases, we must learn how to **delay gratification**, putting in effort now for benefits in the future. One measure of this ability is often referred to as the **Marshmallow Test**: children wait alone in a room with a marshmallow after being told they can eat it whenever they want but will get two marshmallows if they can wait until the researcher returns. This ability for self-imposed delay of gratification in 4 year-olds has been associated with higher ratings of social competence, better ability to cope with frustration, and even higher SAT scores (Mischel, Shoda, & Rodriguez, 1989).

Another ironic effect on motivation comes from punishment, in what we might call the "forbidden fruit" effect. In a study by Elliot Aronson and J. Merrill Carlsmith in 1963, children ranked several toys and then were threatened with either a mild punishment or a severe punishment for playing with a particular toy while the researcher left the room. When the researcher returned, the children ranked the toys again. It turns out that a mild threat of punishment reduced the desirability of that toy, but ironically, a severe threat increased its desirability. Aronson and Carlsmith suggested that the mild threat leads to **insufficient justification** for not playing with the toy. In other words, the children avoid the toy, but since the mild threat doesn't fully justify this avoidance, they also decide that the toy wasn't worth playing with in the first place and desirability is reduced. In the severe threat condition, however, the threat alone is enough to justify avoiding the toy but also serves to increase interest in the toy, making it more desirable. We may wonder how the threat of strict punishments for drug use, infidelity, or other transgressions may actually make these behaviors appear more desirable, perhaps revealing some truth to the expression "you always want what you can't have".

It's not just threats of punishment that can ironically encourage behavior, it seems that actual punishments can also have this effect. Uri Gneezy and Aldo Rustichini (2000) found that day-care centers which began punishing parents with a fee for late pickups actually saw an increase in tardiness. This would likely leave B.F. Skinner scratching his head as to how a punishment could increase a behavior, but thinking in terms of motivation can help us understand what happened. Previously parents were intrinsically motivated to arrive on time in order to avoid feelings of guilt. Arriving late meant taking advantage of the teachers' time and violating a social norm. With the late fee in place, however, this intrinsic punishment was replaced by an extrinsic one, allowing parents to pay the fee rather than feel the guilt. Parents now knew the exact cost of arriving late, leading Gneezy and Rustichini to title their paper "A Fine is a Price".

Given these ironic interactions, we might wonder which is better for managing behavior, intrinsic or extrinsic motivation? If you were managing a group of employees, for instance, would you focus on providing rewards and punishments for their efforts, or would you focus on their sense of satisfaction with the work they do? This relates to **management theory**, and managers can be broadly categorized based on which approach they prefer. **Type X** leaders focus on extrinsic motivators like benefits and punishments, while **Type Y** leaders focus on developing the intrinsic motivation of their workers. Similarly, we can divide leadership into **task-oriented leadership**, which focuses on actual tasks which need to be completed and **relationship-oriented leadership**, which focuses on the social goals of trust or cooperation within a group.

Conscious vs. Unconscious Motivation

When we think about intrinsic and extrinsic motivations for behavior, we must also recognize that we may not always be conscious of motivations. If I asked you why you performed a particular behavior, you might be able to describe your motivation, but perhaps there are things going on under the surface that you aren't aware of. Since Freud's initial ideas about the psychodynamic unconscious, psychologists have considered the possibility of unconscious drives and motivations influencing behavior.

One such unconscious motivation proposed by Henry Murray and further researched by David McClelland was a **need for achievement**. This is a motivation to accomplish tasks, gain mastery, and win. Individuals with a high need for achievement may be motivated to seek out challenges of intermediate difficulty as tasks which are too difficult may lead to failure, while tasks which are too easy won't feel worthwhile or bring a sense of accomplishment.

You may recall Murray's name for his development of the Thematic Apperception Test, described in the previous chapter, in which participants provided storylines and character descriptions based on ambiguous situations. Murray believed that unconscious motivations could be revealed by an individual's responses to the TAT and that repeated themes of success, failure, and competition related to an individual's need for achievement.

David McClelland also suggested other unconscious needs and motivations, including a *need for power* and a *need for affiliation*. He suggested that motives were clusters of cognitions with emotional overtones that organize our behavior and our preferred experiences and goals. We can also see how our present environment influences our motivation for particular behaviors. McClelland referred to an external condition which creates desire for a particular behavior as a **press**, such as how seeing others receive honors can cause people to feel a greater need for recognition. You've probably also experienced a press if you are completely satisfied with a meal and don't feel any hunger, but then you see a dessert tray and are suddenly motivated to keep eating.

This brings us back to food, where the role of unconscious motivations can be seen in research by Brian Wansink which addresses environmental influences on eating behavior. We aren't simply relying on biological hunger signals or conscious decisions about how much to eat, and subtle cues like labels or plate size can have significant effects on how much food people eat. When people are asked why they ate a certain amount of food, they might be able to come up with a plausible explanation, but chances are there were also unconscious processes motivating some of their eating behavior. These cues can also be used to change eating habits for the better, so as Wansink notes in his book *Mindless Eating*, "The best diet is the one you don't know you're on".

Approach and Avoidance Motivations

Another way of categorizing motivations is to consider them as either approach motivations or avoidance motivations. An ***approach motivation*** is a drive to experience a positive outcome, while an ***avoidance motivation*** is a drive to not experience a negative outcome. The relative strength of these motivations may not be equal and some research has suggested that motivations to avoid loss can overpower motivations for gains. In one study, Daniel Kahneman and Amos Tversky (1979) found that participants weren't willing to risk losing $8 on a coin flip, even if a win would pay $10. While rationally these odds favor playing, this demonstrates how we can be more strongly motivated to avoid a loss than gain a win.

These two types of motivation can work together or be in conflict. When we make decisions, we often have multiple options and we must do a sort of mental accounting of approach and avoidance motivations in order to choose. For instance, when making your weekend plans there might be two movies that you'd like to see. In this case, you have ***approach-approach conflict***, because you want the positive experiences of both, but you can only choose one.

You might also experience ***avoidance-avoidance conflict*** when you are faced with choosing between outcomes which are all negative, such as deciding whether to wash the dishes or vacuum the floor.

Finally, you can have ***approach-avoidance conflict*** when a single choice contains both positive and negative motivations. For instance, imagine you've been invited to a party. You want to go because some of your friends are going (approach). At the same time, a few people you dislike will also be at the party, and you don't really want to interact with them (avoidance). Going to the party has positives you don't want to miss, but negatives that can't be avoided, so it's a situation where you're "damned if you do, damned if you don't".

Goals

What's the relationship between goals and motivation? One area of goal setting relates to intrinsic and extrinsic motivation mentioned above. Is a goal driven by internal self-satisfaction, or an external reward? When goals are intrinsically motivated (known as ***self-concordant goals***), individuals are more likely to persevere and they experience greater well-being when the goals are accomplished.

Even when goals are intrinsically motivated, however, we may still have trouble achieving them. One technique to help goal achievement is creation of ***implementation intentions***. Rather than setting a goal and not knowing what to do next, you use *if-then* rules to create situations in which you will perform specific goal-directed behaviors.

For example, creating a rule that you will always review the previous week's psychology notes on Monday afternoons at 4pm creates a specific situation in which you will work on your goal (the goal of learning psychology well). This may help to maintain goal-pursuit even when motivation is lagging (*if* it's 4pm Monday *then* I review, even though I don't feel like it). Now on Monday afternoon you don't need to waste mental effort deciding which subject you should review or what time you should start.

Implementation intentions can also be used to ensure that you don't miss opportunities to make progress toward a goal. For example, creating the rule "*If* I'm waiting in line *then* I will use my flashcard app to review Spanish vocabulary" will help you take advantage of an opportunity to work on a goal that you might otherwise fail to notice. This doesn't mean you need to fill your day with rules for every situation, but I do recommend creating a few implementation intentions to help structure your time and ensure progress on your most important goals.

Chapter Summary – Emotion & Motivation

- Theories of emotion include the *James-Lange Theory*, *Cannon-Bard Theory*, and the *Two-Factor Theory of Emotion*, proposed by *Stanley Schachter* and *Jerome Singer*.

- There are 6 emotional expressions believed to be universal: *joy*, *sadness*, *fear*, *anger*, *surprise*, and *disgust*.

- Early theories of motivation focused on *instincts*, then later *drives*. Research now considers the roles of *conscious*, *unconscious*, *intrinsic*, and *extrinsic* motivations on behavior.

- Hunger is controlled by two main signals which can turn hunger on (*orexigenic*) or turn hunger off (*anorexigenic*). Disorders related to eating behavior include *bulimia nervosa*, *binge-eating disorder*, and *anorexia nervosa*.

- Sex hormones like *testosterone* and *estrogen* play roles in sexual motivation. *William Masters* and *Virginia Johnson* identified 4 stages of the *human sexual response cycle*: *excitement*, *plateau*, *orgasm*, and *resolution*.

- Ironic effects of rewards or punishments on motivation can be seen in *overjustification*, *insufficient justification*, and situations where extrinsic punishments can increase behavior.

- *Self-concordant goals* increase striving and are associated with greater well-being upon accomplishment. *Implementation intentions* can be used to encourage goal-directed behavior.

Notes

Chapter 12
Development

Development

Throughout the previous chapters, we've considered a number of things that help to make you the person you are. Your intelligence, skills, personality, emotions, motivations, and goals are all fundamental for who you are, but how did these come to be? How have you developed physically, cognitively, socially, and morally? How much will you remain the same and how much will you change in the years to come?

These are the questions that developmental psychologists consider in order to better understand how a person progresses through life. We've already seen several examples of theories related to development including Terman's longitudinal study of intelligence, Freud's psychosexual stages, assessments of the stability of personality traits over time, and the lasting impact of early experience in the Dutch Hunger Winter. So chances are you already have a good sense of some of the major themes and challenges of developmental research: Does development occur continuously or in stages? What changes over time and what remains the same? How do genes and environment interact in shaping development? In this chapter we'll look at development more closely and see how theorists have addressed these questions in order to understand development throughout the lifespan.

Changing Challenges

Erik Erikson (1902-1994) viewed the lifespan as a series of eight stages, each with its own *psychosocial task* to be resolved. The first four of these stages were influenced by Freud's Psychosexual Stages, while the next four focused on the challenges of adolescence and adulthood.

In the *oral-sensory stage* (from birth to about age 1) the infant's primary task is establishing *basic trust*, which Erikson believed was primarily related to feeding. The infant learns it can depend on others, and this carries a lasting effect for future social relationships. Next the infant moves to the *muscular-anal stage*, during which the psychosocial task concerns developing a sense of *autonomy* based on successful toilet training. In the *locomotor-genital stage* (from age 3-6) the child learns a sense of *initiative* and independence to explore the world. The fourth stage was a *latency stage*, lasting from age 6 until 12, during which the child learns a sense of *competence* or inferiority based primarily on successful schoolwork.

The remaining four stages begin around puberty and continue through the rest of life. According to Erikson, the main goal of *adolescence* is for teenagers to develop a sense of *identity* (rather than *role confusion*) and this mostly comes from their peer relationships. In *early adulthood* (18-40) the main task is to find *intimacy* through romantic relationships. *Middle adulthood* concerns becoming a productive member of society (or perhaps a *reproductive* member of society by having children) and contributing to future generations, which Erikson referred to as *generativity*. Finally, at *maturity*, (65+) a person's main task is to reflect on life and accept the choices made, resulting in either *ego integrity* (a life well-lived) or regret and despair.

While Erikson's theory provides a reasonable outline for the major challenges of life, we should remember that it is heavily based on certain lifestyles and societal norms (such as schooling, age for childbearing, etc.) and may not apply well to other cultures or individuals who don't follow these social scripts. How well a particular task is resolved is up to the individual, meaning that what constitutes success in identity or ego integrity may vary widely and there are not strict guidelines for assessing accomplishment. Now we'll make our way through the lifespan in more detail, considering the changes and developments that occur over time.

Prenatal Development

We'll begin our journey through the lifespan at the very beginning; *conception*, the joining of the smallest single human cell (the sperm) with the largest single human cell (the egg). This is the genetic lottery; of the approximately 200 million sperm released, just one will find its way into the egg. Many of these 200 million sperm aren't really contenders, as they have defects which prevent them from swimming and many others will fail to swim to the correct fallopian tube. But of about 200 that will come close, one will find the way and break through the surface of the egg. Once this occurs, the egg is sealed by the release of an enzyme which prevents other sperm from penetrating it.

The chromosomes from the sperm and the egg combine to form a single cell, known as a *zygote*. During the *germinal stage*, the first 2 weeks of the zygote's development, the zygote will travel down the fallopian tube and attach itself to the walls of the uterus. This is no easy task and more than half of all zygotes will not survive the trip, with male zygotes (XY) having an increased likelihood of failing.

Once a zygote has attached itself to the uterus it is referred to as an *embryo* and it enters the *embryonic stage*, which lasts from the 2nd to the 8th week. At this point, the embryo is only about one inch long (2.54cm) though it already has a beating heart and the beginnings of arms and legs. Thus far male and female zygotes have been developing in the same way, but during this stage an XY embryo will begin producing *androgens* (male hormones) which will cause it to develop into a male.

Around the 9th week of development, the embryo is beginning to develop a skeleton and muscles and is now referred to as a ***fetus***. The ***fetal stage*** lasts from the 9th week until birth, though development certainly doesn't end there. Unlike many other species, humans are born with a brain that is only 25% of its eventual adult size. This accommodates the physical logistics of giving birth, but more importantly, it gives us greater adaptability because it allows learning and environment to play large roles in brain development.

When we think about the environment's role in development, we have to remember that environment doesn't begin at birth and experiences in the womb are considered environmental influence. The ***placenta*** is the organ which links the bloodstreams of the mother and her offspring and this connection means that mom's environment influences her offspring before birth. A ***teratogen*** (Latin for "monster-maker") is a substance which can harm development. Possible teratogens include lead, mercury, viruses, tobacco, alcohol, and other potentially toxic substances. Heavy drinking by a mother during pregnancy can result in ***fetal alcohol syndrome*** in the child, causing intellectual disability and characteristic facial features including smaller eyelid openings and a smooth *philtrum*, or ridge on the upper lip. Smoking during pregnancy (or even second-hand smoke) also has detrimental effects on the child, including low birth weight and attention and perception problems. The effects of teratogens highlight that early experiences in the womb can have lasting impact on a child's development. In fact, the child can also have lasting impact on the mother, as cells from the fetus can pass back into the mother's body through the placenta and remain for years or even decades, a phenomenon known as *fetal microchimerism*.

Prenatal development also includes learning, and there's evidence that a fetus learns to recognize its mother's voice during this time. In a study by Anthony DeCasper and Melanie Spence in 1986, expectant mothers read a story aloud twice a day during their last weeks of pregnancy and their infants later showed a preference for the sounds of that story over a novel stimulus.

At birth, the fetus has about 100 trillion cells is now an ***infant***. The ***infancy stage*** lasts from birth until age 18-24 months, during which the infant shows rapid development of perceptual and motor skills.

Motor Development

Infants are born with **reflexes**; patterns of motor responses that are triggered by certain types of sensory stimulation. One such reflex is the **rooting reflex**. When an infant's cheek is touched, the infant will turn to move its mouth in that direction. This reflex helps the mother to feed the infant, and it is accompanied by a **sucking reflex**, in which an infant will suck an object placed in the mouth. As the infant's control improves in the first few months, the rooting reflex disappears and the sucking reflex becomes a voluntary behavior.

While we can't predict the exact timing of particular skills, the sequence in which motor skills emerge follows a fairly predictable pattern of **developmental milestones**, such as first crawling, standing, walking, etc. The development of motor skills follows two general rules. The **cephalocaudal rule** (Latin for "head to tail") refers to the fact that motor control starts with head movements, then moves downward to the arms, then feet. The **proximodistal rule** (Latin "near to far") refers to developing control of the trunk, followed by elbows and knees, then finally hands and feet.

Perceptual Development

It can be difficult to assess what an infant perceives, because an infant is unable to tell us. So how can we figure out what's going on in an infant's mind? One way is to use a technique developed by Robert Fantz known as **preferential looking** (or *visual preference*), which is based on the idea that when given a choice between two stimuli, infants will look at the one they prefer or find more interesting. For example, if shown two tiles, one which is a solid color and one which is striped, infants will generally prefer to look at the striped tile. This technique can be used to estimate visual acuity at different distances by seeing when an infant can distinguish a solid tile from a thinly-striped one. Initially, clear vision seems to be limited to a distance of about one foot; not surprising when we consider that is roughly the distance to the mother's face when nursing. Experiments with preferential looking also reveal that infants prefer to look at certain types of stimuli, such as human faces.

A related technique is known as **habituation**. Habituation is based on the fact that we respond strongly to new stimuli and less intensely to repeated stimuli. This means we can see whether an infant considers a stimulus to be novel based on the strength of response. For example, we could see if an infant is able to differentiate two colors by showing one colored tile repeatedly until habituation occurs (response strength decreases). Then we could change the color of the tile and present it again. If the infant stares longer at this new tile, this tells us that the infant has noticed the change. Later we'll see how habituation has been used for more elaborate testing of what infants know about the world.

Brain Development

When thinking back on early years, most people find it impossible to remember much before about the age of 3. Infant brains just don't seem to have the capacity to store episodic memories yet, resulting in this *infantile amnesia*. Sometime around age 3, however, our brains become capable of storing autobiographical memories. This is also when our cognitive development really hits its stride, and we begin making rapid progress in a number of areas. In fact, from age 3 to age 6, children grow billions more synaptic connections than their brains actually use. This ensures that needed connections will be there, and part of normal development is the loss of neurons and neural connections which are not being used (known as *synaptic pruning*).

Mark Rosenzweig, David Krech, Edward Bennett, and Marian Diamond conducted research examining the role of environment on brain development in rats. By measuring the brains of rats who were raised in either an impoverished environment (an empty cage) or an "enriched" environment (a cage with toys, ladders, wheels, and tunnels), they could assess the influence of environment. They found that rats raised in the "enriched" environment had larger brain volume and a greater number of synapses.

This research is probably partially responsible for the onslaught of baby games, toys, and supposed enrichment programs. But how much do these things really enrich a human infant's environment? Probably not much. In the case of the rats, rather than thinking of the wheels and ladders as enriching, these were probably more like a rat's natural environment than the empty cage. "Enrichment" is probably not the best word and maybe something like "less impoverished" would be more accurate. It's likely that the best way to give a rat a bigger brain is not to put it in a cage with toys but to allow the rat to roam free and receive all the stimulation and enrichment the natural environment provides.

So before we rush out to buy Mozart CDs and baby yoga DVDs, we should consider that perhaps the natural environment of sights, sounds, language, and tactile experience is so wildly stimulating that it is already "enriched". If you're currently raising your child in a featureless cage, then sure, throwing in a toy or two would probably help. But in the real world a child is already tackling tough problems; learning to interact, figuring out how language works, coordinating movements and so much more. Given the richness of any normal environment, some background music and another colorful toy probably aren't going to make much difference.

Piaget's Stages of Cognitive Development

Swiss biologist-turned-developmental-psychologist *Jean Piaget* (1896-1980) investigated cognitive development, examining how cognitive abilities progressed throughout childhood. While assessing intelligence in young children, Piaget noticed that the mistakes children made weren't random and certain types of errors were common at certain ages, then seemed to suddenly disappear. This led Piaget to create a stage-based theory of cognitive development, with progress occurring in steps.

Piaget viewed children as little scientists who were building up structures for their knowledge (known as *schema*) which were then maintained or adjusted based on new experiences. Piaget proposed that when children encounter new information, there is a process of either *assimilation*; adding the information to their existing schema, or *accommodation*; changing the schema to account for the new information.

For instance, after seeing a sparrow and being told it is a "bird", a child might develop a schema that small flying things are called "birds". When encountering a pigeon, the child can easily *assimilate* this new stimulus into the existing schema for "bird". When seeing a bat, however, the child will need to *accommodate*, modifying the schema to distinguish that some small flying things are not birds.

The first of Piaget's stages is the *sensorimotor stage*, during which the infant's progress is primarily based on learning how to take in sensory information and how to control body movements. A fundamental concept Piaget believed was learned during this stage is *object permanence*. This is the notion that objects continue to exist even when we can no longer see them. Piaget thought that infants in the sensorimotor stage weren't able to understand this concept, explaining why they make certain types of errors or why a game of peekaboo is enthralling for infants but rather boring for anyone else.

Possible evidence that infants lack object permanence can be seen in the *A-not-B error*. After an object is repeatedly hidden in one location (A) an infant learns to reach for it in that location. Then the infant watches as the object is hidden in a new location (B). Despite watching closely, the infant will then reach for the object where it was last found (A) rather than where he watched it go (B). This suggests that the infant doesn't yet understand how the physical world functions.

Another possible interpretation of the A-not-B error is that infants are not yet able to control and coordinate their movements, since they often look at the **B** location while their arms reach for **A**, indicating that they know where the object is but are unable to inhibit the previously learned motor pattern. This suggests that improvement on the task might not be from improved understanding of object permanence, but from improved ability to suppress previously learned responses (part of what is known as *executive function*).

Piaget believed that infants lacked an understanding of object permanence until about age 2, but research using habituation and preferential looking has suggested that object permanence may exist considerably earlier. Renee Baillargeon, Elizabeth Spelke, and Stanley Wasserman found that 5-month-old infants stared longer at an impossible event than a possible event. In this study, infants seemed surprised when a box failed to stop the movement of a rotating panel, even though the infants could not actually see the box at the time (because it was behind the panel).

This suggests that infants knew the box still existed and expected it to stop the panel's movement. This experiment and others by Baillargeon and Spelke support the view that infant understanding of the physical world is more advanced than Piaget supposed. Similar research by Karen Wynn has found that infants may even have a sense of number. In one experiment, infants were shown 2 dolls which were then hidden behind a screen. A hand reached behind the screen and removed one doll. When the screen was lowered, there were still 2 dolls, and infants as young as 5 months responded to this impossible event by staring longer.

Before age 2 infants also show evidence that they are beginning to develop a sense of ***self-concept***. Around 18 months is when children first pass the ***mark test*** and recognize their own reflections in a mirror (for details see the chapter on consciousness). As children continue to develop, their self-concept becomes more and more complex and they begin to form an identity which includes understanding of their gender, the groups they belong to, and how their traits and skills compare to those of others.

The Preoperational Stage

Around age 2, children are in the ***preoperational stage***, because they don't yet fully understand how the physical world operates. Their perceptual and motor skills will, of course, continue to develop, but now there is greater focus on understanding the world, rather than just perceiving it and moving through it.

One common failure at this stage is difficulty with the concept of ***conservation***. Piaget tested this by using chunks of clay, taking two equal-sized chunks, then rolling one out into a long strip. Though children had initially agreed the pieces were equal, those in the preoperational stage now believed that the longer piece contained more clay. This failure to understand that quantity is conserved even when form changes applies to other situations as well, such as pouring equal amounts of liquid into different-shaped glasses or spreading out a row of objects on a table. Piaget thought the cause of this error was that children weren't yet able to interrelate their schema. In the case of liquid in a glass, children might know that height and width are each important, but they aren't yet able to connect these two schema and so they base their answers on just one.

In addition to figuring out how the world works, children in the preoperational stage also begin to develop a **theory of mind** to learn how others see the world. Around age 2 or 3, children show **egocentrism**, meaning that they are unable to see the world from any viewpoint except their own. Children don't yet understand that other people can have different knowledge, thoughts, and ideas. Piaget demonstrated this by having children view small objects placed on opposite slopes of a model mountain. Despite first-hand experience that the viewpoints differed, children still reported that a viewer on the other side of the mountain could see the objects on the child's side.

Another way of demonstrating egocentrism is through a **false-belief test**, in which characters have different levels of knowledge of a situation. In the *Sally-Anne test*, two dolls, Sally and Anne, are used. The child watches as Sally places a marble in her basket, then leaves the room, so Sally doesn't see Anne move the marble to Anne's basket. Sally then returns, and the child is asked where Sally will look for the marble. Before about age 4, children frequently respond that Sally will look where Anne has hidden the marble, failing to recognize that Sally has no knowledge of Anne moving it.

This might explain the brutal honesty of young children; if you think everyone already knows what you know, there's no need to lie. Once children begin to understand that they can keep secrets, they also realize that they can manipulate the thoughts of others. Evidence for this can be seen in a study conducted by Joan Peskin. In this study, a "mean monkey" puppet asks children which of 2 stickers they want, then, always having first choice, the monkey takes it. Children aged 3 are repeatedly disappointed, as they always tell the monkey which sticker they really want, and so the monkey always takes it and leaves the children with the undesirable sticker. By about age 4 or 5, however, children are able to strategically deceive the monkey about what they want, telling him they want the undesirable sticker so he'll take it, leaving them with the one they really desire. This suggests that children realize they can have thoughts the monkey doesn't know about, and now they can imagine the monkey's viewpoint in order to deceive him. This task may also be related to the development of executive function, because success requires children to inhibit revealing which sticker they really want when they are asked.

Autism spectrum disorder refers to a range of developmental problems related to language, motor skills, and socialization. Autism is sometimes considered a kind of impaired theory of mind, in which sufferers (mostly boys) show less interest in people, are less aware of the emotions, intentions, and beliefs of others, and have difficulty recognizing and expressing emotions. The *Sally-Anne task* mentioned above has been used by Simon Baron-Cohen (cousin of *Borat* actor Sacha Baron-Cohen) and colleagues to assess theory of mind in children with autism, though it's important to note that some children with autism can pass the test, and some children without autism can fail, so results should not be seen as conclusive.

Many children with autism also suffer some degree of intellectual disability and despite depictions in popular culture, only a very small number of autistic children show enhanced skills in areas such as music or mathematics. Autism was initially considered rare, (Baron-Cohen et al suggesting it affected 1 in 2500 children in 1985) but diagnoses have risen dramatically, with some recent estimates as high as 1 in 68 children. This has caused alarm of an autism epidemic as well as accusations of misdiagnosis, with some researchers suggesting that autism has become a catch-all diagnosis for a number of unrelated developmental difficulties, ranging from slower language abilities to low empathy or even frequent tantrums.

Concrete Operational and Formal Operational Stages

Once children have come to understand how the physical operations of the world work, Piaget considered them to be in the ***concrete operational stage***, some time around age 6. Children understand concepts of conservation and recognize that others have different views of the world, but they still struggle with abstract concepts. Children in this stage have difficulty with hypothetical situations and predicting how things will happen given certain abstract rules. Research by Judy DeLoache has shown that at this age children also struggle with tasks involving symbolic representation such as using a model of a room with a miniature toy hidden behind a small couch to determine the location of the toy in the actual room being modeled.

Eventually children develop the ability to think abstractly, entering Piaget's final stage: the ***formal operational stage*** (though Piaget thought some individuals never reach this stage). In this stage, usually beginning around age 11 and continuing throughout the lifespan, children have learned how to think about abstract concepts (such as democracy) and they are able to engage in if-then thinking; such as imagining ways things might happen in the future based on hypothetical changes now.

The Social Environment

While Piaget's stages are able to provide a fairly accurate description of when certain skills emerge in children, they don't really explain how children jump from one stage to the next. ***Lev Vygotsky*** (1896-1934), a Russian developmental psychologist, focused on how social interaction influences a child's development. Vygotsky emphasized a ***zone of proximal development*** which referred to the skills just outside of a child's ability. These are the things that a child cannot do independently, but can accomplish with a little bit of help from a parent or peer. Rather than figuring things out on their own, children have a social environment where others provide ***scaffolding*** to support the direction of their growth. Vygotsky's early death from tuberculosis meant that he was unable to fully complete his work but the concept has been developed and modified by later researchers.

Recognizing the importance of interaction brings us to another important aspect of a child's development; the development of social skills. How do children learn to connect with others?

Attachment and Bonding

One of the first human connections a child makes is with a primary caregiver, usually the mother. How does this connection (known as **attachment**) between mother and child occur?

In some species, the development of this connection isn't left to chance and is hard-wired into the offspring. **Konrad Lorenz** is considered one the fathers of the field of **ethology**; the study of animal behavior. He shared the Nobel Prize in 1973 (along with ethologists Nikolaas Tinbergen and Karl von Frisch) for work on animal instincts, including a phenomenon known as **imprinting**. Lorenz found that upon hatching, goslings would follow the first large moving object they see. There seems to be a **critical period** of about 12 hours after hatching when this imprinting will occur. In nature, the first large moving object seen would be the mother, though Lorenz was able to have goslings attach to other animals, rolling balls, and even himself.

What about other species? Rather than waddling behind, young rhesus monkeys will cling to the fur of their mothers, a literal form of attachment. In the 1950s, **Harry Harlow** was conducting research with rhesus macaques when he discovered that monkeys raised in isolation would cling to cloth diapers as a source of comfort. Harlow decided to raise young monkeys with two surrogate "mothers"; a wire mother which provided food and a cloth mother which did not. This would help to determine whether attachment was due to the mother being a source of food (as many behaviorists believed) or a source of contact comfort. Comfort won, as young monkeys spent most of their time clinging to the "fur" of the cloth mother and would run to this cloth mother when frightened. This suggested that the monkeys had emotionally attached to the cloth mother and were using it as a source of security and comfort.

Harlow's experiments are controversial due to the extent of mistreatment of the young monkeys and Harlow's cold writing style didn't help, as primatologist Robert Sapolsky described "I remember as a student being moved to tears of rage by the savage indifference of his writing". Harlow's other studies included complete isolation in what he called the "pit of despair" and caused psychological disturbance in the monkeys. Harlow's brutality encouraged activists to oppose animal experimentation in order to prevent the type of suffering inflicted on these monkeys. On the bright side, however, these studies improved understanding of how abusive environments and social isolation can inflict psychological damage that continues through life. They also provided clear demonstrations of the importance of touch and comfort for healthy development, overturning earlier parenting advice which had urged parents not to touch or hold their infants too often.

Human infants aren't able to follow their mothers immediately after birth, and they aren't able to physically cling to their mothers either (though they do show a remnant of this with a **_grasp reflex_**; gripping an object which touches the palm tightly enough to briefly support their own body weight). But infants do still form an attachment in the form of an emotional bond. By crying, cooing, making eye contact, and smiling, human infants are able to connect with others and they track who regularly responds to these cues. This is usually the primary caregiver, and the infant will attach to this figure, using him or her as a secure base. This concept of a **_secure base_** is that the infant feels more comfortable exploring the environment in the presence of this person. When frightened or unsure, the infant has learned it can rely on this caregiver to provide assistance.

Mary Ainsworth tested the quality of this attachment by placing infants in a **_strange situation_** in which their secure base was no longer present. While a researcher observed through a one-way mirror, the mother would play with the infant, then exit the room, leaving the infant either alone or, in some variations, with a stranger. After waiting a few minutes to observe the infant's response, the mother would return to the room and the infant's reaction to this reunion would also be observed.

Ainsworth then classified the response styles of the infants as a secure attachment, an avoidant attachment, or an ambivalent attachment (though about 5% of responses don't fit any of these styles and are thus considered **_disorganized attachment_**).

In a **_secure attachment_**, the infant shows distress when the caregiver leaves, but is then effectively comforted upon the caregiver's return. This is the most common attachment type, seen in about 60% of American children. About 20% show an **_avoidant attachment_** (also known as _insecure-avoidant_); they don't show distress when the caregiver leaves and therefore they don't seek comfort during the reunion. Approximately 15% of American children show an **_ambivalent attachment_** (also known as _insecure-resistant_) in which they are distressed when the caregiver leaves, yet the caregiver's return fails to provide comfort. These children may show anger and actively resist the caregiver's attempts at consolation.

After observing these responses from infants, we might naturally wonder what is causing these differences. In the personality chapter we considered that infants show the first signs of personality in their **_temperaments_**, or their patterns of emotional reactivity. Is attachment the first expression of a child's emerging personality? Or perhaps reactions demonstrate the infant's expectations for the caregiver's behavior; preparing for consolation, isolation, or confrontation. Or maybe the attachment type is the result of the parent's ability to read and understand the infant's emotional state, which may then depend on the infant's ability to clearly express that state. As with most questions we face, the answer is probably a mix of all of these factors and you can recall Bandura's _reciprocal determinism_ to consider how temperament may influence and be influenced by experience and environment.

We should also keep in mind that these attachment types are not sharply-defined and may vary across cultures or change over time. Nevertheless, there are some outcomes associated with different attachment types. Secure attachment is associated with better social relationships and better future academic performance compared to ambivalent or avoidant attachments.

Parenting Style

The possible influence of parenting doesn't end at attachment. ***Diana Baumrind*** classified parenting into 3 main styles: Authoritarian, Permissive, and Authoritative.

Authoritarian parenting is strict, with clear rules and harsh punishments. What the parent says goes, and the child is powerless. This type of parenting has been associated with lower social skills and reduced self-esteem in children.

Permissive parenting is on the other end of the spectrum, with few or no rules or punishments. Children can do what they please and parents are neither demanding nor responsive. Children who receive this type of parenting have shown higher levels of aggression and lower levels of maturity.

Authoritative parenting falls in the middle of those extremes and describes parents who are demanding but are also responsive to the child. Rules are set and enforced, but with explanations for why the rules exist and open discussion and possible compromise based on the child's input. This type of parenting is associated with several positive outcomes including higher self-esteem, greater self-reliance, and better social competence.

Eleanor Maccoby and John Martin later added a fourth parenting style to Baumrind's trio, known as ***neglectful parenting*** (also known as *uninvolved parenting*), referring to parents who provide basic needs but are too preoccupied to be responsive or demanding of their children and instead focus most of their attention on other pursuits rather than parenting. This style has been associated with lower levels of social competence and lower school achievement.

As with attachment styles, the outcomes described above are correlational, so we can't assume causation. Children's traits may influence parenting style or children and parents may share genes related to social competence which influence their relationship.

Moral Development

How do we learn what is right and wrong? How do we gain an understanding of morality? **Lawrence Kohlberg** attempted to track the development of morality by posing ethical dilemmas to children and then analyzing the rationales for their answers. Based on interviews with thousands of children of different ages, Kohlberg formulated a stage-based approach for the development of moral reasoning. Kohlberg's model consists of 3 main stages of moral reasoning, each with 2 levels, for a total of 6 levels of moral development.

While Kohlberg's theory is presented in stages, this doesn't necessarily mean that people always use the highest stage of moral reasoning they have reached and different problems and solutions may draw on arguments from earlier stages. Let's take a look at a moral dilemma which Kohlberg used, known as the **Heinz Dilemma** (not to be confused with a Heinz pickle). Here's the dilemma as used by Kohlberg (1981):

A woman was near death from a special kind of cancer. There was one drug that the doctors thought might save her. It was a form of radium that a druggist in the same town had recently discovered. The drug was expensive to make, but the druggist was charging ten times what the drug cost him to produce. He paid $200 for the radium and charged $2,000 for a small dose of the drug. The sick woman's husband, Heinz, went to everyone he knew to borrow the money, but he could only get together about $1,000 which is half of what it cost. He told the druggist that his wife was dying and asked him to sell it cheaper or let him pay later. But the druggist said: "No, I discovered the drug and I'm going to make money from it." So Heinz got desperate and broke into the man's laboratory to steal the drug for his wife. Should Heinz have broken into the laboratory to steal the drug for his wife? Why or why not?

Using this scenario, it doesn't matter whether respondents think that Heinz should or shouldn't have stolen the medicine, what matters is the moral reasoning behind the decision. With this in mind, let's look at each of Kohlberg's stages and consider how someone in each stage might address Heinz's dilemma.

Preconventional Stage

In the **preconventional stage**, morality is generally framed in terms of consequences. **Level 1** is a system of morality based entirely on punishment. If someone is punished, they must be wrong, and if they are not punished then their behavior must be ok. In **Level 2**, the emphasis is on gaining a reward. If you've been rewarded for something, then it must be good.

If you remember what we learned about the *egocentrism* of young children, you might not be surprised to see them think this way. After all, if you think that everyone knows what you know, then punishment or reward should always be swift and certain. No punishment must mean that others know what you did and don't have a problem with it.

Preconventional justifications would focus on whether or not Kohlberg would be rewarded or punished. One might argue that if he steals the drug and saves his wife then his action is justified, or one might argue that if he steals it and gets caught then it is not justified.

Conventional Stage

Rather than specific punishments or rewards, **conventional** morality focuses on societal approval. Consequences don't necessarily reveal morality because of the recognition that some rewards are undeserved and some deserved punishments are never received.

Level 3 morality focuses on conformity to group norms and social approval. *Level 4* focuses on rigid codes for controlling behavior, such as systems of law and order or strict rules of etiquette.

Conventional explanations for Heinz would focus on societal expectations, systems of rules, or codes of conduct. So a level 3 justification for stealing the drug might be that Heinz must be a "good husband" and do anything possible to help his wife (and avoid social condemnation). At level 4, one might argue that stealing the drug is wrong because individuals must obey the law in order to maintain social order.

Postconventional Stage

Kohlberg believed that most people never reached the last two levels of the postconventional stage but instead relied on the rules of society and codes of conduct to guide their moral reasoning (hence the label *conventional*). But for those who reach the ***postconventional stage***, morality is based on overall ethical principles.

In *level 5*, rather than rigid adherence to rules, morality is based upon a "social contract" for the public good. Occasionally circumstances arise in which this contract requires flexibility in order to best serve the public interest. In *level 6*, the individual has come to a personal system of morality which is based on abstract ethical principles.

A response at level 5 might argue that laws don't exist simply to be obeyed; they serve to protect people. In this case, violating a law for something like theft is acceptable if doing so protects a human life. A level 6 argument against stealing the drug might be that Heinz is stealing not from the shopkeeper but from another potential patient. Who is Heinz to decide who lives or dies? Why should his wife's needs come before another patient with the same illness? One might argue that Heinz should see all human life as equally valuable and be glad that the drug will save someone, if not his wife.

These stages correspond to how a person thinks about behavior and aren't meant to imply that one level is more or less moral than another. Kohlberg's stages can be criticized for ignoring the role of culture in how people think about relationships, rules, and social order. Gender may also play a role, and **Carol Gilligan** has proposed that Kohlberg's stages are androcentric because males tend to emphasize justice in their moral reasoning, while females are more likely to focus on relationships and empathy for others. We should also remember that while responses might reveal how a person thinks about the dilemma, they don't necessarily reveal how the person would actually behave in a similar situation.

More recent psychologists such as Jonathan Haidt (pronounced *height*), have argued that in most cases, people don't carefully consider formal arguments when making decisions and instead they rely on **moral intuitions**, which are immediate and mostly unconscious evaluations of right or wrong. Later moral reasoning may be serving to rationalize or justify these feelings, rather than being part of the actual decision-making process.

So where do these moral intuitions come from? Rather than starting from scratch, it seems they use a clever evolutionary trick: emotional experiences developed for physical interactions in the world have been co-opted for use by our decision-making systems. So in terms of emotional response, our reaction to something like incest may be similar to that of finding a rotting animal carcass. The similarity of these experiences can also be seen in the language we use, as we tend to describe acts we think are immoral as gross, repulsive, or disgusting.

Despite these automatic evaluations, there may still be room for reasoning about morality. Based on evidence from fMRI scans while participants think about moral issues, Joshua Greene and colleagues have proposed a dual-process theory with two moral systems; one relying on emotional judgments and the other using rational, calculated judgments. Greene and colleagues found that when moral dilemmas were impersonal they engaged brain areas associated with rational consideration but when people were personally connected to a moral decision, they showed greater activation of their emotional system. These differing systems support the intuitive notion that we are better at rational analysis if we aren't personally involved in a moral decision.

Adolescence

Adolescence marks the transition from childhood to adulthood and thus is a time of great change. Physical changes during puberty are mostly associated with the development of reproductive ability. These changes can be categorized as **primary sex characteristics**, which are changes directly related to reproductive organs, and **secondary sex characteristics** which involve other areas of the body.

Boys begin puberty around age 12, with primary sex characteristics involving growth of the penis, testes, and related internal organs. Secondary sex characteristics in boys include the growth of facial hair, pubic hair, and underarm hair, as well as increased muscle growth and deepening of the voice. Around age 14, boys will experience **spermarche** (pronounced *sperm-AR-key*): their first ejaculation.

Puberty tends to begin earlier in girls, with onset around age 10. Primary sex characteristics are development of the genitals and ovaries, with the experience of **menarche** (pronounced *men-AR-key*), a girl's first menstrual cycle or period, occurring around age 12. Secondary sex characteristics include growth of pubic hair and underarm hair, as well as the development of breasts and widening of the hips.

In both boys and girls, puberty also marks the myelination of the frontal lobes of the brain, although this process won't be completed until around age 25. As we learned in the previous chapter, these brain regions are crucial for self-regulation and emotional control. Increased sexual drives without fully-developed capacities for self-regulation may be partially to blame for the increased impulsivity and risk-taking that are often associated with teenage behavior.

Piaget's *formal operational stage* began around puberty and this means that adolescents have new capacities for hypothetical thinking and abstract reasoning. These new abilities may be applied to teenagers' own lives, as they challenge existing beliefs and conventions. This may cause conflict with parents and other adults, though this conflict is often relatively minor and focused on things like clothing and hair styles, language and slang, or music preferences. Improvement in their cognitive abilities may also be related to the development of more efficient strategies for learning new information and solving problems, as well as improved memory capacity.

Lastly, adolescence is a time of socioemotional change. Adolescents find themselves with greater independence and their primary source of socialization shifts from parents and family to friends and peers. New social, romantic, and sexual experiences and opportunities abound and adolescents must figure out how they fit into this new social world (remember Erikson's *identity* vs. *role confusion*). They may try on multiple roles, eventually finding their own identity, which may also relate to group identities (such as "gamers", "jocks", etc.).

The Development of Sexual Orientation

While psychoanalytic theorists focused on *identification* with a same-sex parent for learning sexual orientation, there's no evidence supporting this early view, and in fact no aspects of parenting have been strongly linked to sexual orientation. Parental sexual orientation doesn't seem to have an influence either, as children are just as likely to identify as homosexual whether they were raised by heterosexual or homosexual parents.

There does seem to be genetic influence on sexual orientation. One study of males found that for dizygotic twins, if one was gay the odds of the other being gay were 22%. For monozygotic twins, however, if one was gay the odds that the other was also gay were 52% (Bailey & Pillard, 1991). Of course, these odds still leave room for environment. Environmental influence during adolescence does not seem to dictate sexual orientation, in fact, in some cultures homosexual behaviors and rituals are a normal part of adolescence, and do not serve to "make" anyone gay in later life. More likely, the influence of environment on sexual orientation comes much earlier, before birth. There's some evidence that levels of prenatal hormones like testosterone may shape or perhaps even determine sexual orientation.

When it comes to the development of sexual orientation, there may also be differences between males and females. Most homosexual males report their first same-sex attraction some time around age 8 and also tend to report feeling that they have always been gay. Homosexual women, however, report less early certainty, supporting the notion that, in general, female sexuality may be more fluid or flexible (referred to as *erotic plasticity*) than male sexuality.

We should also remember that thinking of being gay, straight, or bisexual as an essential part of one's identity is a social construct. We should consider wider possibilities for cultural and individual variation in sexual identity, sexual behavior, and the meaning of same-sex relationships.

Adulthood

It's difficult to assess exactly when "adulthood" begins and this can vary rather widely in different cultures or time periods. In some cases, adulthood may seem to begin just as puberty ends, while in others there may be a long gap before one is considered to have arrived at adulthood. The challenges of adulthood include learning how to develop closeness and intimacy, managing new social and financial obligations, and learning how to care for children and aging parents.

Adulthood also brings physical changes, as physical abilities peak and then begin their gradual decline. Aging brings weight gain, loss of muscle mass, thinning and graying of hair, and decreases in sensory abilities for sight, smell, hearing, and taste.

Cognitive performance also tends to decline with age, though not all cognitive abilities are affected equally. While semantic memory does not show much decline, the ability to access and recall memories can be impaired. Fluid intelligence (for solving new problems) also slowly declines beginning in the early-to-mid twenties. This may seem surprisingly early but crystallized intelligence continues to improve, helping to compensate. Cognitive decline may be influenced by a number of other factors. Reduced effectiveness of other body systems such as kidney function or circulation may contribute, as well as changes in the ability to concentrate and reductions in novel mental stimulation.

More severe cognitive changes may arrive late in life, provided we live long enough to see them. **Dementia** (also known as *senility*) is a category of disorders which cause loss of mental function that is not a normal result of aging. Aging is still associated, however, as dementia affects only about 1% of those over age 65, but may affect as many as 25% of those over age 85. While most cognitive decline from dementia occurs gradually, some people experience more sudden and focused losses due to a series of mini-strokes in the brain (known as *multiple-infarct dementia*).

Alzheimer's disease is a specific type of dementia. *Amyloid plaques* (clusters of protein fragments between neurons) and *neurofibrillary tangles* (twisted protein strands inside neurons) accumulate, damaging or destroying cells. This loss of nerve cells can cause memory problems, disorientation, and difficulty speaking, swallowing, and walking. While some neuron loss in the hippocampus occurs with aging, patients with Alzheimer's disease experience more widespread damage to many areas, shrinking their brains dramatically. Some genetic risk factors have been identified, but there is not yet a clear cause of Alzheimer's disease nor is there is a cure or treatment for reversing damage.

While the cognitive and physical declines of aging cannot be stopped, they can be slowed, with physical exercise being a key strategy. Mental exercise and cognitive activity is likely also a factor, though as we saw in the chapter on intelligence, assessing the effectiveness of brain training is difficult and more research is needed.

Just as adolescents must adapt to a changing social world, adults also face social and emotional changes and transitions. The passionate love of early adulthood gradually gives way to more companionate love. Relationships change, physical and cognitive abilities diminish, and adults must confront the meaning of their lives. Though they tend to live longer than men (by about 5 years) women may be forced to reflect on some of their life choices a bit earlier at the onset of *menopause*; which marks the end of their reproductive abilities.

By old age, the future is short, but generally bright. Elderly adults tend to be less concerned with acquiring new information and skills, and more concerned with emotional goals. The elderly tend to seek out positive emotional experiences, meaning that despite dealing with the many declines of aging, they tend to see an overall increase in well-being.

Chapter Summary – Development

- Developmental psychology considers how traits and behaviors change or remain stable over time, how genes and environment interact, and how goals and challenges vary throughout the lifespan. *Erik Erikson* proposed 8 stages of life, each with a unique challenge to be accomplished.

- Prenatal development begins with **conception**, followed by the **germinal stage**, **embryonic stage**, **fetal stage**, and at birth, the **infancy stage**.

- Jean Piaget proposed a stage theory of cognitive development with 4 stages: **sensorimotor**, **preoperational**, **concrete operational**, and **formal operational**.

- Around age 4 children begin to show less **egocentrism** and more developed **theory of mind**, understanding that others can have differing thoughts, feelings, and intentions.

- Infants show different types of **attachment** to a primary caregiver, including **secure**, **avoidant**, **ambivalent**, or **disorganized attachment**. Parenting styles can be broadly categorized as **authoritarian**, **permissive**, **authoritative**, or **neglectful**.

- *Lawrence Kohlberg* proposed a theory of **moral development** with three main stages: **preconventional**, **conventional**, and **postconventional morality**.

- Adolescence is marked by physical changes of puberty (including **primary** and **secondary sex characteristics**) as well as social and emotional changes that emphasize peers and forming a sense of **identity**. The challenges of adulthood include finding intimacy, contributing to future generations, coping with gradual physical and mental declines, and reflecting on one's life choices.

Notes

Chapter 13
Social Psychology

Social Context

In this chapter, we'll consider how groups, culture, and social context influence thoughts, feelings, and behavior. You may wonder about the difference between social psychology and sociology. *Social psychology* studies the influence of social context, mostly by examining how this context influences the behavior of individuals. *Sociology*, on the other hand, tends to focus on the influence of social factors on larger groups of people, such as social or economic classes, genders, or entire ethnic groups.

Social psychological research (and other types of psychological research) can be broadly categorized into *basic research*, which refers to gaining knowledge simply for increased understanding, and *applied research*, which refers to research that aims to improve some aspect of human society. As we'll see, social psychology tackles a number of issues with important social implications and hopefully increased knowledge can be used to better the world.

Social psychologists use some research methods that aren't as common in other areas. They may engage in *archival studies*, which consist of examining past records in order to look for patterns and cultural or historical trends. This may involve studying newspaper accounts, medical records, diaries, or statistics like the number of website hits or search queries over a certain time period.

Another type of study which is common in social psychology is an *observational study*. This type of research involves observing and recording natural behaviors that occur in the real world. One type is a *field experiment*, in which researchers control an aspect of the environment and then measure how people respond to different manipulations. It's important to remember, however, that while these situations help to demonstrate actual behaviors in the real world (high *external validity*), researchers are unable to control many other aspects of the environment and these other variables may influence results. There are also *subject variables* such as gender, ethnicity, or cultural background, which may influence behavior but which psychologists cannot possibly assign or manipulate.

The Role of Culture

Globalization has made the world a smaller place, and it's more important than ever to understand differences as cultures collide, compete, and hopefully, cooperate. How does culture shape how we think, feel, and behave?

How can we consider a variable as broad as culture? One way of doing this is to focus on **cultural dimensions**, which refer to particular ways that cultures can differ. From 1967 to 1973, Geert Hofstede, a Dutch researcher, conducted pioneering work on cultural dimensions by surveying 117,000 IBM employees in more than 50 countries. By surveying people whose cultures differed but who were likely similar in their education levels, income, and job status, Hofstede looked for patterns in how people thought and believed differences between cultures could be seen in 5 cultural dimensions:

individualism/collectivism – how much a culture emphasizes individual efforts versus group ties

masculinity/femininity – high masculinity refers to large differences in gender roles and a focus on competition and material success while high femininity refers to more equal gender roles and a focus on cooperation and quality of life

uncertainty avoidance – tolerance for ambiguity versus clear expectations for behavior

power distance – how close people feel to the power structure of their society

time orientation – focus on the past and tradition (short-term orientation) versus focus on the future and adaptability (long-term orientation)

Hofstede added an *indulgence/restraint* dimension in 2010 based on how much a culture allows for the gratification of desires and fun. It's important to remember that these dimensions don't predict specific behavior or reflect the views of all individuals within a culture, they refer to overall tendencies and ways of thinking.

The Self and Others

In the chapter on personality, we recognized that people have a *self-concept* and this is partially developed by comparing ourselves to others. This is known as ***social comparison theory***, and it was proposed by Leon Festinger. Festinger suggested that we tend to look to others in order to understand ourselves, particularly when we are in a state of uncertainty. When we aren't sure of our own traits and abilities, we examine the traits and abilities of others in order to figure out where we fit in.

Who are the others that we compare ourselves to? We tend to focus on people who are relevant to us in some way. In other words, we don't necessarily compare ourselves to the best, but instead to those who are around us. So if you want to figure out where you stand in terms of athletic ability, you'll probably start by comparing yourself to the other players in the pick-up basketball games you join, rather than comparing yourself to Michael Jordan. Similarly, you probably assess your intellectual prowess by comparing yourself to your classmates, rather than Isaac Newton or Albert Einstein. When it comes to attractiveness, however, media exposure may make us feel that stunningly attractive people are all around us, distorting our sense of comparison and making us feel inadequate.

Our sense of self is also inextricably tied to the groups that we are a part of. We can see ourselves as at least partially defined by our social relationships (i.e. a mother, a sibling, a student leader, or a social organizer). Our self-esteem and pride may be tied to the failures and successes of these groups, known as ***social identity theory***.

This can be seen in what's known as ***basking in reflected glory***. This refers to emphasizing our group membership as part of our identity when a group has been successful. This was demonstrated in an observational study by Robert Cialdini and others at several universities which found that on the Mondays following a weekend football game, students were more likely to wear clothing with the school insignia if the team had won than if they had lost, even though these students were not on the football team. We see the same in devoted sports fans, who proudly grab their share of reflected glory at the end of a game by exclaiming "We won! We won!", though as Jerry Seinfeld noted; "No, *they* won. *You* watched". While victory can bring reflected glory, this is only half the story, and losses may cause distancing from the losing team or "*cutting off reflected failure*".

Just how much we tie ourselves to certain groups brings us back to the cultural dimension of *individualist* versus *collectivist* cultures. The United States is considered to be highly individualist, with an emphasis on self-reliance, achieving personal goals, and satisfying personal needs. Other cultures may be more group-oriented, with a focus on the importance of maintaining relationships and achieving group harmony. Perhaps some insight into the individualist nature of American culture can be seen in team sports. Although wins in basketball, baseball, and football are always achieved through group effort, there is still a tendency to glorify individual players (why else have MVP awards?). We might also see this individualist attitude in the business world, as CEOs are idolized (or condemned) for results that have come from the work of hundreds or thousands of employees.

How Do We Know Our Attitudes?

When it comes to understanding ourselves, we might think that we're aware of all our feelings and beliefs, though hopefully other chapters have encouraged you to be critical of this idea. We're subject to biases and there can be a large disconnect between our attitudes and our behavior.

In the 1930s, while anti-Asian sentiment was high, Richard LaPiere traveled over 10,000 miles throughout the United States with a Chinese-American couple. Along the way, LaPiere and his companions didn't experience much discrimination in the many restaurants, campgrounds, and hotels they visited, and they were denied service only once. Following the trip, however, LaPiere sent letters to the establishments they had previously visited, asking if they would accept Chinese customers and 90% of respondents indicated they would not. This demonstrates that actual behavior doesn't always match stated attitudes. Of course, this disconnect between expressed attitudes and actual behavior could work in the opposite direction, with many people proclaiming that they are not prejudiced, though their behavior may not always match their expressions of equality.

Another disconnect between attitudes and behavior was famously created in an experiment by *Leon Festinger* and *James Carlsmith* in 1959. Participants spent an hour in the lab completing several boring tasks (turning wooden pegs and filling, emptying, then refilling a tray with wooden spools). Following this boredom, however, some participants were asked to lie to the next participant (actually a confederate) in the waiting room, telling her that the experiment was interesting and fun. For this additional help, these participants were given either $1 or $20 (a decent sum in 1959). As they were leaving the building, participants were asked to do a follow-up interview with the psychology department to find out about their experience. Part of this interview included asking how enjoyable the tasks were. Participants who had not been asked to lie admitted that the tasks were boring, but how did the liars feel? Did lying for $1 or $20 influence how participants felt about the experiment?

It did, but perhaps not in the way you might expect. Those who had just been paid $20 to say the experiment was fun stated that actually, it wasn't. Those who had been paid only $1 to lie, however, said the experiment had been engaging and worthwhile. This brings us back to an idea from the chapter on motivation, which is **insufficient justification**. A little white lie in exchange for $20 seems like a deal anyone should take, but lying just to get $1 is a bit unsettling. Rather than admitting they had been easily bought, these participants justified the lie by thinking maybe it wasn't a lie after all.

Based on this research, Festinger and Carlsmith proposed the theory of **cognitive dissonance**, which suggests that when we hold conflicting attitudes or we engage in behavior that doesn't match our attitudes, this creates discomfort that must be resolved, either by changing behavior or changing attitudes. In the case above, lying to a stranger for only $1 created dissonance and this dissonance was resolved by changing an attitude (I didn't lie, because the experiment was actually fun). The $20 group, however, already had enough justification for lying and therefore experienced less dissonance and did not need to change the attitude (I lied, but hey, for $20, who wouldn't?).

In another example of cognitive dissonance, Leon Festinger, Henry Riecken, and Stanley Schachter infiltrated a cult which believed that the world was going to end on a certain date (detailed in their book *When Prophecy Fails*.). The researchers assumed that the world would not end, and wanted to see how members of the cult would deal with this massive amount of cognitive dissonance. After all, these members so firmly believed the end was nigh that they had quit their jobs, given away their possessions and dedicated themselves to the group. As you might guess, the world did not end. How did these members deal with this incredible amount of cognitive dissonance? Did they admit to their foolishness and say "wow, I really shouldn't have done that"?

Of course not. Instead, they reduced dissonance by believing that actually, it was *because* of their behaviors and *because* of their beliefs that the world was spared. Rather than weakening their beliefs, the failure of their prophecy strengthened their convictions and rather than fools, they viewed themselves as saviors.

If you're wondering how to use dissonance for your own personal benefit, perhaps you can try what's known as the **Benjamin Franklin effect**. Franklin wasn't just a brilliant entrepreneur, inventor, and statesman, he was also quite a talented social psychologist, who found a way to use dissonance in his favor. When he felt that someone didn't like him, he would find a way to ask that person for a favor, such as borrowing a book he knew they owned. Franklin found that if the request was accepted, the person in question would be left wondering why he did Franklin a favor if he didn't like him. To eliminate this dissonance and justify the behavior, he might decide that Franklin mustn't be so bad after all. As Franklin wrote, "He that has once done you a kindness will be more ready to do you another, than he whom you yourself have obliged".

The Presence of Others

Norman Triplett noticed that bicyclists tended to be faster when they raced against other opponents than when they raced alone, so he had children use reels in pairs or alone to see if this influenced their speed. This idea that the presence of others improves performance is known as ***social facilitation***. Though the strength of Triplett's early data (published in 1898) has been questioned by modern statistical methods, other researchers have found supporting evidence for social facilitation.

Sometimes, however, the presence of others can cause us to choke and perform worse. Why does this occur? It seems that it's a matter of practice. When a task is simple or well-learned, the additional arousal of others can boost performance. When a task is complex, however, the presence of others can hinder performance. J.W. Michaels and colleagues (1982) found that skilled pool players performed better with 4 people watching than when alone, while amateurs missed more shots and played more poorly when others were observing. It's not just humans that experience these effects. In fact, Robert Zajonc, Alexander Heingartner, and Edward Herman (1969) found that cockroaches running in a straight line (simple task) ran faster with others than when alone, but when placed in a maze (complex task) they were slower in the presence of others and made more mistakes.

When we work in groups, the presence of others can cause us to reduce effort, a phenomenon known as ***social loafing***. This occurs when individuals work together and individual contributions are difficult to measure. Max Ringelmann found that a group of individuals pulling on a rope generated far less force than the sum of each individual pulling alone would predict. Lone individuals pulled with an average force of about 139 lbs. Groups of 8, however, only generated an average of 546 lbs, meaning that each individual's contribution was about 68 lbs, approximately half of the effort when alone. Alan Ingham and colleagues used confederates pretending to pull a rope and demonstrated that individuals put forth less effort when they believed others were helping. You've probably experienced this first-hand when the work for a group project just doesn't seem to get done. When individual contributions cannot be easily measured and everyone will receive the same grade, there may be an incentive for members to loaf.

Conformity

Seeing what others are doing or hearing what others think can influence how we think, feel, and behave, and this process may be subtle or it may be glaringly obvious. Our desire to fit in with a group can result in **conformity**; following an indirect social pressure to go along with a group's attitude or behavior.

Turkish-American psychologist Muzafer Sherif (pronounced *sher-reef*) used a perceptual illusion to demonstrate the influence of others on our thoughts and behaviors. The illusion, known as the **autokinetic effect**, occurs when a person looks at a small spot of light in a dark room. In this situation, the spot of light will appear to move, even though it is actually stationary. How much it appears to move, however, is subjective. Some people report it moving only an inch or two, while others may think that it moves as much as one foot. Sherif used this variability to investigate how hearing other people's estimates influenced an individual's perception of the movement. By having people look at the same spot in groups of 3, Sherif found that answers would gradually converge over several trials. In other words, people who thought the light only moved an inch or so increased their estimates (after hearing others give higher answers), while those who initially gave high estimates lowered their answers, causing the group to reach a consensus in the middle. Even though no estimates were said to be "right" or "wrong", the participants were using information from others to guide their decision-making, and this is known as **informational influence.**

In 1951, **Solomon Asch** conducted studies in which participants were asked to match line lengths of a stimulus line to one of three possible answers. Unbeknownst to the participants, however, all five of the others in the room were confederates working for the experimenter. After a few trials, these confederates began to give unanimously incorrect answers. Would these responses influence the participant enough to give the wrong answer too? Would you be swayed?

Asch found that in about one third of the critical trials, individuals went along with the group and gave incorrect responses. In follow-up interviews after the experiment, he found that people went along with the group for one of two reasons. In some cases, people really believed that the group was correct. They thought maybe they were viewing the lines from a strange angle or that the others had better vision. Asch referred to this as **private acceptance** because the individuals really believed that the group's answer was accurate.

1   2   3

Other participants, however, believed that the group was wrong but didn't want to stand out. By declaring the correct answer, the participant would essentially be telling everyone else in the room they were incorrect and taking a stand didn't seem to be worth it. In this case, participants engaged in **public compliance**; going along with the group answer, even though they believed it was incorrect. Rather than using other answers as information about the correct answer, these participants used the views of others to establish how they should behave, known as **normative influence**. This normative influence could easily be disrupted, however, and the presence of just one confederate disagreeing with the others (giving the correct answer) greatly reduced the rate of conformity, even though participants claimed that this "social supporter" had not influenced their answers (though they did rate this person as more likable).

While it might be surprising how readily participants went along with the group, you may still ask, "who cares?". Who really cares about the length of lines and whether the answer is 1, 2, or 3? Does this tell us about conformity in real life? This is a valid concern for conformity research. We want to know about real life behaviors, and we aren't often asked to judge line lengths in an inconsequential task. What happens when people really care about being right? How much does the desire to be accurate and the importance of the task affect levels of conformity?

In order to investigate this, Robert Baron, Joseph Vandello, and Bethany Brunsman (1996) created a task in which participants were motivated to give the correct answer and were also led to believe that the task was important. The task was to identify a criminal in a lineup after viewing a photo very briefly. Participants who performed best would receive an additional $20 (increasing the desire to be accurate) and participants were also told that the results of the study would be used by law enforcement and judges in considering future eyewitness testimony (increasing importance of the task). Participants could hear the answers given by others (who were confederates) though the order in which they answered was rotated in order to reduce suspicion (only the occasions in which the participant answered last were actually used). So if the confederates all gave a wrong answer, would you expect the participants to conform?

It turns out that the increased desire for accuracy and the perceived importance of the task actually served to increase the rate of conformity from 35% to 51% when the task was made more difficult (participants were given less time to view the images). How could this be? The researchers suggested that because the task was difficult, and because participants wanted to do well, they tended to rely on the informational influence of others. If you really aren't sure of the correct answer and you want to increase your odds of being right, it might make sense to rely on the judgments of others, especially if those judgments seem to be unanimous.

Compliance and Persuasion

While conformity can be considered an indirect influence on our behavior (we feel a pressure to conform even though no one is specifically asking us to), we are also influenced by more direct attempts to modify our attitudes or behaviors. We can be encouraged to comply with requests or be persuaded to engage in certain behaviors.

One model for thinking about how persuasion works involves two different systems; a central route and a peripheral route. The **central route** refers to careful consideration of options and conscious effort to weigh the pros and cons, while the **peripheral route** refers to mostly unconscious processing and snap judgments. So a salesman telling you all about the fuel efficiency and safety ratings of a car is appealing to central route processing, while a salesman showing off the sexy, sleek look of the car would be appealing to peripheral route processing. As you might guess from your knowledge of unconscious influences and the System 1 / System 2 distinction discussed in the chapter on decision-making, the peripheral route to persuasion is the one that most advertisers appeal to. It should come as no surprise that advertisements filled with bikini-clad women aren't trying to convince you that a particular beer is the most rational choice.

One way of encouraging others to comply is to use what we've already learned about cognitive dissonance. This can be done through the **foot-in-the-door technique**, in which you begin by making a small request that is easily accepted, followed by a larger request, which is now more likely to be accepted than if you had started with it.

In a classic study of this technique, researchers found that more people were willing to erect a "Drive Carefully" sign on their front lawns if they had previously been asked to sign a petition for safe driving, rather than if the sign was the first request. This technique works because people like consistency (to avoid dissonance) so they're more likely to agree with consistent requests. If I've already said that I support safe driving, it becomes harder to say no to the sign because that would be inconsistent with my previous behavior.

Of course, you've likely been using this technique for years when trying to get compliance from your parents. You don't start by suggesting an entire day's worth of fun activities, you start small; "Can I go to a friend's house for a little while?", then "Can I stay for dinner?", then "can I stay to watch a movie", then "can we have a sleepover?".

In contrast to the foot-in-the-door technique, the **door-in-the-face technique** begins with an overly-large request (which is rejected), followed by a much smaller request which is more likely to be accepted (given how trivial it appears compared to the first request). So if I were to ask you to give me $1,000 you would probably scoff, but if I then asked for $10 it wouldn't seem so bad and you just might agree.

Robert Cialdini and colleagues demonstrated the effectiveness of the door-in-the-face technique by approaching strangers on the street and asking them to volunteer their time. Sometimes researchers started with a large request: would you be willing to volunteer to help juvenile delinquents for 2 hours every week for at least the next 2 years? Not surprisingly, the researchers did not get any volunteers. This request was followed with a smaller (though still fairly large) request: would you volunteer to take a group of juveniles to the zoo for a field trip next weekend? Cialdini and colleagues found that if the smaller request (zoo trip) was asked first, only 17% of respondents agreed. But if it came after the much larger request, 50% of respondents were willing to chaperone.

So why does the door-in-the-face technique work? It's related to the reason why the next technique works, so hold tight and see if you can work out the reason for both of these.

While shopping in the grocery store, you've probably found yourself on the receiving end of some free samples. What a lovely person this food corporation is, charitably distributing foodstuffs to hungry shoppers everywhere! Well, not quite. Social psychologists would refer to this as a **not-so-free sample**, because there is indeed a cost (and not just to the food company). You've experienced this cost yourself, standing there awkwardly as you smile and feel the mounting pressure to purchase.

What's going on here? What's happening is that when someone does something nice for you, you feel that you have an obligation to return the favor, known as the **norm of reciprocity**. This norm is so deeply ingrained that even when we stop and consider that the worker giving us the sample isn't personally paying for it and probably doesn't care what we put in our grocery cart, the pressure to buy remains.

How does the norm of reciprocity help explain the door-in-the-face technique? Reducing the larger request is a way of doing the other person a favor (by asking for less) and it shows a willingness to compromise. As a result, the person being asked may feel the need to reciprocate by accepting the now smaller request.

This also occurs in the ***that's-not-all technique***, in which you are given an additional bonus or incentive for making a purchase, making it seem as though the seller is doing you a favor. Jerry Burger (1986) tested this at a bake sale by selling a cupcake and a small bag of cookies for $0.75, or selling a cupcake alone for $0.75, but giving the customer a "free" bag of cookies with the purchase, with the second approach resulting in greater sales.

Obedience to Authority

Perhaps the most famous research in all of psychology is ***Stanley Milgram***'s investigation of obedience to authority, conducted in the early 1960s at Yale. Each participant came into the lab, where another participant was also waiting. A researcher had them select a slip of paper, assigning one to the role of teacher and the other to the role of learner. The learner was then strapped into a chair and told that he would receive electric shocks in response to incorrect answers. The teacher was taken next door and seated in front of a large shock machine. The teacher's job was to read a series of multiple choice word-pair questions to the learner (via microphone), then administer increasingly powerful electric shocks as punishment for any incorrect responses. With each additional wrong answer, the teacher would move to a new switch on the machine, increasing the strength of the shock by 15 volts. The initial shock was only 15 volts, and the machine had switches leading up to 450 volts, along with labels "moderate", "danger: severe shock", and, for the last two switches, "XXX".

Milgram wanted to find out just how many participants would continue giving the shocks all the way up to 450 volts, despite cries of protest, complaints of heart trouble, and eventual silence from the learner on the other side of the wall. If participants verbally protested, the experimenter would insist that everything was fine, the shocks didn't cause permanent damage, and that the experiment must go on. Milgram surveyed psychiatrists, who estimated that only about 1% of people would continue to obey the experimenter but Milgram found that 67% of participants in the original study went all the way to 450 volts.

While Milgram conducted many variations which manipulated aspects of the situation (proximity to the learner, presence of the experimenter, presence of other teachers, etc.) to observe effects on obedience, note that the "standard" version recounted above isn't actually an experiment (no manipulation of an independent variable) and is a demonstration of how people behave in a particular situation. While there have always been ethical concerns over the intense stress and potential psychological harm to participants (making replication difficult), Gina Perry found evidence that participants were not always properly debriefed after the study (detailed in her book "Behind the Shock Machine"). Milgram's "de-hoaxing" may have sometimes showed the learner smiling and unharmed at the end, without ever revealing that the shocks weren't real.

The standard interpretation of Milgram's study is that most people would be willing to harm or potentially kill a stranger just because a man in a lab coat instructed them to. This fit in well with related theories of the time, such as Hannah Arendt's notion of the "***banality of evil***", which suggested that evils and atrocities like the Holocaust were mostly carried out by ordinary people. Monsters and megalomaniacs aren't necessary for evil to occur, just regular people following orders.

This interpretation has been questioned and some researchers have reconsidered the meaning of Milgram's results. Some participants may have known the experiment was a hoax but continued anyway, out of curiosity. Milgram's own data suggested that nearly half of the participants had some doubts about whether the setup was real. Were some participants "obeying" the experimenter like actors following a director, accepting a role and playing along to see where it led? Others may have thought the shocks were real but trusted the experimenter's assurances that they were not dangerous.

We should also remember that the entire experimental environment was orchestrated by Milgram to maximize obedience. Concluding that people are blindly obedient ignores Milgram's carefully-constructed script, his casting of the experimenter and learner, the weeks of rehearsal, and the repeated obstruction of participants' verbal protests. "Obedience" is a broad term, and many participants argued with the experimenter, certainly a form of disobedience. Textbook accounts may also leave out the active role that many participants played in attempting to reduce the shocks to the learner either by accentuating the correct answer while reading the prompts or by tapping the shock button as quickly as possible, both of which could be considered forms of disobedience.

Even if we accept Milgram's interpretation that continuing represents obedience, participants could be considered to be obeying the scientific process, rather than the man in the lab coat. Belief that science is conducted for noble purposes, that those conducting it minimize risks, and that Yale researchers can be trusted could all contribute to participants' behaviors. Don Mixon has suggested that Milgram's results are really measurements of the good faith the general public has in science and those who conduct it. But of course "67% of participants trust Yale researcher" doesn't make for a great headline.

These criticisms and re-interpretations aren't meant to completely discount Milgram's findings. The results were certainly surprising and perhaps show how readily we cede responsibility to others in ambiguous situations. But we should be careful not to oversimplify or draw far-reaching conclusions about human nature on the basis of some bizarre requests in a Yale basement. The comparisons between Milgram's results and the horrors of the Holocaust trivialize real-life atrocities and imply that obedience itself is evil. Thinking of obedience as shocking-a-stranger-to-death ignores its potentially positive role in many situations. While we may sometimes be led astray, it's usually a wise choice to obey parents and teachers, follow the laws of society, and heed the instructions of physicians.

Attraction

Why are we attracted to some people and not others? Why do you have the friends you have? One rather straightforward answer is proximity: we tend to become friends with people that are near us. So your childhood friends are far more likely to be other kids who attend the same school, rather than kids from a remote village in Peru. This effect continues, and your friends in college are likely to be those who live in the same dorm you do, adult life will have you socializing with neighbors and workmates, and old age will have you befriending the other residents of your retirement community.

Of course, proximity alone isn't really enough, as you could live directly above a neighbor without interacting but frequently see someone who lives 3 apartments away on the same hallway. To clarify this difference from simple proximity, the term **propinquity** can be used to refer to people that are near you that you actually encounter more often.

If you recall the **mere-exposure effect**, you'll recall that we tend to like things that we're familiar with or that we've seen more often and this certainly applies to attraction. Seeing a face more often will tend to make you like that face more. In fact, you can even demonstrate this mere-exposure effect by looking at your own face. Compare two identical images of your face, but with one flipped to a mirror image and consider which you think looks better. You're likely to choose the mirrored version, since that's what you see most often. This may explain why you see so many mirror-inverted selfies and Snapchats, as users are likely to consider those versions of themselves more attractive. Ironically, friends would probably prefer the non-mirrored versions, since that's what they are used to seeing.

Similarity

It's also true that we like people who are more similar to ourselves and we're likely to have a partner with a similar background, known as **homogamy**. Married couples tend to be similar in many ways, and in fact they tend to grow more and more similar over time. When others share our views it helps to confirm that our views are accurate and correct. While it isn't the case that opposites attract, there is evidence for a *Romeo-and-Juliet effect*, in which parental opposition to a teenage relationship can serve to intensify it.

Attractiveness

Of course, I'd be hard-pressed to write a section on why we are attracted to other people without mentioning the fact that some people are just more physically attractive than others. Being attractive matters, in fact, it matters in ways that it probably shouldn't. It's not just the case that people who are physically attractive attract others, they are also assumed to have a number of other positive traits, known as the *halo effect*. So we have a tendency to think that physically attractive people are smarter, more capable, more outgoing and social, and have higher self-esteem. Or as Norm MacDonald joked "women say they like guys with a sense of humor, but it turns out they just laugh at handsome guys." When it comes to persuasion and advertising, the halo effect may explain why attractive celebrities are frequently used to promote unrelated products, as their attractiveness might make us think they are more knowledgeable than they are.

While we might like to think personality trumps looks, the truth is that physical appearance is one of the best predictors of why people are attracted to one another. These positive effects of physical attractiveness raise the question, what is attractive? Are there universal laws of attractiveness, or is beauty really in the eye of the beholder?

For both genders, symmetry is important. Symmetry of face (and body) is a sign of good health, indicating that development hasn't been hindered by genetic defect, disease, infection, or a parasite. When it comes to specific facial features, gender differences emerge and attractive female features are often those seen as "cute" (such as large eyes, a small nose, and a pointed chin) while attractive male features are more "dominant" (such as a thick brow, a sharp jaw, and a broad chin).

In women, a body shape that is considered to be universally attractive is a waist-to-hip ratio of about 0.7, meaning that the waist is 70% of the size of the hips. For males, a ratio of about 0.9 relates to attractiveness, though in this case it refers to the hip-to-shoulder ratio, with the shoulders being broader than the hips, creating an inverted triangle shape. Of course, we want our offspring to be healthy, but we also want them to be attractive. This will give them a better chance of passing on their (and our) genes. If we think in terms of our genes, the attractiveness of a potential mate is so compelling because in a way, it signals our chance at immortality.

Outside of physical characteristics, another way of increasing attraction is *self-disclosure*. Revealing personal details strengthens relationships and draws people together. Revealing more about yourself can actually cause you to feel closer and more attracted to the person to whom you divulge your secrets. So next time you want to draw someone in and cause them to like you more, try to tactfully skip the small talk: the more they reveal about themselves, the more they may end up liking you.

Disposition or Situation?

How do we understand the behavior of other people? Rather than focusing on a person's traits (or their *disposition*) as we did in personality psychology, we'll now include a focus on the *situation* the person is in. We'll begin with **Attribution Theory**, which refers to how we understand the cause of events. So if I watch a person walking down the street and that person suddenly trips and falls down, how might I explain this occurrence?

The **Fundamental Attribution Error** (FAE) refers to a tendency to attribute the causes of behavior to disposition rather than situation. This means I'm likely to conclude that the person fell because she is clumsy, rather than concluding that a cracked sidewalk was to blame. Similarly, I may conclude that a student hasn't turned in homework because he's lazy, rather than thinking that situational factors outside of his control were the cause.

The FAE was demonstrated in a study by Lee Ross, Teresa Amabile, and Julia Steinmetz which involved a quiz game. In the study, participants observed two others play; one person was the quizmaster and the other was the contestant, and these roles were chosen at random. The quizmaster's job was to think of random trivia questions that the contestant would be unable to answer correctly.

Rather than recognizing that the random assignment of roles and the nature of the task caused one person to appear more knowledgeable than the other, participants concluded that the quizmasters were actually more intelligent than the contestants. Even when we have clear information that should protect us from making the Fundamental Attribution Error, it still has a tendency to occur.

It's not just about seeing game show hosts as more knowledgeable (you think you're pretty smart, don't you Trebek?) this same effect occurs for actors and their roles, explaining why people might feel uneasy meeting Robert Englund or why Leonard Nimoy titled his first autobiography *I Am Not Spock*. Although we rationally know that actors are not the roles they play, we still have a tendency to fall into this trap, perhaps thinking that they portray a role so well because they are indeed similar to the character.

Why Does the FAE Occur?

One reason that the FAE may be common is that it allows us to generate explanations quickly and easily. So when a student doesn't turn in a homework assignment and the teacher wants to know why, the simplest answer is to just blame the student for being lazy and move on. Attempting to understand the situational context requires a great deal more effort and investigation, while focusing on disposition allows the question to be answered right away. Lazy student, case closed.

Even if we try to understand the situation, as an outside observer we don't have access to all of the situational information and this may cause *actor-observer bias*. The student (actor) can easily see all the situational factors which made completing the assignment impossible, while the teacher (observer) just sees an empty-handed student. When explaining behavior, if we are the actor, situation stands out, but if we are the observer, disposition seems to dominate.

Culture may also play a role in the fundamental attribution error and some cultures may be less prone to it. Cultures which emphasize fate over self-reliance or interdependence over independence may be less inclined to think of individuals as solely responsible for what happens to them.

The fundamental attribution error can cause problems when it comes to explaining why bad things happen to people. If we have a tendency to attribute cause to the dispositions of individuals, this also means we may blame them when things go wrong. We do this in part because we like to think that the world is a fair place, known as the *just-world bias*. We'd like to think that people get what they deserve, that negative actions will be punished and good deeds rewarded. In actuality, however, we must accept that the world is not just. Bad things happen to good people and good things happen to bad people. It's scary to think that no matter how good of a person you are, you could still be the victim of a horrible crime or accident or suffer from an incurable illness, all through no fault of your own. This idea is so discomforting that we might prefer to put our just-world blinders back on, blaming victims of sexual assaults, assuming carelessness explains all car accidents, or thinking that good karma will ward off cancer.

Impression Formation

How do we form impressions of other people? How long does it take to form an impression of someone? As you might guess from your knowledge of heuristics, we tend to form impressions very quickly. ***"Thin slices" theory*** suggests that we form impressions in a matter of seconds. In one study by Nalini Ambady and Robert Rosenthal, 10-second silent video clips of professors were rated by participants, and the mean of these ratings was shown to be a reliable predictor of the professors' actual end-of-semester student evaluations. Similar studies have found that people can predict big five personality scores (openness to experience, conscientiousness, extraversion, agreeableness, and neuroticism) fairly well within a matter of seconds.

One interpretation of this is that we are both fast and surprisingly accurate when it comes to forming impressions. It could be the case, however, that this consistency results because our first impressions shape subsequent impressions and may be resistant to change. We have to remember the possibility of confirmation bias, as once we start thinking someone has a particular trait, we may find ourselves looking for it and ignoring any evidence to the contrary. This was demonstrated in a study by Harold Kelley in which students were given a description of a guest speaker which included either that he was rather "warm" or rather "cold". This early description then influenced the students' ratings of the speaker, even though they all witnessed the same lecture.

If first impressions are so important, why don't we just throw out all those convoluted course evaluation forms and lengthy personality assessments? Thin slices can be accurate, but they can also be horribly inaccurate, and our level of confidence may not help us figure which is occurring. We *can* make judgments in the blink of an eye, but that doesn't mean that we *should*. More information gives us the chance to revise those initial impressions as we attempt to minimize confirmation bias and avoid self-fulfilling prophecies, in which initial expectations cause expected behaviors to occur.

Stereotypes, Prejudice, and Discrimination

The fact that we rapidly form impressions of others using little information means that we have a tendency to rely on *stereotypes*, expectations and inferences based on categories. Stereotypes emerge as a result of our mental ability to quickly categorize information and draw conclusions. Stereotyping isn't a big deal for most categories, but when it comes to categorizing people, this process causes problems. It can lead to *prejudice*, when our attitudes and evaluations of others are based on their group membership, and *discrimination*, when our behavior toward others is influenced by their group membership.

Not to be outdone by the name of the Fundamental Attribution Error, the ***Ultimate Attribution Error*** (***UAE***) suggests that not only do we assume disposition as an explanation for an individual's behavior, we also tend to apply that disposition to all members of that individual's group. So if I see a Korean person helping someone, not only might I assume that this individual is kind (the FAE), I might also assume that all Koreans are kind (the UAE). A stereotype has been formed.

This error might be more pronounced when it comes to groups we don't have much information about. So if this is the only Korean person I've ever seen, it's more likely I'll think this way. On the other hand, if I've personally met hundreds of Koreans in the past, then I might not be as likely to jump to this conclusion (because I have lots of other information to go on). You may want to keep this in mind if you're a traveler, particularly if your ethnicity or nationality is rare in the area you're visiting. Like it or not, you really do become a representative of where you are from. If you're the only American locals have ever met, your behaviors may exert undue influence on their perceptions of all Americans.

We're all members of many different groups, but how easily do these groups form? ***Henri Tajfel*** proposed ***minimal group*** theory; that groups can form rapidly on the basis of trivial classifications. This was demonstrated by having teenage boys view artwork from either Paul Klee or Wassily Kandinsky (two artists with similar styles). After rating the paintings, boys were placed into either the Klee group or the Kandinsky group, supposedly on the basis of their preferences but they were actually randomly assigned.

Next, individuals were asked to choose how points (which were worth money) were distributed to other members of the two groups. Rather than maximizing points for everyone (getting the most money out of the experimenters) or maximizing total points for their own group, boys preferred arrangements maximizing difference between the groups, so their own group got more points *relative* to the other group, demonstrating an ***in-group bias***.

If these group biases occur in minimal groups which are easy to join, what happens when groups are difficult to join? Based on what we've learned already about cognitive dissonance, social pressures, and group formation, we may be able to better understand how barriers to entry can actually make a group seem more appealing and can increase group solidarity among members.

One way groups increase solidarity is through ***hazing*** or harsh initiation rites. If you could just walk up to any fraternity or sorority house and instantly become a member, you might check out one or two parties, make small talk with a few members, then move along with your social life and never really look back. If, however, you were forced to endure rituals, rites, and ridicule in order to earn your membership, those same parties might be imbued with greater camaraderie, excitement, and fun. When you find yourself thinking "I went through all that for *this*?", insufficient justification and cognitive dissonance may just make you feel that *this* is actually the best party in town.

All Alike?

Not only do we show a preferential bias for members of our own groups, we are better able to recognize in-group members as individuals who vary from one another. When it comes to outsiders we tend to suffer from a bias known as ***out-group homogeneity***, which refers to the tendency to see them as all being the same and having similar preferences, behaviors, and thoughts.

So while an American might think that "all Germans are alike", it's quite unlikely that a German would think this way. You may recognize that individuals at your own school are quite varied in their tastes, preferences, and thoughts, but you might consider members of another school to be more uniform. Our detailed knowledge of our in-group helps us to see that it is composed of individuals, while our limited knowledge of out-group members causes us to ignore their differences.

This reduction of identity and seeing others as more alike also relates to ***dehumanization***, in which we stop seeing members of an out-group as people. Unfortunately, history is filled with examples of people being likened to rats, dogs, apes, cockroaches, pigs, snakes, locusts, or worse. While insulting to the recipients of these slurs, the greater damage comes in thinking of them as less than human.

This dehumanization can reduce feelings of empathy, making it easier to inflict harm upon them and reducing the stress of doing so. With this in mind, it's not surprising that opponents and victims of war are frequent targets of dehumanization. Those fighting for the opposition are frequently viewed as cold, interchangeable machines devoid of human sentiment and emotional experience. Dehumanization may also lead to greater mutilation of enemies and the macabre collection of "war trophies", including skulls, scalps, teeth, or ears.

Improving Group Relations

What can we do to improve group relations? In the real world, group conflicts may have decades, centuries, or millennia of events contributing to them, and this means that even experts may not know where to begin. But what about creating a simple form of group conflict and then testing strategies for reducing it? This is precisely what **Muzafer Sherif** and colleagues did at a boys' summer camp in 1954. Upon arriving at the camp in Oklahoma's Robber's Cave State Park, each of the 22 boys found out he was part of a group, the Eagles or the Rattlers.

While the Eagles and Rattlers were initially focused on bonding with group members through activities like hiking and swimming, the two groups were soon put into competition. This was to see if hostilities between the groups increased when they competed for scarce resources, known as **realistic conflict theory**. As the Eagles and Rattlers competed for prizes in tug-of-war, baseball, football, and other activities, hostilities quickly escalated, from name-calling and flag-burning to cabin-raiding, theft, and even fist-fights between the boys. Within a matter of days these groups of boys had come to despise one other.

Now that the researchers had created prejudice, what could be done to reduce it? One early theory, known as **contact theory**, suggested that groups just need to interact more and spend more time together. This contact would allow everyone to get to know each other better, ending stereotypes and building bonds that transcend group alliances. For the Eagles and Rattlers, however, contact alone was not enough. They maintained strict segregation when forced together and engaged in several food fights when group meals were attempted.

Researchers turned to another approach, creating **superordinate goals**, goals which could only be achieved if members of both groups worked together. The two groups of boys were forced to work together on tasks such as repairing the water supply and pulling a "broken-down" food truck. Following these tasks, hostilities lessened, and the boys began intermingling and forming new friendships. By the final night of camp a few days later, they were all singing, roasting marshmallows, and looking forward to sharing a bus back to Oklahoma City (during which the Rattlers even used a $5 prize they had previously won to buy malted milks for everyone).

Attitudes That Aren't Expressed

While the boys in Sherif's study openly expressed their dislike for Eagles or Rattlers (like sports fans yelling "Yankees Suck!"), negative attitudes and prejudices for race or gender are not always so obvious. Most people, whether they are racist or not, know that appearing racist is generally a bad thing, so they don't openly express negative attitudes they hold, making these attitudes difficult to study.

One way of getting around this is to measure negative associations in a way that participants can't control or hide. The ***implicit association test*** (***IAT***) does this by measuring how quickly participants are able to associate certain items. To assess racial associations, participants are instructed to press a key with one hand when they see either a positive word (like "love") or a white face, and to press a key with the other hand when they see either a negative word (like "terrible") or a black face. The participant is repeatedly timed completing this task and a version of the task with the opposite pairings (one key for black faces and positive words, the other key for negative words and white faces).

Researchers using this type of task have revealed that many participants perform slightly slower when black faces are paired with positive words, suggesting an implicit association between black faces and negative words. The IAT has also been used to assess attitudes for a number of other possible negative associations for age, sexual orientation, gender, and other groups. You can try the implicit association test yourself at **www.implicit.harvard.edu**.

Results from this test don't indicate active prejudice or discrimination, just possible unconscious associations. These associations may occur as a result of exposure to stereotypes, even if we don't actually believe the stereotypes. We should hesitate to judge anyone (or ourselves) based on IAT results alone, as having these associations doesn't mean that a person acts on them. Nevertheless, they suggest subtle, unconscious influence that might be shaping thought and behavior.

What Can We Do?

Evidence of implicit associations doesn't tell us what we can do to reduce them. How can we overcome societal stereotypes and associations that may not even be conscious? We may even end up worrying that we have some negative implicit associations that could "leak out" and cause us to be seen as prejudiced. Despite holding what I believe to be egalitarian views, as a white male I might feel hesitant to join a group discussion on race or gender, out of fear that I may inadvertently say something that could be interpreted as racist or sexist. This kind of fear might cause me to avoid these situations, and this avoidance means I'll have less experience and feel less comfortable if I do try to participate. Is this why it's so hard to discuss these issues?

How can we overcome this tendency? Claude Steele and colleagues uncovered one way by asking college undergraduates to prepare for a discussion group on racial profiling. After seeing photos of the two other students they were going to meet with, participants were asked to arrange the chairs in the meeting room while the researcher went to get the other members for the discussion. When white participants believed they were going to meet with black students to discuss racial profiling, they placed the chairs farther apart than if they believed they were meeting with other white students, a physical representation of their discomfort.

One intervention, based on Carol Dweck's work on mindset, was to tell participants beforehand that feeling uncomfortable was natural, encouraging them to view the discussion as an opportunity for growth and learning how to discuss controversial issues with people who may have different viewpoints. For participants given this growth-mindset approach to the discussion, the race gap in chair placement disappeared.

Group Dynamics

How do group opinions differ from individual opinions? In other words, if a group of people get together to express an opinion, will that opinion be the same as the average of each of the group members?

What tends to happen in group decision-making is that the opinion of the group starts to shift away from the average of the group members' opinions and move toward extremes, known as ***group polarization***. To illustrate how this happens, imagine that students are going to evaluate a teacher, whom they all feel slightly positive about. Before submitting their individual evaluations, they have a discussion, and all of these slightly-positive messages strengthen the idea that this teacher is actually quite good. One student mentions that homework isn't excessive, another that lectures are at least mildly entertaining, and another that grading is fair. These aren't glowing reviews but these multiple positive messages may be enough to push each individual's evaluation a bit higher. Of course, this can also work in the other direction, causing a group to become more negative than members were initially. Groups may also take larger risks than the individuals would, a kind of group polarization known as ***risky shift***.

What happens when evidence is mixed? Charles Lord, Lee Ross, and Michael Lepper found that rather than moderating opinions, mixed results or inconclusive findings may actually strengthen views. Groups of people either for or against capital punishment were exposed to evidence that adoption of the death penalty was associated with an increase in the murder rate in some states, in addition to evidence showing a decrease in the murder rate in other states. People on each side viewed the research supporting their own view as better conducted and more convincing, meaning that the same mixed results served to strengthen the views of both groups.

Why do groups sometimes make terrible decisions? Why didn't the US military predict the attack on Pearl Harbor? How is it that John F. Kennedy's administration approved an invasion of Cuba so far-fetched it should have been obvious it would fail? These aren't examples of hindsight bias, as early warnings and criticisms were present at the time, but were largely ignored. ***Irving Janis*** investigated a number of catastrophic group decisions and proposed they resulted from ***groupthink***, a term he coined based on the *newspeak* and *doublethink* of George Orwell's *1984*.

Janis outlined a number of factors that increased the risk of groupthink, which included having a strong or charismatic leader members want to impress, members of the group believing that they are highly intelligent or talented, and dissenting opinions being minimized, disregarded, or suppressed. These factors result in greater conformity, an illusion of invulnerability, and stereotyped views of outsiders or the opposition. Since Janis's first description, the role of groupthink has been considered in other fiascoes, from NASA's failed Challenger launch in 1986 to the US invasion of Iraq in 2003.

Crowd Behavior

What about when larger groups of people make bad decisions? When crowds of fans overturn cars, looters rob local shops, and rioters destroy property? What causes the apparent madness of crowds?

Just being part of a crowd can have physiological effects on your body, stimulating the sympathetic nervous system and raising heart rate and blood pressure. Ask your average pedestrian if they would ever encourage a stranger to commit suicide, and chances are very few people will say yes. Leon Mann's archival research found, however, that crowds of people frequently chant "jump!" to those contemplating suicide on buildings and bridges. What causes this callous disregard for a life? Mann noted that this phenomenon tended to occur when it was dark, the crowd was large, and the "jumper" was far away.

What these factors accomplish is increased ***deindividuation***, a feeling that one is no longer an individual but a part of a group. One factor that increases feelings of deindividuation is ***physical anonymity***. When people feel that their identity is unknown, they feel less like individuals and feel less responsible for their actions.

You may have experienced this feeling yourself when wearing a costume that conceals your identity. In fact, research by Ed Diener and colleagues considered how anonymity and group size might influence children's behavior on Halloween. With the help of 27 homes in the Seattle area, these researchers were able to manipulate the level of anonymity that children experienced by either having the host ask children who they were (or not) and where they lived (or not). Children then had an opportunity to violate the stated "one candy" rule and take extra. Deindividuation was lowest, and so was theft (7.5%), when a child had provided a name and address and was trick-or-treating alone. When children remained anonymous and were in a group, however, 57% stole candy.

The Stanford Prison Study

Another one of the most famous studies in psychology is the Stanford Prison Study. Philip Zimbardo and colleagues randomly assigned healthy college-aged volunteers to play the roles of prisoners or guards in a mock prison created in the basement of the psychology building at Stanford University. Mock arrests were conducted by real police and prisoners were handcuffed, fingerprinted, given short robe-like uniforms and small ankle chains on one leg, and placed in shared "cells". Guards were given mirrored sunglasses, uniforms, and batons, and they worked 8-hour shifts at the prison but were otherwise free to go. Zimbardo himself acted as the prison superintendent, instructing guards to break the will of the prisoners and maintain authority.

While the study was scheduled to last for 2 weeks, it was discontinued after 6 days because several prisoners experienced emotional breakdowns and guards were mistreating prisoners. Zimbardo has argued that this demonstrates the power of the situation in shaping behavior, causing otherwise normal people to act as sadistic guards or powerless prisoners.

So what should we make of these "results"? While Zimbardo has claimed that this study reveals how the environment exerts a powerful influence on individuals and their behavior, it doesn't really help us to understand why some guards were more sadistic than others, or why some chose to help and support prisoners rather than dominate them. While it may be true that environment can exert a powerful influence on individuals and their behaviors, in this case it might be nothing more than **demand characteristics**. As Peter Gray wrote, "This is a study of prisoners and guards, so their job clearly is to act like prisoners and guards—or, more accurately, to act out their stereotyped views of what prisoners and guards do. Surely, Professor Zimbardo, who is right there watching them (as the Prison Superintendent) would be disappointed if, instead, they had just sat around chatting pleasantly and having tea."

This brings up a broader issue in social psychology. Many "classic" studies are flawed ethically and methodologically, and yet they remain required readings and must-know theories of human behavior. Their power comes from their ability to present stories we can latch onto, though these stories often leave out the inaccuracies, the alternate explanations, and the conflicting evidence. These are the studies that make for great lecture introductions, and capture attention by asking if you would shock a stranger or abuse a prisoner. While it is certainly easier to focus on studies that sum behavior up into neat bullet points, I encourage you to think more deeply about the complexity of social, psychological, and cultural issues. Ask questions, and don't settle for simplified answers.

The Bystander Effect

Another famous example in social psychology is the case of Kitty Genovese, who was murdered in 1964. According to newspaper accounts at the time, dozens of witnesses saw the attack from their windows and heard her pleas for help, though none came to her assistance or even called the police, and this indifference became known as the **bystander effect**. Questions have arisen about the initial reports of the crime, suggesting that many neighbors could not have actually seen Genovese and that several who heard her cries did in fact contact the police.

Evidence for the bystander effect doesn't come solely from Genovese's murder, however, and other examples of bystander apathy can be found, both in real-life situations as well as laboratory demonstrations. In a study by John Darley and Bibb Latané (1968), students participating in a discussion with others via intercom heard a student have a seizure. When participants believed they were the only ones hearing the student in distress, 85% rushed out to find help. When they believed that four others also heard the seizure, only 31% went for help and they waited longer before doing so. In another study by Latané and Darley (1968), participants were completing forms in a conference room when smoke began to enter the room from a vent. When alone, 75% of participants left the room to report the smoke, but when in a roomful of passive others (confederates), only 10% got up to report the smoke. This suggests that the bystander effect isn't just about failing to help others, it can even include failing to help oneself.

Unfortunately real life provides other examples of the bystander effect, such as when 2 year-old Wang Yue was run over by 2 different vehicles in Foshan, China in 2011. She lay in the street for seven minutes while over a dozen pedestrians walked by before someone finally called for help. Seeing situations like this, we may feel the truth in Elie Wiesel's assertion that "the opposite of love isn't hate, it's indifference".

Why Don't People Act?

One reason people don't act is that there are costs to getting involved. These costs can be great (harm or even death) and may discourage people from acting. In China, many blame the Peng Yu incident for discouraging bystander intervention, making it financially costly to help. In 2006, 26-year old Peng Yu assisted a 65-year old woman to the hospital after she fell and broke her hip while boarding a bus. In recognition, Peng Yu was accused of causing her injuries and ordered by a judge in Nanjing to pay the woman over $6000. In the studies by Darley and Latané, however, seeking help isn't particularly risky, so what is holding people back?

One thing that holds people back is that situations are often ambiguous and it's unclear what people should do. People may look to other bystanders, who are also doing nothing, and decide that nothing must be the appropriate response. This is referred to as *pluralistic ignorance*, as each person assumes others know more about the situation, so if they know more and aren't acting then there's no need to act.

The number of bystanders also plays a role, and the larger the crowd, the less likely an individual will help. This is known as the *diffusion of responsibility*. If you were the only person to witness someone being injured, you would feel the full force of responsibility to help, because you know that as the only bystander, if you don't help, no one will. In a crowd, however, this feeling of responsibility is dispersed among all of the bystanders, who each wait for someone else (perhaps someone more knowledgeable) to step in.

Prosocial Behavior

While the previous section may have you feeling a bit down about human nature, it's not all doom and gloom. There's also a good deal of prosocial behavior going on, and every day people help one another. When bad things happen, people come together and offer physical, financial, and emotional support. What causes this **altruism**, in which people help others without regard for their own welfare?

2 Brothers or 8 Cousins

You may have heard attempts to explain altruism which claim that animals sometimes act for the "good of the species". This sounds nice, but it seems instead that individuals act for the good of their genes. And remember that those genes don't just belong to the individual. Families share genes, so helping family helps an individual's genes survive too, and this is known as **kin selection**. Saving yourself ensures the survival of 100% of your genes, but saving a sibling is equivalent to 50% of your genes surviving (while a cousin shares 12.5% of "your" genes). We could think of the decision to make the ultimate sacrifice as simple math, which is why J.B.S. Haldane joked that he would lay down his life for 2 brothers or 8 cousins.

This isn't just about laying down your life, kin selection applies to producing the next generation of genes as well; help your brother find that special someone and you're passing on some of your own genes by proxy (though you may later be asked to babysit). Of course, most people don't consciously calculate their genetic relationships in deciding whether or not to help someone. Rather than just genes, this system relies on who feels like family (known as *nurture kinship*). So you could have adopted siblings or close friends you'd make sacrifices for long before you'd help those cousins from Kansas you met once.

While kin selection may explain some altruism, people often help those who aren't kin and who they've never met before. What's going on here? We could be cynical and assume that people help because they want something in return; a reward, social approval, or others returning a favor in the future (known as **reciprocal altruism**). Or maybe they want that "warm glow" of helping. This "warm glow" could be argued to be selfish, but if it helps helping happen, maybe it's not a bad thing.

Considering what we've learned about social pressures in this chapter, we could also argue that people help because of a *social-responsibility norm*, in which societal expectations for generosity and helping behavior encourage altruism. Empathy may also play a role, and the *empathy-altruism hypothesis* suggests that people are more likely to help when they empathize with people in need.

Despite aggression and daily violence inflicted by humans on one another around the world, our ability to work together remains the greatest strength of our species. We need one another and groups accomplish far more than any individual could achieve alone. Each day, people unite to help one another and to share resources, time, and stories. For all the potential prejudice and conflict groups can create, we wouldn't be here today if it weren't for our natural desire to join with others. We evolved in a world of small tribes, but now the globe feels smaller while the number of people we can connect with is larger than ever. The more we can identify with one another and put aside minor differences, the greater the problems we can overcome and the accomplishments we can achieve.

Chapter Summary – Social Psychology

- Social psychology considers how society and culture influence an individual's thoughts, behaviors, and sense of self.

- The presence of others can boost performance (**social facilitation**), while group efforts can sometimes encourage people to slack off (**social loafing**).

- Pressure to behave in certain ways may come indirectly from a group (**conformity**), from specific requests (**compliance / persuasion**), or from direct orders (**obedience**).

- We tend to be more attracted to those we see and interact with often (**propinquity**) as well as those who display signs of health and fertility through facial features (**symmetry**) and body shapes.

- We tend to make assumptions about disposition when explaining individual behavior (**FAE**) and we may apply these assumptions to other group members (**UAE**).

- Our tendency to take mental shortcuts can lead us to **stereotype** others, which can influence our evaluations (**prejudice**) and our behaviors (**discrimination**).

- Individual evaluations can be shifted by **group polarization**, and **groupthink** can result in disastrous decision-making.

- Despite the cold indifference of the **bystander effect**, prosocial behaviors and **altruism** are common in human interaction, and every day people come together to help one another.

Notes

Chapter 14
Stress & Health

Health Psychology

In this chapter we'll be considering **health psychology**; the study of how psychological factors influence health, illness, and recovery. This will include attempting to uncover the **etiology**, or the origin or causes, of illness (*aetiology* if you prefer the British spelling). This is no easy feat and answers won't be clear, as many psychological factors are hard to measure precisely. As a result, we'll frequently see how certain factors (such as stress) increase or decrease risk of an illness, though we can't say they directly cause the illness.

A closely related area of study is **epidemiology**, which refers to studying the frequency, distribution, and causes of illness. We need to be careful because this is an area in which we can't readily rely on experimentation when it comes to risk factors for most diseases and this limits our ability to draw conclusions about causality. Obviously we can't go around exposing participants to potentially harmful stimuli to see if they develop ulcers, cancer, or heart disease. Instead, we often have to rely on **retrospective studies**. These studies look into the past of a person who has already been diagnosed with a particular illness. It's far easier to find people who have ulcers and then find out about their pasts than it is to measure people now and then wait for some of them to get ulcers later. This can create a problem for stress research, because once people have an illness they may have a tendency to misrepresent their previous levels of stress (I must have been really stressed, after all, now I've got all these damn ulcers).

Another problem here is that if we measure many factors and many health outcomes, relationships may appear which are purely coincidental. This can be a problem for conclusions about mortality (which has many possible causes and can't be replicated in a particular patient) so we should be careful when considering interventions that claim to increase or decrease longevity. If several elderly patients in a study die this can drastically change the apparent longevity of the groups, even if the causes of these deaths were unrelated. This may also explain why we often see epidemiological studies with opposing conclusions (Is red wine good or bad? What about coffee? Or eggs?)

Occasionally we have **prospective studies**, which collect data from a large number of healthy people and then track who gets diagnosed with which diseases later. By following participants over time (known as **longitudinal research**), researchers can see how illnesses develop and how risk factors change throughout a person's life. Unfortunately, these types of studies are rather rare. This is in part because we've gotten so good at beating infections that most deadly illnesses today are those that accumulate slowly over the course of decades (such as heart disease, cancer, diabetes, etc) meaning that longitudinal studies are incredibly time-consuming and prohibitively expensive to conduct.

The Psychology of Illness

Walter Cannon (whose name you may recall from the *Cannon-Bard Theory of Emotion*) investigated reports of "*voodoo death*" in traditional cultures around the world. In these cases, a shaman or community leader placed a curse on an individual, who subsequently died. Cannon suggested that this was the result of over-activation of the sympathetic nervous system, causing the victim to die from the stress and anxiety of being cursed. It's difficult to say for sure that stress is the cause of voodoo death (also referred to as "*psychophysiological death*" to avoid cultural insensitivity), as a shaman could curse a person who was already ill, use poison (ensuring success and encouraging others to believe), or it could be the case that after being cursed the person is shunned from society, leading to dehydration and starvation.

Can our beliefs really cause us to become sick? You might think of **psychogenic illnesses**, which are "illnesses originating from the mind". We have to be careful because there have been illnesses considered to be psychogenic until the discovery of a new virus, bacterium, hormone, or receptor suddenly makes them "legitimate" and suspicion is no longer cast on the patient's mind. We could also consider cases of **psychosomatic illness**, which is when symptoms arise from thoughts or beliefs about illness. This doesn't necessarily indicate that the illness is caused by psychological factors (it may still have an underlying biological cause) but that symptoms are expressed or worsened by psychological factors, such as stress increasing the severity of asthma attacks.

In this chapter we'll see how psychological factors like stress can influence the immune system's ability to function, a field known as **psychoneuroimmunology**. This field looks at the relationships between stress, psychological factors, immune function, and health.

What is Stress?

You're undoubtedly familiar with the concept of stress, but like many psychological variables we've seen, you may find it difficult to come up with a precise definition. What exactly is stress and how can we go about measuring it?

Walter Cannon coined the term *"fight or flight response"* to consider how we react to threats in the environment (you may also recall that a "freeze" response has since been added). Cannon was one of the first researchers to use the term "stress" when referring to something that evoked this response. The term stress was used frequently by Hans Selye (who we'll learn more about later), though his use was criticized because the same word was used for both cause and effect (stress causes stress).

To clarify things a bit, Selye introduced the term ***stressor*** to refer more specifically to something that causes a ***stress response***. So we can say that a ***stressor*** is something that is a threat to our safety or something that places demands on our resources. This could be as obvious as a bear chasing us through the woods or as subtle as tinges of nervousness before a first date.

The ***stress response*** is our physiological reaction to stressors, and involves activation of the sympathetic nervous system. As we'll see throughout this chapter, this response is well-suited for dealing with some stressors but not so great for others.

Despite these more specific labels, the general term stress is still used quite frequently. Thinking in terms of stressors and how we respond to them means that ***stress*** can refer to our physiological and psychological response to stressors, which can originate from the environment or from within our own minds. Now let's look at these two aspects of stress in more detail.

Types of Stressors

We can understand emotions and personality traits by comparing them rather than carefully defining them and the same can be done with stressors. Thomas Holmes and Richard Rahe (1967) created the ***Social Readjustment Rating Scale*** to compare how stressful different life events are perceived to be. On the very top end of this scale are incredibly traumatic events such as being raped, being diagnosed with a terminal illness, or dealing with the death of a close friend or family member. Below these highly stressful events are mid-level stressors such as getting into a physical fight, making a speech, experiencing sleep deprivation, or getting a new job or moving to a new city. At the bottom end, we have minor stressors such as being sick with a common cold, participating in an athletic event, going on a first date, or fighting traffic in your morning commute.

Individual differences also play a role in determining whether something is a stressor. Our level of stress depends on our interpretation of the situation. A particular stimulus might be considered stressful to some people and not-so-stressful to others. The same traffic jam may frustrate one person (who is running late for a crucial meeting) but not bother the driver next to her in the slightest.

We can also consider the role that frequency plays in stress. While major stressors are hopefully infrequent, some minor stressors become daily hassles which occur repeatedly or continuously. These **chronic stressors** can be particularly problematic when they evoke a stress response day after day, without giving the body a chance to recover. A related type of stressor is an **environmental stressor,** which refers to something in the environment that continuously evokes a stress reaction. Children attending schools located on flight paths have been shown to have higher blood pressure and lower resilience than their peers in quieter learning environments. Crowding is another environmental stressor and people show a physiological response to cramped living conditions or being packed like sardines in a subway car.

The Stress Response

While Cannon's expression "fight or flight" is still frequently used, there's growing recognition of other responses to threats and Shelley Taylor has proposed possible gender differences in the stress response. Women may be less likely to "fight" or act aggressively in the face of a threat (though they certainly can do so), and Taylor's research has focused on a **tend and befriend response**. This refers to a greater focus on relationships, empathy, and group cohesion in the face of a threat. This response has been linked to the release of the hormone oxytocin in response to threats, which occurs for both genders but may be stronger in females. Research by Mara Mather and colleagues in 2010 found that women showed greater activation of brain areas associated with face recognition and empathy when stressed. For now, we'll focus on the "fight or flight" aspect of the stress response and look closer at the roles of brain regions, neurotransmitters, and hormones in regulating this process during and after exposure to a stressor.

The activation of the sympathetic nervous system occurs along the **HPA axis**, which refers to the **Hypothalamus**, **Pituitary gland**, and **Adrenal glands**. While the pituitary gland is referred to as the "master gland", the brain is the true master and the hypothalamus releases hormones that tell the pituitary what to do. In the case of the stress response, the hypothalamus releases a hormone known as **CRH** (*corticotropin releasing hormone*). CRH tells the pituitary gland to release **ACTH** (*adrenocorticotropic hormone*), which travels in the bloodstream to the adrenal glands, which release the **catecholamines** (pronounced *cat-a-coal-a-means*) **epinephrine** and **norepinephrine,** which activate the sympathetic nervous system. It's easier to remember that epinephrine and norepinephrine are released by the adrenal glands if you remember their British names; *adrenaline* and *noradrenaline.*

The adrenal glands also release a group of steroid hormones known as *glucocorticoids*. As we'll see, these *glucocorticoids* (such as *cortisol*) play a fundamental role in the stress response and are one of the keys for understanding how stress can negatively affect the body. These hormones help to mobilize energy resources (increasing *gluc*ose in the bloodstream) and prepare for possible injury by reducing inflammation. The stress response emphasizes immediate needs so processes that don't help you survive right now are put aside. Digestion, growth, reproduction and sex drive (now is not the time to look for a mate!) are for long-term projects that won't matter if the current crisis isn't averted. Using energy for these during an emergency would be, as the saying goes, rearranging deck chairs on the Titanic.

You may be familiar with cortisol's pharmaceutical name: *hydrocortisone*, used in creams to reduce itchiness, swelling, and inflammation from rashes or insect bites though you may also know that overly-frequent use of hydrocortisone can cause skin damage. This is a good example for thinking about glucocorticoids; in small doses they can be beneficial but bring them out too often and they end up doing more harm than good.

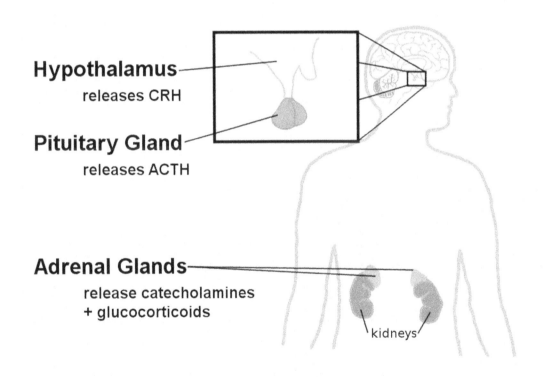

Hypothalamus
releases CRH

Pituitary Gland
releases ACTH

Adrenal Glands
release catecholamines
+ glucocorticoids

kidneys

Homeostasis (Greek *homeo* – "similar" and *stasis* – "stand") is the idea that the body works to maintain an optimal state. But when it comes to stress, how can we think about using the same response for different scenarios? How can the stress response help if you're too cold and also help if you're too hot? How can you have an optimal point for something like blood pressure if it depends on the situation?

To help correct this, we can consider an adjusted theory of homeostasis known as allostasis. *Allostasis* (from the Greek *allo* - "variable") recognizes that the optimal state is not a set point but a range. Your optimal blood pressure for sitting on the couch watching Netflix is quite different from your optimal blood pressure for running a marathon. In fact, your "optimal" blood pressure will be changing more often than you might think, even needing to adjust for behaviors like standing up from the couch. (People with *Shy-Drager* syndrome fail to produce an adequate stress response and can faint from an inability to cope with the drop in blood pressure created by standing up). Allostasis recognizes that "optimal" covers a wide range of possibilities depending on context. Essentially allostasis is the idea that our bodies are always adjusting to maintain a consistent level of function (sometimes expressed with the phrase "constancy through change").

Hans Selye (*sell-yay*) was a Hungarian endocrinologist who was born in Vienna but spent most of his professional career in Canada. He's considered one of the pioneers of stress research but Selye didn't set out to study stress. He began his work by trying to understand the effects of an ovarian extract on rats. He found that rats repeatedly injected with the extract developed swollen adrenal glands, a smaller thymus, shrunken lymph glands, and *peptic ulcers*, which are holes in the lining of the stomach. These initially seemed to be effects of the extract but control rats given saline injections also developed these symptoms. Selye theorized that it was the chronic stress of painful injections that was causing these effects. He then subjected rats to many different stressors (cold exposure, heat exposure, trauma, infection) and found that chronic stress reliably enlarged adrenal glands, shrunk the thymus and lymph glands, and created peptic ulcers.

Based on this research, Selye proposed a general three-stage process of adaptation to any stressor, which he called *General Adaptation Syndrome* (*GAS*). The first stage of GAS is *Alarm*, in which the body mobilizes resources to confront the threat. If the stressor continues for an extended period of time, the body enters the second phase, known as *Resistance*. In this phase, the body adapts to the high level of arousal by drawing on muscle and fat to maintain energy while shutting down sex drive and processes for digestion and growth in order to conserve resources. If the stress continues, Selye believed the body enters the final phase of GAS, *Exhaustion*, during which the body's ability to resist collapses and the stressor causes organ damage, aging, or even death. You might create a mnemonic for **G**eneral **A**daptation **S**yndrome's 3 stages (**A**larm, **R**esistance, **E**xhaustion) such as "People with **GAS ARE** stressed."

While Selye was correct in identifying how various stressors could mobilize a similar response in the body, later research has shown that the stress response is not identical for all stressors. While there are many similarities, different stressors can have different physiological signatures. Selye's last stage (exhaustion) hasn't held up to scrutiny either. Stressors don't exhaust the body's resistance and then cause damage, it's actually the continued stress response itself that damages the body. Stressors like cold exposure weren't causing Selye's rats to develop ulcers, the rats' own stress responses were responsible. This is where that class of steroid hormones known as glucocorticoids come into play. These hormones mobilize energy but can cause damage and weaken the immune system if the body isn't given a chance to recover. In order to better understand this process, we'll need to take a closer look at the immune system and how it functions.

The Immune System

The immune system is the body's defense against intruders, pathogens, and injury, acting as a surveillance and protection system that is distributed throughout the entire body. A great deal of the work is done by white blood cells known as lymphocytes. **Lymphocytes** come in two main types: **T-cells**, which originate from the thymus (thus the **T**), and **B-cells**, which originate from the **b**one marrow. Lymphocytes identify invaders then produce antibodies to fight them off. Other cells in the immune system include **macrophages** (Greek for "big eaters") which consume invaders and damaged cells, as well as **natural killer cells** which destroy other cells.

So how does the stress response disrupt immune function? Those glucocorticoids we mentioned earlier (released by the adrenal glands during the stress response) can interfere with the immune system by slowing white blood cell formation and altering the function of lymphocytes, which increases susceptibility to infection and weakens the body's ability to fight invaders and repair itself. Sheldon Cohen and colleagues (1998) had healthy volunteers complete a stress survey, then gave them nasal drops containing a cold virus. They found that those who had reported chronic stress were more likely to become sick from the virus. Excessive glucocorticoids can also cause degeneration of neurons in the hippocampus and increase fat storage (particularly in the abdomen) which raises the risk of obesity and associated illnesses (heart disease, metabolic syndrome, type-II diabetes, etc.)

In order to do their jobs properly, it's vital that lymphocytes, macrophages, and natural killer cells can tell the difference between the "good guys" (your own healthy cells) and the "bad guys" (invaders and damaged cells that need to be removed). This is no easy task, and it's possible for errors to occur. This happens in **autoimmune disorders** such as rheumatoid arthritis or psoriasis. In these disorders, the immune system incorrectly determines that healthy cells represent threats, and then tries to destroy them. How are these autoimmune disorders treated? Patients are given massive doses of glucocorticoids, suppressing the immune system and reducing symptoms (though potentially causing other problems in the process).

Chronic stress can also cause shortening of **telomeres**, segments of DNA on the ends of chromosomes which control cell division. As telomeres shorten, the process of cell division is inhibited or eventually blocked completely. Telomeres naturally shorten with aging, but chronic stress accelerates this process, explaining why stress can make people appear to age rapidly. Mothers caring for chronically ill children showed shorter telomere length (as well as lower white-blood cell count) the longer they had been caring for the child.

Psychological Components of Stress

The stress response seems pretty well-designed for physical stressors, preparing our bodies to flee or fight threats. But we also face psychological stressors, and the stress response isn't particularly well-designed for these, as we usually can't run from them or physically fight them off.

Unlike other species, we're able to *anticipate* threats and experience a stress response from anticipation alone. Your average gazelle on the savannah would certainly be stressed by the presence of a lion, but you probably won't find a gazelle experiencing a major stress response from thinking that maybe one day next week it will need to sprint from a lion. Yet we can manage to mount a stress response just by thinking about stressful situations. Just imagining having to make a presentation in class might be enough to make your heart race and your palms feel sweaty.

Because we can think about them at any time, anticipated threats can easily become chronic stressors. Once a gazelle escapes the lion's clutches it can recover from the stress of the event, which probably won't happen every day. For us, however, anticipated stressors can be non-stop, from family pressures to recurrent concerns related to school, work, finances, or our societal standing. If these stressors are flooding our bodies with glucocorticoids day after day, we can end up with the same problems Selye's rats faced.

Stress and Health

We'll begin with one problem Selye's rats had: peptic ulcers. In the middle of the twentieth century, doctors knew that *gastritis* (inflammation of the stomach lining) led to ulcers, but they couldn't figure out what was causing gastritis in the first place. People who were stressed had more ulcers, so the assumption was that stress caused gastritis, which then caused ulcers. The only way to treat gastritis was to tell patients to reduce their stress and give them antacids to reduce some symptoms. It wasn't until 1982 that Australian researchers Barry Marshall and Robin Warren identified a bacteria, *Helicobacter pylori*, which was implicated in the formation of peptic ulcers (work for which they received the Nobel Prize in 2005). To prove the point, Marshall himself drank a petri dish containing a pure *H. pylori* culture which caused nausea and (crucially) gastritis within a matter of days. Physicians no longer had to deal with vaguely telling patients to reduce stress and could instead place blame for gastritis (and later ulcers) squarely on a microbial cause.

While it's still possible to develop gastritis and ulcers without *Helicobacter pylori* being present, *H. pylori* is extremely common and it's estimated that about 50% of people worldwide play host to it, most without symptoms or ulcers. In fact, the presence of *H. pylori* may even reduce the risk of other illnesses for some people. So why doesn't half the world suffer from gastritis and ulcers? Now we're back to the role of stress. Chronic stress weakens the immune system and this influences the body's ability to control levels of *H. pylori*. Chronic stress distracts the guards, allowing the bacteria to proliferate, as well as reducing the body's ability to repair damage the bacteria causes.

The stress response reduces digestion and part of the way this works is by reducing blood flow to the stomach (in order to increase blood flow to skeletal muscles). This reduction in blood flow means that the stomach is temporarily less able to repair itself. Do this day after day, and you might just find yourself developing symptoms of gastritis. This same pattern is seen with other invaders which are always in the body but are more likely to cause symptoms during periods of stress. Herpes (including cold sores), shingles, and periodontal disease (such as gingivitis) are all more likely to flare up when stress is high and immune function is low.

Stress, Personality, and Heart Disease

Cardiologists Meyer Friedman and Ray Rosenman first proposed that there was a personality type associated with greater risk of heart disease. This **Type-A behavior pattern** refers to people who are competitive and ambitious, feel a constant sense of time urgency, and become easily angered and hostile. In contrast, those with a **Type-B behavior pattern** have a more laid-back approach to life and are more cooperative, easy-going, patient, and less prone to sudden hostility or aggression.

Type-A people feel that there's never enough time to do everything, so they quickly become frustrated or angry when confronted with a traffic jam, a line at the grocery store, or a long wait at the doctor's office. In fact, part of the inspiration for investigating the relationship between personality and heart disease resulted from Friedman and Rosenman having to replace the armrests on the chairs in their waiting room frequently, as apparently their cardiac patients had a tendency to fidget; impatiently rubbing, squeezing, and pulling at the fabric of the chairs. Initial research by Friedman and Rosenman found that people with a Type-A personality had 7x more heart disease than their relaxed and easy-going Type-B peers.

In order to understand exactly how stress increases the risk of heart disease, we need a brief primer on what **cardiovascular disease** is. **Atherosclerosis** (from the Greek *athera* "gruel" + *scleros* "hard"), also known as *arteriosclerosis*, refers to the buildup of plaque on the walls of arteries. The walls become thick and hardened by inflammation and the gradual accumulation of white-blood cells, foam cells (macrophages filled with lipids), and cholesterol. This buildup of plaque increases blood pressure, so blood whips through arteries faster, potentially furthering damage and inflammation.

If a section of plaque is unstable, it can break off and this clot then enters blood circulation where it can block a blood vessel or an artery (this possibility increases as arterial walls thicken). If the blockage occurs in a coronary artery, it is a *myocardial infarction*, or a heart attack. If it occurs in a blood vessel in the brain, it is a *stroke*. This means that atherosclerosis increases the risk of both of these potentially-fatal outcomes, and the frequent blood pressure spikes of Type-A personality further increase risk. Later research has suggested that it's not so much the time urgency or ambition of Type-A that increases risk, but the frequent anger. Impatience may wear down armrests, but hostility increases heart rate and blood pressure and causes greater wear-and-tear on one's arteries.

Understanding exactly how much additional risk Type-A personality carries is difficult, however, because the hostile actions of Type-A individuals may relate to other factors. Their *negative affectivity* (more anger, contempt, fear, disgust, and nervousness) not only activates their stress response more often, it also makes it more likely that others will be hostile to them (this can be referred to as *transactional hostility*). This means that others are less likely to provide social support, and a lack of social support is another risk factor for cardiovascular disease.

If Type-A personality hit a little too close to home for you, the good news is that it's possible to change by adopting stress management strategies. If you're not particularly Type-A yourself, you may still have to resist responding in kind when others initiate hostility. But when people are leaning on their car horns or berating others for trivial errors and minor delays, you might just find yourself feeling bad for them (and their poor arteries) and hoping they learn better ways to cope with stress.

Perceived Control

Determining whether something is stressful has two main parts. The first, or ***primary appraisal***, involves asking the question "is this a threat or not?". If not, there's no need to activate the stress response.

If something has been determined to be a threat, the next step in the appraisal process is ***secondary appraisal***, which refers to figuring out how to respond to the threat by asking the question, "can I do anything about it?". Stressors which can't be managed or controlled create a greater stress response.

The answer to whether or not we can control a stressor might not always be straightforward. In fact, two people may answer this question differently for the same stressor. So the level of ***perceived control*** varies. This is the difference between the student who experiences stress over an impending exam and studies more (exerting control over the outcome) versus the student who feels powerless, experiencing stress but feeling that nothing can be done about it.

David Glass and Jerome Singer (1972) conducted a series of studies which exposed participants to predictable or unpredictable noises, then had the participants work at tasks requiring concentration, such as proofreading or solving puzzles. In some variations, after initial noise exposure participants were told there was a switch they could use to turn off the noise, while other participants did not have this control. The participants with access to the switch showed better performance on the tasks, even though they never actually used the switch (there weren't any noises after the switch was shown to them), supporting the idea that perceived control can reduce the effects of some stressors. It seems that participants with access to the switch felt they were prepared for the potential stressor, and this allowed them to focus on the tasks more fully. Other research has linked greater perceived control in the workplace to higher work satisfaction, improved well-being and work performance, and greater immune function.

Learned Helplessness

In a series of well-known studies, **Martin Seligman** and Steven Maier placed dogs in a box that gave them electric shocks. Some dogs were able to turn the shocks off, while other dogs had no control. When later placed in a box in which all dogs could escape the shocks (by jumping over a divider) those who had previously been unable to avoid shocks did not attempt to escape. They seemed to have given up hope and sat there accepting the new shocks. These dogs perceived that they had no control over this stressor and this was named *learned helplessness*.

Learned helplessness has been replicated in rats, fish, insects, primates, and humans. In one study, Donald Hiroto and Martin Seligman found that human participants initially presented with an inescapable noise later showed slower learning for a task that could turn the noise off. Rats taught to be helpless seem to be depressed; they spend less time grooming, have disturbed sleep patterns, show less interest in sex and food, engage in self-mutilation (by biting themselves), and, to bring us back to the stress response, they have elevated levels of glucocorticoids in their bloodstreams.

Seligman and Maier also found that laboratory-raised dogs learned to be helpless more easily than dogs who had been caught by the pound (and had presumably been roaming free). This suggests that learning a sense of control in other areas can build resistance to helplessness, perhaps because one realizes that while the shocks are bad, they are just one situation in which control has been lost. Laboratory animals may have reduced control over many other aspects of their lives, increasing their risk of developing helplessness.

Stress and the Social Hierarchy

How much control we have over our environment may depend on our position in the *social hierarchy*. Those who are high status may feel (or actually have) a greater sense of control over many aspects of their lives, reducing their stress response to some stressors. This isn't the case in all species, however, and sometimes it's not so good to be the king, particularly if the hierarchy is unstable. Holding the highest rank may mean that one is constantly challenged. In these cases, having to fend off rivals day after day takes its toll, and higher status is associated with higher levels of glucocorticoids.

So where do humans fit in? Drawing conclusions about the role of rank for humans can be difficult for a number of reasons. In many human hierarchies, we aren't competing for vital resources like food, but for luxury products, prestige, and perceived importance. We may confuse rank with personality traits associated with dominance, such as those traits we saw in Type-A personality, which contribute to stress. It can also be difficult to assess control in human hierarchies, such as for middle-managers who feel they have increased responsibilities but reduced control.

Despite these difficulties, it does seem that for humans being on top can provide a sense of control that mitigates stress. This may explain why high-ranking British civil servants get sick less often than their subordinates and show reduced risk of several illnesses (see Marmot et al, 1978 and Rossum et al, 2000). It may also explain why Oscar-winners tend to live an average of 4 years longer than their nominated-but-non-winning peers.

In contrast, low *SES* (*socioeconomic status* - a combination of education, income, and occupation) is associated with poorer health. Poverty represents the greatest risk factor in all of behavioral medicine and the stressors of poverty include physical stressors (hunger, manual labor, increased work-related accidents and injuries, chronic sleep deprivation from working multiple jobs), psychological stressors (lack of control, financial worries, fewer resources to deal with problems that arise), and environmental stressors (noise, pollution, poor housing conditions, crowding, high-crime neighborhoods).

Once basic needs are met, however, understanding how status influences us is complicated by the fact that humans don't have one single hierarchy that influences all aspects of life. Our lives are varied and we are all members of multiple hierarchies, from family and friend groups, to school and the workplace, to hobbies and leisure activities. We may be high-ranking in some of these hierarchies and near the bottom of others. Just knowing someone's station at work doesn't tell us much if that person is more concerned with status in a different social hierarchy. The guy who just barely managed to finish a community 5K run after recovering from a long illness may feel he's on top of the world, while the competitive runner who thought he'd get first but came in second may feel utterly defeated.

The Downsides of Control

A stronger sense of control isn't always better and there are situations in which perceived control increases stress. Sherman James identified one damaging relationship with perceived control which he labeled *John Henryism*; the belief that one can overcome any challenge with enough effort. James coined the term after interviewing a patient of his with *hypertension* (high blood pressure) named John Henry Martin. Like the legendary African-American railroad worker whose efforts to outwork a steam-powered spike driver ended in his victory and his death, John Henry Martin cared about success and believed he could control all outcomes if he just worked hard enough. While this might sound like an empowering example of an internal locus of control, the truth is that not everything can be controlled by one's work ethic, no matter how strong it may be.

Individuals with John Henryism (frequently working-class African-Americans) believe they just need to push themselves harder, and tend to blame themselves for failures or shortcomings. When it comes to overcoming societal prejudice, discrimination, and injustice, however, it's not always the case that one can simply work harder. The message that managing these issues is a matter of individual effort is not only unfair, it's dangerous. There's a price to be paid for the continuous coping involved in confronting a stressor like prejudice day in and day out. Trying one's best to monitor social interactions for prejudice, avoid confirming negative stereotypes, and work to make up for discrimination takes its toll. James found that ratings on traits of John Henryism (agreeing with statements such as *"When things don't go the way I want them to, that just makes me work even harder"*) were associated with greater cardiovascular reactivity to stress, and increased risk of hypertension. More recent research has also suggested that disadvantaged children with a high sense of self-control show more rapid immune cell aging (see Miller et al, 2015).

We might also wonder how choice influences our perception of control. As Barry Schwartz notes in his book "The Paradox of Choice", sometimes having more options makes choosing all the more difficult. We seem to have more autonomy and control over our lives than ever before, but this greater perceived control introduces greater responsibility. We may feel that we are to blame when things go wrong, perhaps we could have avoided this if we had just made better choices. If you're unhappy in a world where you seem to have unlimited choice, the implication is that you've chosen poorly and your unhappiness is your own fault.

Control and Blame

Sometimes it's better to have greater cognitive flexibility; the ability to switch locus of control from internal to external, depending on circumstances. In other words, if you've accomplished something, it's probably good to feel that you had a sense of control so you can take credit for it, but when something terrible happens to you for no good reason, blaming yourself isn't going to help and will worsen stress. In these cases we need to switch to an external locus of control, accepting our lack of control and placing blame outside ourselves (fortunately most of us tend to show this ***self-serving bias***; taking credit for our successes and blaming failures on others).

While it's true we have control over some factors related to our health (exercise, diet, etc.) that control is limited. When bad things happen, sometimes it's best to realize you had no way of preventing them. The same can be true when bad things happen to others. We should avoid the just-world bias that causes us to blame victims of disease as if they somehow deserve their suffering. Sure, treat people well and they're likely to treat you well, but the rest of the universe is indifferent. Microbial invaders don't care how kind you are, cancer doesn't believe in karma, and life-altering injuries can happen to anyone in an instant. These are facts we must learn to live with, and more importantly, facts we must remember when we see others fall ill.

One more thing about blame. Later in this chapter we'll see strategies for coping with stress, but before we do, I'd like to note that those recommendations are mostly for minor-to-moderate stressors. They are not cure-all approaches and they don't address social and economic origins of stress. Thinking of stress as a *cause* of illness (rather than a *risk factor*) can unintentionally place blame on people for being sick. Suggesting that people struggling with the overwhelming stress of poverty just need to relax, go for a jog (through crime-ridden neighborhoods), or eat healthier (when neighborhood stores only stock processed foods) implies that if they don't, their stress is their own fault. While we might not like to admit it, the impact of poverty on health can't easily be smiled or meditated away and expecting that it can places an additional burden on those who most need help.

Stress-Related Disorders

PTSD (*Post-Traumatic Stress Disorder*) is a psychological disorder in which patients show 4 main types of symptoms. These symptoms include *intrusive thoughts,* memories, nightmares, and "flashbacks" of traumatic events, *heightened physiological arousal* (such as hypervigilance, sleep disturbance, and increased startle response), *avoidance* of memories, thoughts, feelings, or situations related to the trauma, and *negative mood and cognition,* which may include emotional numbing, guilt, memory and concentration problems, or suicidal thoughts. Symptoms must persist for at least one month in order to warrant diagnosis. While it was previously classified as an anxiety disorder, the DSM-5 now classifies PTSD within trauma and stress-related disorders.

This disorder has historically been associated with military combat, described as "shell shock" during WWI, and "combat fatigue" during WWII, and has frequently been diagnosed in the victims, witnesses, and perpetrators of war. PTSD is associated with other traumatic events such as assault, domestic abuse, rape, hostage situations, natural disasters, and terrorist attacks, which can result in diagnoses for victims or for others who must face these scenarios (police officers, firefighters, emergency response teams, and other health workers).

Not everyone who confronts these extreme stressors develops PTSD, so what other risk factors are relevant? It shouldn't be surprising that other risk factors relate to stress, such as low socioeconomic status, other preexisting mental disorders, prior childhood abuse and trauma, and low social support.

Another possible risk factor relates to physiology and the nervous system, as greater sensitivity to glucocorticoids and smaller hippocampal volume have been indicated in predicting the likelihood of developing PTSD in response to extreme stress. To examine whether hippocampal volume was a consequence of PTSD or an existing risk factor, Mark Gilbertson and colleagues looked at pairs of identical twins in which one twin saw active combat and the other did not, finding that twins with smaller hippocampal volume were more likely to develop PTSD if exposed to combat situations. Research by Douglas Bremner has found that PTSD seems to cause permanent shrinking of the hippocampus. So it may be the case that smaller hippocampal volume is a risk factor, but also a consequence of PTSD. Surprisingly, people with PTSD tend to show lower levels of glucocorticoids, but this may be because they are more sensitive to glucocorticoids. PTSD also increases one's risk of heart disease and asthma (not surprising given their relationship with stress).

How Do Some People Handle Stress So Well?

As with Type-A or Type-B behavior patterns, we might think about responsiveness to stress as a personality trait. Susanne Kobasa first referred to the ability to withstand stress as **hardiness** in her initial studies of business executives who seemed to thrive in stressful circumstances, and this trait has since been studied in a number of other high-stress jobs, including military special forces, police officers, firefighters, and even students facing academic stress.

Kobasa identified three main traits of people who were **hardy** (or *stress-resistant*), which can be remembered as the **3 C**s of **c**oping:

Commitment – Stress-resistant people show an active involvement with life, believing that their pursuits are important and meaningful.

Challenge – Rather than seeing change (and the stress the comes with it) as a threat, these individuals view change as an opportunity for continuous growth and improvement.

Control – Hardy people believe that they have causal influence over their life and that their behaviors make a difference.

You might recall some other ideas from personality that seem relevant here such as Julian Rotter's *locus of control* or Albert Bandura's *self-efficacy*. Hardiness can also been seen as a factor in understanding **resilience** and those who are hardy are more likely to survive or even thrive in the face of adversity. Life-changing accidents and injuries, loss of loved ones, and episodes of severe trauma represent extreme circumstances of stress and hardiness may play a role in how individuals respond and recover. There's also evidence that resilient people not only recover from traumatic events but experience **post-traumatic growth**, finding a greater sense of purpose and meaning for their lives and feeling stronger as a result of the challenges they have overcome.

Can Hardiness be Increased?

Is hardiness a fixed personality trait, or are there ways to develop it? The research is encouraging and hardiness training may help people learn how to respond to stress in more positive ways. Training to improve hardiness tends to focus on three main techniques.

Reappraisal of the stressful stimulus or situation to consider how it could be better or worse, followed by consideration of what could be done to ensure that the better version happens. This helps the person to create a plan and increases perceived control.

Focusing helps a person get unstuck from the belief that they have no control by focusing on how stress feels in the body, which emotions are involved, and how these can be compensated for. When things are out of our hands, we can still exert control over our response to uncontrollable events and circumstances.

Compensatory self-improvement emphasizes how a person could improve from a stressful experience, either by learning how to overcome the stressor, or by using the experience to learn more about the self.

Salvatore Maddi has studied the effectiveness of hardiness training and one study found that students taught these approaches showed GPA improvements which continued for 2 years after the training, suggesting a long-term benefit.

Stress Management

No matter how much we know about stress, we can't evade it. But stress isn't something we need to hide from, it's something we need to learn to live with. This means we need effective strategies for managing stress and coping with the inevitable stressors we will face.

There are three main ways of managing stress: *appraisal-focused coping* refers to reconsidering one's appraisal of a stressor (maybe this isn't a stressor), *problem-focused coping* refers to confronting a stressor head on and finding strategies to eliminate or reduce it (it is a stressor but I can overcome it), and *emotion-focused coping* refers to managing stress by focusing on one's emotional response to it, rather than on the stressor itself (it is a stressor, I can't overcome it, but I can deal with the emotions it causes).

If John is stressed by his Spanish class, one way he might deal with this is to reappraise the situation and decide not to care about his grades for this class and then he won't be stressed. This would be appraisal-focused coping. If Susan is stressed by Spanish class and she responds to this stress by creating flashcards, rereading assignments, and organizing review sessions with classmates, this would be an example of problem-focused coping. If Bill is regularly stressed by unavoidable traffic in his morning commute, he may confront this problem by using this time in the car to listen to his favorite podcasts. The stressor (traffic) is still there, but Joe has changed his emotional response to it (perhaps even enjoying this time spent in the car).

Another way of approaching emotion-focused coping is to calm physiological reactivity to stressors. This might be done in the form of medications (such as anti-anxiety drugs which reduce activation of the stress response) or through relaxation techniques and physical exercise, both of which can reduce reactivity.

Gary Schwartz pioneered the use of **biofeedback**, a technique that involves monitoring heart rate or muscle tension in order to learn greater control over these processes which are normally unconscious. By using a device to monitor heart rate or muscle tension, a person can learn how to consciously reduce the stress response. It seems that fancy biofeedback equipment isn't necessary for these benefits, and Herbert Benson has shown that simply sitting quietly and focusing on relaxation can evoke a **relaxation response**, in which heart rate, breathing, and muscle tension are reduced and immune function is boosted.

Exercise

If we think about how stress prepares our body for movement and action, there's an intuitive logic to moving and using the energy that has been mobilized as a way of calming the stress response. This turns out to be true, and physical exercise is an excellent method for managing stress.

People who exercise regularly show greater feelings of self-efficacy, more energy, and they tend to be more extraverted and sociable. These types of correlations could work in the other direction (self-efficacy and energy cause you to exercise) but we can experimentally have people exercise and then see these effects occur. Physical exercise seems to improve psychological well-being, and just 10 minutes of aerobic exercise has been demonstrated to improve mood. Regular exercise reduces the risk of many chronic illnesses and has been used as an effective intervention for a number of mental illnesses including depression and anxiety disorders. Exercise has been shown to increase **neurogenesis**, the creation of new neurons, in the hippocampus. You may be familiar with "runner's high", which refers to the release of **endorphins**, the body's natural painkillers, following a bout of exercise. These endorphins (as well as *enkephalins*) boost mood, relieve pain, and improve quality of sleep.

Ironically, while exercise is an effective strategy for relieving stress, stress can become a barrier which prevents people from exercising. Feeling that they have too much work and too little time, people may fail to get adequate exercise, even though it would help to reduce their overall stress level (and improve their health). Exercise can be a way of exerting control and feeling a greater sense of self-efficacy, though it's important to note that this only refers to voluntary exercise. Rats given the opportunity to engage in exercise by running on a wheel show reductions in glucocorticoid levels, but those forced to exercise (for the same amount of time) show increases in their glucocorticoid levels.

As with perceived control, it might be possible to have too much of a good thing. While moderate exercise is associated with increased testosterone in males, those who run more than 40 miles per week actually show higher glucocorticoid levels and lower reproductive function (decreased testosterone production and smaller testes). Females who engage in excessive exercise also show reductions in reproductive function, including delayed onset of puberty and *amenorrhea* (cessation of menstruation). Overexercise can also lead to decreased bone density in both males and females (probably caused by the elevated glucocorticoid levels).

Moderate exercise may engage multiple aspects of stress management, providing people with a sense of control over their lives and their health. Exercise can also provide a source of social engagement and group cohesion, whether in the form of an organized team or just a jogging partner. Social support is another component of stress management, and this means that exercising with a friend may allow you to fight stress on two fronts.

Social Support and Stress

Social support, which refers to feeling loved, valued, and connected with others, is an important factor for coping with stress. Social support can come in a variety of forms. It may be in the form of *tangible support*, such as cooking a meal for someone, it might be *informational support*, such as providing advice or suggestions to a friend, or it could simply be *emotional support*, helping to comfort someone who is struggling. There's a balance between support and control, however and in some cases, it may be better for social support to be *invisible support*, particularly when assistance could be seen as a threat to self-esteem or perceived control.

Sometimes being there "just in case" might be all that is needed. As with *perceived* control, sometimes there's a benefit from *perceived* support, even if that support is not actually used. In other words, knowing there's a friend you could call might help, even if you never actually pick up the phone.

When it comes to identifying the benefits of social support we need to remember that those who enjoy the greatest social support may have other traits related to their ability to manage stress, such as greater social skills and social competence, which may help reduce their anxiety. We should also consider that not all social support is positive and others may encourage negative thinking patterns or harmful behaviors like smoking, alcohol consumption, or drug use. It's also possible for support to be intrusive, violating our privacy and increasing, rather than reducing, stress levels. We can probably all imagine at least one person we'd rather not be around while dealing with stress.

The benefits of social support in the face of acute stress can be demonstrated in the lab. In one study, women were exposed to the threat of electric shocks to the ankle while in an fMRI scanner which monitored their brain activity. Women who were alone showed the highest threat response activation, those who held a stranger's hand showed a slight reduction in activation, and those who held their husband's hand showed the greatest reduction of the threat response. In fact, this reduction was greatest in those couples who had reported a high quality of marriage (see Coan, Schaefer, & Davidson, 2006).

Being a member of a group can provide "***social capital***", which refers to a sense of community, trust, and reciprocity among members. When members of a community see each other as equals, there's less hierarchy, reductions in exerting dominance over others, and a greater sense of looking out for one another. This all sounds great, but we have to remember that groups can provide social capital to members in a way that is harmful to others. There's a risk that what's great for members can still be destructive to society as a whole, if tight-knit groups become intolerant, prejudiced, or actively discriminatory against outsiders.

The "Faith Factor"

Religious communities and spirituality can provide a form of social support and those who express greater religiosity or spirituality tend to have better health outcomes, recover faster from illnesses and live longer. This may be in part because religion provides a way of thinking about the world and reappraising the meaning of stressful events. It may help increase perceived control over the otherwise uncontrollable. Devotion, piety, and the practice of rituals can provide ways of exerting control over the vicissitudes of life. Even when control seems impossible, one might trust that there's a deity keeping watch. When bad things do happen, faith may be of benefit, provided that one sees the misfortune as a challenge (my devotion is being tested) or part of an overall plan (there's a reason for my suffering).

Like many topics in this chapter, religiosity can be a double-edged sword. Those who struggle with their faith in hard times, or who see their misfortunes as punishments from an angry god show higher levels of stress. Believing that illnesses represent karmic comeuppance or that strength of faith can overcome cancer can cause people to blame victims and make them feel they deserve their illnesses. As with other sources of social support, religious groups may become insulated, shun outsiders, or engage in discrimination, inflicting more stress and hardship on the rest of the world.

Positive Psychology and Well-Being

Positive psychology is seen as a counterpoint to the study of illness and mental disorder. By considering the traits, behaviors, and cognitions of those who thrive, we may uncover the sources of health and well-being. Recognizing that happiness can mean many things to many people, researchers in positive psychology prefer to use the term *subjective well-being* rather than "happiness" (though the latter still seems superior for best-selling book titles). We've already seen a few cognitive and behavioral strategies for improving health and well-being, now we'll take a look at some of the other areas of research in positive psychology.

Optimism

In addition to hardiness, there are other personality traits associated with well-being. One of these is *optimism*, which refers to a tendency to "expect the best", even in negative circumstances. In contrast, *pessimism* refers to the expectation that things will continue to be bad, or get worse. Optimism appears to be slightly heritable, though this doesn't necessarily mean that one's level of optimism can't be changed. Martin Seligman has proposed "learned optimism" as an opposing strategy to his "learned helplessness" discussed earlier.

Optimism is associated with a number of positive health outcomes and patients with higher levels of optimism prior to surgery have been shown to have better post-operative health and faster recovery (see Scheier et al, 1999). As for whether optimism can be learned, Seligman and Gregory Buchanan found that college students who attended 16 hours of learned optimism training reported fewer health problems and had lower incidence of depression than a control group over the following 18 months.

The Role of Environment

How much does our external environment influence our well-being? Would you be happier if you were living in a palace rather than an apartment, or driving a luxury coupe instead of a clunker? Environmental changes can make us happier, but this may not last as long as we expect.

Even extreme changes in environment don't seem to cause long-term changes in happiness, perhaps best demonstrated by Brickman, Coates, and Janoff-Bulman's study of lottery winners and paraplegics. While these major life events did cause short-term changes in happiness, people tended to revert back to their previous levels of happiness. This suggests that despite some peaks and valleys, we have a "*happiness set point*" which isn't strongly influenced by our environment.

Daniel Gilbert has suggested that we have a kind of "psychological immune system" that we aren't usually aware of. We think we know what will make our future selves happy but our ability to predict our future emotional states (known as *affective forecasting*) is actually quite poor. As a result we end up chasing the things we think will make us happy rather than focusing on those things that can actually raise our well-being.

Buying Happiness?

Perhaps the most obvious thing that people chase in search of happiness is money. Poverty is devastating and can decrease well-being in a number of ways, so being able to meet basic needs and have some financial security can indeed boost happiness. But more and more wealth does not mean more and more happiness. And of course, we all already know this, as the struggles of celebrities and the super-rich are popular tabloid fodder, and remind us that money doesn't solve all problems.

Research by Daniel Kahneman has suggested that after about $70,000 per year, increased wealth shows **diminishing returns** (or *diminishing marginal utility* for the economists reading this) meaning that as you earn more, each dollar contributes less to improving well-being.

It seems that as we move up, we adjust to our new surroundings and they no longer boost our well-being. This idea that we continually adjust to our new positive experiences is referred to as the **adaptation level phenomenon** or, more memorably, the **hedonic treadmill**. Making more money doesn't necessarily make you happier because as you move up, you start comparing yourself to those who make even more than you do. Essentially you move up to the next level of comparison. When you make $25,000/year then earning $75,000 seems like just what you need, but once you're making $75,000 you start comparing yourself to people making more and wishing you could reach $100,000.

This kind of social comparison is key for understanding well-being. It's not just a matter of having "enough", it's about defining what "enough" is based on the people around you. In this way, it's not so much actual deprivation that makes many Americans unhappy, it's their feeling of **relative deprivation** when they compare themselves to those who are doing better, known as **upward comparison**. A perfectly functional old Toyota that gets you everywhere you need to go doesn't feel like the luxury it is when you park it in a lot filled with Mercedes.

One way to reduce feelings of relative deprivation is to consider those people who are worse off than you are, known as **downward comparison**. That Toyota starts looking like a luxury again when you remember that some people can't afford a car at all. Or that the vast majority of human beings who have ever lived never had access to a car in their entire lives. It's tough to feel bad for yourself when you realize there are millions or even billions of people around the world who would gladly trade places with you right now, and that's not including all those who have previously lived and died before our modern times. The lifestyles of kings and emperors would happily be traded for air-conditioning, antibiotics, and whatever this Internet thing is.

So what can we do to boost our well-being in a lasting way? Are there interventions which can raise our happiness set-points and then keep them there? Indeed there are, and some will come as no surprise. Physical exercise, performing acts of kindness, and regularly experiencing and expressing **gratitude** have all been shown to raise people's overall level of well-being in the long-term.

Finding Balance

Perhaps the key to understanding this chapter is to recall the concept of allostasis: finding balance in a world that never stops shifting, finding stability by always moving. Stress is inevitable, so we can only hope to find balance among tides which constantly turn.

Feel a sense of control over life, but recognize when control is out of your hands. Allow ambition to drive achievement without fueling hostility. Manage stress through exercise, but don't overdo it. Encourage strength, support, and social capital within your communities, but avoid the temptation to disparage outsiders. Balance optimism with acceptance, strive to improve while savoring what you have, and use downward comparison to feel grateful without developing a sense of superiority.

Chapter Summary – Stress & Health

- *Health psychology* studies the relationship between psychological factors and health.

- *Stress* is a general term that can refer to *stressors*, threats to well-being, as well as the physiological *stress response* of the body, which occurs along the *HPA-axis* and involves the release of *catecholamines* and *glucocorticoids.*

- *Hans Selye* proposed a response to chronic stress called *General Adaptation Syndrome*, which consisted of 3 stages: *Alarm*, *Resistance*, and *Exhaustion*.

- The *immune system* protects the body from invaders and illness but can be suppressed by over-activation of the stress response, primarily due to the effects of *glucocorticoids*.

- Stress has been linked to increased risk of several illnesses, including cardiovascular disease, peptic ulcers, respiratory illnesses, arthritis, and depression, as well as stress-related psychological disorders such as *Post-Traumatic Stress Disorder*.

- Individuals differ in their responses to stress, and those who show *hardiness* are able to manage stress better than others. *Coping* strategies for stress may be *appraisal-focused*, *problem-focused*, or *emotion-focused*.

- *Positive psychology* examines the sources of health and wellness, uncovering how environment, wealth, and social comparison influence well-being.

Notes

Chapter 15
Psychological Disorders

Psychopathology

Now we'll finally be turning our attention to the scientific study of mental disorders or **psychopathology** (from the Greek *psyche* - "mind" *pathos* - "suffering" and *logos* - "study"). This chapter will cover approaches to defining abnormality, the challenges of diagnosis, and the main classifications and criteria for **psychological disorders**; illnesses of the mind which cause distressful thoughts, feelings, or emotions.

What is Normal?

If we want to study abnormality, how do we decide which behaviors, thoughts, or emotions are normal? Of those that are abnormal, how do we decide which should be considered disorders?

One way of determining abnormality is familiar to us already: using a normal distribution or bell curve to determine *statistical abnormality*. If you measure a trait in a large enough sample of people, chances are you'll find some people who are several standard deviations from the mean and thus could be considered abnormal. If you measured height, you might find extremes at either end represent abnormalities related to illness or disease, such as *dwarfism* or *gigantism*. But just because something is statistically abnormal doesn't mean that it is a problem. Having green eyes is statistically abnormal (only about 2% of people) but this doesn't mean it is an illness that needs to be treated. Similarly, if depression becomes common among many people, it will still be considered a disorder that needs to be treated.

For these reasons, statistical abnormality alone cannot determine whether something is a mental illness. People vary in many ways, but only some variations are considered to be disorders. How do we determine which differences represent disorders, and which represent acceptable variations? We shouldn't forget that some behaviors previously classified as disorders, such as homosexuality (listed as a disorder until 1973), are no longer viewed as such, demonstrating how thinking can change on acceptable variations in people and their behaviors.

If societal views can influence whether something is defined as a mental illness or not, we might wonder if all disorders are societal inventions. **Thomas Szasz** argued just that, claiming that mental illness is a myth created by some members of society to control others. Szasz has argued that "problems in living" don't necessarily indicate "disease". Mental illnesses involve judgment and thus are inherently tied to a social context, not just a biological one. Though Szasz first wrote these arguments more than 50 years ago, many of his criticisms still stand and there are not yet objective biological tests for the diagnosis of mental disorders.

Mental illness is diagnosed according to a ***medical model***. This means that disorders or syndromes are considered to be clusters of ***symptoms***; features believed to indicate disease. Symptoms can be categorized as ***positive symptoms***, which are not seen in healthy people, or ***negative symptoms***, which refer to the absence of behaviors that are common in most people. Terms for negative symptoms can often be identified by the prefix ***a-*** or ***an-***, Greek for "not" or "without", as in *anhedonia* - "without pleasure", a loss of pleasure that can be a symptom of depression.

Just as your physician looks at a combination of symptoms (cough, sore throat, and fever) to identify an illness such as influenza, a psychiatrist considers a particular combination of symptoms to diagnose a mental disorder. As with other illnesses, symptoms may overlap, which can make diagnosis difficult. Is your fever a sign of influenza or some other infection? Is your sleep disturbance the result of a sleep disorder, or is it related to some other disorder such as depression? This becomes even more complicated when we consider that mental illnesses are often ***comorbid***, meaning that more than one illness may be present at one time.

Approaches to Understanding Mental Illness

One approach to understanding mental illness focuses on physiology, suggesting that psychological disorders arise from problems in the body. This is known as the *somatogenic hypothesis.* Or we may consider how thoughts and psychological factors could play a role in causing mental disorders, known as the *psychogenic hypothesis.* Finally we could consider the role of culture, society, and experience, and adopt a *learning* perspective.

As you might guess, none of these approaches should be seen as THE approach to understanding mental illness. All of these factors may play a role in the development, progression, and possible treatment of mental illness, leading us to a ***biopsychosocial approach*** (or *multicausal model*).

This approach includes considering the role that gender plays in mental illness. While gender differences can be observed in many illnesses, the underlying causes for these differences are not clear. They may result from differences in hormones, thinking patterns, or societal expectations and cultural pressures, all of which can vary by gender. Males and females may experience different levels of ***stigma***, or feelings of disgrace, attached to seeking help or showing certain emotions. There may be unspoken cultural rules for how men and women express symptoms and how those symptoms are interpreted. All of these may play a role in the emergence, diagnosis, and treatment of mental illness.

The Ds of Disorder

When it comes to deciding if certain symptoms are part of a disorder, you can remember the three D's of disorder: **d**eviance, **d**ysfunction, and **d**istress.

Deviance refers to thoughts or behaviors which are considerably different from normal and are uncommon or unacceptable. Would most people do this if they were in a similar situation? Defining deviance necessarily involves social and cultural norms: screaming at the top of your lungs and dancing violently might be normal at a rock concert, but this behavior would probably be considered deviant in a lecture hall.

Dysfunction refers to maladaptive behaviors which interfere with the ability to live a normal life. Thoughts, behaviors, or emotions that impair the formation of social relationships, cause occupational difficulties, or disrupt daily life would be considered dysfunctional.

Distress refers to causing pain or making a person upset. Some deviant or even dysfunctional behaviors are not distressing and thus may not represent disorders. In some cases, however, distress may be felt by others rather than the person with the disorder (as in *antisocial personality disorder* in which the person's disregard for others doesn't distress the person with the disorder but may harm others).

There are a few other D-words that can relate to diagnosis. *Danger*, to oneself or others could range from the extremes of suicide or homicide to the mundane like failure to take care of one's health or maintain a clean and safe living environment. Potential symptoms are considered based on their *duration*. So depressed mood lasting for a day or two is not considered a symptom (even though it causes distress and dysfunction), but it can become a symptom if it lasts for several weeks.

Keep in mind that many symptoms of mental illness are common and their diagnostic usefulness comes not from their mere existence but from their frequency and severity. One challenge of diagnosis is determining just how severe or persistent potential symptoms are during brief consultations. Limited information can lead to misdiagnosis, but multiple lengthy consultations could unnecessarily delay treatment for those who need it.

While psychiatrists frequently use carefully designed inventories with specific questions and limited options for responses, they also use *semi-structured interviews* with open-ended questions to assess symptoms and signs of mental illness. We might see psychiatrists as torn between the need for objectivity (with the dry checklist mentality that entails) and the need to connect with patients on a human level in order to encourage trust and openness (despite the subjectivity this can create). The same can be said for all physicians; bedside manner matters and plays a role in the description and interpretation of symptoms, compliance with treatment regimens, efficacy of treatment, and overall patient well-being.

Difficulties of Diagnosis

In 1973, **David Rosenhan** published a study which disrupted the mental health community and questioned the ability of psychiatrists to recognize and diagnose mental illness, the way patients were treated, and the long-term consequences of mental health diagnoses.

8 healthy pseudo-patients (3 women and 5 men) went to 12 different hospitals and claimed to be hearing voices saying things like "empty", "hollow", and "thud" (these words were chosen specifically because there were not any recorded cases matching them). Based on the one symptom of hearing voices, a diagnosis of *schizophrenia* was given 11 times (and a diagnosis of *manic-depressive psychosis* was given once) and the pseudo-patients were all admitted. The pseudo-patients gave false names and occupations to disguise that some of them worked in the mental health field but truthfully answered other questions during their assessments. Rather than raising skepticism, these otherwise-normal personal histories were frequently interpreted as pathological.

One explanation for this is that most people who seek consultation with a psychiatrist are assumed to need help. Healthy people don't usually decide to spend an afternoon waiting in the emergency room just for something to do, and the same is assumed to be true for those at a mental health facility. With this in mind, it may seem fair that psychiatrists assume an illness and focus their energies on figuring out which one to diagnose, rather than questioning whether there is any illness at all.

Once admitted, the patients faced the challenge of convincing staff they were sane in order to be released. This was no easy task and length of hospitalization ranged from 7 to 52 days, with an average of 19 days. Immediately upon admission, the patients claimed that their symptoms were gone and they behaved "normally" (though Rosenhan notes they may have shown some anxiety and fear, since they weren't expecting to actually be admitted so readily). Normal, sane behaviors such as keeping a journal were often interpreted as symptoms by staff. Ironically, Rosenhan noted that other patients were often more attuned to the sanity of the pseudo-patients than the psychiatrists and nurses, and said things like "You're not crazy. You're a journalist, or a professor (referring to the continual note-taking). You're checking up on the hospital."

None of the 12 hospitals recognized any of the pseudo-patients as fakers. Rather than casting doubt on the original diagnosis, discharge often led to "schizophrenic – in remission" on records, revealing the stickiness of labels in mental health. Labels can take a lasting place in medical records and allow stigma to follow patients for years after symptoms have been successfully treated. When our physical bodies heal we have no problem dropping the names of illnesses that have previously plagued us, so we don't call you "broken-legged" or "chicken pox-ic" for years after you've healed. Yet with mental health, there's a tendency to consider disorders as lasting traits, meaning that one-time diagnoses can become part of patients' identities, prolonging symptoms and reducing feelings of control.

Rosenhan's study helped remind psychiatrists of the many assumptions they were making. In fact, Rosenhan suggested he would send more pseudo-patients to hospitals in the future. Several facilities claimed to have identified dozens of these fakers in the months that followed, only for Rosenhan to reveal that he hadn't actually sent any.

The DSM-5

The main classification system for mental illness in the United States is the **DSM-5**, the *Diagnostic and Statistical Manual of Mental Disorders – 5th edition*, released in 2013. This manual describes the symptoms and prevalence of each mental disorder as well as other associated features and how similar disorders can be differentiated from one another. You may notice that the DSM-5 does not use roman numerals like earlier editions (*DSM-III* or *DSM-IV*). More frequent incremental updates will be labeled like software updates such as 5.1, rather than V.I, which would look confusingly similar to the roman numerals for 6. The DSM-5 is not the only system of classification, and the ICD-10 (International Statistical Classification of Diseases and Related Health Problems – 10th edition) is more commonly used for clinical purposes in Europe. An updated 11th edition of the ICD is scheduled to be released in 2018 (after being pushed back multiple times).

The DSM-5 attempts to focus on objective criteria; symptoms which are observable, reliable, and easily counted. But this can be difficult when it comes to how patients describe their thoughts and emotions, if they are able to describe them at all. Patients may not have insight into their own symptoms and may be unable to recognize or explain them, meaning that a psychiatrist must make inferences. Patients may also have a tendency to misrepresent their symptoms, emphasizing or downplaying certain behaviors, feelings, or thoughts.

The monist assumption that everything psychological results from underlying physiology applies to mental illness, but this doesn't mean we should assume biological *defects* are the cause of all abnormality. We should accept that well-functioning biology can still give rise to behaviors which are deemed abnormal. This may explain why there are not yet any medically valid physiological tests for the illnesses described in the DSM-5. In other words, no blood test or brain scan can be used to diagnose depression, schizophrenia, or obsessive-compulsive disorder. While there are biological factors associated with mental illnesses (such as neurotransmitter levels, hormone levels, etc.) these associations are not used to diagnose illness in the way that a blood test can diagnose anemia or hepatitis. While mentally ill people are often said to suffer from a "chemical imbalance", no measurement of chemicals takes place during diagnosis, nor have any researchers provided a clear description of what an appropriate balance would be.

Without these kinds of objective criteria for diagnosis, reliability can become a problem. Will two psychiatrists seeing the same symptoms reach the same diagnosis? Aaron Beck and colleagues (1962) found that when pairs of psychiatrists assessed 153 patients then made independent diagnoses, only 54% of these diagnoses were in agreement. Reliability can also be an issue across cultures. John Cooper and colleagues showed video-taped clinical interviews of patients to psychiatrists in New York and London in 1972. They found that based on the same video of the same patient, psychiatrists in the US were twice as likely to give a diagnosis of schizophrenia while those in the UK were twice as likely to diagnose the same symptoms as an affective disorder (such as depression or bipolar disorder). DSM updates have made an attempt to make criteria clearer in order to address these problems and ensure that the same diagnosis is reached regardless of which psychiatrist a patient visits.

The push for greater objectivity for the DSM-5 led to removal of the previous axial system and this represents a controversial ideological shift. In previous editions, the axial system included other potentially relevant medical illnesses as well as factors such as poverty and social support. While many psychiatrists and counselors consider mental illness part of a complex biopsychosocial process, the diagnostic criteria in the DSM-5 place less emphasis on how psychological or social factors contribute to disorders.

In addition to listing symptoms, the DSM-5 provides information on the prevalence of most disorders, usually expressed as a percentage. The **prevalence** tells us how frequently a disorder occurs, either over the course of one's life (*lifetime prevalence*) or during a particular time period (*point prevalence*). For example, the point prevalence of bulimia nervosa is much higher for teenage girls and young women than for older women. If a woman has not suffered from bulimia before age 40, her risk of developing the disorder drops considerably. Most of the prevalence estimates provided in the DSM-5 are based on 12-month periods of time, indicating the percentage of people in the population with that diagnosis during the course of a single year, so lifetime prevalence estimates will often be higher than 12-month prevalence estimates.

To be clear, prevalence refers to the total number of cases of an illness at a given time. This differs from **incidence**, which refers to the number of *new* cases which have appeared in a given time period. Prevalence tells us how widespread an illness is, not the risk of contracting it. Imagine a virus outbreak with high incidence only in a particular year (say 2014). If this infection takes longer than a year to cure, then in 2015 incidence could be low (very few new cases) even though the prevalence would still be high (many people are still infected).

The DSM-5 also indicates **comorbidity**, listing disorders that are frequently diagnosed in the same patient. We can't simply add prevalence rates to estimate how many total people are diagnosed with mental illnesses because disorders tend to be more highly concentrated among a smaller group of people who are each diagnosed with several disorders.

While there are genes which predispose people to certain mental illnesses like depression or schizophrenia, genes are not fate and are not solely responsible for these illnesses. The ***diathesis-stress model*** for mental illness suggests that people may have a predisposition for a disorder (or a *diathesis*) but that environmental or psychological events (*stress*) cause the disorder to be expressed (or not). The level of predisposition and the amount of stress needed to reach a threshold will vary for different individuals, explaining why the same environmental stressor can trigger a disorder in some people but not others.

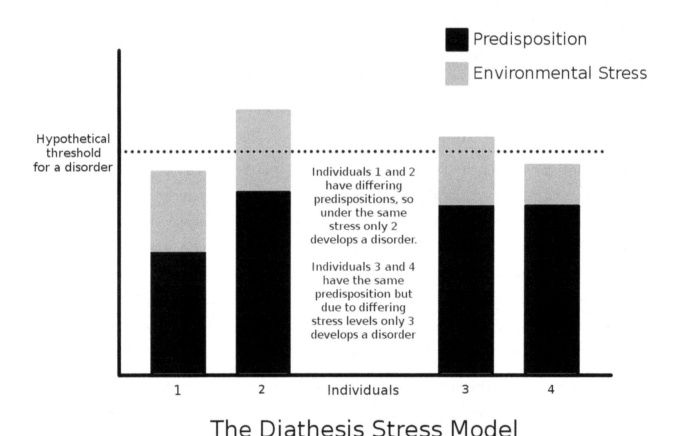

Hypothetical threshold for a disorder

Individuals 1 and 2 have differing predispositions, so under the same stress only 2 develops a disorder.

Individuals 3 and 4 have the same predisposition but due to differing stress levels only 3 develops a disorder

Predisposition
Environmental Stress

1   2   Individuals   3   4

The Diathesis Stress Model

This graph is oversimplified, however, as environment may influence gene expression (*epigenetics*) and genes may influence response to environmental stress. This interaction can be seen in a study by Avshalom Caspi and colleagues (2003) which found that versions of a serotonin transporter gene may influence an individual's response to stress. This means that people with a particular version of the gene are at greater risk for depression, but only if they also experience certain levels of stress.

The Role of Culture

What role does culture play in the prevalence, expression, and understanding of mental illness? Culture can determine which behaviors are considered abnormal. Refusing to leave the house alone could be seen as a symptom of *agoraphobia* for a woman in the US, but in some cultures this behavior might be the result of expectations and pressures, rather than a sign of internal dysfunction. The DSM-IV listed *culture-bound syndromes*, which were disorders considered to be culturally or geographically localized. One such disorder was *koro*, an intense anxiety that the penis is retracting into the body and will cause death (women may have symptoms of *koro* related to retraction of the nipples, breasts, or labia), though there are not any actual physiological changes. Most cases of *koro* have occurred in Southeast Asia, though it has also been reported in West Africa.

The DSM-5 has done away with the term "culture-bound syndrome" and replaced it with three terms for discussing the role of culture on mental illness: **cultural syndromes** which tend to co-occur among individuals in specific groups, **cultural idioms of distress** for how groups express symptoms or syndromes, and **cultural explanations of distress or perceived causes**, which are culturally-recognized meanings or etiologies for symptoms, illness, or distress.

Other cultural syndromes include *dhat* (semen-loss anxiety) in India, *ataque de nervios* "nerve attack" in Latin America, and 神经衰弱 *shénjīng shuāiruò* or "nerve weakness" in China. Are these specific disorders based on culture, or are these just differing expressions of the same universal disorders? Do disorders like *shénjīng shuāiruò*, which emphasizes nerves and the physical body, provide a way for people to sidestep the stigma associated with mental illness in their culture?

Shénjīng shuāiruò and ataque de nervios carry complex cultural baggage, but a diagnosis of depression provides a clear path to treatment: prescription of antidepressant medication. Is replacing cultural ideas of illness with universal disorders a way for pharmaceutical companies to increase their global reach? This cynicism isn't unfounded. A marketing campaign by GlaxoSmithKline in Japan introduced the idea of mild depression as a common problem and sales in the country quintupled between 1998 and 2003. We shouldn't be too cynical, however, as this campaign may have helped to raise awareness and reduce stigma, both of which may have improved people's lives.

DSM-5 Disorders

In the next sections, we'll see disorders from several categories of the DSM-5, as well as their symptoms, prevalence, and associated factors. In looking over symptoms, remember that not all symptoms are necessary for a diagnosis. Usually, there will be a specified minimum number of symptoms for each criteria relevant to a diagnosis. Where do these numbers come from? These numbers were chosen by the DSM committee, based on discussion and voting as to how many symptoms are needed to meet a criteria. So if we ask why 5 symptoms are needed for a particular disorder, rather than only 4 or instead of 6, there's not always an objective research-based answer. To be fair, the DSM recognizes this problem, generally by having an unspecified disorder listed for those people who meet many of the symptoms of a disorder but do not fulfill the full criteria for diagnosis.

The DSM-5 recognizes 10 classes of substances which are known to cause symptoms of other disorders. If symptoms appear within 1 month of intoxication or withdrawal from these medications, drugs, or toxins, symptoms may represent a **substance/medication induced disorder**. (It is also noted that some toxins or hallucinogenic drugs may cause neurocognitive or perceptual symptoms which persist for longer than one month). This means that there are diagnoses in the DSM-5 which many people would qualify for at some point but which do not really represent mental illness. These include *alcohol intoxication* (for which the DSM-5 gives an estimated 12-month prevalence of 70% among college students), *caffeine intoxication*, *cannabis intoxication*, and *tobacco withdrawal*.

Before we begin discussing the symptoms of particular disorders, it's important that we remind ourselves that many symptoms are common. We should avoid falling ill to **medical student's disease**: in which medical students begin to feel they have all the symptoms they are learning about. The information in this chapter is to help you understand mental illnesses, **not** diagnose them. Just as you may see symptoms in yourself, you may see potential symptoms in others but you should avoid making assumptions about their mental health.

As you learn these diagnostic terms, remember that they shouldn't be thrown into everyday conversation as adjectives. These disorders represent real struggles for many people. Saying things like "I have to wash my hands, I'm so OCD" or "I'm so anorexic" because you didn't eat much at a meal can trivialize the suffering of others, or worse, discourage them from seeking help.

I've tried to provide a broad overview of mental illness, so some disorders are included for reference purposes. Don't be overwhelmed or feel you need to memorize all of the disorder names, symptoms, and prevalence estimates. This list isn't meant to be comprehensive but it should give you a better understanding of the categories of mental illness and the symptoms associated with particular disorders. Remember that not all symptoms are necessary for a diagnosis and that severity, duration, and levels of distress are important when considering any possible symptoms.

Anxiety Disorders

A ***specific phobia*** refers to an irrational fear of a specific object or situation. While many people experience fear in the presence of snakes or spiders, people with a phobia experience an intense panic reaction; elevated heart rate, sweating, and difficulty breathing. One exception to this response occurs in specific phobias for blood, injury, or injections, in which patients show an elevated disgust response, rather than a fear response, so the sight of blood or a needle can result in fainting.

Specific phobias are characterized by *irrational* fear, meaning that the reaction occurs when the person is not in any danger, such as when looking at an image of the object. Of course, a fear of snakes, spiders, and other potentially dangerous stimuli is rational in some circumstances, and the fact that these specific phobias are common suggests an evolutionary link. ***Preparedness theory*** suggests that there has been an evolutionary advantage to learning some fear associations more easily than others. The DSM-5 gives a 12-month community prevalence in the US of 7-9% with women twice as likely as men to be diagnosed. Point prevalence is highest for 13-17 year-olds (16%) and lower for children (5%) and adults (3-5%).

You've probably seen exotic terms for specific phobias (i.e. *arachnophobia* – fear of spiders) but these terms are not part of the DSM-5. These are created using the Greek word for an object + *phobia*, creating familiar terms like *claustrophobia* – fear of enclosed spaces, as well as obscure terms like *triskaidekaphobia* – fear of the number 13 or *coulrophobia* – fear of clowns (which I'm pretty sure everyone has). For more, check out www.phobialist.com, unless of course you have *epistemophobia*- fear of knowledge.

Social anxiety disorder (also known as *social phobia*) is a phobia for situations which carry a threat of scrutiny or evaluation, or the anticipation of these situations. Social situations almost always cause some anxiety and social situations with high risk of judgment may be avoided (such as meeting new people or public speaking).

Social anxiety disorder is associated with substance abuse (alcohol or other drugs) as a means of coping with social situations. The 12-month prevalence estimate is about 7% in the US, though estimates in other countries are considerably lower (median of 2.3% in European countries). Age of onset is usually between 8 and 15 years old, and prevalence is roughly equal for men and women.

Panic disorder is characterized by the occurrence of *panic attacks*; sudden episodes of heart palpitations, difficulty breathing, sweating, trembling, and a sense of terror that one is having a heart attack, going crazy, or dying. Unlike specific phobias, which are triggered by particular objects or situations, panic attacks occur unpredictably. This can cause anxiety over the possibility of having an attack in an embarrassing or dangerous situation. Attacks may occur consistently (once every week or two), or frequently (daily) for a short period of time, followed by weeks or months without incident. The estimated 12-month prevalence in the US and Europe is 2-3% with a female to male ratio of 2:1.

One specific phobia which has its own diagnostic criteria and label is *agoraphobia*. Sometimes translated as a "fear of open spaces" (from the Greek *agora* - "marketplace" or "public square") this phobia refers to avoidance of situations in which it would be difficult to escape danger or receive assistance. This may include open spaces like fields or parking lots but it can also include enclosed spaces, public transportation, or crowds. People with agoraphobia tend to withdraw to places where they feel safe and may not leave their homes or bedrooms for days or weeks. Agoraphobia is often comorbid with panic disorder, as the fear of public panic attacks can cause people to become isolated. Agoraphobia has a 12-month prevalence of 1.7%, is twice as common in women, and occurs most during late adolescence to early adulthood.

Unlike specific phobias, panic disorder, or agoraphobia, all of which occur as episodes of intense anxiety, *generalized anxiety disorder* (*GAD*) refers to a condition in which anxiety is ever-present. This anxiety is not related to specific causes or may be caused by a wide range of situations, from continuous worry about loved ones to constant nervousness at work. This uncontrollable anxiety causes sufferers to feel on edge and can lead to irritability, difficulty concentrating, sleep disturbance, and fatigue. GAD has a 12-month prevalence of 0.9% for adolescents and 2.9% for adults. GAD is slightly more common in females, and males with GAD show greater comorbidity with substance use disorders.

Separation anxiety refers to persistent and excessive fear or anxiety when separated from home or from attachment figures. While temporary anxiety when separated from a caregiver indicates secure attachment in infants, separation anxiety is "developmentally inappropriate" and lasts for at least 4 weeks in children or 6 months in adults, resulting in significant impairment in social, academic, or occupational functioning. 12-month prevalence of separation anxiety is highest in infants (4%), lower in adolescents (1.6%), and lowest for adults (0.9-1.9%).

Trauma and Stressor Related Disorders

As mentioned in the chapter on stress, ***Post-Traumatic Stress Disorder*** (***PTSD***) involves recurrent, involuntary, and intrusive memories of traumatic events. In order to receive a diagnosis, one has to have experienced a traumatic event (not via television, movies, or video-games) or had repeated extreme exposure to aversive details (such as police officers or first-responders encountering victims, handling human remains, etc.).

Symptoms of PTSD typically emerge within 3 months of exposure to the traumatic event, though they may be delayed. Sufferers of PTSD often feel or act as if the event is occurring again and these dissociative reactions are referred to as "***flashbacks***". Sufferers may avoid related stimuli, show a heightened startle response, and develop negative beliefs and distorted cognitions such as "my nervous system has been destroyed".

The lifetime prevalence of PTSD is about 8%, with a 12-month prevalence of 3.5%. Prevalence is higher for certain groups such as military veterans, firefighters, medical personnel, police officers, and victims of rape, assault, combat, or captivity. While PTSD is commonly associated with men (especially military veterans), a greater number of sufferers are women who are victims of rape or violence. 80% of PTSD sufferers also meet the diagnostic criteria for another disorder, such as a depressive or anxiety disorder, or a substance use disorder.

While PTSD is a long-term effect of trauma, the short-term effects of traumatic events may lead to ***acute stress disorder***; feelings of depersonalization and guilt which occur within 1 month of the event. Prevalence varies by event and acute stress disorder is estimated to affect 13-21% of those involved in vehicular accidents, 6-12% of those in industrial accidents, and 20-50% of victims of rape, assault, or mass shootings.

Other stressful events such as breakups, divorces, occupational problems, natural disasters, or even retirement can cause people to have emotional or behavioral symptoms and a level of distress which is considered out of proportion to the severity of the stressor. This may be diagnosed as ***adjustment disorder*** if distress causes impairment of social or occupational functioning. This disorder is considered to be a common psychological response to diagnosis of other serious medical disorders and illnesses and has an increased risk of suicide.

Obsessive-Compulsive and Related Disorders

Obsessive-Compulsive Disorder (***OCD***) consists of two main symptoms: *obsessions* (recurrent, unwanted thoughts) and *compulsions* (repetitive behaviors). Common themes for obsessive thinking are thoughts of contamination, fears of harming others, or a need for symmetry and balance. OCD has a prevalence of about 2% and affects men and women equally. When untreated, OCD has a high comorbidity with depression.

To better understand the plight of OCD sufferers, imagine the brief anxiety you might experience from a thought such as "my hands are contaminated" after you've touched something unsanitary. You quickly find a place to wash your hands, the anxiety fades, and you move on to other thoughts. Now imagine that after you washed your hands, the anxiety didn't go away. This might compel you to wash again, and yet you still feel anxious and have thoughts of contamination. In order to reduce the obsessive thoughts and anxiety, you might begin performing compulsive behaviors which you know are irrational but seem to help, such as washing your hands multiple times, avoiding touching certain objects like doorknobs, or engaging in repetitive behaviors to distract yourself.

Previously considered a type of Obsessive-Compulsive Disorder, ***hoarding disorder*** now warrants its own diagnosis. The main symptom of hoarding is a difficulty parting with personal possessions (even those that are worthless) that is not due to obsessive thoughts, brain injury, autism, or decreased energy. This accumulation of clutter can cause congestion of the person's living area if others do not intervene and may cause social or occupational impairments or make it difficult to maintain a safe living environment.

80-90% of patients with hoarding disorder show *excessive acquisition*, acquiring items for which there is no available space. Some may also show *animal hoarding*, acquiring a number of pets for which they are unable to provide minimal standards of nutrition, sanitation, and care. Surveys indicate a prevalence of 2-6% for hoarding disorder affecting both genders equally. Hoarding is 3x more prevalent in older adults (age 55-94) and 75% of people with a hoarding disorder diagnosis have a comorbid mood or anxiety disorder such as major depressive disorder (50%) or OCD (20%).

The main symptom of **Body Dysmorphic Disorder** (formerly *dysmorphophobia*) is a preoccupation with perceived flaws or defects in physical appearance which are slight or not noticeable to others. These are commonly skin issues (scars, wrinkles, etc), but may be related to hair, teeth, facial features, or areas of the body. This preoccupation may lead to intrusive thoughts or repetitive behaviors (like mirror checking, excessive grooming, or reassurance-seeking) which are difficult to control and cause significant distress or social impairment. There may also be distorted thoughts such as "I look deformed" and self-ratings which range from feeling "unattractive" to feeling that one is a "monster". While preoccupation with a flaw may lead to cosmetic surgery, only an estimated 7-8% of cosmetic surgery patients meet the diagnostic criteria for body dysmorphic disorder. The estimated prevalence is 2.4% in the US, affecting slightly more females than males. It is often comorbid with major depressive disorder.

Somatic Symptoms and Related Disorders

This category of disorders replaces the *somatoform disorders* section of the DSM-IV. Two of the disorders in this category used to share the label *hypochondriasis,* which referred to a false belief in illness (which is not clear from the Greek roots for "under" and "cartilage", which reference medieval beliefs about the location of melancholy under the sternum). This term has been divided into two disorders, which are differentiated based on whether or not somatic symptoms are present. Some patients previously diagnosed with *hypochondriasis* could now be diagnosed with *somatic symptom disorder* (if somatic symptoms are present) or *illness anxiety disorder* (if somatic symptoms are mild or non-existent).

Somatic Symptom Disorder refers to excessive thoughts, feelings, or behaviors related to somatic symptoms or associated health concerns. This leads to anxiety and sufferers devote excessive time and energy to symptoms and health concerns. Preoccupation with illness may become a focus of identity for the patient. While attention to symptoms may be excessive, the suffering of these patients is authentic and the most common somatic symptom is persistent pain, though normal bodily sensations may also be misattributed to illness. The estimated prevalence is 5-7% and is likely higher in females, who tend to report somatic symptoms more often than males.

Illness anxiety disorder involves excessive worry and anxiety that one has an illness, though one does not necessarily have any somatic symptoms of that illness (differentiating it from *somatic symptom disorder* above). There is still a high level of anxiety over health issues and preoccupation with illness, though potential symptoms are mild or non-existent. 12-month prevalence is similar for males and females and estimates range from 1.3 to 10%. Patients are frequently encountered in medical settings rather than mental health settings, since they believe they have a physical illness, not a psychological disorder. They may receive repeated negative diagnostic test results from multiple physicians and still persist in a belief in illness, though it's important not to be dismissive, as sometimes a patient may actually have a physical illness that is simply not being detected accurately.

Conversion disorder (also *functional neurological symptom disorder*) provides fascinating and puzzling case studies in neurology. This disorder is characterized by altered voluntary motor or sensory function and symptoms or deficits which cannot be explained by other disorders or are incompatible with other neurological diseases. These may include weakness, paralysis, abnormal movement or tremors, difficulty swallowing or speaking, and even seizures or loss of sensory function such as deafness or blindness. Physiological causes for these deficits cannot be found, and patients are not faking, so they are considered to be "functional" symptoms, or they may be labeled "psychogenic" (though as we've seen, the label "psychogenic" can be misleading, as underlying physiological mechanisms may exist but haven't been identified yet). Conversion disorder is quite rare, so prevalence is unclear but there are an estimated 2 to 5 cases per 100,000 people, affecting 2-3x more females than males.

Dissociative Disorders

Dissociation refers to a separation of some thoughts or experiences from conscious awareness. While dissociation may seem like a particularly bizarre symptom, you've probably experienced a few types of dissociation in everyday life. If you've ever felt unsure whether you did something or just thought about doing it, became so involved in a fantasy it felt real, driven a car and "lost time" or forgotten about part of the trip, talked to yourself when alone, or felt that a part of your body wasn't your own, then you've experienced dissociation, though likely not to the degree of the disorders below.

Dissociative experiences can also occur under the influence of drugs, such as blacking out from alcohol consumption or from the use of painkillers or anesthetics, whether having your wisdom teeth removed or falling into the "k-hole" reported by recreational users of ketamine, though you'll recall that the DSM-5 considers substance or medication induced symptoms differently than those which arise from internal dysfunction.

Dissociative amnesia refers to selective or global memory loss of autobiographical information, which may include a loss of identity. This is not ordinary forgetting such as misplacing your keys, it's forgetting where you live, who your family members are, or even who you are. Onset tends to be sudden and is typically preceded by a traumatic event. 12-month prevalence is estimated to be about 1.8% in the United States and dissociative amnesia is more than twice as common in women. In the US, nearly 50% of homicide cases involve defendants claiming to have memory loss for some or all of the events in question, though it's unclear whether this figure shows the extreme stress of those circumstances or a popular strategy by defense lawyers to reduce culpability. Amnesia occurring as a result of a physical injury (such as a blow to the head) would not be considered symptomatic of dissociative amnesia.

In some cases, dissociative amnesia and loss of identity is accompanied by what is known as a *fugue state* or a ***dissociative fugue***, in which a person loses his identity, moves to a new location, and adopts a new identity. This new identity replaces the former one, and the person may have no recollection of prior life events, though these may be successfully recovered later. A character experiencing a fugue state is a somewhat common plot device for television shows, such as the *Archer* 4th season opener *"Fugue and riffs"* which began with Sterling Archer in a fugue state working at *Bob's Burgers* – a nod to the fact that actor H. Jon Benjamin voices the lead characters of both shows.

Dissociative Identity Disorder (**DID**), previously known as *Multiple Personality Disorder* (*MPD*), refers to a dissociation of identity which creates two or more distinct personality states. This disrupts the continuity of self and agency, and may also create gaps in memory. Some have suggested that this disorder manifests itself as possession in some cultures, though the DSM-5 diagnostic criteria clarify that symptoms should not be part of accepted cultural or religious practices. Some sufferers of DID may not be aware of their dissociative symptoms due to dissociative amnesia.

Prevalence is difficult to estimate, though the DSM-5 mentions a small community study with a 12-month prevalence estimate of 1.5% that was similar across genders. Other estimates, however, have been lower and suggest greater prevalence among women. Dissociation may be an attempt at coping with overwhelming experiences or traumatic events and an estimated 90% of DID sufferers previously experienced childhood abuse. This figure can be questioned, however, as some sufferers' memories of abuse were only uncovered through therapy, raising the possibility that these repressed memories or symptoms of DID were suggested by the therapist. DID is comorbid with PTSD, depression, anxiety, and substance use disorders and risk of suicide is high.

Depersonalized/Derealization Disorder refers to experiences of unreality or detachment, and the feeling that one is an outside observer of one's thoughts, feelings, sensations, body, or actions (often called an *out-of-body experience*). This may cause thoughts that one has no self or is no one. Some sufferers report knowing they have feelings, but not actually feeling them. This can cause diminished sense of agency for one's thoughts and actions and an altered sense of time. Derealization is a sense of unreality or detachment from surroundings, feeling that one is in a fog, dream, or bubble. Derealization may include sensory distortions such as altered distance or size of objects or voices sounding muted. Episodes of derealization may last for a few hours or as long as several days.

This disorder has a prevalence of about 2% and is equal for both genders. Despite the apparently bizarre symptoms, it's estimated that about half of all adults will briefly experience an episode of these symptoms at some point, though not severe enough to warrant a diagnosis.

Neurodevelopmental Disorders

This category of disorders refers to those with onset in the developmental period. These include things like intellectual disability, communication disorders (language, speech, stuttering, social communication), specific learning disorders (dyslexia, dyscalculia), and motor disorders (tic disorders and Tourette's syndrome).

Autism Spectrum Disorder (also discussed in the development chapter) refers to a range of developmental problems related to language, motor skills, and socialization, including difficulty with recognizing facial expressions and other non-verbals. Those with autism may have problems understanding social relationships, have fixated interests, insist on rigid routines and rituals, or show repetitive motor behaviors such as hand-flapping or repeatedly saying idiosyncratic phrases.

Prevalence has increased rapidly in recent years, with the DSM-5 estimating prevalence at about 1% worldwide, though it is not clear whether this is due to the expansion of diagnostic criteria, increased awareness of the disorder, new methodology for assessment, or a true increase in the disorder. Autism spectrum disorder is 4 times more common in males than females and 70% of those diagnosed have a comorbid disorder (such as intellectual disability).

Attention Deficit/Hyperactive disorder (ADHD) consists of two main symptoms: problems with attention, and hyperactivity. *Attention* problems include failures to pay attention to detail, carelessness, difficulty organizing tasks, following through, or sustaining attention, and frequent distraction and forgetfulness. Inattention is frequently accompanied by *hyperactivity*, which can be seen in frequent fidgeting, squirming, restlessness, and running and climbing in inappropriate situations. There may also be signs of *impulsivity*, such as frequent interrupting or intruding on others in conversations, games, and activities, or behaviors that lack foresight or impulse control. This combination of inattention and hyperactivity interferes with normal functioning or development.

Population surveys estimate prevalence of about 5% in children. Symptoms usually appear before age 12 and there's a 2:1 ratio of males to females. Adult ADHD is estimated to have a prevalence of only 2.5%, suggesting that people "grow out" of this disorder (or perhaps "grow into" improved executive function). A study of nearly one million Canadian schoolchildren indicated that the younger children are for their grade, the more likely they are to be diagnosed with ADHD. This suggests that faulty comparisons by grade (rather than age), are causing relative immaturity to be mistaken for illness (see Morrow et al, 2012).

Schizophrenia Spectrum and Other Psychotic Disorders

In popular culture, *schizophrenia* is frequently confused with *Dissociative Identity Disorder*, likely due to the origins of the term, from the Greek *schizo* - "split" and *phren* - "mind", coined by Swiss psychiatrist Eugen Bleuler. In schizophrenia, however, splitting refers to a disintegration of mental functions rather than a splitting of personalities or identities. Positive symptoms include *delusions* (false beliefs), *hallucinations* (perceptions of things not actually present), *disorganized thought and speech*, and abnormal motor behavior (*catatonia*). Negative symptoms include diminished emotional expression, *anhedonia* (lack of pleasure), *alogia* (diminished speech output), *avolition* (decrease in self-initiated purposeful activities), and *asociality* (decrease in social activities). Diagnostic criteria include at least 2 of the symptoms above which persist for at least one month (though some signs must persist for at least 6 months). Patients with schizophrenia may lack awareness of their symptoms, making it difficult to encourage them to seek treatment.

Cognitive symptoms include memory problems, difficulty with executive function and attention, and **psychosis**, which refers to losing contact with reality, resulting in bizarre beliefs and perceptions. Some patients with schizophrenia experience **catatonia**, locking the body into unusual positions which may be held for hours. Sometimes these postures are rigid and immovable, but at other times they may show **waxy flexibility**, in which the patient will maintain a body position but can be bent or moved by another person and will then hold the new position. While there is evidence of brain differences in neuroimaging, cellular architecture, white matter connectivity, and gray matter volume when comparing those with schizophrenia to healthy individuals, there are not currently any radiological or laboratory tests for schizophrenia, and it is only diagnosed through observation and assessment of symptoms.

The lifetime prevalence of schizophrenia is estimated to be around 0.3-0.7%. The sex ratio differs in different populations and may be influenced by interpretation of symptoms, with negative symptoms emphasized in males while mood symptoms may be emphasized in females. Whether these differences represent variations in the disorder itself or variations in expectations is not yet clear. Expression of symptoms may also be influenced by cultural or religious practices, such as hallucinations of hearing "god's voice" or delusions of having supernatural powers. Schizophrenia is comorbid with substance use disorders, though substance use may represent a consequence rather than a cause of schizophrenic symptoms. Approximately 50% of patients with schizophrenia use tobacco, suggesting it may be a type of self-medication for managing some symptoms. Some researchers have suggested that schizophrenia could be classified as a neurodevelopmental disorder, with the possibility that brain development during childhood is responsible for the symptoms which emerge later (most frequently in adolescence or early adulthood).

Despite depictions in popular culture, the vast majority of schizophrenia sufferers are not aggressive or violent and they are far more likely to be victims of violence or mistreatment rather than perpetrators. Schizophrenia carries an elevated risk of suicide; nearly 20% of sufferers will attempt suicide and 5-6% will complete suicide.

Feeding and Eating Disorders

Pica (from the Latin for "magpie", a reference to the bird's indiscriminate eating) refers to repeated and persistent (at least one month) eating of nonfood substances with little or no nutritional value. The minimum age for diagnosis is 2 years (so the fact that babies try to put everything in their mouths doesn't count) and the eating behavior must be "developmentally inappropriate". In addition, the nonfood items must not be part of a culturally supported practice with spiritual, medicinal, or social value, such as *geophagia* (earth-eating) by women in South Africa who believe consuming clay improves skin softness. Common items on the pica menu include paper, soap, cloth, hair, string, wool, soil, chalk, paint, gum, metal, pebbles, charcoal, ash, starch, and ice. Pica is often comorbid with autism spectrum disorder and intellectual disability.

Binge-eating disorder is a new addition to the DSM-5 as a separate eating disorder. Binge-eating refers to episodes of eating until uncomfortably full, feeling a lack of control over eating, and feeling disgusted, depressed, or guilty after, resulting in distress but without any inappropriate compensatory behaviors (such as vomiting, using laxatives, or exercising excessively). Binge-eating episodes are defined as eating an amount of food definitely larger than most individuals would eat in similar circumstances (so Thanksgiving doesn't count) and in a discrete period of time (such as 2 hours, rather than snacking all day). To warrant diagnosis of the disorder, episodes of binge-eating must occur at least once a week for at least 3 months. 12-month prevalence is estimated at about 1.6% for females and 0.8% for males.

The main symptom of *anorexia nervosa* is an intense fear of gaining weight or becoming fat, which leads to extreme restriction of energy intake. This can result in very low body weight, with severe cases showing a BMI below 15 (a BMI of 18.5 is considered the lower limit for "normal" body weight in adults). Though the word *anorexia* comes from the Greek for "without appetite", sufferers do still experience hunger. Other symptoms include disturbed experience of body shape or weight (believing they are fat or overweight despite clear evidence to the contrary), depressed mood, social withdrawal, insomnia, low sex drive, and loss of bone mineral density. Some women also experience *amenhorrhea*, or cessation of their menstrual cycle.

Anorexia nervosa can be further specified as restricting type or binge-eating/purging type. The binge-eating/purging type is differentiated from bulimia nervosa based on body weight, as a diagnosis for bulimia nervosa occurs within the normal body weight range, while anorexia nervosa is diagnosed if bingeing and purging is accompanied by low body weight.

12-month prevalence of anorexia nervosa is estimated to be about 0.4% for young women. Anorexia nervosa overwhelmingly affects females, with a female to male ratio of 10:1. Anorexia nervosa is comorbid with bipolar disorder as well as depressive and anxiety disorders. Considered one of the deadliest of all mental illnesses, anorexia diagnosis carries a roughly 6-fold increase in mortality due to consequences of starvation in addition to an elevated risk of suicide, which accounts for 1 in 5 anorexia deaths.

Bulimia nervosa is an eating disorder characterized by binge-eating followed by inappropriate compensatory behaviors, such as vomiting, fasting, using laxatives, diuretics, or medications, or excessive exercise at least once a week for at least 3 months. Individuals with bulimia nervosa often have negative self-evaluations based on their body shape and weight and negative emotions often precede episodes of binge-eating, during which sufferers feel they cannot control their behavior. Unlike the low body weight of anorexia nervosa, bulimia nervosa is associated with body weight that is normal to overweight. 12-month prevalence is estimated to be 1-1.5%, mostly in young females, with a female to male ratio of 10:1. Depressive symptoms and mood disturbance are also common, as well as substance use, particularly the use of stimulants in an attempt to control appetite and weight.

Depressive Disorders

The primary symptom of *major depressive disorder* is a depressed mood most of the day, every day, for at least a two week period. In addition to depressed mood, sufferers also experience decreased interest or pleasure in most activities (*anhedonia*), and may also show changes in appetite (and body weight) and sleep disturbances such as *hypersomnia*, sleeping for long periods of time, or insomnia, which often occurs in the form of early awakening followed by inability to return to sleep despite feeling tired. Many sufferers also experience fatigue and a slowing of motor activity, referred to as *psychomotor retardation*. Cognitive symptoms include thoughts of worthlessness (which may be extreme enough to be considered delusional – such as "my brain is rotting" or "I am the worst person in the world"), difficulty concentrating and making decisions, and in some cases, suicidal thoughts.

Sufferers may also find themselves persistently and repetitively thinking about minor past failures or how depressed they currently feel, and this *rumination* may worsen symptoms and feelings of helplessness. As Sylvia Plath's character Esther Greenwood described, "Wherever I sat — on the deck of a ship or at a street cafe in Paris or Bangkok — I would be sitting under the same glass bell jar, stewing in my own sour air." Some patients with major depressive disorder report feeling "blah" or having no feelings, while others may emphasize somatic symptoms such as aches, pains, or fatigue that occurs without any physical exertion.

The estimated 12-month prevalence of major depressive disorder is 7% and it is 3 times more common in young adults (18-29) than those over 60. The lifetime prevalence of depression has been estimated to be as high as 7-12% in males and 20-25% in females (Kessler, 2005). Each major depressive episode increases the odds of a subsequent episode; 50-60% of patients who experience one episode will experience a second, of those 70% will experience a third, and of those 90% will experience a fourth.Women with depression are more likely to *attempt* suicide than males, though males are more likely to *complete* suicide. This is because males tend to chose methods such as jumping from a building or using a firearm, while females are more likely to use methods with greater odds of rescue, such as pill ingestion or wrist-cutting. It's worth noting that when depression is extreme, risk of suicide is low. Suicide risk actually rises as severely depressed patients start feeling better. In the depths of depression, patients may lack the energy or motivation to carry out potential suicide plans but a dangerous combination occurs when fatigue fades and suicidal thoughts remain.

Episodes of depression may be further specified if they occur in certain patterns such as a **seasonal pattern** (also known as *seasonal affective disorder*) in which episodes occur during fall or winter and may be related to decreased levels of sunlight. **Peripartum onset** (commonly called *postpartum depression* though it often begins before childbirth) refers to depressive episodes in women which occur during pregnancy or in the 4 weeks following childbirth and may be related to hormonal changes. Peripartum depression may also include panic attacks, agitation, and in extreme cases, desire to harm oneself or the newborn child.

While major depressive disorder tends to occur in episodes of depression which come and go, **persistent depressive disorder** (formerly *dysthymia*) refers to a depressed mood most of the day, more days than not, for at least 2 years. 12-month prevalence is estimated to be about 0.5% and it's possible to have persistent depressive disorder coupled with periods of major depressive disorder, specified as **persistent depressive disorder with major depressive episodes** (which was formerly referred to as *double depression*).

Bipolar and Related Disorders

As the name suggests, disorders in this category are characterized by two extremes (or poles) of behavior: depressive episodes and manic episodes. Previously classed as "mood disorders" (a category that is no longer in the DSM-5), bipolar disorders now have their own category. Part of the reason for this re-categorization is that some extremes of behavior seen in these disorders do not involve mood.

Bipolar I disorder refers to having (not necessarily alternating) manic episodes and major depressive episodes. A ***manic episode*** is a period of time lasting at least one week, most of the day, every day, characterized by inflated self-esteem, grandiosity, decreased need for sleep (such as 3 hours/night), increased goal-directed activities as well as behaviors with potential painful consequences (buying sprees, sexual promiscuity, foolish investments), and talkativeness, which often shows ***flight of ideas***, abruptly switching from one topic to another.

Diagnosis of a ***major depressive episode*** lasting at least 2 weeks follows the same criteria listed previously for major depressive disorder.

Kay Redfield Jamison, an expert on bipolar disorder, has written a number of popular books on the disorder and her own personal experiences suffering from it are described in "An Unquiet Mind". The term "bipolar" was introduced in the DSM-IV to replace the previous name "*manic-depressive disorder*", though Jamison has criticized the newer term for downplaying the existence of ***mixed states***: periods of dark depression and simultaneous agitation, energy, and aggression.

12-month prevalence for bipolar I is 0.6% and it is slightly more common in males, with a male/female ratio of 1.1:1. The mean age of onset is 18. Bipolar I carries a risk of suicide which is 15x greater than that for the general population. Approximately 25% of all completed suicides are by bipolar I patients.

Bipolar II disorder is a combination of major depressive episodes and hypomanic episodes. ***Hypomanic episodes*** are less extreme than manic episodes, last for at least 4 days, and are not severe enough to cause social or occupational impairment. Bipolar II has a 12-month prevalence rate of about 0.8% in the United States (0.3% internationally) with usual age of onset during the mid-20s.

Because bipolar II often begins with a depressive episode, misdiagnosis as major depressive disorder is possible until the emergence of a hypomanic episode. About 5-15% of those diagnosed with bipolar II later experience a full-blown manic episode, which results in a diagnosis change to bipolar I. Misdiagnosis of depression for bipolar I or bipolar II is dangerous because antidepressant drugs can actually trigger manic episodes. Suicide risk for bipolar II is also quite high, and roughly 1 in 3 sufferers attempt suicide.

In addition to bipolar I and bipolar II, this category includes *cyclothymic disorder*, which refers to chronic fluctuating mood disturbances with periods of hypomanic and depressive episodes which are not frequent, severe, or long-lasting enough to fully meet the criteria for a bipolar diagnosis.

Personality Disorders

A *personality disorder* indicates a pattern of behavior beginning around adolescence or early adulthood which differs from cultural expectations, is resistant to change and stable across time and situations, and which causes significant distress or impairment. The DSM-5 recognizes 10 distinct personality disorders which can only be diagnosed after the age of 18 and are organized into 3 different clusters based on their similarities.

Cluster A refers to personalities which are generally considered to be odd or eccentric, *Cluster B* refers to those which are considered dramatic, emotional, or erratic, and *Cluster C* refers to those which are anxious or fearful. One may also be diagnosed with a personality change due to physiological effects from another medical condition (such as brain damage) or have traits of several personality disorders but not meet full criteria for a specific disorder, diagnosed as an *unspecified personality disorder*.

DSM-5 Personality Disorders

Cluster	Disorder	Pattern
A	Paranoid	Distrust or suspicion of others
A	Schizoid	detachment from social relationships, reduced range of emotional expression
A	Schizotypal	acute discomfort in close relationships, cognitive or perceptual distortions, and eccentricities of behavior
B	Antisocial	disregard and violation of others' rights
B	Histrionic	excessive emotionality and attention-seeking
B	Narcissistic	grandiosity, need for admiration, and lack of empathy
B	Borderline	instability of relationships and self-image, high impulsivity
C	Dependent	submissive and clinging behavior, excessive need to be taken care of
C	Avoidant	social inhibition, feelings of inadequacy, sensitivity to negative evaluations
C	Obsessive-Compulsive	preoccupation with orderliness, perfectionism, and control

In the chapter on personality, we saw the complexity of accurately measuring personality traits, and we should keep this in mind when considering personality disorders. We may also wonder if calling some traits disorders is really just a way of labeling people with personality traits we don't like. At what point does narcissism stop just being an annoying trait and become a disorder?

Prevalence of personality disorders varies by cluster, and the prevalence estimate for disorders in cluster A is about 5.7%, cluster B is 1.5%, and cluster C is 6%. This represents an overall prevalence estimate of about 9.1% for any personality disorder, though this estimate includes the co-occurence of more than one personality disorder in the same patient.

If you've read Susanna Kaysen's memoir *Girl, interrupted* (or you've seen the film starring Winona Ryder and Angelina Jolie), borderline personality disorder was the diagnosis that Kaysen received upon her entrance to McLean hospital, where she stayed for 18 months in 1967.

Since we don't have a chapter dedicated to criminal psychology in this book (as it is not covered in most introductory classes), I thought I'd take a moment to point out the relationship between ***antisocial personality disorder***, ***psychopathy*** and ***sociopathy***. These terms have a great deal in common, and this is partly because the term *psychopathy* was used in early editions of the DSM but was replaced by *antisocial personality disorder* starting with the DSM-III. Adding to the confusion is the term *sociopath*, which is used interchangeably with *psychopath* by many, but not all, psychiatrists, criminologists, and forensic psychologists. Some prefer to use the term *sociopath* to emphasize those who are less able to mask their disregard for others and whose antisocial behaviors seem to stem from environment rather than genes but this is certainly still up for debate. *Antisocial personality disorder* uses the diagnostic criteria of the DSM-5 while psychopathy is often diagnosed using the ***Psychopathy Checklist – Revised (PCL-R)***, a 20-item scale developed by Robert Hare. While most psychopaths will also meet the criteria for antisocial personality disorder, it's possible (and fairly common) to have a diagnosis of antisocial personality disorder without meeting the PCL-R criteria for psychopathy. Since personality disorders aren't diagnosed until age 18, those under 18 showing cruelty, violation of the rights of others, and lack of guilt and empathy may be diagnosed with ***conduct disorder***.

Neurocognitive Disorders

The DSM-5 also has a category for neurocognitive disorders which include Alzheimer's Disease, Traumatic Brain Injury (TBI), Parkinson's Disease, and prion-related diseases, which result from the accumulation of misfolded proteins known as *prions* (pronounced *pree-ons*) which damage brain cells (diseases include Creutzfeldt-Jakob disease, Kuru, and fatal familial insomnia). While the core focus of diagnosis for these disorders is on cognitive deficits, these disorders are somewhat unique in that several of them have clear biological markers that can be identified through brain scans and genetic testing.

Paraphilic Disorders

The DSM-5 also has a category for 8 ***paraphilic disorders*** (from the Greek *para* - "abnormal" and *philos* - "fondness"), which refer to intense, persistent sexual interests which are not considered to be normal. These include voyeuristic disorder, exhibitionistic disorder (showing one's genitals), frotteuristic disorder (touching or rubbing against a non-consenting individual), sexual masochism disorder, sexual sadism disorder, pedophilic disorder, transvestic disorder, and fetishistic disorders focused on specific body parts or inanimate objects.

Some behavioral symptoms of paraphilic disorders can be criminal offenses (such as exhibitionism, frotteurism, and pedophilia). Having a paraphilia does not necessarily mean diagnosis, and the paraphilia must also involve distress, which often comes from the potential harm to self or others that might occur from satisfying the paraphilia.

Chapter Summary - Psychological Disorders

- Definitions of normality may vary, but the **medical model** of mental illness focuses on symptoms which are considered **deviant**, **dysfunctional**, and **distressful**.

- **David Rosenhan**'s study with pseudo-patients revealed problems of **validity** in diagnosing disorders, as well as problems associated with labeling patients.

- Culture may play a role in how people define syndromes, describe symptoms, or explain the causes of disorders.

- The **diathesis-stress model** considers the interaction of genes and environment in producing mental illness.

- The **Diagnostic and Statistical Manual of Mental Illness - Fifth Edition** or **DSM-5** lists the **symptoms**, **prevalence**, **comorbidity**, and associated features of psychological disorders.

- Categories of disorders in the DSM-5 include **anxiety** disorders, **obsessive-compulsive** disorders, **dissociative** disorders, **depressive** disorders, **schizophrenic** disorders, **eating** disorders, **bipolar** disorders, **personality** disorders, and others.

Notes

Chapter 16
Treatment

Treatment of Mental Illness

In general, the goal of treatment is to change thoughts, behaviors, or emotions. This means that in order to consider the possibility of treatment, we must believe that change is possible. For most of human history, the conditions for people suffering from psychological disorders made it virtually impossible for them to improve. Sufferers have been persecuted and subjected to cruel practices; trapped not only in their own minds, but also in physical restraints. Unfortunately, today a large number of mentally ill people remain locked away in penitentiaries, being penalized rather than protected, and tortured rather than treated.

Despite this, treatment is better than it ever has been. As a society, we owe a great debt to early reformers such as Philipe Pinel (1745-1826), who called for exercise, fresh air, and the removal of chains and shackles from the mentally ill in France, and Dorothea Dix (1802-1887), who called for the creation of mental health hospitals in the United States and advocated for more humane treatments for the mentally ill. In the past few decades, stigma has been further reduced and care has been greatly improved, but there is still progress to be made.

Mental Health Professionals

Psychiatrists hold an MD (or a DO – *Doctor of Osteopathic medicine*) and are licensed physicians who specialize in mental health issues. They are able to prescribe medications and usually work in hospitals, institutions, or their own private practices. *Neurologists* also hold an MD (or DO) and are physicians who specialize in the brain and nervous system. *Clinical psychologists* hold a Ph.D (or a Psy.D) and specialize in psychotherapy. They do not usually have prescription privileges, though this is beginning to change in some places. *Counseling psychologists* hold a master's degree or a Ph.D in counseling and usually specialize in mild to moderate mental health issues, providing things like family and couples therapy, grief counseling, or career counseling. *Clinical social workers* hold a 2-year master's degree in social work and may also have specialized training in certain types of counseling. They may work in a variety of settings including mental health facilities, substance-abuse clinics, veterans' affairs centers, and child welfare agencies.

Why Treat Mental Illness?

This may seem like an obvious question, but while psychological disorders are, by definition, distressing to sufferers, this is not the only reason for treatment. Psychological disorders carry many other costs as well, which include costs to the individual (including social, financial, and occupational costs) as well as costs to society in the form of lost productivity, absenteeism, and costs of treatments and institutions. It has been estimated that anxiety disorders alone cost the United States an estimated $42.3 billion dollars each year.

Treatment for all?

Now that treatment is more humane and more widely available than ever before, it may come as a surprise that many people who are suffering are not currently receiving treatment. Why doesn't everyone get treated?

In some cases, people may not recognize that they need to be treated. Misconceptions about mental illness may cause people to suffer without feeling that they are "bad enough" to need treatment. Or they may believe that their symptoms are personal weaknesses that must be overcome. Of those that do recognize the need for treatment, they may not always be willing or able to receive help and well-trained mental health professionals may not be readily available. Even where help is available, people may not be well-informed of treatment options.

Recognition, availability, and awareness of options are not the only barriers to proper mental health treatment. Stigma still exists, and some potential patients may not seek treatment due to the acknowledgment of mental illness it entails. There are also bureaucratic hurdles which must be overcome, and some sufferers who are willing and able to seek treatment may face wait lists, financial difficulties in paying for treatments or getting insurance, linguistic or cultural barriers, or problems getting appropriate treatments for their particular illnesses.

Ethics of Treatment

There are also ethical implications when it comes to considering treatment. Ideally, every person who needed treatment would recognize the need and freely choose to be treated, but unfortunately this is not the case. Should some people be forced to undergo treatment? Thomas Szasz noted that while we might hope to view psychiatrists as agents of the mentally ill, there are situations in which they act as the agents of others; family and friends of the ill, law enforcement, private organizations, or courts.

Though the DSM-5 has slightly reduced the total number of disorders compared to the DSM-IV-TR, critics still claim that it represents a *medicalization* of daily life which causes otherwise normal aspects of the human condition to be seen as symptoms of illness requiring treatment. Are pharmaceutical companies too eager to push (and profit from) the sale of drugs to an increasingly large number of patients?

For instance, the DSM-5 removed the bereavement exclusion for depression, meaning that previously you couldn't be diagnosed with depression if your symptoms followed the loss of a loved one, but now you can be. Critical psychiatrists have questioned whether we should be attempting to medicate away some negative emotions, regardless of how painful they may be. Which kinds of suffering are the "right" kinds of suffering and which should be treated? Should we make this decision for other people? How do we say that one person's suffering is appropriate and necessary and another's should be chemically blunted? Which of the slings and arrows of life should we be forced to bear, and which should be pharmaceutically excised?

Treatment Options

The two main branches of treatment are psychotherapy and biomedical interventions. The term *psychotherapy* covers a broad range of therapies including psychoanalysis, humanistic therapy, cognitive therapy, behavioral therapy, and *eclectic* therapies, which combine elements of multiple types of psychotherapy (and may also use biomedical treatments). *Biomedical* interventions include the use of medications, stimulation, and in some cases, surgery.

Psychoanalysis

Freud's psychoanalytic approach to treatment was based on gaining insight into the unconscious. A combination of free association, dream analysis, and interpretation (sometimes called the "talking cure") was used to resolve conflicts and reduce anxiety, which Freud believed were the source of mental illness. Freud thought that patients may initially show *resistance* to therapy, to avoid confronting the unconscious, but that this could be overcome by "working through" conflict over time. As resistance faded, Freud believed that a process of *transference* would occur, in which patients would redirect some strong feelings (love, hatred, etc.) onto the therapist, who could then work to resolve these feelings. Traditional psychoanalysis is not commonly practiced today, though some aspects of it remain, particularly in *interpersonal therapy*, which focuses on improving relationships.

Humanistic Therapy

The humanistic approach grew out of psychoanalysis but emphasized a more positive view of human nature and focused on striving for improvement rather than battling unconscious forces. The ***person-centered therapy*** (also known as client-centered therapy) of ***Carl Rogers*** focused on developing self-awareness and self-acceptance. The goal of therapy was personal growth rather than a "cure" and conscious thoughts were considered to be more important than unconscious influences.

The therapist's role in this humanistic approach was to offer acceptance and genuine reactions to the patient, with the assumption that the patient would realize the correct path toward growth. In order to facilitate this, the therapist would provide empathy and ***unconditional positive regard***, attempting to understand the patient's experience and reflect it back in a positive way. This was accomplished by ***active listening***, in which the therapist would listen to clients, then echo, clarify, and acknowledge their views, allowing them to gradually gain greater awareness.

Frederick "Fritz" Perls developed a humanistic approach called ***Gestalt therapy***, which drew inspiration from the Gestalt psychologists of the early 20th century. The goal of gestalt therapy was for a patient to confront thoughts, behaviors, and feelings, take full responsibility for them, and integrate them into a coherent whole (*gestalt*). This was accomplished using a variety of techniques, most notably the "***empty-chair technique***", in which the patient imagined another person (mother, father, etc.) in an empty chair and talked openly, imagining and role-playing responses from that person.

Behavioral Therapy

The behaviorist approach to therapy is based on the learning principles of classical and operant conditioning, emphasizing that inappropriate responses can be extinguished and more constructive behaviors can be learned in their place.

Aversion therapy stops problematic behaviors by using classical conditioning. By pairing maladaptive behaviors with punishment, they can be extinguished. For example, the drug Antabuse (don't worry, it doesn't involve abusing ants), or *disulfiram*, can be used to discourage alcohol consumption. If alcohol is consumed while on Antabuse, this causes nausea and vomiting, even after only one drink. These negative consequences can discourage potential drinkers from breaking their sobriety. While this can be successful in the short-term, it may not be as effective long-term because it doesn't teach coping strategies or reduce cravings for alcohol so users may stop taking the drug to avoid the negative consequences.

Behavioral techniques have greater success when it comes to extinguishing unwanted emotional responses. ***Exposure therapy*** is an effective intervention for overcoming phobias and anxiety. This therapy involves repeatedly confronting a feared stimulus or situation in order to decrease negative emotional responses to it.

Counterconditioning refers to overcoming a negative response (such as fear) to a stimulus by repeatedly pairing the stimulus with something that evokes a positive response. In 1924, Mary Cover Jones described using this approach to rid a boy named Peter of his rabbit fear but it did not become a widespread therapeutic technique until it was popularized by ***Joseph Wolpe*** a few decades later. Wolpe's exposure therapy used a process of ***systematic desensitization***, teaching a person to remain relaxed in the face of increasingly threatening stimuli. In the case of a snake phobia, a person would be taught relaxation techniques, then would practice using these techniques while thinking about a snake, then viewing an image of a snake, then a real snake (known as ***in vivo exposure***), until the person was eventually able to hold a live snake without showing a fear response. Throughout this process the therapist would also serve as a model for appropriate behavior, handling the snake without showing fear.

In vivo exposure is not always practical, so modern exposure therapy also uses virtual reality to simulate situations which are costly or difficult to recreate, allowing patients to learn how to decrease their unwanted emotional responses to situations like combat or airplane travel.

More recent research has demonstrated that the progressive relaxation techniques taught by Wolpe are not essential to this process, and unwanted emotional responses will naturally tend to fade following exposure. Rather than systematic desensitization, some therapists use ***flooding***, in which the patient is immediately confronted with a "worst-case" scenario rather than gradually building up the intensity of the stimulus. While jarring, this approach can be effective and may shorten the time needed to extinguish the unwanted emotional response.

Exposure therapy can also be used for other types of disorders by preventing behaviors. In the case of OCD, patients might be exposed to a situation (putting their hands in dirt) but not be allowed to engage in the behavior they would usually respond with (washing their hands). This approach, known as ***response prevention***, forces patients to learn new ways of coping with the anxiety they feel in order to break out of their usual responses.

The principles of operant conditioning can also be used for behavior modification and shaping desired behaviors. In a **token economy**, people are given rewards (such as tokens) for completing desired behaviors, and these tokens can then be redeemed for other rewards such as television watching, special meals, or trips. This approach can be used to boost social interaction in children with autism, or for skills training that can allow people with disorders or disabilities to become self-sufficient and live on their own. What happens when the token economy is no longer there to reward behaviors? In many cases, the behaviors and skills being taught are designed to be rewarding for their own sake. So when a person has learned how to interact well with others or how to fill out the forms necessary to pay bills or order food, these now have real-life rewards that replace the token economy training.

Cognitive Therapy

Cognitive therapy focuses on thinking patterns associated with particular disorders and aims to improve reasoning, self-control, and responses to events, giving patients new ways of thinking.

The goal of **Aaron Beck**'s **Cognitive Therapy** was to identify distorted views about the *self*, *others*, and the *world* (which Beck referred to as the **cognitive triad**) then correct these views by challenging the beliefs behind them. Beck taught patients to avoid **catastrophizing**, or imagining the worst possible consequences of minor events (i.e. "I failed my math test, so I'm not going to get into college, which means my life is ruined"). The role of the therapist was to gradually reveal these faulty thinking patterns, then challenge them, allowing patients to become more aware of their thoughts and how to change them.

Albert Ellis used a more direct approach, and in his **Rational Emotive Behavior Therapy**, the therapist would point out errors in a patient's thinking, then work to resolve them. In both cognitive therapy and rational emotive behavior therapy, the goal is **cognitive restructuring**, getting patients to question their beliefs, assumptions, and predictions about the world, then encouraging them to replace these with more realistic and positive ways of thinking. Modern cognitive therapists may draw inspiration from both Beck and Ellis, in addition to using other techniques such as mindfulness meditation in order to teach patients how to detect cognitive and emotional issues before they become problems.

Cognitive-Behavioral Therapy (CBT)

As the name suggests, *Cognitive-Behavioral Therapy* is a combination of techniques from both cognitive and behavioral approaches, in addition to some unique features. CBT is problem-focused and action-oriented, meaning that it has a narrow focus for which areas of thinking need to be improved and it provides a structured program of behaviors for progress. Programs are flexible and can be tailored to each individual patient, and the purpose of the exercises is made clear to the patient, creating a sense of transparency. The patient and therapist meet with a specific agenda of problems to focus on, then work to restructure thinking in those areas. At the end of a session, the patient is given "homework" assignments to be completed before the next meeting, creating a relationship more like teacher-student than therapist-client. For example, a patient with OCD might work with a CBT therapist to recognize when obsessive thinking patterns occur, then create a list of alternative behaviors designed to interrupt these patterns. This approach can be effective, and PET scans have shown changes in the brain activity of OCD patients over time (Schwartz et al, 1996), reminding us that psychological interventions influence biology.

Group Approaches

Some types of therapy are conducted in groups. *Couples therapy* works with partners to improve communication, deal with sexual dysfunction, domestic violence, or address specific problems that may influence the relationship (such as one person being diagnosed with depression). *Family therapy* considers the system of relationships that has an influence on each of the individual members of a family. These family dynamics may play a role in some illnesses, such as parental pressures or sibling rivalries contributing to a teenage girl's development of an eating disorder.

In *group therapy*, multiple people work on their own independent problems in a shared setting. This group format encourages social behaviors and social skills and it allows participants to get feedback from multiple people. Group therapy can be beneficial and it provides individuals with an opportunity to relate to others and reduce feelings of isolation or stigma associated with a disorder. In addition, group sessions with a single therapist and multiple participants are more cost-effective, reducing financial strain on individuals.

There are downsides to the group format, however, and all individuals in the group may not have similar needs, so treatments will necessarily be less focused. Group dynamics can also become negative if some members dominate discussions or make others uncomfortable and this may be difficult for a therapist to control. Patients may lose the incentive to improve if some behaviors are now seen as normal in the context of their new group, such as bulimia patients feeling that purging is common or that it is not a big deal because now they know many others who admit to doing it. Patients may also learn negative techniques from others, such as new methods of purging or how other patients with anorexia hid their weight loss from family and friends.

Self-Help and Support Groups

Like formal group therapies, self-help and support groups provide cost-effective and supportive groups for sufferers of specific problems, from alcoholism (AA) and gambling (Gambler's Anonymous) to social phobias (Toastmasters). These groups can provide support, reduce isolation, and foster a sense of community and public commitment to change. Often these group meetings are not run by trained therapists or counselors, which means some advice may be counter-productive, and in extreme cases, groups can become insular, encourage radical views, or even form cults.

Biomedical Treatments

One of the earliest biological interventions for the mentally ill was *trephining* (also known as *trepanning*) which involved drilling a hole in the skull in order to release the demons or spirits trapped within. Evidence of this practice (skulls with holes that show partial healing and bone growth) dates back as far as 6000BC. We've come a long way since then and **psychopharmacology** (the study of drug treatments for influencing emotions, thoughts, and behaviors) is far less invasive. Nevertheless, medications shouldn't be thought of as "magic bullets" for treating mental illness and their broad effects come with some costs.

Antipsychotic Medications

One of the first antipsychotic medications (also known as *neuroleptics*) for treating schizophrenia resulted from work to develop an antihistamine and was discovered in 1951. The result, chlorpromazine (Thorazine), and the other drugs which followed, thioridazine (Mellaril), and haloperidol (Haldol) would fundamentally change the nature of treatment for psychotic disorders. These medications, which rendered patients euphoric and docile, led to mass **deinstitutionalization** in the 1950s and 60s, releasing millions of patients and reducing hospitalization for mental illness by two-thirds. Release is not synonymous with cure, however, and many of these former patients were later unable to care for themselves, and ended up destitute and often homeless.

The main way these drugs work is by blocking dopamine activity, which led to the **dopamine hypothesis** that schizophrenia results from distorted dopamine signaling in the brain. While these early medications were able to reduce positive symptoms such as hallucinations, they weren't effective for negative symptoms such as emotional numbing or social withdrawal. These drugs have side effects which include sluggishness, tremors, twitches, weight gain (with increased risk of obesity and diabetes), and **tardive dyskinesia**; uncontrollable facial tics and twitches. Some patients experience *akathisia* (Greek for "unable to sit"), a painful restlessness and agitation which causes them to pace constantly in an effort to reduce pain and which can be severe enough to cause patients to refuse treatment. Newer drugs, known as *atypical antipsychotics* such as clozapine (Clozaril) risperadone (Risperadil) and olanzepine (Zyprexa), work on both dopamine and serotonin systems, are more successful in reducing cognitive and perceptual distortions, and tend to have fewer side effects.

Anti-anxiety Medications

Anti-anxiety medications (or *anxiolytics*) help to reduce anxiety and can aid the extinction of learned fears. **Benzodiazepines** are anti-anxiety drugs which work on the GABA system. Benzodiazepines take effect within minutes to reduce heart rate and anxiety. Side effects include drowsiness and problems with memory and coordination. While effective for reducing arousal and slowing heart rate, these drugs can be dangerous when combined with alcohol (which can lead to a fatal drop in blood pressure) and also carry high risk of addiction, dependency, and withdrawal. Sudden cessation of benzodiazepines results in symptoms of withdrawal that include increased heart rate, shakiness, insomnia, agitation, and anxiety. Common benzodiazepines include diazepam (Valium), lorazepam (Ativan), and alprazolam (Xanax). Due to growing recognition of risks, these drugs are now prescribed more cautiously and in lower dosages than they once were.

Given the side effects and potential for dependence, we may wonder if these drugs really treat anxiety or if they merely mask symptoms. Are people popping pills rather than learning coping strategies? While one could argue that these drugs are helping more people than ever before (prescriptions for anxiolytics doubled between 1995 and 2005) there's a possibility they are being over-prescribed for anxiety that isn't severe enough to warrant drug treatment.

Antidepressant Medications

One of the first drugs for depression was *iproniazid*, a treatment for tuberculosis which had the side effect of making patients euphoric (though it caused higher incidence of hepatitis and was discontinued). Iproniazid was the first of a class of antidepressants known as **monoamine-oxidase inhibitors** (**MAOI**s). Monoamine-oxidase is an enyzme which breaks down monoamines (which include serotonin, dopamine, and norepinephrine), so inhibiting this enzyme may boost levels of these neurotransmitters. Unfortunately, blocking this enzyme also causes a host of side effects, including dizziness, and loss of sexual interest. It also has a dangerous interaction with food containing *tyramine* (common in fermented foods, cheese, and alcohol) and can lead to *hypertensive crisis* (extremely high blood pressure), which means that a very strict diet must be followed. Given these side effects and risks, MAOIs are rarely prescribed today.

The next class of antidepressants, introduced in the 1950s, were **tricyclic antidepressants** (**TCA**s), which are named for their three-ringed chemical structure and include imipramine (Thorazil) and amitriptyline (Elavil). These drugs block reuptake of serotonin and norepinephrine but they come with a number of side effects (including dry mouth, rash, blurred vision, and increased heart rate) and the potential for fatal overdose. Patients must be gradually weaned off of these drugs to avoid anxiety, headache, nausea, insomnia, and motor disturbances, so these drugs are rarely prescribed today.

The success of early antidepressants lent credence to the ***catecholamine hypothesis***, put forth by Joseph Schildkraut in 1965, contending that depression resulted from a decrease in catecholamines, which include dopamine, epinephrine, and norepinephrine. This later gave way to the ***serotonin hypothesis***, which focused on the possible role of serotonin deficiency in depression.

Perhaps the best-known class of antidepressants are the ***SSRI***s, or ***selective serotonin reuptake inhibitors*** which include fluoxetine (Prozac), citalopram (Celexa), paroxetine (Paxil) and sertraline (Zoloft). These drugs block reuptake of serotonin back into presynaptic neurons, increasing the availability of serotonin to postsynaptic neurons. Side effects include nausea, agitation, and sexual dysfunction, and there is also a potential for withdrawal symptoms. The most recently developed class of antidepressants, known as *atypical antidepressants,* are less focused on serotonin and may also influence norepinephrine or dopamine. These include venlafaxine (Effexor), nefazodone (Serzone), and bupropion (Wellbutrin), among others.

Despite direct-to-consumer advertising implying that antidepressants correct a serotonin imbalance, researchers don't fully understand why antidepressants work (and they don't work for everyone). Effects on neurotransmitter levels occur quickly, but results for patients often don't appear for several weeks after beginning treatment. In addition, depleting serotonin in healthy individuals does not seem to directly lower mood. Imbalance or simple deficiency does not seem to be an adequate explanation for depression and some recent research focuses on the possible role of ***neurogenesis***, the creation of new neurons, in treating depression.

Despite their name, antidepressants are used to treat other categories of illness as well, including anxiety disorders, eating disorders, obsessive-compulsive disorder, and ADHD. Pharmaceutical companies often change the brand name, packaging, and pill colors to avoid consumer associations with antidepressants. So Eli Lilly's drug Sarafem, for Premenstrual Dysphoric Disorder, is actually Prozac and GlaxoSmithKline's smoking-cessation drug Zyban is actually Wellbutrin.

Bipolar Medications

Antidepressants are not prescribed for bipolar disorders, because although they can boost mood they can also trigger manic episodes. Medications for bipolar I and bipolar II are known as ***mood stabilizers***, the most commonly prescribed of which is ***lithium***. Approximately 60-70% of bipolar patients respond to drug treatments, which can prevent manic episodes, reduce depression, and decrease the risk of suicide. Side effects of lithium include nausea and weight gain. Levels of lithium in the blood naturally fluctuate, so patients must use blood monitoring to adjust dosages, as high levels can affect kidney and thyroid function. Lithium is also teratogenic, meaning that it can't be taken during pregnancy due to the potential for harm to the fetus. Valproate, an anticonvulsant drug, can also be used in treating bipolar disorders, though it carries a potential for liver damage.

Evaluating Drug Treatments

How should we evaluate drug therapies? Even with medications that have been shown to be effective, finding the correct drug and dosage for each individual patient is a process of trial and error, and in many cases the exact mechanisms of a drug's effects are unknown. Are these treatments correcting problems, or are they merely relieving symptoms? The presence of side effects means drug treatments can be accused of trading one symptom for another, without necessarily addressing the real causes of an illness.

For these reasons, medications shouldn't be seen as standalone treatments. They are often prescribed in addition to psychotherapy in order to help address the underlying causes of symptoms as well as provide patients with greater feelings of control compared to just popping pills and hoping for the best. CBT has been found to be as effective as medication for some disorders, including panic disorder and depression, but effectiveness can be even higher when CBT is combined with medication.

Combining therapies can represent a challenge, however, as it often involves coordinating treatments with multiple practitioners, such as a psychotherapist conducting CBT and a psychiatrist prescribing dosages for medications. Some areas have adopted rules allowing psychologists to prescribe drugs such as antidepressants even though these psychologists don't have the same medical training as psychiatrists. This is a controversial policy, though we may also worry when we consider that the majority of antidepressant prescriptions come from primary care physicians (who are not specialists in mental illness) rather than psychiatrists.

Other Biological Treatments

Medications aren't the only biological methods of treating mental illness, though the following treatments are much less common.

Electro-convulsive therapy (***ECT***), first used in 1938, is a method of delivering brief electric shocks to the brain. Despite popular depictions as a torturous process (as in the film *One Flew Over the Cuckoo's Nest*), ECT is administered with muscle relaxants to reduce spasms, and patients are put under general anesthesia before the procedure begins. ECT is mostly used as a treatment for those who have not responded to other treatments. Of these, approximately 80% show improvement with ECT, though the exact mechanism for why this improvement occurs is not clear. It may be that the mini-seizures created by ECT have calming effects on some brain regions, or that they stimulate neurogenesis. Side effects of ECT are generally mild and consist of short-term memory loss, headaches, and muscle aches.

A newer, non-invasive form of brain stimulation is ***transcranial magnetic stimulation***. A magnetic coil is used to pass a current through the left or right prefrontal cortex for a short period of time. TMS has fewer side effects than ECT and does not cause short-term memory loss, though it can cause mild headaches and a slight increase in seizure risk. Once again, the exact reason for the effectiveness of TMS is not known, but it may be that TMS helps to increase the likelihood of certain neurons firing, or it may be that it helps to create new neural circuits or improves long-term potentiation (LTP).

Phototherapy uses a box that directs bright light onto the face for 30 minutes each morning. Despite the idea of light healing illness sounding a bit like quackery, this technique actually works for lifting seasonal pattern depression (seasonal affective disorder) by influencing hormone levels.

The *leucotomy* developed by Egas Moniz and popularized as the *lobotomy* by Walter Freeman has a terrible reputation which was certainly well-earned, and it is banned in many places. But other types of ***psychosurgery*** remain in use, though they are quite rare and because they are irreversible, are only used as last resorts for severe cases. Unlike Freeman's imprecise ice-pick wiggling, modern techniques destroy connections between specific brain areas and include the *cingulotomy* (which focuses on the area between the *cingulate gyrus* and the *corpus callosum*) for depression and OCD, and the *anterior capsulotomy* (focusing on the *caudate nucleus* and *putamen*) for OCD.

Another type of psychosurgery is ***deep brain stimulation*** (***DBS***). Electrodes are implanted in the brain, a pacemaker to control them is implanted in the chest, and stimulation helps to control areas of brain activity. DBS has been used for Parkinson's disease, chronic pain, Tourette's syndrome, tremors, OCD, and even depression.

Effectiveness of Treatment

How do we know when a treatment has worked? This might seem like a simple question (did the patient get better?) but it is actually quite complex and difficult to answer with certainty.

The first problem is that sometimes patients show natural improvement and symptoms of a disorder go away on their own. The illness may have simply run its course (known as ***spontaneous remission***), or symptoms may have gone from their very worst back to average (known as ***regression to the mean***). People tend to seek treatment when they are feeling really bad, so just returning to average may make it seem like a treatment has been effective.

Patient Perspectives

Things get even more complicated when we consider all the aspects of receiving treatment that may play a role in how a patient feels. These are known as **nonspecific treatment effects** and include things like the doctor or therapist's confidence, feeling a greater sense of control (due to the decision to seek help), avoiding alcohol or changing one's diet (to avoid interactions with medication), or building a warm relationship with a therapist who also wants to see improvement (known as the "**therapeutic alliance**"). All of these factors may play a role in a patient's recovery and make it difficult to assess how much the specific treatment is actually contributing.

Another problem is the **placebo effect**, and just believing that one is receiving treatment can be enough to cause improvement. This means that patients receiving medication should be compared to similar patients receiving drug treatments that don't contain any medication. This helps to assess which results are from the medication and which are from believing one is taking medication. Of course, patients can become suspicious and side effects can indicate to a patient that they are getting the "real" drug, distorting results. At the same time, it's possible for patients in the placebo group to experience side effects and this is known as the **nocebo effect**; an inert substance causing negative effects.

Reconstructive memory can also influence effectiveness. Patients who haven't really improved may falsely remember their symptoms as having been worse before. Patients may be biased to believe that their efforts were worthwhile, convincing themselves they are at least a little better now or that without their therapist or doctor they would have been much worse off. It's also possible that some patients come to depend on the therapeutic relationship and attempt to prolong treatment. **Malingering** refers to claiming symptoms continue after they have faded, in order to continue receiving care, attention, and sympathy and this can distort the apparent effectiveness of treatment.

Clinician Perspectives

You might think that clinicians would be better able to avoid the biases that influence patient perceptions of improvement, but this isn't necessarily the case. Therapists are likely to have a bias toward believing their treatments work. In addition, they may be prone to only counting the positives, hearing and repeating success stories from patients whose lives were turned around, but forgetting those patients who never made progress or stopped treatment. In fact, therapists may think that patients who left treatment and never returned were "cured", when perhaps these patients simply started seeing other therapists.

All of these effects and biases open the door for pseudo-therapies with true believers, both practitioners and patients. These approaches, from homeopathy and herbal medicines to energy fields and eye-movement desensitization, may be nothing more than nonspecific treatment effects resulting from the misplaced hope and trust of patients and the good intentions and empathy offered by providers.

Treatment Studies

So how do we establish whether treatments are effective? There are *outcome studies*, which aim to determine whether patients actually get better, and *process studies*, which attempt to pinpoint why a treatment works in order to refine it.

Hans Eysenck called out the apparent ineffectiveness of psychotherapy treatment in 1952, noting that while roughly two-thirds of patients improved, two-thirds of those not treated also improved. Treatments have become more effective in the last 6 decades, and the average patient who receives treatment today is likely to be better off than 80% of those who do not receive treatment. While this is good news, keep in mind that this figure can be misleading, since by definition the "average" untreated patient will be better off than 50% of untreated patients. Nevertheless, treatment does provide an advantage, and those who receive treatment tend to improve more rapidly and are less likely to relapse.

Comparing Effectiveness

Studies which compare treatment, no treatment, and placebo-treatment groups can evaluate the success of interventions. **Well-established treatments** or "empirically-supported" treatments are those which have repeatedly been shown to outperform placebo treatments, while **probably-efficacious treatments** are those which have shown some success but may not yet have enough supporting research.

Ideally we could use double-blind placebo studies to assess all treatments, but when it comes to psychotherapy it's difficult or impossible to provide a "placebo" treatment. One way around this is to have a control group of patients who have been diagnosed but who don't receive treatment right away, known as a **wait-list control** group, which is then compared to patients who did receive treatment during the same time period. This isn't a perfect solution, however, as the anxiety of waiting may contribute to the control group's symptoms, while placebo and nonspecific treatment effects may influence the treatment group.

Placebo studies are easier to conduct with medications, but results have not always been flattering. In 1998, Irving Kirsch and Guy Sapirstein conducted a meta-analysis of the effectiveness of antidepressants and found that 75% of their apparent effectiveness was likely due to the placebo effect. When unpublished trials from the FDA were obtained and analyzed, Kirsch and colleagues reported that for most patients, the difference between antidepressants and placebo was too small to have a clinically significant difference in outcome.

Another problem for assessing and comparing treatments is comorbidity. How should we compare the treatment of "pure" and "mixed" cases? How should a therapist or psychiatrist approach the treatment of multiple disorders? Should one disorder be prioritized or should simultaneous treatment be attempted? How will this influence efficacy? Will side effects of one disorder's treatment influence the symptoms of another disorder?

Given just how difficult it is to assess if a single treatment works, it's even more challenging to determine the "best" treatments for any particular disorder, particularly when we consider that the effectiveness of individual therapists using the same approach may vary widely. Nevertheless, when it comes to certain problems we do have some ideas of which treatments are most effective. Phobias and panic disorders tend to respond well to behavioral treatments that teach specific strategies. Moderate depression tends to respond well to CBT as well as medications like SSRIs. Cognitive and behavioral treatments don't seem to be particularly effective for bipolar disorders, which means medication is often a vital first step, and the same is true for schizophrenia and severe depression.

Lifestyle Changes

The treatments discussed in this chapter have considered how behaviors, thoughts, and biology can be modified to improve mental health. But these haven't specifically addressed lifestyle factors that may contribute to mental illness. Would we be surprised at the development of physical or mental illness in a sleep-deprived person who feels disengaged at work, socially-isolated at home, and who lives a sedentary lifestyle and eats a poor diet? Might mental illness be a natural response to these negative lifestyle factors?

We can think of positive lifestyle changes as ways of coping with stressful circumstances before they result in illness, as well as ways of combating some symptoms. Many of these habits have been mentioned previously in other chapters, and for good reason. Proper sleep, exercise, a healthy diet, relaxation techniques, and social support can help us to cope with stress and can improve our quality of life.

As previously mentioned, relaxation techniques can boost immune function, and practicing mindfulness meditation may even teach a sort of **anti-rumination**, allowing us to recognize and redirect negative thoughts when they occur. Aerobic exercise has repeatedly been shown to be as effective as drug treatments for moderate depression and unlike medications, aerobic exercise has side effects which are positive (improved sleep, increased strength and energy, enhanced sex drive, reduced risk of obesity and diabetes, etc.). Exercise has also been shown to be effective at preventing relapse of depression, and a study by Michael Babyak and colleagues (2000) found that an exercise-only group had the lowest rate of relapse, even lower than the exercise + SSRI treatment group.

These lifestyle changes are not a substitute for all treatment and I'm not suggesting that one can jog away schizophrenia or meditate through a manic episode. What I am suggesting is that these behaviors may help to treat some symptoms, and possibly help prevent the development of illness. These strategies can also help to remind us that mental health isn't confined to psychiatric institutions and therapists' offices. Just as infectious diseases can be controlled by inoculating people who aren't sick, mental illness can be addressed by preventing the development of disorders in healthy individuals.

This is not just about encouraging habits to make ourselves healthier or happier. When we understand the factors that increase risk of mental illness, we see that the burdens of poverty, unemployment, homelessness, discrimination, and poor access to healthcare are not just issues of social justice, they are mental health issues too. Helping others to increase competence and control, improve mood and self-esteem, and build resilience doesn't just benefit those individuals, it benefits our society as a whole.

Chapter Summary - Treatment

- Stigma, availability of treatment, and awareness of options may influence whether or not people receive treatment for mental illness.

- *Psychotherapy* includes psychoanalytic, humanistic, behavioral, cognitive, cognitive-behavioral (CBT), and group therapies.

- Common medications for treating psychological disorders include ***antipsychotics***, ***anti-anxiety drugs***, ***antidepressants***, and ***mood stabilizers***.

- Other biomedical interventions include ***electro-convulsive therapy*** (***ECT***), ***transcranial magnetic stimulation*** (***TMS***), ***phototherapy***, ***psychosurgery***, and ***deep-brain stimulation*** (***DBS***).

- Assessing the effectiveness of treatment can be difficult due to ***nonspecific treatment effects***, the ***placebo effect***, ***reconstructive memory***, ***malingering***, and ***clinician bias***.

- Lifestyle changes to incorporate exercise, meditation, better sleep and eating habits, and social support may be effective in relieving some symptoms and preventing the development of mental illness.

Notes

Thanks for Reading!

Congratulations for making it through this rather dense guide. I hope that it has helped you to have a better grasp of these concepts. I encourage you check out the free resources at **www.psychexamreview.com!**

In the pages that follow you'll find lists of key terms, as well as references and recommended readings for each chapter. Thanks again for reading, and I wish you all the best in your study of psychology!

History and Approaches – Key Terms

Plato

Aristotle

nativism

philosophical empiricism

nature / nurture

René Descartes

dualism

monism

phrenology

Franz Josef Gall

structuralism

introspection

Wilhelm Wundt

Edward Titchener

functionalism

William James

Charles Darwin

natural selection

Sigmund Freud

unconscious

psychoanalytic approach

behaviorism

B.F. Skinner

cognitive

evolutionary psychology

developmental psychology

neuroscience (cognitive/behavioral)

social psychology

industrial-organizational psychology

cultural psychology

abnormal psychology

psychiatrist

clinical psychology

counseling psychology

Research Methods - Key Terms

demand characteristics

social desirability

Hawthorne Effect

skepticism

Robert Rosenthal and Kermit Fode

observer bias

double-blind study

property

measure

operational definition

construct validity

predictive validity

case study

survey

reporting bias

population

sample

stratified sampling

random sampling

opportunity sample

representative sample

illusory correlation

confirmation bias

correlation

scatterplot

correlational coefficient

third variable

matched sample

matched pair

illusory correlation

theory

hypothesis

experiment

manipulation

independent variable

dependent variable

placebo effect

random assignment / random allocation

self-selection

confounding variable

controls

descriptive statistics

central tendency

mean

median

mode

variance

range

standard deviation

normal curve

frequency distribution

inferential statistics

statistical significance

p-value

effect size

internal validity

replication

external validity / ecological validity

artificiality

informed consent

debriefing

Biological Bases of Behavior – Key Terms

reductionism

parsimony

neuron structure

dendrites

soma (cell body)

axon

myelin

Nodes of Ranvier

multiple sclerosis

glial cells

terminal button

ion channel

vesicles

neurotransmitters

resting potential

action potential

all-or-none principle

refractory period

synapse

acetylcholine

dopamine

GABA

serotonin

reuptake

enzyme deactivation

autoreception

Alzheimer's disease

Parkinson's disease

reward area (*nucleus accumbens*)

Structure of the Nervous System

Central Nervous System

Peripheral Nervous System

somatic division

autonomic division

sympathetic nervous system

hormone

parasympathetic nervous system

Phineas Gage

Paul Broca

aphasia

electroencephalogram (EEG)

computerized axial tomography (CAT scan)

magnetic resonance imaging (MRI)

positron emission tomography (PET scan)

functional magnetic resonance imaging (fMRI)

Brain Structures

hindbrain

medulla

reticular formation

cerebellum

pons

midbrain

tectum

tegmentum

forebrain

subcortical structures

thalamus

hypothalamus

limbic system

amygdala

hippocampus

pituitary gland

basal ganglia

cerebral cortex

hemispheres

corpus callosum

contralateral control

frontal lobe

parietal lobe

temporal lobe

occipital lobe

somatosensory cortex

motor cortex

split-brain patients

Roger Sperry and Michael Gazzaniga

Genes and Heritability

gene

chromosome

DNA

genome

behavioral genetics

monozygotic

dizygotic

heritability score

molecular genetics

chromosomal abnormalities

Down Syndrome

Turner Syndrome

Klinefelter Syndrome

Phenylketonuria (PKU)

Sensation and Perception Key Terms

sensation

transduction

perception

psychophysics

absolute threshold

just-noticeable difference (JND)

Weber's Law

signal detection theory

noise

hit, miss, false alarm, correct rejection

response criteria

vision

cornea

iris

pupil

lens

retina

accommodation

photoreceptors

rods

cones

fovea

blindspot

retinal ganglion cell

bipolar cell

lateral inhibition

receptive fields

mach bands

Young-Helmholtz Trichromatic Theory

Opponent Process Theory of Color

color afterimage

hearing

pinna

tympanic membrane / eardrum

ossicles

cochlea

basilar membrane

stereocilia

place code

auditory nerve

vestibular system

semicircular canals

haptic perception

mechanoreceptors

pressure, texture, pattern, vibration

thermoreceptors

nocireceptors

contralateral control

somatosensory cortex

A-delta fibers

C-fibers

referred pain

olfaction

odorant molecules

olfactory receptor neuron (ORN)

glomeruli

olfactory bulb

anosmia

taste

papilla

tastant molecules

taste bud

microvilli

taste pores

gustatory cell

salty, sweet, bitter, sour, umami

synesthesia

Gestalt laws

closure

proximity

similarity

continuity

simplicity

common fate

perceptual constancy

size constancy

brightness constancy

shape constancy

depth cues

monocular cues

linear perspective

texture gradient

interposition

shading

binocular disparity

convergence

motion parallax

optic flow

Müller-Lyer illusion

carpentered-world hypothesis

Learning – Key Terms

learning

behaviorism

classical conditioning

Ivan Pavlov

neutral stimulus

unconditioned stimulus

unconditioned response

conditioned stimulus

conditioned response

acquisition

extinction

spontaneous recovery

stimulus generalization

stimulus discrimination

second-order / higher-order conditioning

John B. Watson & Rosalie Rayner

"Little Albert" study

aversive conditioning

learned taste aversion

biological preparedness

operant conditioning

Edward Thorndike

Law of Effect

instrumental learning

B. F. Skinner

positive reinforcement

negative reinforcement

primary reinforcer

secondary reinforcer

positive punishment

negative punishment / omission training

operant box / "Skinner box"

chaining

shaping

continuous reinforcement

intermittent reinforcement

schedules of reinforcement

fixed-ratio schedule

variable-ratio schedule

fixed-interval schedule

variable-interval schedule

superstition

David Premack / Premack Principle

Keller & Marian Breland

instinctual drift

Rescorla-Wagner Model / Contingency Model

observational learning

Albert Bandura

"Bobo doll" study

modeling

vicarious reinforcement

latent learning

Edward Tolman

cognitive map

abstract learning

Wolfgang Köhler

insight learning

Memory – Key Terms

encoding

storage

retrieval

3-box model

sensory memory

George Sperling

iconic memory

echoic memory

selective attention

short-term memory

George Miller

the "magical number 7"

organizational encoding

chunking

rehearsal

working memory

long-term memory

declarative / explicit memory

episodic memory

semantic memory

non-declarative / implicit memory

procedural memory

Daniel Schacter

transience

Hermann Ebbinghaus

forgetting curve

absentmindedness

blocking

tip-of-the-tongue experience

misattribution

source memory

false recognition

cryptomnesia

suggestibility

Elizabeth Loftus

reconstructive memory

bias

consistency bias

egocentric bias

persistence

flash-bulb memory

state-dependent memory

hippocampus

anterograde amnesia

retrograde amnesia

patient H.M.

long-term potentiation (LTP)

NMDA

serial position effect

primacy

recency

testing effect

distributed review

massed practice

spaced-repetition software (SRS)

overlearning

levels of processing

self-referential effect

retrieval cue

spreading activation

Method of Loci / Roman Room / Journey Method

Link / Keyword Method

Language and Cognition – Key Terms

B.F. Skinner

Noam Chomsky

language acquisition device (LAD)

linguistics

phonemes

morphemes

phonological rules

accent

syntactical rules

fast-mapping

telegraphic speech

overgeneralization / overregularization

The Wug Test

critical period

genetic dysphasia

interactionist approach

linguistic relativity hypothesis / Whorf-Sapir hypothesis

concepts and categories

prototype

exemplar theory

mental set

functional fixedness

convergent thinking

divergent thinking

overconfidence

illusory superiority / Wobegon effect

belief bias

belief perseverance

algorithm

heuristic

Amos Tversky & Daniel Kahneman

availability heuristic

representativeness heuristic

framing effect

sunk-cost fallacy

recognition heuristic

States of Consciousness – Key Terms

René Descartes

mind-body problem

Cartesian Theater

philosophical zombie

problem of other minds

Thomas Nagel

minimal consciousness

self-consciousness

mark test

"hard problem" of consciousness

unity

intentionality

selectivity

transience

cocktail-party phenomenon

dichotic listening task

selective attention

change blindness

inattentional blindness

thought suppression

dual-process theory

System 1

System 2

priming

mere-exposure effect

circadian rhythm

zeitgeber

suprachiasmatic nucleus

pineal gland

melatonin

sleep cycle

EEG (electroencephalogram)

alpha waves

NREM stage 1

theta waves

hypnagogic imagery

hypnic jerk

NREM stage 2

sleep spindle

K-complex

NREM stage 3

delta waves

slow-wave Sleep

REM

paradoxical sleep

sleep deprivation (chronic, acute)

insomnia

sleep apnea

sleepwalking / somnambulism

night terrors

REM behavior disorder

narcolepsy

cataplexy

polyphasic sleep

Sigmund Freud

manifest content

latent content

dream interpretation

activation-synthesis hypothesis

information processing theory

memory consolidation

lucid dreaming

agonist

antagonist

homeostasis

neuroadaptation

tolerance

dependency

withdrawal

psychological addiction

stimulant

depressant

narcotic

opiates

hallucinogen

hypnosis

hypnotic suggestibility

analgesia

post-hypnotic amnesia

role theory of hypnosis

dissociation theory of hypnosis

focused attention meditation

mantra

mindfulness meditation

relaxation response

Intelligence and Testing – Key Terms

reification

Charles Spearman

factor analysis

g-factor

Louis Leon Thurstone

primary mental abilities

Howard Gardner

multiple intelligences

prodigy

savant

acquired savant syndrome

Robert Sternberg

triarchic theory of intelligence – analytical, creative, practical

emotional intelligence

fluid intelligence

crystallized intelligence

psychometrics / psychometrician

power test

speed test

achievement test

aptitude test

validity

construct validity

face validity

content validity

criterion-related validity

concurrent validity

predictive validity

reliability

split-half reliability

test-retest reliability

equivalent form reliability

standardized

standardization sample

representative sample

norms

Francis Galton

Alfred Binet

Binet-Simon test

mental age

Intelligence Quotient (IQ)

ratio IQ score

deviation IQ score

Lewis Terman

Stanford-Binet Intelligence Scale

Wechsler Adult Intelligence Scale (WAIS)

Wechsler Intelligence Scale for Children (WISC)

Wechsler Preschool and Primary Scale of Intelligence (WPPSI)

percentile score

intellectual giftedness

intellectual disability (ID)

Down Syndrome

Fragile X syndrome

Williams Syndrome

Phenylketonuria (PKU)

eugenics

Robert M. Yerkes

artificial selection

Flynn Effect

self-fulfilling prophecy

tracking

Head Start Program

fixed vs. growth mindset

stereotype threat

identity contingencies

transcranial direct current stimulation (tDCS)

transcranial magnetic stimulation (TMS)

Ritalin, Modafinil, Adderall

nootropics

dual-n-back task

Personality – Key Terms

nomothetic

idiographic

humors

Sigmund Freud

unconscious

dream interpretation

free association

parapraxis / Freudian slip

libido

id

pleasure principle

ego

reality principle

superego

Psychosexual Stages

fixation

Oral Stage

oral fixation

Anal Stage

anal-retentive type, anal-expulsive type

Phallic Stage

Oedipus Complex

castration anxiety

identification

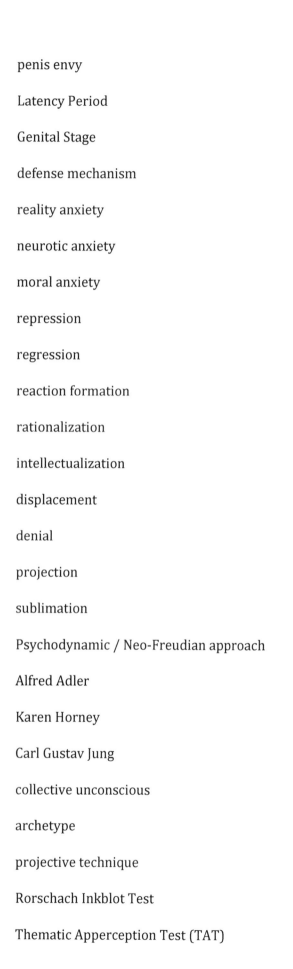

penis envy

Latency Period

Genital Stage

defense mechanism

reality anxiety

neurotic anxiety

moral anxiety

repression

regression

reaction formation

rationalization

intellectualization

displacement

denial

projection

sublimation

Psychodynamic / Neo-Freudian approach

Alfred Adler

Karen Horney

Carl Gustav Jung

collective unconscious

archetype

projective technique

Rorschach Inkblot Test

Thematic Apperception Test (TAT)

self-report

implicit assessment

Forer Effect / Barnum Effect

Minnesota Multiphasic Personality Inventory (MMPI)

cardinal dispositions

central traits

secondary traits

authoritarianism

factor analysis

Hans Eysenck

Introversion/Extraversion

Psychoticism

The Big Five / Five Factor Model

Openness to Experience

Conscientiousness

Extraversion

Agreeableness

Neuroticism

personality profile

experience sampling

intrapersonal functioning

Behavioral Approach System (BAS)

Behavioral Inhibition System (BIS)

temperament

personal constructs

person variables

self-schema

self-serving bias

person-situation controversy

existential psychology

terror management

mortality salience

humanistic psychology

Abraham Maslow - self-actualization

Carl Rogers

fully-functioning person

unconditional positive regard

Wobegon Effect / Illusory Superiority

self-concept

reciprocal determinism

self-efficacy / efficacy expectancy

internal vs. external locus of control

self-perception theory

self-esteem

Myers-Briggs Type Indication (MBTI)

Emotion and Motivation – Key Terms

multidimensional scaling

valence

physiological arousal

James-Lange Theory of Emotion

Cannon-Bard Theory of Emotion

Stanley Schachter & Jerome Singer - Two-Factor Theory of Emotion

appraisal

misattribution of arousal

Klüver-Bucy Syndrome / temporal lobe syndrome

nucleus accumbens / "reward area"

amygdala

fast pathway / "low road"

slow pathway / "high road"

lobotomy

emotional regulation

reappraisal

universality hypothesis

Paul Ekman

joy, sadness, anger, fear, surprise, disgust

facial-feedback hypothesis

display rules

hedonic principle

motivation

instinct

drive

drive reduction theory

homeostasis

primary drive

secondary drive

opponent process theory of motivation

arousal theory

Yerkes-Dodson Law

flow

orexigenic

anorexigenic

orexin

lateral hypothalamus

ghrelin

ventromedial hypothalamus

leptin

bulimia nervosa

binge-eating disorder

anorexia nervosa

obesity

set point theory

metabolism / basal metabolic rate

Dutch hunger winter

sexual motivation

estrus

William Masters & Virginia Johnson - Human Sexual Response Cycle

excitement, plateau, orgasm, resolution

refractory period

Abraham Maslow

hierarchy of needs

intrinsic vs. extrinsic motivation

overjustification effect

delay of gratification

Marshmallow Test

insufficient justification

management theory

Type Y vs. Type X leadership

task-oriented vs. relationship oriented leadership

need for achievement

press

approach vs. avoidance motivation

approach-approach conflict

avoidance-avoidance conflict

approach-avoidance conflict

self-concordant goals

implementation intentions

Development – Key Terms

Erik Erikson

oral-sensory, muscular-anal, locomotor-genital, latency

adolescence, early adulthood, middle adulthood, maturity

psychosocial task

prenatal development

conception

zygote

germinal stage

embryo - embryonic stage

androgens

fetus - fetal stage

placenta

teratogen

fetal alcohol syndrome

infant - infancy stage

reflex

rooting reflex

sucking reflex

developmental milestones

cephalocaudal rule

proximodistal rule

preferential looking / visual preference

habituation

infantile amnesia

synaptic pruning

Jean Piaget

schema

assimilation

accommodation

sensorimotor stage

object permanence

A-not-B error

executive function

self-concept

mark test

preoperational stage

conservation

theory of mind

egocentrism

false-belief test

autism spectrum disorder

concrete operational stage

formal operational stage

Lev Vygotsky

zone of proximal development

scaffolding

ethology

Konrad Lorenz

imprinting

critical period

Harry Harlow

grasp reflex

secure base

Mary Ainsworth

strange situation

secure attachment

avoidant attachment / insecure-avoidant attachment

ambivalent attachment / insecure-resistant attachment

disorganized attachment

temperament

Diana Baumrind

authoritarian parenting

permissive parenting

authoritative parenting

neglectful parenting

Lawrence Kohlberg

Stages of Moral Development

Heinz Dilemma

preconventional

conventional

postconventional

moral intuitions

primary sex characteristics

secondary sex characteristics

spermarche

menarche

sexual orientation

cognitive decline

menopause

dementia

Alzheimer's disease

Social Psychology – Key Terms

social psychology

sociology

basic research

applied research

archival studies

observational studies

field experiment

subject variables

Geert Hofstede

cultural dimensions

individualism/collectivism

masculinity/femininity

uncertainty avoidance

power distance

time orientation

social comparison theory

social identity theory

basking in reflected glory

Leon Festinger & James Carlsmith

insufficient justification

cognitive dissonance

Benjamin Franklin Effect

social facilitation

social loafing

conformity

autokinetic effect

informational influence

Solomon Asch

private acceptance

public compliance

normative influence

compliance / persuasion

central route

peripheral route

foot-in-the-door technique

door-in-the-face technique

not-so-free sample

norm of reciprocity

that's-not-all technique

obedience

Stanley Milgram

banality of evil

attraction

propinquity

mere-exposure effect

homogamy

halo effect

self-disclosure

attribution theory

disposition

situation

Fundamental Attribution Error (FAE)

actor-observer bias

just-world bias

impression formation

"thin-slices" theory

stereotype

prejudice

discrimination

Ultimate Attribution Error (UAE)

Henri Tajfel

minimal group

in-group bias

hazing

out-group homogeneity

dehumanization

Muzafer Sherif

Robber's Cave study

realistic conflict theory

contact theory

superordinate goals

implicit association test

group polarization

risky shift

Irving Janis

groupthink

deindividuation

physical anonymity

Stanford Prison Study

bystander effect

pluralistic ignorance

diffusion of responsibility

prosocial behavior

altruism

kin selection

reciprocal altruism

Stress and Health – Key Terms

health psychology

etiology

epidemiology

retrospective studies

prospective studies

longitudinal research

Walter Cannon

voodoo death / psychophysiological death

psychogenic illness

psychosomatic illness

psychoneuroimmunology

fight or flight response

stressor

stress response

social readjustment rating scale

chronic stressor

environmental stressor

tend and befriend response

HPA axis

hypothalamus

pituitary gland

adrenal glands

corticotropin releasing hormone (CRH)

adrenocorticotropic hormone (ACTH)

catecholamines

epinephrine

norepinephrine

glucocorticoids

cortisol

homeostasis

allostasis

Hans Selye

peptic ulcer

General Adaptation Syndrome (GAS)

Alarm, Resistance, Exhaustion

immune system

lymphocytes

T-cells, B-cells

macrophages

natural killer cells

autoimmune disorder

telomeres

Helicobacter pylori

Type-A behavior pattern

Type-B behavior pattern

cardiovascular disease

atherosclerosis / arteriosclerosis

perceived control

primary appraisal

secondary appraisal

Martin Seligman

learned helplessness

social hierarchy

socioeconomic status (SES)

John Henryism

cognitive flexibility

self-serving bias

post-traumatic stress disorder (PTSD)

hardiness

resilience

post-traumatic growth

reappraisal

focusing

compensatory self-improvement

appraisal-focused coping

problem-focused coping

emotion-focused coping

biofeedback

relaxation response

neurogenesis

endorphins

social support

social capital

faith factor

positive psychology

subjective well-being

optimism

pessimism

happiness set-point

diminishing returns

adaptation level phenomenon / hedonic treadmill

relative deprivation

upward comparison

downward comparison

gratitude

Psychological Disorders – Key Terms

psychopathology

psychological disorders

etiology

Thomas Szasz

medical model

symptoms – positive / negative

biopsychosocial approach

stigma

deviance

dysfunction

distress

David Rosenhan

DSM-5

prevalence

incidence

comorbidity

diathesis-stress model

cultural syndromes

cultural idioms of distress

cultural explanations of distress or perceived causes

substance / medication induced disorder

medical student's disease

Anxiety Disorders

specific phobia

preparedness theory

social anxiety disorder (social phobia)

panic disorder

panic attack

agoraphobia

generalized anxiety disorder (GAD)

separation anxiety

Trauma and Stressor Related Disorders

post-traumatic stress disorder (PTSD)

flashbacks

acute stress disorder

adjustment disorder

Obsessive-Compulsive and Related Disorders

obsessive-compulsive disorder

hoarding disorder

body dysmorphic disorder

Somatic Symptoms and Related Disorders

somatic symptom disorder

illness anxiety disorder

conversion disorder

Dissociative Disorders

dissociative amnesia

dissociative fugue

dissociative identity disorder (DID)

depersonalized / derealization disorder

Neurodevelopmental Disorders

autism spectrum disorder

attention deficit / hyperactive disorder (ADHD)

hyperactivity

impulsivity

Schizophrenia Spectrum and other Psychotic Disorders

schizophrenia

delusion

hallucination

disorganized thought / speech

psychosis

catatonia

waxy flexibility

Feeding and Eating Disorders

pica

binge-eating disorder

anorexia nervosa

bulimia nervosa

Depressive Disorders

major depressive disorder

anhedonia

psychomotor retardation

rumination

seasonal pattern (seasonal affective disorder)

peripartum onset (postpartum depression)

persistent depressive disorder

Bipolar and Related Disorders

bipolar I

manic episode

flight of ideas

mixed states

bipolar II

hypomanic episode

cyclothymic disorder

Personality Disorders

Cluster A, B, C

unspecified personality disorder

paranoid

schizoid

schizotypal

antisocial

histrionic

narcissistic

borderline

dependent

avoidant

obsessive-compulsive

psychopathy / sociopathy

Psychopathy Checklist – Revised (PCL-R)

conduct disorder

Neurocognitive Disorders

Alzheimer's disease

traumatic brain injury

Parkinson's disease

prion-related diseases

Paraphilic Disorders

voyeuristic disorder

exhibitionistic disorder

frotteuristic disorder

sexual masochism disorder

sexual sadism disorder

pedophilic disorder

transvestic disorder

fetishistic disorder

Treatment – Key Terms

psychiatrist

neurologist

clinical psychologist

counseling psychologist

clinical social worker

psychotherapy

biomedical treatment

psychoanalysis

resistance

transference

interpersonal therapy

humanistic therapy

Carl Rogers

person-centered therapy / client-centered therapy

unconditional positive regard

active listening

Fritz Perls

Gestalt therapy

empty-chair technique

Behavioral therapy

aversion therapy

exposure therapy

counterconditioning

Joseph Wolpe

systematic desensitization

flooding

token economy

cognitive therapy

Aaron Beck

cognitive triad

catastrophizing

Albert Ellis

rational emotive behavior therapy

cognitive restructuring

Cognitive-Behavioral Therapy (CBT)

couples therapy

family therapy

group therapy

self-help / support groups

psychopharmacology

antipsychotic medication / neuroleptics

deinstitutionalization

dopamine hypothesis

anti-anxiety medication / anxiolytics

benzodiazepines

antidepressant medications

monoamine-oxidase inhibitor (MAOI)

tricyclic antidepressant (TCA)

catecholamine hypothesis

serotonin hypothesis

selective serotonin reuptake inhibitor (SSRI)

mood stabilizers

lithium

electro-convulsive therapy (ECT)

transcranial magnetic stimulation (TMS)

phototherapy

psychosurgery

deep brain stimulation

spontaneous remission

regression to the mean

nonspecific treatment effects

therapeutic alliance

placebo effect

nocebo effect

malingering

outcome studies

process studies

well-established treatments

probably-efficacious treatments

wait-list control group

anti-rumination

References and Recommended Reading

In preparing this series, I read thousands of pages from several editions of psychology textbooks, student guides, teacher resources, and online materials, in addition to completing coursework, listening to podcasts, and reading journal articles to better understand and explain the concepts presented here. This is not an academic research publication and to keep it in a student-friendly format that is easy to read, I decided not to create extensive footnoting or referencing in the text itself. That said, the following have been excellent sources of information, and I am indebted to all of the authors below for their clarity, insight, and information. I have listed specific journal articles for all individual studies mentioned in this text, as well as other recommended reading for students interested in exploring subjects in more detail.

General resources for all chapters

Gleitman, H., Gross, J., & Reisberg, D. (2011) Psychology (8th ed.) New York, NY: W.W. Norton & Company, Inc.

Myers, D. (2010). *Myers' Psychology for AP* (1st ed.). New York, NY: Worth.

Myers, D. (2013). Psychology (10th ed.). New York, NY: Worth.

Schacter, D.L., Gilbert, D.T., & Wegner, D.M. (2009) *Psychology.* New York, NY: Worth.

Spielman, R.M., Dumper, K., Jenkins, W., Lacombe, A., Lovett, M. & Perlmutter, M. (2014). *Psychology*. Houston, TX: OpenStax. Available at: https://openstaxcollege.org/textbooks/psychology

Weseley, A., & McEntarffer, R. (2010). *AP® Psychology* (4th ed.). Hauppauge, N.Y.: Barron's Educational Series.

Chapter 1

Shorto, R. (2009). *Descartes' bones: A skeletal history of the conflict between faith and reason* (First Vintage Books edition). New York: Vintage Books.

Recommended Reading:

Eliot, C. W. (Ed.) (1937) *The Harvard Classics, Vol. 11: Origin of Species, Darwin.* New York, N.Y.: P.F. Collier & Son.

Chapter 2

Olson, R., Verley, J., Santos, L., & Salas, C. (2004) What we teach students about the Hawthorne studies: A review of content within a sample of introductory I-O OB textbooks. *Industrial- Organizational Psychologist*, 41(3), 23-39

Roethlisberger, F., & Dickson, W. (1939). *Management and the worker: An account of a research program conducted by the Western Electric Company, Hawthorne Works, Chicago.* Cambridge, Mass.: Harvard University Press.

Rosenthal, R. & Fode, K.L. (1963). The effect of experimenter bias on the performance of the albino rat. *Behavioral Science*, 8, 183-89.

Recommended Reading:

Randi, J. (1982). *Flim-flam!: Psychics, ESP, unicorns, and other delusions*. Buffalo, N.Y.: Prometheus Books.

Shermer, M. (2002). *Why people believe weird things: pseudoscience, superstition, and other confusions of our time. Rev. and expanded.* New York: A.W.H. Freeman/Owl Book.

Chapter 3

Benson, H., and Klipper, M.Z. (2000). *The Relaxation Response - Updated and Expanded* (25th Anniversary Edition) New York: HarperTorch.

De Carlos, Juan A; Borrell, José (2007). A historical reflection of the contributions of Cajal and Golgi to the foundations of neuroscience. *Brain research reviews 55* (1), 8–16.

Haas, L. F. (2003). Hans Berger (1873-1941), Richard Caton (1842-1926), and electroencephalography. *Journal of Neurology, Neurosurgery & Psychiatry, 74*(1), 9.

Macmillan, M., & Lena, M. (2010). Rehabilitating Phineas Gage. *Neuropsychological Rehabilitation, 20*(5), 641-658.

Ratiu, P., Talos, I., Haker, S., Lieberman, D., & Everett, P. (2004). The Tale of Phineas Gage, Digitally Remastered. *Journal of Neurotrauma. 21*(5): 637-643.

Varki A, Altheide TK (2005). Comparing the human and chimpanzee genomes: searching for needles in a haystack. *Genome Research 15* (12): 1746–58

Recommended Reading:

Dawkins, R. (1989). *The Selfish Gene* (New ed.). Oxford: Oxford University Press.

Ramachandran, V.S. & Blakeslee, S. (1998). *Phantoms in the Brain*. New York: HarperCollins.

Open Course Recommendations:

Robert Sapolsky - Human Behavioral Biology course - Stanford University

David Cox - Fundamentals of Neuroscience – MCB80x – HarvardX

Chapter 4

Jillette, P., Teller, & 4 others (Writers). (2005). The Best [Television series episode]. In *Penn & Teller: Bullshit!* Showtime Networks.

Ramachandran, V.S. & Hubbard, E.M. (2001). Psychophysical investigations into the neural basis of synaesthesia. *Proceedings of the Royal Society of London, B,268*, 979-983.

Segall, M., Campbell, D. and Herskovits, M. J., (1966). The Influence of Culture on Visual Perception. New York: The Bobbs-Merrill Company.

Recommended Reading:

Sacks, O. (1995). *An anthropologist on Mars: Seven paradoxical tales*. New York: Knopf.

Open Course Recommendation:

Stuart Anstis - Sensation and Perception (PSYC 102) course - University of California at San Diego.

Chapter 5

Bandura, A., Ross, D., & Ross, S. (1961). Transmission Of Aggression Through Imitation Of Aggressive Models. *The Journal of Abnormal and Social Psychology,* 575-582.

Bandura, A., Ross, D., & Ross, S. (1963). Imitation Of Film-mediated Aggressive Models. *The Journal of Abnormal and Social Psychology,* 3-11.

Bhatt, R., Wasserman, E., Reynolds, W., & Knauss, K. (1998). Conceptual behavior in pigeons: Categorization of both familiar and novel examples from four classes of natural and artificial stimuli. *Journal of Experimental Psychology: Animal Behavior Processes,* 219-234.

Breland, K., & Breland, M. (1961). The Misbehavior Of Organisms. *American Psychologist,* 681-684.

Garcia J., Kimeldorf D., & Koelling R. (1955) Conditioned aversion to saccharin resulting from exposure to gamma radiation. *Science,* 122(3160): 157-8.

Garcia, J., & Koelling, R. (1966) Relation of cue to consequence in avoidance learning. *Psychonomic Science, 4,* 123-124.

Premack, D. (1959). Toward empirical behavior laws: I. Positive reinforcement. *Psych Rev., 66,* 219-233

Skinner, B. (1947). 'Superstition' In The Pigeon. *Journal of Experimental Psychology,* 168-172.

Tolman, E. C., & Honzik, C. H. (1930). Introduction and removal of reward, and maze performance in rats. *University of California Publications in Psychology.*

Tolman, E. C., Ritchie, B. F., & Kalish, D. (1946). Studies in spatial learning. I. Orientation and the short-cut. *Journal of Experimental Psychology, 36,* 13-24.

Tolman, E. C. (1948). Cognitive maps in rats and men. *Psychological review,* 55(4), 189.

Watanabe, S., Sakamoto, J., & Wakita, M. (1995) Pigeon's discrimination of paintings by Monet and Picasso, *Journal of the Experimental Analysis of Behavior, 63,* pp. 165–174

Watson, J., & Rayner, R. (1920). Conditioned Emotional Reactions. *Journal of Experimental Psychology, 3,* 1-14.

Recommended Reading:

Burgess, A. (1986). *A Clockwork Orange.* New York: Norton.

Skinner, B. (1976). *Walden Two.* New York: Macmillan.

Chapter 6

Anderson, J. (1983). A Spreading Activation Theory Of Memory. *Journal of Verbal Learning and Verbal Behavior,* 261-295.

Atkinson, R. & Shiffrin, R. (1968). Human memory: A proposed system and its control processes. In Spence, K.W.; Spence, J.T. *The psychology of learning and motivation (Volume 2).* New York: Academic Press. pp. 89–195.

Craik, F., & Lockhart, R. (1972) Levels of Processing: A Framework for Memory Research. *Journal of Verbal Learning and Verbal Behavior* 11: 671-684.

Loftus, E., & Pickrell J. (1995). The formation of false memories. *Psychiatric Annals* 25: 720–725.

Loftus, E., & Palmer, J. (1974). Reconstruction of automobile destruction: An example of the interaction between language and memory. *Journal of Verbal Learning and Verbal Behavior,* 585-589.

Miller, G. (1956). The Magical Number Seven, Plus Or Minus Two: Some Limits On Our Capacity For Processing Information. *Psychological Review,* 81-97.

Morris, R., Anderson, E., Lynch, G., & Baudry, M. (1986). Selective Impairment Of Learning And Blockade Of Long-term Potentiation By An N-methyl-D-aspartate Receptor Antagonist, AP5. *Nature,* 774-776.

Paivio, A (1969). Mental Imagery in associative learning and memory. *Psychological Review,* 76(3), 241-263.

Scoville, W., & Milner, B. (1957). Loss of recent memory after bilateral hippocampal lesions. *Journal of Neurology, Neurosurgery and Psychiatry* 20 (1): 11–21.

Sperling G. (1960) The information available in brief visual presentations. *Psychological Monogr.* 74:1-29.

Tulving, E. (1966) Subjective Organization and Effects of Repetition in Multi-Trial Free-Recall Learning. *Journal of Verbal Learning and Verbal Behavior,* Volume 5.

Recommended Reading:

Foer, J. (2011). *Moonwalking with Einstein: The art and science of remembering everything.* New York: Penguin Press.

O'Brien, D. (1993). *How to Develop a Perfect Memory.* London: Pavilion.

Schacter, D. (2001). *The Seven Sins of Memory: How the mind forgets and remembers.* Boston: Houghton Mifflin.

Wearing, Deborah (2005) The man who keeps falling in love with his wife. Available at: http://www.telegraph.co.uk/news/health/3313452/The-man-who-keeps-falling-in-love-with-his-wife.html

Chapter 7

Adams, P., & Adams, J. (1960). Confidence in the recognition and reproduction of words difficult to spell. *The American journal of psychology* 73: 544–552.

Berko, Jean (1958). The Child's Learning of English Morphology. *Word*: 150–177.

Chomsky, N. (1959). A Review of Skinner's Verbal Behavior. *Language* 35 (1): 26–58.

Evans, J. St. B.T., Barston, J.L., & Pollard, P. (1983). On the conflict between logic and belief in syllogistic reasoning. *Memory and Cognition* 11: 295–306.

Goldstein, D., & Gigerenzer, G. (2002). Models Of Ecological Rationality: The Recognition Heuristic. *Psychological Review,* 75-90.

Johnson, E., & Goldstein, D. (2003) Do Defaults Save Lives? *Science*, Vol. 302, pp. 1338-1339.

Kahneman, D., & Tversky, A. (1979). Prospect theory: An analysis of decisions under risk. *Econometrica* 47 (2): 263–291.

Lord, C., Lepper, M., & Preston, E. (1984). Considering the opposite: A corrective strategy for social judgment. *Journal of Personality and Social Psychology*, 47, 1231-1243.

Maslow, A. (1966). *The psychology of science; a reconnaissance,*. New York: Harper & Row. p.15.

Pilkington, K. (Presenter) (2010) China [Television series episode]. In *An Idiot Abroad* British Sky Broadcasting.

Ramírez-Esparza, N., Gosling, S. D., Benet-Martínez, V., Potter, J., & Pennebaker, J. W. (2006). Do bilinguals have two personalities? A special case of cultural frame switching. *Journal of Research in Personality*, 40, 99-120.

Ross, L., Lepper, M., & Hubbard, M. (1975). Perseverance In Self-perception And Social Perception: Biased Attributional Processes In The Debriefing Paradigm. *Journal of Personality and Social Psychology,* 880-892.

Ross, M., Xun, W., & Wilson, A. (2002). Language And The Bicultural Self. *Personality and Social Psychology Bulletin,* 1040-1050.

Skinner, B. (1957). *Verbal behavior*. New York: Appleton-Century-Crofts.

Tversky, A., & Kahneman, D. (1973). Availability: A heuristic for judging frequency and probability. *Cognitive Psychology* 5 (2): 207–232.

Tversky, A., & Kahneman, D. (1974). Judgment under uncertainty: Heuristics and biases. *Science* 185 (4157): 1124–1131.

Tversky, A., & Kahneman, D. (1981). The framing of decisions and the psychology of choice. *Science* 211 (4481): 453–458.

Recommended Reading:

Ariely, D. (2010). *Predictably irrational: The hidden forces that shape our decisions*. New York: Harper Perennial.

Pinker, S. (2007). *The Stuff of Thought: Language as a window into human nature*. New York: Viking.

Kahneman, D. (2011). *Thinking, Fast and Slow*. New York: Farrar, Straus and Giroux.

Chapter 8

Drowsy Driving Facts and Stats from the National Sleep Foundation and the National Highway Traffic Safety Administration. Retrieved February 7, 2015, from http://drowsydriving.org/about/facts-and-stats/

Bargh, J., Chen, M., & L. Burrows. (1996). Automaticity of social behavior: Direct effects of trait construct and stereotype activation on action. *Journal of Personality and Social Psychology*, 71, 230-244

Cherry, E. (1953). Some Experiments On The Recognition Of Speech, With One And With Two Ears. *The Journal of the Acoustical Society of America,* 975-975.

Green, J.P., & Lynn, S.J. (2005). Hypnosis vs. relaxation: Accuracy and confidence in dating international news events. *Applied Cognitive Psychology*, 19, 679- 691.

Heider, F, & Simmel, M. (1944). An experimental study of apparent behavior. *American Journal of Psychology, 57,* 243–259.

Hobson, J. A., & McCarley, R. (1977). The Brain as A Dream State Generator: An Activation-Synthesis Hypothesis of the Dream Process. *The American Journal of Psychiatry* 134 (12): 1335–48.

Nagel, T. (1974). What Is It Like to Be a Bat? *The Philosophical Review,* 435-450.

Ricard, M., Lutz, A., & Davidson, R.J. (2014) Mind of the Meditator. *Scientific American, 311(5),* 38-45

Simons D., & Chabris C. (1999) Gorillas in our midst: sustained inattentional blindness for dynamic events. *Perception* 28(9), 1059 – 1074

Simons, D., & Levin, D. (1998), Failure to detect changes to people during a real-world interaction, *Psychonomic Bulletin and Review* 5 (4): 644–649

Stampi, C. (1989) Polyphasic sleep strategies improve prolonged sustained performance: A field study on 99 sailors. *Work & Stress, 3, 1,* 41-55.

Van Gulick, R. (2014) Consciousness. *The Stanford Encyclopedia of Philosophy* (Spring 2014 Edition), Edward N. Zalta (ed.), URL = <http://plato.stanford.edu/archives/spr2014/entries/consciousness/>.

Wamsley, E., Tucker, M., Payne, J., Benavides, J., & Stickgold, R. (2010). Dreaming Of A Learning Task Is Associated With Enhanced Sleep-Dependent Memory Consolidation. *Current Biology,* 850-855.

Wegner, D. M., Schneider, D. J., Carter, S., & White, T. (1987). Paradoxical effects of thought suppression. *Journal of Personality and Social Psychology, 53,* 5-13.

Zeidan, F., Grant, J., Brown, C., Mchaffie, J., & Coghill, R. (2012). Mindfulness meditation-related pain relief: Evidence for unique brain mechanisms in the regulation of pain. *Neuroscience Letters,* 165-173.

Recommended Reading:

Benson, H. (1975). *The Relaxation Response.* New York: Morrow.

Freud, S., & Crick, J. (1999). *The Interpretation of Dreams.* Oxford: Oxford University Press.

LaBerge, S., & Rheingold, H. (1990). *Exploring the World of Lucid Dreaming.* New York: Ballantine Books.

Sacks, O. (2012). *Hallucinations.* New York: Alfred A. Knopf.

Wegner, D. (2002). *The Illusion of Conscious Will.* Cambridge, Mass.: MIT Press.

Zinn, J. (2004). *Wherever You Go, There You Are.* London: Piatkus.

Chapter 9

Allaire, J. C. & 74 others. (2014, October 20). A Consensus on the Brain Training Industry from the Scientific Community. Retrieved January 25, 2016, from http://longevity3.stanford.edu/blog/2014/10/15/the-consensus-on-the-brain-training-industry-from-the-scientific-community/

Arvey*, R. D., & 51 others. (1994, December 13). Mainstream science on intelligence. *Wall Street Journal,* p. A–18.

* note – this reference appears incorrectly in several textbooks under the name *Avery*, though the first signatory was Richard *Arvey*. The article was republished later as: Gottfredson, Linda S. (1997). Mainstream Science on Intelligence: An editorial with 52 signatories, history, and bibliography. *Intelligence* **24**: 13–23

Deary, I. J., & Stough, C. (1996). Intelligence and inspection time: Achievements, prospects, and problems. *American Psychologist,51*(6), 599-608.

Dickens, W. T., & Flynn, J. R. (2001). Heritability estimates versus large environmental effects: The IQ paradox resolved. *Psychological Review, 108*(2), 346-369.

Dickens, W. T., & Flynn, J. R. (2006). Black Americans Reduce the Racial IQ Gap: Evidence From Standardization Samples. *Psychological Science, 17*(10), 913-920.

Fung, B. (2012, May 17). Eureka! When a Blow to the Head Creates a Sudden Genius. Available at: http://www.theatlantic.com/health/archive/2012/05/eureka-when-a-blow-to-the-head-creates-a-sudden-genius/257282/

Galton, F. (1869). *Hereditary genius*. Macmilan and Co., London.

Full text (public domain) available at http://galton.org/books/hereditary-genius/

Gottfredson, L. S., & Deary, I. J. (2004). Intelligence Predicts Health and Longevity, but Why? *Current Directions in Psychological Science, 13*(1), 1-4.

Gould, S. J. (1980) "Women's Brains" from The Panda's Thumb, *W.W. Norton, pp. 152-159.*

Gould, S. J. (1982). A nation of morons. *New Scientist, 6, 349-352*

Halpern, D. F. (1997) Sex differences in intelligence: Implications for education. *American Psychologist, 52*(10), 1091-1102.

Herrnstein, R. J., & Murray, C. A. (1994). *The bell curve: Intelligence and class structure in American life.* New York: Free Press.

Hurley, D. (2014). *Smarter: the new science of building brain power.* New York: Plume.

Jaeggi, S. M., Buschkuehl, M., Jonides, J., & Perrig, W. J. (2008). Improving fluid intelligence with training on working memory. *Proceedings of the National Academy of Sciences, 105*(19), 6829-6833.

Lerner, R. M. (1992). *Final solutions: Biology, prejudice, and genocide.* University Park, PA: Pennsylvania State University Press.

Neisser, U., Boodoo, G., Bouchard, T. J., Jr., Boykin, A. W., Brody, N., Ceci, S. J., et al. (1996). Intelligence: Knowns and unknowns. *American Psychologist, 51,* 77–101.

Plomin, R., DeFries, J. C., Knopik, V. S., & Neiderhiser, J. M. (2013). *Behavioral genetics* (6th ed.). New York: Worth.

Reis, J., Schambra, H. M., Cohen, L. G., Buch, E. R., Fritsch, B., Zarahn, E., Celnik, P. A., & Krakauer, J. W. (2009). Noninvasive cortical stimulation enhances motor skill acquisition over multiple days through an effect on consolidation. *Proceedings of the National Academy of Sciences, 106*(5), 1590-1595.

Rosenthal, R., & Jacobson, L. (1968). Pygmalion in the classroom. *The Urban Review, 3*(1), 16-20.

Steele, C. M., & Aronson, J. (1995). Stereotype threat and the intellectual test performance of African Americans. *Journal of Personality and Social Psychology, 69*(5), 797-811.

Sternberg, R. J., Grigorenko, E. L., & Kidd, K. K. (2005). Intelligence, Race, and Genetics, *American Psychologist 60*(1): 46–59.

Recommended Reading:

Dweck, C. S. (2006). *Mindset: The new psychology of success.* New York: Random House.

Gladwell, M. (2007). None of the above: What IQ doesn't tell you about race. *The New Yorker.* Available at: http://www.newyorker.com/magazine/2007/12/17/none-of-the-above

Steele, C. (2011). *Whistling Vivaldi: How stereotypes affect us and what we can do.* New York: W.W. Norton & Company.

Chapter 10

Bettelheim, B. (1983). *Freud and man's soul.* New York: A.A. Knopf.

Bettelheim, B. (1982). Reflections: Freud and the Soul [as perceived in America]. *New Yorker. 68*(2), 52-93.

Bouchard, T. J., & Loehlin, J. C. (2001). Genes, evolution, and personality. *Behavioral Genetics, 31,* 243–273.

Larson, R., & Csikszentmihalyi, M. (2014). The Experience Sampling Method. *Flow and the Foundations of Positive Psychology,* 21-34.

Mischel, W. (1968). *Personality and assessment.* New York: Wiley.

Plomin, R., DeFries, J. C., Knopik, V. S., & Neiderhiser, J. M. (2013). *Behavioral genetics* (6th ed.). New York: Worth.

Pittenger, D. J. (1993) Measuring the MBTI. . .And Coming Up Short. *Journal of Career Planning and Employment, 54* (1) 48-52.

Rorschach, H. (1927). *Rorschach Test – Psychodiagnostic Plates.* Cambridge, MA: Hogrefe Publishing Corp.

Recommended Reading:

Carver, C. S., & Scheier, M. F. (2012). *Perspectives on Personality* (7th edition). Boston: Pearson.

Emre, M. (2015). Uncovering The Secret History Of Myers-Briggs. Available at: http://digg.com/2015/myers-briggs-secret-history

Chapter 11

Achtziger, A., Gollwitzer, P. M., & Sheeran, P. (2008). Implementation Intentions and Shielding Goal Striving From Unwanted Thoughts and Feelings. *Personality and Social Psychology Bulletin, 34*(3), 381-393.

Carlsmith, J. M., & Aronson, E. (1963). Some hedonic consequences of the confirmation and disconfirmation of expectancies. *The Journal of Abnormal and Social Psychology, 66*(2), 151-156.

Deci, E. L., Koestner, R., & Ryan, R. M. (1999). A meta-analytic review of experiments examining the effects of extrinsic rewards on intrinsic motivation. *Psychological Bulletin, 125*(6), 627-668.

Dutton, D. G., & Aron, A. P. (1974). Some evidence for heightened sexual attraction under conditions of high anxiety. *Journal of Personality and Social Psychology, 30*(4), 510-517.

Geller, L. (1982). The failure of self-actualization theory: A critique of Carl Rogers and Abraham Maslow. *Journal of Humanistic Psychology, 22 (2), 56-73*

Gneezy, U., & Rustichini, A. (2000). A Fine is a Price. *The Journal of Legal Studies, 29*(1), 1-17.

Hirstein, W.; Ramachandran, V.S. (1997). Capgras syndrome: a novel probe for understanding the neural representation of the identity and familiarity of persons. *Proceedings of the Royal Society B: Biological Sciences* 264 (1380): 437–444.

Kahneman, D., & Tversky, A. (1979). Prospect Theory: An Analysis of Decision under Risk. *Econometrica, 47*(2), 263.

King, B. M. (2006). The rise, fall and resurrection of the ventromedial hypothalamus in the regulation of feeding behavior and body weight. *Physiology and Behavior* 87 (2): 221–244.

Lazarus, R. S., & Alfert, E. (1964). Short-circuiting of threat by experimentally altering cognitive appraisal. *The Journal of Abnormal and Social Psychology, 69*(2), 195-205.

Lepper, M. R., Greene, D., & Nisbett, R. E. (1973). Undermining children's intrinsic interest with extrinsic reward: A test of the "overjustification" hypothesis. *Journal of Personality and Social Psychology, 28*(1), 129-137.

Masters, W. H., & Johnson, V. E. (1966). *Human sexual response*. Boston: Little, Brown and Company.

Mischel, W., Shoda, Y., & Rodriguez, M. (1989). Delay of gratification in children. *Science, 244*(4907), 933-938.

Olds, J., & Milner, P. (1954). Positive Reinforcement Produced By Electrical Stimulation Of Septal Area And Other Regions Of Rat Brain. *Journal of Comparative and Physiological Psychology, 47*(6), 419-427.

Roseboom, T. J., Meulen, J. H., Ravelli, A. C., Osmond, C., Barker, D. J., & Bleker, O. P. (2001). Effects of prenatal exposure to the Dutch famine on adult disease in later life: An overview. *Molecular and Cellular Endocrinology, 185*(1-2), 93-98.

Sheldon, K. M., & Elliot, A. J. (1999). Goal striving, need satisfaction, and longitudinal well-being: The self-concordance model. *Journal of Personality and Social Psychology, 76*(3), 482-497.

Solomon, R.L. and Corbit, J.D. (1974). An Opponent-Process Theory of Motivation: I. Temporal Dynamics of Affect. *Psychological Review 81*(2), 119–145.

Strack, F., Martin, L. L., & Stepper, S. (1988). Inhibiting and facilitating conditions of the human smile: A nonobtrusive test of the facial feedback hypothesis. *Journal of Personality and Social Psychology,54*(5), 768-777.

Whalen, P. J., Rauch, S. L., Etcoff, N. L., McInerney, S. C., Lee, M. B., & Jenike, M. A. (1998). Masked presentations of emotional facial expressions modulate amygdala activity without explicit knowledge. *Journal of Neuroscience, 18,* 411–418.

Yerkes, R. M., & Dodson, J. D. (1908). The relation of strength of stimulus to rapidity of habit-formation. *Journal of Comparative Neurology and Psychology, 18*(5), 459-482. This paper is public domain and available here: http://psychclassics.yorku.ca/Yerkes/Law/

Zajonc, R. B. (1980). Feeling and thinking: Preferences need no inferences. *American Psychologist, 35*(2), 151-175.

Zamiska, N. (2007). In China, Brain Surgery Is Pushed on the Mentally Ill. *Wall Street Journal,* pp 1,10. Available at: http://www.wsj.com/articles/SB119393867164279313

Recommended Reading:

Csikszentmihalyi, M. (1990). *Flow: The psychology of optimal experience.* New York: Harper & Row.

Damasio, A. R. (1994). *Descartes' error: Emotion, reason, and the human brain.* New York: Putnam.

Dutch Famine Birth Cohort Study – Academic Medical Centre site at www.dutchfamine.nl

McGonigal, K. (2012). *The willpower instinct: How self-control works, why it matters, and what you can do to get more of it.* New York: Avery.

Wansink, B. (2006). *Mindless eating: Why we eat more than we think.* New York: Bantam Books.

Open Course Recommendations:

Kelly Brownell - The Biology, Psychology, and Politics of Food – Yale University

Robert Sapolsky - Human Behavioral Biology – Stanford University

Chapter 12

Ainsworth, M. D. S., Blehar, M. C., Waters, E., & Wall, S. (1978). *Patterns of attachment: A psychological study of the strange situation.* Hillsdale, NJ: Erlbaum.

Bailey, J. M., & Pillard, R. C. (1991). A Genetic Study of Male Sexual Orientation. *Archives of General Psychiatry, 48*(12), 1089.

Baillargeon, R., Spelke, E. S., & Wasserman, S. (1985). Object permanence in five-month-old infants. *Cognition, 20*(3), 191-208.

Baron-Cohen S., Leslie A.M., & Frith, U. (1985). Does the autistic child have a 'theory of mind'?. *Cognition 21* (1), 37-46.

Baumrind, D. (1967). Child care practices anteceding three patterns of preschool behavior. *Genetic Psychology Monographs, 75*(1), 43-88.

Decasper, A. J., & Spence, M. J. (1986). Prenatal maternal speech influences newborns' perception of speech sounds. *Infant Behavior and Development, 9*(2), 133-150.

Deloache, J. S. (2000). Dual Representation and Young Children's Use of Scale Models. *Child Development, 71*(2), 329-338.

Deloache, J. S. (2005). Mindful of Symbols. *Scientific American, 293*(2), 72-77.

Gilligan, C. (1982). *In a different voice: Psychological theory and women's development.* Cambridge, MA: Harvard University Press.

Greene, J.D., Sommerville, R.B., Nystrom, L.E., Darley, J.M., & Cohen, J.D. (2001). An fMRI investigation of emotional engagement in moral judgment. *Science, 293,* 2105-2108.

Hammack, P. L. (2005). The Life Course Development of Human Sexual Orientation: An Integrative Paradigm. *Human Development,48*(5), 267-290.

Harlow, H. F. (1958). The nature of love. *American Psychologist, 13,* 573–685.

Kohlberg, L. (1963). Development of children's orientation towards a moral order (Part I). Sequencing in the development of moral thought. *Vita Humana, 6,* 11–36.

Kohlberg, Lawrence (1981). *Essays on Moral Development, Vol. I: The Philosophy of Moral Development.* San Francisco, CA: Harper & Row.

Peskin, J. (1992). Ruse and representations: On children's ability to conceal information. *Developmental Psychology, 28*(1), 84-89.

Rosenzweig, M. R., Krech, D., Bennett, E. L.,Diamond, M. C. (1962). Effects of environmental complexity and training on brain chemistry and anatomy: A replication and extension. *Journal of comparative and physiological psychology* 55 (4): 429–437.

Rosenzweig, M. R. (1984). Experience, memory, and the brain. *American Psychologist, 39,* 365–376.

Recommended Reading:

Bloom, P. (2010, May 05). The Moral Life of Babies. Available at: http://www.nytimes.com/2010/05/09/magazine/09babies

Blum, D. (2002). *Love at Goon Park: Harry Harlow and the science of affection.* Cambridge, MA: Perseus Pub.

Sapolsky, R. M. (2004). *Why zebras don't get ulcers* (3rd ed.). New York: Holt

Chapter 13

Ambady, N., & Rosenthal, R. (1993). Half a minute: Predicting teacher evaluations from thin slices of nonverbal behavior and physical attractiveness. *Journal of Personality and Social Psychology, 64,* 431–441.

Asch, S. E. Effects of group pressure upon the modification and distortion of judgments. In Guetzkow, H. E., (1951). Groups, leadership and men; research in human relations. , (pp. 177-190). Oxford, England: Carnegie Press.

Asch, S.E. (1955). Opinions and social pressure. *Scientific American,* 193, 31–35.

Baron, R. S., Vandello, J. A., & Brunsman, B. (1996). The forgotten variable in conformity research: Impact of task importance on social influence. *Journal of Personality and Social Psychology, 71*(5), 915-927.

Burger, J. M. (1986) Increasing compliance by improving the deal: The that's-not-all technique. *Journal of Personality and Social Psychology, Vol 51(2),* 277-283.

Cialdini, R. B., Vincent, J. E., Lewis, S. K., Catalan, J., Wheeler, D., & Darby, B. L. (1975). Reciprocal concessions procedure for inducing compliance: The door-in-the-face technique. *Journal of Personality and Social Psychology, 31,* 206–215.

Cialdini, R.B., Borden, R.J., Thorne, A., T., Walker, M. R., Freeman, S., & Reynolds, S. L. (1976). Basking in reflected glory: Three (football) field studies. *Journal of Personality and Social Psychology, 34*(3), 366-375.

David, L., Masters, B., & Shaw, B. (Writers). (1994). The Chaperone [Television series episode]. In *Seinfeld.*

Darley, J. M., & Latané, B. (1968). Bystander intervention in emergencies: diffusion of responsibility. *Journal of Personality and Social Psychology* 8 (4): 377–383.

Diener, E., Fraser, S., Beaman, A., & Kelem, R. (1976). Effects of deindividuation variables on stealing among Halloween trick-or-treaters. *Journal of Personality and Social Psychology, 33 (2),* 178-183

Festinger, L. & Carlsmith, J. M. (1959). Cognitive consequences of forced compliance. *Journal of Abnormal and Social Psychology, 58,* 203-210. Available at http://psychclassics.yorku.ca/Festinger/index.htm

Festinger, L., Riecken, H. W., & Schachter, S. (1956). *When prophecy fails.* Minneapolis: University of Minnesota Press.

Franklin, B., & Pine, F. W. (1916). *Franklin's autobiography.* New York: Henry Holt and Company. Available at www.gutenberg.org/ebooks/20203

Freedman, J. L., & Fraser, S. C. (1966). Compliance without pressure: The foot-in-the-door technique. *Journal of Personality and Social Psychology, 4*(2), 195-202.

Goff, P. A., Steele, C. M., & Davies, P. G. (2008). The space between us: Stereotype threat and distance in interracial contexts. *Journal of Personality and Social Psychology* 94, 91–107.

Gray, P. (2013). Why Zimbardo's Prison Experiment Isn't in My Textbook. Available at: www.psychologytoday.com/blog/freedom-learn/201310/why-zimbardo-s-prison-experiment-   isn-t-in-my-textbook

Greenwald, A. G., McGhee, D. E., & Schwartz, J. L. K. (1998). Measuring individual differences in implicit cognition: The Implicit Association Test. *Journal of Personality and Social Psychology 74*, 1464–1480.

Greenwald, A. G., Nosek, B. A., & Banaji, M. R. (2003). Understanding and using the Implicit Association Test: I. An `improved scoring algorithm. *Journal of Personality and Social Psychology 85*, 197–216.

Haney, C., Banks, C., & Zimbardo, P. G. (1973). Interpersonal dynamics in a simulated prison. *International Journal of Criminology and Penology, 1*, 69–97.

Ingham, A. G., Levinger, G., Graves, J., Peckham, V. (1974). The Ringelmann effect: Studies of group size and group performance. *Journal of Experimental Social Psychology 10*(4), 371–384.

Janis, I. L. (1982). *Groupthink: Psychological studies of policy decisions and fiascoes.* Boston: Houghton Mifflin.

Kelley, H. H. (1967). Attribution theory in social psychology. In D. Levine (Ed.), *Nebraska Symposium on Motivation.* (Vol. 15, pp. 192–238). Lincoln: University of Nebraska Press.

Kravitz, D.A., Martin, B. (1986) Ringelmann rediscovered: The original article. *Journal of Personality and Social Psychology, 50(5)*, 936-941.

Latane, B., & Darley, J. M. (1968). Group Inhibition of Bystander Intervention in Emergencies. *Journal of Personality & Social Psychology, 10*(3), 215–221.

Lord, C., Ross, L., and Lepper, M. (1979). Biased Assimilation and Attitude Polarization: The Effects of Prior Theories on Subsequently Considered Evidence, *Journal of Personality and Social Psychology*, 37 (11): 2098-2109.

Mann, L. (1981) The baiting crowd in episodes of threatened suicide. *Journal of Personality and Social Psychology 41 (4)*, 703-709

Michaels, J. W., Blommel, J. M., Brocato, R. M., Linkous, R. A., & Rowe, J. S. (1982). Social facilitation and inhibition in a natural setting. *Replications in Social Psychology, 2*, 21-24.

Milgram, S. (1963). Behavioral study of obedience. *Journal of Abnormal and Social Psychology, 67,* 371–378.

Milgram, S. (1974). *Obedience to authority.* New York: Harper & Row.

Ross, L., Amabile, T. M., & Steinmetz, J. L. (1977) Social roles, social control, and biases in social perception processes. *Journal of Personality and Social Psychology, 35,* 485-494.

Sherif, M. (1935). A study of some social factors in perception. *Archives of Psychology, 27 (187)* 17-22.

Sherif, M., Harvey, O.J., White, B.J., Hood, W., & Sherif, C.W. (1961). *Intergroup Conflict and Cooperation: The Robbers Cave Experiment.* Norman, OK: The University Book Exchange. pp. 155–184. Available at: http://psychclassics.yorku.ca/Sherif/

Stroebe, W. (2012). The truth about Triplett (1898), but nobody seems to care. Perspectives on Psychological Science, 7, 54-57.

Strube, M. J. (2005). What did Triplett really find? A contemporary analysis of the first experiment in social psychology. *American Journal of Psychology, 118,* 271-286.

Tajfel, H. (1970). Experiments in intergroup discrimination. *Scientific American, 223,* 96–102.

Zajonc, R. B., Heingartner, A., Herman, E. M. (1969). Social Enhancement and Impairment of Performance in the Cockroach. *Journal of Personality and Social Psychology 13 (2),* 83–92.

Recommended Reading:

Buss, D. M. (2003). *The evolution of desire: Strategies of human mating.* New York: Basic Books.

Cialdini, R. B. (2000). *Influence: Science and practice* (4th ed.). New York: Morrow.

Dweck, C. S. (2006). *Mindset: The new psychology of success.* New York: Random House.

Perry, G. (2012). Behind the shock machine: The untold story of the notorious Milgram psychology experiments. Brunswick, Vic: Scribe Publications.

Schwartz, B. (2004). *The paradox of choice: Why more is less.* New York: Ecco.

Steele, C. (2011). *Whistling Vivaldi: How stereotypes affect us and what we can do*. New York: W.W. Norton & Company.

Peng Yu details: http://www.danwei.org/law/common_sense_decency_and_crowd.php

Wang Yue story: http://www.bbc.com/news/world-asia-pacific-15401055

Chapter 14

Coan, J. A., Schaefer, H. S., & Davidson, R. J. (2006). Lending a hand: Social regulation of the neural response to threat. *Psychological Science, 17,* 1032– 1039.

Cohen, S. (1980). Aftereffects of stress on human performance and social behavior: A review of research and theory. *Psychological Bulletin, 88*(1), 82-108.

Cohen, S., Frank, E., Doyle, W. J., Skoner, D. P., Rabin, B. S., & Gwaltney, J. M., Jr. (1998). Types of stressors that increase susceptibility to the common cold in healthy adults. *Health Psychology, 17,* 214–223.

Brickman, P., Coates, D., & Janoff-Bulman, R. J. (1978). Lottery winners and accident victims: Is happiness relative? *Journal of Personality and Social Psychology, 36,* 917–927.

Diener, E., Lucas, R. E., & Scollon, C. N. (2006). Beyond the hedonic treadmill: Revising the adaptation theory of well-being. *American Psychologist, 61*(4), 305-314.

Emmons, R. A., & Mccullough, M. E. (2003). Counting blessings versus burdens: An experimental investigation of gratitude and subjective well-being in daily life. *Journal of Personality and Social Psychology,84*(2), 377-389

Epel, E. S., Blackburn, E. H., Lin, J., Dhabhar, F. S., Adler, N. E., Morrow, J. D., & Cawthon, R. M. (2004). Accelerated telomere shortening in response to life stress. *Proceedings of the National Academy of Sciences, 101*(49), 17312-17315.

Friedman, M., & Rosenman, R. H. (1974). *Type A behavior and your heart.* New York: Knopf.

Gilbertson, M. W., Shenton, M. E., Ciszewski, A., Kasai, K., Lasko, N. B., Orr, S. P., et al. (2002). Smaller hippocampal volume predicts pathological vulnerability to psychological trauma. *Nature Neuroscience, 5,* 1242–1247.

Glass, D. C., & Singer, J. E. (1972). *Urban stress.* New York: Academic Press.

Hanson, C. J., Stevens, L. C., & Coast, J. R. (2001). Exercise duration and mood state: How much is enough to feel better? *Health Psychology, 20,* 267–275.

Hiroto, D. S., & Seligman, M. E. P. (1974) Generality of learned helplessness in man. *Journal of Personality and Social Psychology, 31*(2), Feb 1975, 311-327.

Holmes, T. H., & Rahe, R. H. (1967). The social readjustment rating scale. *Journal of Psychosomatic Research, 11,* 213–318.

James, S. (1994) "John Henryism and the health of African-Americans," *Culture, Medicine and Psychiatry 18,* 163.

Kahneman, D., & Deaton, A. (2010). High income improves evaluation of life but not emotional well-being. *Proceedings of the National Academy of Sciences, 107,* 16489–16493.

Kobasa, S. (1979). Stressful life events, personality, and health: An inquiry into hardiness. *Journal of Personality and Social Psychology, 37,* 1–11.

Maddi, S. R., Harvey, R. H., Khoshaba, D. M., Fazel, M., & Resurreccion, N. (2009). Hardiness training facilitates performance in college. *Journal of Positive Psychology, 4,* 566–577.

Marmot, M. G., Rose, G., Shipley, M., & Hamilton, P. J. (1978). Employment grade and coronary heart disease in British civil servants. *Journal of Epidemiology & Community Health, 32*(4), 244-249.

Marshall, B. J. (2005). Barry J. Marshall Autobiographical page at http://www.nobelprize.org/nobel_prizes/medicine/laureates/2005/marshall-bio.html

Marshall B.J., Armstrong J.A., McGechie D.B., Glancy R.J. (1985) *Attempt to fulfil Koch's postulates for pyloric campylobacter. Medical Journal of Australia, 142*(8), 436-439

Mather, M., Lighthall, N. R., Nga, L., & Gorlick, M. A. (2010). Sex differences in how stress affects brain activity during face viewing. *NeuroReport, 21,* 933–937.

Miller, G. E., Yu, T., Chen, E., & Brody, G. H. (2015). Self-control forecasts better psychosocial outcomes but faster epigenetic aging in low-SES youth. *Proceedings of the National Academy of Sciences, 112*(33), 10325-10330.

Mochon, D., Norton, M. I., & Ariely, D. (2008). Getting off the hedonic treadmill, one step at a time: The impact of regular religious practice and exercise on well-being. *Journal of Economic Psychology, 29*(5), 632-642.

Moriya, M., Uehara, A., Okumura, T., Miyamoto, M., & Kohgo, Y. (2011). Stress-induced hemorrhagic gastric ulcer after successful Helicobacter pylori eradication: Two case reports. *Journal of Medical Case Reports, 5*(1), 252.

Rossum, C. T. (2000). Employment grade differences in cause specific mortality. A 25 year follow up of civil servants from the first Whitehall study. *Journal of Epidemiology & Community Health, 54*(3), 178-184.

Scheier, M. F., Matthews, K. A., Owens, J. F., Schulz, R., Bridges, M. W., Magovern, Sr., G. J., et al. (1999). Optimism and rehospitalization after coronary artery bypass graft surgery. *Archives of Internal Medicine, 159*, 829–835.

Seligman, M. E. P., Maier, S. F. (1967) Failure to escape traumatic shock. *Journal of Experimental Psychology, 74*(1), 1-9.

Seligman, M. E. P. (1972). Learned helplessness. *Annual Review of Medicine* 23 (1): 407–412

Selye, H. (1936). A Syndrome produced by Diverse Nocuous Agents. *Nature, 138*(3479), 32-33.

Szabo, S., Tache, Y., & Somogyi, A. (2012). The legacy of Hans Selye and the origins of stress research: A retrospective 75 years after his landmark brief "Letter" to the Editor of Nature. *Stress, 15*(5), 472-478.

Taylor, S. E., Klein, L. C., Lewis, B. P., Gruenewald, T. L., Gurung, R. A. R., & Updegraff, J. A. (2000). Biobehavioral responses to stress in females: Tend-and-befriend, not fight-or-flight. *Psychological Review*, 107, 411–429.

Recommended Reading:

Benson, H. (1975). *The Relaxation Response*. New York: Morrow.

Gilbert, D. (2005). *Stumbling on Happiness*. New York, NY: Vintage Books.

Hamblin, J. (2015). The Paradox of Effort. Available at: http://www.theatlantic.com/health/archive/2015/07/the-health-cost-of-upward-mobility/398486/

Lyubomirsky, S. (2008). *The how of happiness: A scientific approach to getting the life you want*. New York: Penguin Press.

Ratey, J. J., & Hagerman, E. (2008). *Spark: The revolutionary new science of exercise and the brain*. New York: Little, Brown.

Sapolsky, R. (2004) *Why Zebras Don't Get Ulcers (3rd edition)*. New York: Henry Holt.

Seligman, M. E. P. (2002). *Authentic happiness: Using the new positive psychology to realize your potential for lasting fulfillment*. New York: Free Press.

Taylor, S. E. (2015). *Health psychology* (9th ed.). New York, NY: McGraw Hill.

Open Course Recommendation:

Tal Ben-Shahar – Positive Psychology – Harvard University

Chapter 15

American Psychiatric Association (2013). *Diagnostic and statistical manual of mental disorders: DSM-5*. Washington, D.C. American Psychiatric Association.

Arcelus, J., Mitchell, A. J., Wales, J., & Nielsen, S. (2011). Mortality rates in patients with Anorexia Nervosa and other eating disorders. *Archives of General Psychiatry, 68*(7), 724-731.

Beck A.T., Ward C.H., Mendelson M, Mock J.E., & Erbaugh J.K. (1962). Reliability of psychiatric diagnosis. A study of consistency of clinical judgments and ratings. *American Journal of Psychiatry*. 119, 351-7.

Caspi, A., Sugden, K., Moffitt, T. E., Taylor, A., Craig, I. W., Harington, H., McClay, J., Mill, J., Martin, J., Braithwaite, A., & Poulton, R. (2003). Influence of life stress on depression: moderation by a polymorphism in the 5-HTT gene. *Science*, 301(5631), 386-389.

Cooper, J. E., Kendell, R.E., Gurland, B.J., Sharpe, L., Copeland, J.R.M, & Simon, R. (1972). Psychiatric Diagnosis in New York and London. Maudsley Monograph, no 20. Oxford: Oxford University Press.

Hare, R. (1996). Psychopathy and Antisocial Personality Disorder: A Case of Diagnostic Confusion. Available at: http://www.psychiatrictimes.com/antisocial-personality-disorder/psychopathy-and-antisocial-personality-disorder-case-diagnostic-confusion

Kessler, R. C., Berglund, P., Demler, O., Jin, R., Merikangas, K. R., & Walters, E. E. (2005). Lifetime Prevalence and Age-of-Onset Distributions of DSM-IV Disorders in the National Comorbidity Survey Replication. *Archives of General Psychiatry, 62*(6), 593-602.

Morrow, R. L., Garland, E. J., Wright, J. M., Maclure, M., Taylor, S., & Dormuth, C. R. (2012). Influence of relative age on diagnosis and treatment of attention-deficit/hyperactivity disorder in children. *Canadian Medical Association Journal, 184*(7), 755-762.

Reed, A. (Writer). (2013). Fugue and riffs [Television series episode]. In *Archer*. FX Network.

Rosenhan, D. (1973). On being sane in insane places. *Science, 179,* 250–258.

Schulz, K. (2004) Did Antidepressants Depress Japan? Available at http://www.nytimes.com/2004/08/22/magazine/did-antidepressants-depress-japan.html

Szasz, T. (1960). The Myth of Mental Illness. *American Psychologist, 15,* 113-118. Available at: http://psychclassics.yorku.ca/Szasz/myth.htm

Woywodt, A., & Kiss, A. (2002). Geophagia: The history of earth-eating. *Journal of the Royal Society of Medicine, 95*(3), 143-146.

Recommended Reading:

Hare, R. D. (1999). *Without conscience: The disturbing world of the psychopaths among us*. New York: Guilford Press.

Jamison, K. R. (1995). *An unquiet mind*. New York: A.A. Knopf.

Kaysen, S. (1994). *Girl, interrupted*. New York: Vintage Books.

Plath, S. (1971). *The bell jar*. New York: Harper & Row.

Ronson, J. (2011). *The psychopath test: A journey through the madness industry*. New York: Riverhead Books.

Chapter 16

Akagi, H., & Kumar, T. M. (2002). Lesson of the week: Akathisia: Overlooked at a cost. *BMJ* 324 (7352): 1506–7.

Amick H.R., Gartlehner G., Gaynes B. N., Forneris C., Asher G.N., Morgan L.C. & 7 others. (2015) Comparative benefits and harms of second generation antidepressants and cognitive behavioral therapies in initial treatment of major depressive disorder: systematic review and meta-analysis. The BMJ. 2015;351:h6019. 2

Babyak, M., Blumenthal, J. A., Herman, S., Khatri, P., Doraiswamy, M., Moore, K., Craighead, W. W., Baldewics, T. T., & Krishnan, K. R. (2000). Exercise treatment for major depression: Maintenance of therapeutic benefit at ten months. *Psychosomatic Medicine, 62,* 633–638.

Barlow, D. H., Gorman, J. M., Shear, M. K., & Woods, S. W. (2000). Cognitive-behavioral therapy, imipramine, or their combination for panic disorder: A randomized controlled trial. *Journal of the American Medical Association, 283*(19), 2529–2536.

Becker, S., & Wojtowicz, J. M. (2007). A model of hippocampal neurogenesis in memory and mood disorders. *Trends in Cognitive Sciences, 11,* 70–76.

Blumenthal, J. A., Smith, P. J., & Hoffman, B. M. (2012). Is Exercise a Viable Treatment for Depression? *ACSM's Health & Fitness Journal, 16*(4), 14–21.

Eysenck, H.J. (1952). The Effects of Psychotherapy: An Evaluation. *Journal of Consulting Psychology, 16,* 319-324. Available at: http://psychclassics.yorku.ca/Eysenck/psychotherapy.htm

Jacobs, B. L., van Praag, H., & Gage, F. H. (2000). Adult brain neurogenesis and psychiatry: A novel theory of depression. *Molecular Psychiatry, 5,* 262–269.

Jones, M. C. (1924). A Laboratory Study of Fear: The Case of Peter. *Pedagogical Seminary, 31*, 308-315. Available at: http://psychclassics.yorku.ca/Jones

Khan, A., Redding, N., & Brown, W. A. (2008)"The persistence of the placebo response in antidepressant clinical trials." *Journal of Psychiatric Research, 42* (10), 791– 796.

Kirsch, I., & Sapirstein, G. (1998). Listening to Prozac but hearing placebo: A meta-analysis of antidepressant medication. *Prevention & Treatment, 1*(2). doi:10.1037/1522-3736.1.1.12a

Kirsch, I., Moore, T. J., Scoboria, A., Nicholls, S. S. (2002). The emperor's new drugs: An analysis of antidepressant medication data submitted to the U.S. Food and Drug Administration. *Prevention & Treatment 5* (1). doi:10.1037/1522-3736.5.1.523a

Lacasse, J. R., & Leo, J. (2005). Serotonin and Depression: A Disconnect between the Advertisements and the Scientific Literature. *PLoS Med PLoS Medicine, 2*(12). doi:10.1371/journal.pmed.0020392

Ruhé, H. S., Mason, N. S., & Schene, A. H. "Mood Is Indirectly Related to Serotonin, Norepinephrine and Dopamine Levels in Humans: a meta-analysis of monoamine depletion studies." Molecular Psychiatry, 12 (2007): 331–359.

Schildkraut, J. J. (1965). The catecholamine hypothesis of affective disorders: A review of supporting evidence. *American Journal of Psychiatry, 122,* 509–522.

Schwartz, J. M., Stoessel, E. W., Baxter, L. R., Jr., Martin, K. M., & Phelps, M. E. (1996). Systematic changes in cerebral glucose metabolic rate after successful behavior modification treatment of obsessive-compulsive disorder. *Archives of General Psychiatry, 53,* 109–113.

Recommended Reading:

Davies, J. (2013). *Cracked: The unhappy truth about psychiatry*. New York; Pegasus.

Mukherjee S. (2012) Post-Prozac Nation: The Science and History of Treating Depression. *New York Times Magazine.* Available at: http://www.nytimes.com/2012/04/22/magazine/the-science-and-history-of-treating-depression.html.

A

A-not-B error, 276
absolute threshold, 76
abstract learning, 116
accommodation, 80 (visual), 276 (Piaget)
acetylcholine, 54, 55
action potential 50-52
activation-synthesis model, 177
actor-observer bias, 308
addiction, 180
Adler, Alfred, 226
adrenal gland, 328-329
agonist, 55
agoraphobia, 362
agreeableness, 233
Ainsworth, Mary, 281
allostasis, 330, 347
altruism, 262, 319
Alzheimer's disease, 54, 288, 378
amnesia, 128, 129, 183, 275, 367
amygdala, 63, 86, 250
anhedonia 56, 352, 369, 372
anorexia nervosa, 259, 371
antagonist, 55, 56, 179
anti-anxiety medication (anxiolytics), 180, 341, 392
antidepressant medication, 375, 392, 393
antipsychotic medication (neuroleptics), 391
anxiety disorders, 361-362
aphasia, 59
appraisal, 249-250, 252, 334, 340-341
approach-avoidance motivations, 266
arousal theory, 257
Asch, Solomon, 299
assimilation, 276
atherosclerosis, 333
attachment, 280-282, 362
attention, 123, 126
attention deficit / hyperactive disorder (ADHD), 369
attraction, 249, 287, 305-306
attribution theory, 307
authoritarianism, 231, 237
autism spectrum disorder, 278-279, 368
autoimmune disorder, 331
autonomic division, 57-58
availability heuristic, 154
aversion therapy, 386

B

Bandura, Albert, 112-113, 239, 340
Barnum effect, 230, 242
basilar membrane, 84
basking in reflected glory, 295

Baumrind, Diana, 282
Beck, Aaron, 357, 388
Behavioral Approach System (BAS), 235
behavioral genetics, 69,
Behavioral Inhibition System (BIS), 235
behavioral therapy, 386-387
behaviorism, 14, 103
belief bias, 152
Benjamin Franklin effect, 297
benzodiazepines, 56, 180, 392
big five, 233
Binet, Alfred, 198
bipolar disorders, 374-375, 393
blocking, 126
Bobo doll study, 112-113
body dysmorphic disorder, 365
Broca, Paul, 59
bulimia nervosa, 259, 357, 371-372
bystander effect, 317-318

C

C-fibers, 86
Cannon-Bard Theory of Emotion, 248
Cannon, Walter, 248, 326
carpentered-world hypothesis, 99
catatonia, 369-370
catecholamines, 328, 393
central nervous system, 57
central route persuasion, 301
cerebellum, 63, 129
cerebral cortex, 63-64
chaining, 108
change blindness, 167
Chomsky, Noam, 141, 143
chromosome, 68, 70, 272, 332
chunking, 124, 130, 136
circadian rhythm, 170-171, 176
classical conditioning, 103-106, 386
cochlea, 84
cocktail-party phenomenon, 166-167
cognitive dissonance, 297, 301, 311
cognitive map, 115
cognitive therapy, 388
Cognitive-Behavioral Therapy (CBT), 389, 394, 398
comorbidity, 357, 398
compliance, 301-302
computerized axial tomography (CAT scan), 60
confirmation bias, 28, 309
conformity, 299-300
confounding variable, 35
conscientiousness, 233-234
conservation, 277 (Piaget)
consistency bias, 127

contact theory, 312
contralateral control, 64, 66, 67, 85
convergence, 80, 97
convergent thinking, 151
conversion disorder, 366
coping, 340-341, 343, 399
corpus callosum, 64, 66, 68
correlational studies, 28-31
cortisol, 173, 329
counterconditioning, 387
critical period, 145-146, 280
crystallized intelligence, 192, 288
cultural dimensions, 294
cultural syndrome, 359

D

Darwin, Charles, 13, 15, 197, 206, 253
deep brain stimulation, 395
defense mechanism, 224-225
dehumanization, 311-312
deindividuation, 316
delay of gratification, 264
delusions, 369
demand characteristics, 21, 24, 26, 34, 317
dependent variable, 34-35, 39
depersonalized / derealization disorder, 368
depressant 55-56, 179-181
depressive disorders, 372-373
depth cues, 96-98
Descartes, René, 9, 163
descriptive statistics, 35-37
deviation IQ score, 198
diathesis-stress model, 358
diffusion of responsibility, 318
discrimination, 310
dissociative identity disorder (DID), 367
divergent thinking, 151
door-in-the-face technique, 302
dopamine, 54, 56, 63, 180, 235, 391-393
double-blind study, 24, 398
Down Syndrome, 70, 204
drive, 256-257
DSM-5, 356-357, 360
dual-process theory, 168
dualism, 9, 10, 12
Dutch hunger winter, 260

E

eating disorders, 259, 371-372
Ebbinghaus, Hermann, 125, 131-132
EEG (electroencephalogram), 60, 171
effect size, 38
egocentric bias, 127

egocentrism, 278, 284
Ekman, Paul
electro-convulsive therapy (ECT)
electroencephalogram (EEG), 394
Ellis, Albert, 388
emotional intelligence, 191
emotional regulation, 252
empiricism, 8
empty-chair technique, 386
encoding, 121, 124-125, 128, 135
endorphins, 181, 342,
epidemiology, 325
epinephrine, 248, 328, 392
episodic memory, 124
Erikson, Erik, 271-272
estrus, 261
etiology, 325,
eugenics, 206-207
evolutionary psychology, 15, 236, 253, 259, 261, 361
executive function, 276, 278, 369
existential psychology, 237
exposure therapy, 387
extraversion, 232-233, 242
Eysenck, Hans, 232, 235, 397

F

facial-feedback hypothesis, 253
factor analysis, 189, 192, 231
femininity, 294
Festinger, Leon, 295-297
fetal alcohol syndrome, 273
fight or flight response, 57, 326, 328
fixed vs. growth mindset, 212, 314
flash-bulb memory, 128
flashback, 339, 363
flooding, 387
flow, 258
fluid intelligence, 192, 288
Flynn Effect, 210-211
foot-in-the-door technique, 301-302
forebrain, 62
forgetting curve, 125
Fragile X syndrome, 204
framing effect, 155
frequency distribution, 37
Freud, Sigmund, 13, 176-177, 220-227, 385
functional fixedness, 151
functional magnetic resonance imaging (fMRI), 60
functionalism, 12-13
Fundamental Attribution Error (FAE), 307-308

M

magnetic resonance imaging (MRI), 60
major depressive disorder, 372-373, 392, 399
malingering, 396
manic episode, 374
mark test, 164, 277
Marshmallow test, 264
masculinity, 294
Maslow, Abraham, 238, 262
Masters, William, 261
matched pair/sample, 31-32
mean, 35
median, 36
medical model, 352
meditation, 184-185
melatonin, 170
mental set, 151
mere-exposure effect, 169, 305
method of loci, 133-137
midbrain, 63
Milgram, Stanley, 303
Miller, George, 124
minimal group, 310-311
misattribution, 126-127 (memory), 249(arousal)
mode, 36-37
modeling, 113
monoamine-oxidase inhibitor (MAOI), 392
mood stabilizers, 393
moral development, 283-285
morpheme, 142
mortality salience, 237
motivation, 63, 212, 250, 256-257, 260, 262-266
Müller-Lyer illusion, 99
multiple sclerosis, 51
myelin, 51
Myers-Briggs Type Indication (MBTI), 242-243

N

narcolepsy, 175
narcotic, 181
nativism, 8
natural selection, 13
need for achievement, 265
neurogenesis, 342, 393-394
neuroticism, 232-233
night terrors, 174
nocireceptors, 85
nodes of Ranvier, 48, 51
nootropics, 214
norepinephrine, 55-56, 328, 392-393
norm of reciprocity, 302
normal curve, 37, 201

NREM sleep, 171
nucleus accumbens, 63, 250-251

O

obedience, 303-304
object permanence, 276-277
observational learning, 112-113
observer bias, 23-24
obsessive-compulsive disorder, 364-365, 393
openness to experience, 233
operant conditioning, 106-110, 386-388
operational definition, 24-25, 32, 39-40
opponent process theory, 83 (color), 257 (motivation)
optimism, 345
orexin, 258
ossicles, 84
out-group homogeneity, 311
overgeneralization, 144
overjustification effect, 263

P

p-value, 38-39
panic disorder, 362
paraphilic disorders, 378
parasympathetic nervous system, 58, 184, 262
parenting style, 282
Parkinson's disease, 63, 378, 395
Pavlov, Ivan, 103-105
perceived control, 334-335, 337, 340, 343
percentile score, 201
perceptual constancy, 96
peripheral nervous system, 57
peripheral route to persuasion, 301
Perls, Fritz, 386
persistence, 128 (memory)
personality disorders, 375-377
phenylketonuria (PKU), 71, 205
phoneme, 141
phonological rules, 142
photoreceptors, 80
phrenology, 11
Piaget, Jean, 276-279
pica, 371
pineal gland, 9, 170
pituitary gland, 64, 328-329
placebo effect, 34, 182, 396, 398
positive psychology, 345-347
positron emission tomography (PET scan), 60
post-traumatic stress disorder (PTSD), 128, 339, 363
power test, 192
prejudice, 310
Premack Principle, 111
preparedness theory, 361

About the Author

Michael Corayer earned his Bachelor's degree in Psychology from Harvard in 2006. Michael taught Advanced Placement and International Baccalaureate Psychology courses at an international school in Shanghai, China from 2008 until 2015. He writes for www.psychexamreview.com, a resource for students of psychology, and hosts a YouTube channel (PsychExamReview) featuring tutorial videos.

CPSIA information can be obtained
at www.ICGtesting.com
Printed in the USA
LVHW061621250721
693637LV00005B/47